"Young adults need guidance and so do those who desire to help them mature into healthy adulthood. This book provides a lucid overview of the current research regarding emerging adulthood as well as accessible guidelines for reaching this generation with the gospel. The authors make a strong case for why the church should take emerging adulthood research *and* emerging adults more seriously. Most refreshing, the central motivation behind *Spiritual Formation in Emerging Adulthood* is not the desire to grow a church or young adult program, but to see young people grow up in Christ."

—**Derek Melleby,** director, CPYU's College Transition Initiative; author of *Make College Count: A Faithful Guide to Life and Learning;* coauthor of *Learning for the Love of God: A Student's Guide to Academic Faithfulness*

"David Setran and Chris Kiesling have written a marvelous book that seasons social science research with biblical and theological wisdom. Each chapter covers critical features of the complexities of emerging adult development and the authors' guidance on mentoring alone is worth the price of the book. This book is well conceived and ably written. I highly recommend *Spiritual Formation in Emerging Adulthood.*"

—**Steve Rankin,** Southern Methodist University

"Recognized for their judicious scholarship and reflective ministry practice, Setran and Kiesling offer a comprehensive guide to both understanding and ministering among emerging adults in their faith journeys. *Spiritual Formation in Emerging Adulthood* pulsates with a passion to nurture young adults toward growing faithfulness and conformity to the image of Christ. This is practical theology of spiritual formation at its best."

—**S. Steven Kang,** Gordon-Conwell Theological Seminary

SPIRITUAL FORMATION IN EMERGING ADULTHOOD

A Practical Theology for College and Young Adult Ministry

DAVID P. SETRAN | CHRIS A. KIESLING

Baker Academic

a division of Baker Publishing Group
Grand Rapids, Michigan

Published by Baker Academic
a division of Baker Publishing Group
P.O. Box 6287, Grand Rapids, MI 49516-6287
www.bakeracademic.com

Printed in the United States of America

Library of Congress Cataloging-in-Publication Data
Setran, David P.
    Spiritual formation in emerging adulthood: a practical theology for college and young adult minustry / David P. Setran, Chris A. Kiesling
        p.   cm.
    Includes bibliographical references and index.
    ISBN 978-0-8010-3956-0 (pbk.)
    1. Spiritual formation. 2. Young adults—Religious life. 3. Church work with young adults.
I. Title
BV4511.S48 2013
259′.25—dc23   2013010860

Portions of chapter 5 were first published in fall 2011 as "Getting a Life: Vocational Discernment in the Post-Christian World" in the *Christian Education Journal* (vol. 8, no. 2, pp. 345–63). They are included here with permission.

13   14   15   16   17   18   19   7   6   5   4   3   2   1

Contents

Acknowledgments   vii

Introduction   1

1. Faith: The Emerging Adult Landscape   11

2. Spiritual Formation: Reversing Moralistic Therapeutic Deism   29

3. Identity: Internalization, Refusal, and Engagement   55

4. Church: Forming an Ecclesiological Vision   81

5. Vocation: Purpose and Providence   111

6. Morality: Training the Dispositions of the Soul   139

7. Sexuality: Forming a Sexual Ethic   161

8. Relationships: Pitfalls and Pathways   185

9. Mentoring: Past, Present, and Future   205

Conclusion   231

Notes   241

Index   275

Acknowledgments

As with everything in our lives, this book is a product of grace, given by God and spread through others. We would like to thank our students, those who shaped these pages through their insights and questions. As we have taught and shared life with them through joyous and hard times, our passion for emerging adult ministry has been continually rekindled. While our students' stories may be veiled in the abstractions of these pages, their particular stories are engraved on our hearts.

This book also bears the marks of encouraging and supportive colleagues. I (David) am so thankful for department colleagues—Barrett, Scottie, Jim, Tom, Dan, Dave, Laura, and Kathleen (and TA Kristal)—who enrich my life and my thinking in so many ways. My (Chris) gratitude extends in ever-widening circles to those who inhabit my theological homeland, especially my area colleagues—Ellen, Jim, and Beverly—and my dean, Anne Gatobu. Our home institutions, Wheaton College and Asbury Theological Seminary, have provided the nourishing context for all that we have been able to accomplish here.

We are indebted to the Baker Academic team, those who have worked to bring this book to fruition. Thanks in particular go to Bob Hosack for catching and shaping the vision, and assembling a magnificent editorial and marketing team to guide us to the finish line.

A brief word of gratitude cannot begin to express our thanks to our families. I (David) want to thank my parents for launching me so well into adulthood and for their continued passion for Christ and for my work. I am also grateful to my children—Parker, Anna Joy, Owen, and Emily—for providing daily opportunities to experience the love of Jesus. Meeting my wife, Holly, was the greatest blessing of my own emerging adult years. Her love and support are overwhelming and I thank God for allowing me to live life with my best friend.

I (Chris) also want to express my abiding gratitude to my parents. Whatever I have become can be attributed to the forming center they have provided. And I am so thankful for my wife, Suzanne, with whom I celebrated twenty-five years of marriage while writing this book. She presses beauty, order, and faithfulness into my life. My boys, Daniel and Samuel, make fatherhood one of my most privileged roles.

Our passion for this stage of life is linked to our own stories of emerging adulthood and the people—teachers, mentors, family members, and pastors—who invested in us at this formative life stage. We dedicate the following pages to them, hoping that many will be inspired to do the same in their own spheres of influence.

Introduction

Remember your Creator during your youth: when all possibilities lie open before you and you can offer all your strength intact for his service. The time to remember is not after you become senile and paralyzed! Then it is not too late for your salvation, but too late for you to serve as the presence of God in the midst of the world and the creation. You must take sides earlier—when you can actually make choices, when you have many paths opening at your feet, before the weight of necessity overwhelms you.

Jacques Ellul[1]

So the time of late adolescence, which has received the least attention in Christian education literature, has actually become the period in the life cycle that poses the most far-reaching challenges to church and theology.

Friedrich Schweitzer[2]

In the United States, the years between the ages of 18 and 30 have long been heralded for their formative potential. Even a surface analysis of this period reveals a dizzying array of critical life tasks: choosing a college, choosing a life calling and vocation, moving away from home for the first time, buying or renting a home, making independent financial decisions, choosing and maintaining church commitments, forging new friendships and relationships with members of the opposite sex, and embracing the potential for singleness, engagement, marriage, and parenting. These years also mark a crucial stage for developing a worldview and faith stance amid a wide array of competing perspectives. This time of life is often attended by the need to assume ownership of one's faith and to select mentors and communities capable of

1

challenging and nurturing that faith over the long haul. Many of the choices made in these areas shape the contours of the rest of the life span, serving as gateways to future meaning, lifestyle, and mission. In short, this is the time when the fabric of life is woven together into a discernible—and increasingly solidified—pattern.

While the importance of this age span has often been acknowledged, however, it is critical to recognize that the experience of these years has changed dramatically in recent times. Most prominently, the last fifty years have witnessed a gradual delaying of traditional adult milestones. Sociologists have marked this shift by monitoring five key social events: leaving home, finishing school, becoming financially independent, getting married, and having children. The Research Network on Transitions to Adulthood and Public Policy reports that in 1960, more than two-thirds of young adults had attained all five of these markers by the age of 30; by the year 2000, this was true of less than half of females and less than a third of males.[3] Seventy percent of 25-year-old women had attained these markers in 1960, but only 25 percent in 2000. The later timing of these traditional adult responsibilities has reconfigured the typical "shape" of life between the ages of 18 and 30. As sociologist Christian Smith helpfully comments, "Half a century ago, many young people were anxious to get out of high school, marry, settle down, have children, and start a long-term career. But many youth today face almost a decade between high school graduation and marriage to spend exploring life's many options as singles, in unprecedented freedom."[4]

In the American context, a number of social and cultural factors have fueled delays in traditional adulthood. First, and perhaps most importantly, a growing number of individuals in this age group are delaying marriage. The average ages of first marriage in 1960 stood at roughly 20 for women and 22 for men. Now, approximately fifty years later, the average woman marries at age 26 while the average man waits until he is nearly 28.[5] This delay can be explained in part by a second social change: the expansion and extension of higher education. In the shift from a manufacturing-based economy to one anchored by technical and service sectors, higher education is often required to enhance career opportunities and earn a solid income. Therefore, while about 38 percent of high school graduates attended college in 1960, that number has now risen to approximately 70 percent. About a third of college graduates also attend graduate school, thereby extending schooling into the mid-to-late twenties. It is important to note that this change is even more dramatic for women. Women now constitute 58 percent of all undergraduate students in the United States, and they also constitute 50 percent or more of the students in medical schools, law schools, and business schools.[6] With higher education filling the early years of the twenties and beyond, other responsibilities—including career, marriage, and parenting—are put on hold.

For both men and women, economic factors are critical. In a changing global economy, many in this age range explore multiple career options and change jobs frequently, diminishing the stability usually desired before entering into the commitments of marriage and parenting. Less likely to begin and maintain a lifelong career with a single company, many feel a perpetual need for educational and geographical flexibility, postponing other kinds of commitments until they achieve some sense that they have found their vocational niches. When coupled with the need to repay sizable student loans, these factors often postpone the financial independence that is thought to be the prerequisite for settling down.[7]

In addition to these structural issues, personal concerns are also at play. As Smith reports, middle- and upper-class parents seem a bit more willing to finance these delays, providing the economic safety net necessary for young people to "find their place" educationally and vocationally.[8] Parents may provide a geographical safety net as well. Increasingly, twentysomethings are living at home during school or returning home after their schooling to relieve financial pressure while they seek to gain the education and skills required for a career. In a culture of high divorce rates, delays in marriage and parenting may also be linked to fears of marital failure. Particularly for children of divorced parents and those who have experienced such realities close up, delayed marital commitment can seem a wise safeguard against the disappointments of a fractured family. Finally, the cultural tolerance for premarital sexuality and the advent of easy and reliable birth control methods have broken the perceived link between marriage and sexuality. In a culture where sexual taboos have been abolished and where reproductive consequences have been removed, marriage is no longer viewed as a necessary precursor to sexual intimacy.[9] While this is obviously less true in Christian contexts, the church is far from immune to these shifts.[10]

These changes, according to many psychologists and sociologists, have actually paved the way for a genuinely new phase of the American life course. In 2000, psychologist Jeffrey Arnett posited a new life stage—"emerging adulthood"—to describe the growing chasm between adolescence and the completion of traditional adult milestones.[11] Between age 18 and the late twenties, he argues, emerging adults are characterized by five interrelated characteristics. First, they are actively engaged in identity formation, exploring personal meaning in love, work, and worldview. Second, they live lives marked by instability: regularly moving, changing jobs, and revising their life plans. Third, they tend to be very focused on themselves, free from parents' oversight and yet also free from significant responsibilities to others. Fourth, they feel "in between," recognizing that they have transcended adolescence and yet unsure if they have achieved full adult status. Finally, they see this time period as an "age of possibilities," optimistic about the future and desirous of keeping all of their options open.[12] "Having left the dependency of childhood and adolescence, and having not yet entered the enduring responsibilities that are normative in adulthood," Arnett notes, "emerging adults often explore a variety of possible life directions in love, work, and worldviews."[13]

While many of these emerging adult changes can be exhilarating, they also tend to produce a great deal of anxiety. Because many of the stable and scripted road maps of the adult life course have vanished, there is little clear direction on how to proceed through the twenties. In a period of instability, continual change, and new freedom, the weight of personal responsibility can be overwhelming. The uncertainty and volatility of this decade, coupled with the loss of clear expectations, often results in fear, depression, emotional paralysis, and various forms of addiction and escapism. While the midlife crisis during the forties and fifties is often a result of stagnancy and monotony, the so-called quarterlife crisis is linked to the pressure of developing a life plan in the absence of strong social cues and supports.[14]

How does all of this relate to the Christian vision of growth, maturity, and kingdom responsibility? Over the last ten years, a number of scholars and practitioners have embraced the language of emerging adulthood and attempted to analyze the religious dimensions of "twentysomething" life in light of these new social and cultural variables. The news about this age group is mixed. On the troubling side, by measures of both belief and practice, emerging adults are less religious than all other age groups. Smith, Robert Wuthnow, and others contend that emerging adults often lack purposeful engagement with Christian formation. Disrupted by the transitions and distractions in their lives, many in this age group diminish the faith commitments and practices that defined their childhood and adolescent years.[15] This is perhaps most visible in declining church participation, a reality that leaves emerging adults untethered to supportive Christian community at this formative stage of life.[16]

Other challenges are equally daunting. Emerging adults have been described as "morally adrift," devoid of clear boundaries for right and wrong outside of personal opinion.[17] Others highlight their tendency to engage in risk behaviors such as reckless driving, binge drinking, and drug abuse.[18] Many point to their sexually permissive and promiscuous relationships, evidenced by a "hookup" culture concerned chiefly with personal gratification.[19] Some indicate that emerging adults view this stage of life as a decade set apart for pleasure and personal exploration, ignoring the missional call of vocational responsibility.[20]

In all of these areas, many identify a pervasive pattern of individualism, a primary reliance on what Smith has labeled the "sovereign self."[21]

Yet despite these troubling indicators, there are also some very hopeful signs. For example, various authors have identified among emerging adults a renewed passion for social justice and compassion for the downtrodden. According to journalist Colleen Carroll, many desire to bring the redemptive power of the gospel to bear on a broader range of personal and social issues.[22] In addition, some authors point to a renewed desire among Christian emerging adults to forge connections with the traditions of the Christian faith. Both Carroll and Robert Webber, for example, have described a trend among young professionals to embrace traditional liturgical forms and strict moral and doctrinal creeds as a counterpoint to the diffuse permissiveness of contemporary American culture.[23] Furthermore, many are indeed seeking mentors to nourish and guide their faith journeys. As they begin the process of evaluating former commitments and developing new ideals, emerging adults desire guides who will support their growth, challenge and critique where needed, and cast a vision for the future.[24]

Undoubtedly, there is exciting promise and potential for emerging adults to bring renewal to the church and the world. They are primed at this time of life to consider new ideas and dream about future possibilities. Emerging adults tend to be idealistic, energetic, and passionate about their pursuits. Many great revivals and missionary movements throughout history, in fact, were birthed through the irrepressible zeal of emerging adults.[25] They tend to be what Andy Crouch has called "culture makers," people poised to immerse themselves in creative opportunities for connecting gospel truths to a variety of cultural contexts.[26] Of course, this energy and enthusiasm can be misguided and can disorient older church members who desire continuity and stability. However, when tethered to the internal compass of biblical truth and directed by encouraging mentors, this passion can serve as a potent force for spiritual renewal. Part of our calling as mentors to young adults is to unleash some of this "potential energy" into channels through which the kingdom can infiltrate church and world to the glory of God.

We therefore see emerging adulthood as a time of formidable challenge and yet great opportunity. Our backgrounds are in college and young adult ministry. We have spent most of our professional lives working on college campuses. For more than a decade, we have both been teaching undergraduates and graduate students, including a large number who desire to minister among the members of this age group. We have seen emerging adults abuse their newfound freedom, falling victim to sexual struggles, substance abuse, and relational chaos. We have seen students swayed by intellectual currents that erode the foundations of their faith. We have observed the development of cynicism in which joy and enthusiasm is stripped away by recurring patterns of callousness and apathy. Yet we also find a longing among young people today to find mentors who will listen to their stories and walk alongside them as they embrace new challenges. We have been amazed at their willingness to address the monumental challenges of our day: caring for orphans, setting up barriers to human trafficking, building relations with villages in developing countries, and embracing leadership challenges in churches worldwide. Amid all of the disruptions, distractions, and cultural distortions, we have witnessed deep spiritual transformation that awakens and sustains a passionate pursuit of Christian discipleship.

Living in the midst of such activity, in roles that privilege us to watch these tensions unfold in the lives of emerging adults, we are prompted to ask two central questions. First, what does the gospel have to offer emerging adults as they are formed through the adult transition? Second, what do emerging adults shaped by the gospel have to offer to the church and the world?[27] In other words, we want to discern how emerging adults can be spiritually formed within communities marked by a countercultural biblical and theological narrative. We also want to propose how emerging adults' gospel-shaped lives can offer truth, healing, and hope to the body of Christ and to the larger world.

Despite the critical nature of this life stage and a host of new cultural challenges, emerging adult spiritual formation has been largely neglected as a topic of purposeful inquiry. Books related to Christian education and spiritual growth tend to focus on children and youth, the groups over which the church possesses more "comprehensive" influence. Books written on issues related specifically to emerging adult faith tend to fall into three main categories. First, popular books written to emerging adults provide sage wisdom regarding issues of character, use of time and money, relational intimacy, and biblical faithfulness.[28] Second, books written about the "next generation" furnish sweeping portraits of the cultural changes influencing emerging adults in the "postmodern era." Based largely on examinations of cultural and philosophical trends, these works help us think more carefully about the ways in which the church relates to emerging adults growing up in cultures distinct from those of previous generations.[29]

Third, a growing academic literature grants us incisive analyses of cultural and demographic trends as well as faith development stage theories for emerging adults. Recent sociological works, such as Smith's *Souls in Transition* and Wuthnow's *After the Baby Boomers*, provide quantitative and qualitative perspectives on emerging adult church attendance, denominational affiliation, beliefs, spiritual practices, and cultural patterns related to dating, marriage, consumerism, and entertainment.[30] Those with more of a psychological orientation, including Sharon Parks's *Big Questions, Worthy Dreams*, James Fowler's *Becoming Adult, Becoming Christian*, and Arnett's *Emerging Adulthood*, focus on documenting the changing internal worlds of emerging adults.[31] These sociological and psychological works provide us with critical data about the institutional and internal dynamics of emerging adult life in the twenty-first century.[32]

With this present work, we seek to fill a gap in the existing literature. We desire to provide a "practical theology" for college and young adult ministry, one that combines important scholarship, a Christian theological vision, and attentiveness to concrete ministry applications. With an eye to the link between theory and practice, we look specifically at the formative emerging adult issues of spiritual formation, identity, church involvement, vocation, morality, relationships and sexuality, and mentoring. In each area, we describe present reality as a starting point for understanding the matrix of forces shaping the transition to adulthood in today's culture. We also seek to interpret these conditions, specifying some of the key factors underlying these trends. Finally, turning to Scripture, theology, and other academic disciplines, we provide Christian perspectives on these issues and delineate key postures and practices designed to facilitate spiritual formation in these areas. By providing descriptive, interpretive, normative, and pragmatic insights on these topics, we hope to better equip college and young adult ministers, professors, pastors, student development professionals, parents, and laypeople in their work among emerging adults in this formative life stage.[33]

In chapters 1 and 2, we address spiritual formation during these formative years. Chapter 1 looks at the current landscape of emerging adult spiritual formation, documenting the widespread spiritual "slump" at this time of life and tracing the personal, cultural, and theological barriers that challenge growth in Christ. One of those challenges stems from the default faith position Smith has called "Moralistic Therapeutic Deism," a perspective defined by vague moral goodness, an appeal to personal fulfillment, and a God who is distant and called on only in times of trouble.[34] Chapter 2, therefore, sets forth a vision of emerging adult spiritual formation that confronts this imposter religion at each point. Proposing an approach that seeks inner transformation, costly discipleship, and embodied disciplines that facilitate communion with God, we hope to cast a vision for emerging adult formation that describes the contours of the "with God" life at the cusp of adulthood.[35]

In chapter 3, we look carefully at the evolving nature of emerging adult identity formation. As social movements through the past fifty years have largely liberated people from ascribed identities, emerging adults today are offered an almost unlimited array of possible life choices.[36] Attaining adult identity is now a highly self-directed process, where allegiances to institutions and family are often relinquished in the pursuit of individualization. However, with fewer prescribed social roles and with increased pressure to become one's own person, anxiety multiplies. In this chapter, we describe a Christian perspective on identity formation, highlighting both the individual and cultural processes by which a strong identity is formed. At this time of life, emerging adults move beyond authority-bound structures and begin owning and internalizing faith commitments. Yet this process, we contend, is fostered not by complete autonomy and separation from authority structures but within "communities of truth" that bestow Christian identity on emerging adults.[37] We draw from the biblical narrative of Daniel to emphasize two dynamic processes, refusal and engagement, as important directives in fostering this kind of Christian identity.

Having advocated for the critical importance of authoritative community in developing Christian identity, we turn in chapter 4 to a consideration of the church. Christian leaders and academics have spoken a great deal about the detachment of emerging adults from faith communities. While some blame local churches and others focus their attacks on emerging adults themselves, the result is clear: a loss of corporate spiritual formation. In this chapter, we look at the research documenting emerging adult disengagement from the church, noting diverse sources and consequences of this troubling reality. We then look biblically and theologically at the critical importance of corporate Christian formation, describing the key components of an "ecclesiological vision" for emerging adults. Finally, we offer practical suggestions for emerging adults and for churches seeking to enhance their focus on this formative period of life.

Since the church is missional by its very nature, this ecclesiological vision is inextricably linked to the development of Christian vocational commitments during emerging adulthood. Chapter 5, therefore, looks at the development of a sense of calling and life purpose at this critical stage. The cultural priority given to personal exploration and self-actualization in these years tends to make this a journey linked tightly to personal identity and fulfillment. The vast proliferation of options and choices has further complicated the vocational journey and challenged commitment and contentment along these lines. In this chapter, therefore, we seek to provide a Christian vision of vocation and calling that is grounded in God's redemptive purposes and in his providential hand in emerging adults' lives. We then demonstrate the critical importance of such a vision for assisting emerging adults in vocational discernment.

Closely related to vocational discernment is consideration of the moral framework within which an emerging adult makes life choices. This is our focus in chapter 6. As in other domains, the cultural elevation of individualism has worn thin any communal fabric of morality to guide emerging adults. The resultant posturing of morality for most twentysomethings is a reliance on moral intuition attributed to early childhood socialization, coupled with a consequentialism that regards wrong only that which causes harm to another. Rarely does the current cultural ethos compel emerging adults to curb self-interest for the sake of the common good or for missional service in the world. In this chapter, we provide a moral formation framework that attempts to move beyond both permissiveness and a legalistic reliance on rules. Instead, we commend a virtue-centered approach that promotes habituated dispositions of the soul linked to the larger Christian narrative. We then conclude by offering five pathways as viable means of deepening moral formation among emerging adults.

Linked to issues of both faith and morality, chapters 7 and 8 explore emerging adult romantic relationships and sexuality. Most emerging adults envision themselves eventually settling into a monogamous marriage relationship. However, the strategies to secure this hope can be full of devastating misadventures. Chapter 7 traces historical and cultural shifts in the ways intimate relationships are structured. Looking particularly at the increasingly sexualized nature of the emerging adult "hookup" culture, we also explore the influence of delayed marriage and cohabitation on the shape of such interactions. With this background established, we then outline the broad strokes of an emerging adult sexual ethic that grounds virtuous sexuality in the covenant relationships manifested by God and his people and by the "one-flesh" union of husband and wife. Chapter 8 then looks more specifically at how leaders can help emerging adults navigate such relationships by exploring their histories of attachment and sexuality, by gaining a deeper awareness of such issues as singleness, dating, cohabitation, and early marriage, and by understanding the relationships between physical, social, and spiritual intimacy.

As we consider the various themes mentioned in this book, chapter 9 will provide a concluding framework for effective mentoring among emerging adults. After delineating the challenges to forming mentoring relationships with emerging adults, the proposed framework describes mentoring as facilitating postures of (1) "remembering"—looking back on God's faithful past action in history and in their own lives, (2) "attending"—looking around and within for God's present work in their lives and in the world, and (3) "envisioning"—looking forward to a future that is anticipated both in their sanctified imaginations and in the examples of those already demonstrating adult faithfulness. Since emerging adulthood represents an important "hinge" moment, attention to past, present, and future can provide a holistic sense of God's work in their lives and a growing capacity to locate their stories within the broader story of God.

In the end, therefore, we hope to provide guidance both for Christian thinking about emerging adulthood and for walking alongside emerging adults in their faith journeys. In many ways, we hope to say something substantive about what it means to be spiritually formed *into adulthood*. Within the life span, the twenties represent what one author has called "the stem cell of human development, the pluripotent moment when any of several outcomes is possible."[38] It is an important moment in which beliefs, perspectives, and habits are being etched within the soft wax of life. We desire the gospel to make its stamp before the wax has hardened. So we ask the following questions: What are the unique opportunities and challenges that emerging adulthood provides for the process of spiritual formation? How can emerging adults enter deeply into processes of formation that will serve as gateways to lives of growing faithfulness and conformity to the image of Christ? How can mentors shepherd emerging adults as they construct paths of meaning, purpose, and mission in these formative years?

Ultimately, we hope that the answers to such questions will furnish a compelling mandate for ministry to emerging adults, one that takes seriously both the perils and the promises of this life stage. Emerging adulthood can be a wonderful "runway" enabling individuals to take off into a life of productive service for the kingdom of God.[39] For others, it can be a very difficult and lonely journey, accompanied by depression, anxiety, diffused identity, failed intimacy, vocational "false starts," and stagnation. We hope that the perspectives offered in these pages will provide a window into the very meaning of adulthood in Christian perspective and also provide wisdom for emerging adult mentors in college, church, and world.

1 | Faith

The Emerging Adult Landscape

The terrible thing, the almost impossible thing, is to hand over your whole self—all your wishes and precautions—to Christ. But it is far easier than what we are all trying to do instead. For what we are trying to do is to remain what we call "ourselves," to keep personal happiness as our great aim in life, and yet at the same time be "good." We are all trying to let our mind and heart go their own way—centered on money or pleasure or ambition—and hoping, in spite of this, to behave honestly and chastely and humbly. And that is exactly what Christ warned us you could not do. As He said, a thistle cannot produce figs. If I am a field that contains nothing but grass-seed, I cannot produce wheat. Cutting the grass may keep it short: but I shall still produce grass and no wheat. If I want to produce wheat, the change must go deeper than the surface. I must be ploughed up and re-sown.

C. S. Lewis[1]

"Fine." That seemed to be Jim's go-to reply when asked about his spiritual life. Twenty-seven years old and a former student of David's, Jim had spent the previous hour excitedly recounting some of his key accomplishments since graduation. After a transitional year at home, he had completed a master's program, started a new romantic relationship, and landed a job with a great salary and benefits. He was beginning to think seriously about marriage and looking forward to the prospect of buying a house in one of the city's better neighborhoods. He noted repeatedly that he was enjoying his new freedom and attempting to make the most of each day, soaking in all that the city had to offer: concerts, museums, parties, and sporting events. "It's been a whirlwind," he remarked, "but I'm loving every minute of it."

Jim's eager posture dropped significantly, however, when asked about his faith. "It's fine," he noted, stating that he still held firmly to his college-age beliefs. Jim had been a solid disciple of Jesus as an undergraduate, involved in various ministries and eager to share his faith with others. In the years after graduation, he had not been able to find a good church, and he didn't know many people who attended church on a weekly basis. He said that he still read his Bible, though not with the regularity that marked his college days. Graduate school had been so intense that he found himself unable to get involved in ministries or evangelism. "I still believe the same things," he suggested without prompting. "I still have my faith. I just don't have a ton of time to give to it right now, but that day will come again soon. I'm doing fine."

"Fine." That word, in many ways, seems an apt description of the spiritual formation landscape during the years of emerging adulthood.

The "Religious Slump" of Emerging Adulthood

While each story is unique, Jim's account is certainly characteristic of larger trends. Research on emerging adulthood is fairly consistent in proclaiming this to be a stage marked by widespread religious decline in the areas of belief, behavior, and the subjective inner life. On the cognitive level, there appears to be a moderate erosion of basic belief in the orthodox tenets of the Christian faith. While 78 percent of 18- to 23-year-olds claim to believe in God without reservation—certainly a sizable majority—this represents about a 7 percent drop when compared with American teenagers. Furthermore, this decline is actually sharper among those who spent their teen years within the church. Conservative Protestants, for example, see an 8 percent decline in belief in God while mainline Protestants see a more precipitous 17 percent decline.[2] In every religious tradition, emerging adult belief in God is also lower than belief in God for those over the age of 30.[3] Fewer emerging adult Protestants see God as a "personal being involved in the lives of people today" while a growing number identify God as "not personal, something like a cosmic life force."[4] Basic belief in God's existence and personal involvement, therefore, reaches its lowest point in the years after high school.

When it comes to more specific beliefs, the drift from orthodoxy is still pronounced. A declining number of conservative and mainline emerging adult Protestants believe in a divine "judgment day," and fewer believe in the existence of angels and divine miracles. Members of this age group are also more likely than any other to disavow Jesus's sinlessness and to doubt his bodily resurrection.[5] Among evangelicals, those between the ages of 18 and 30 are significantly less likely to view the Bible as the literal Word of God and more likely to approve of homosexuality than their older counterparts.[6] While other beliefs—such as the reality of life after death and the existence of heaven and hell—seem to remain fairly stable or even increase from the teen years through older adulthood,[7] the larger picture indeed demonstrates what sociologist Christian Smith identifies as "general shifts away from certainty about God . . . and definite belief in other traditional, 'biblical' teachings."[8]

Even when basic beliefs remain intact, there is widespread recognition that religion declines in subjective importance during the emerging adult years. When comparing 18- to 23-year-olds with those between the ages of 13 and 17, the National Survey of Youth and Religion (NSYR) found significant declines in the percentage agreeing that faith was "very important" in daily life, coupled with a strong increase in the number claiming that faith was either "not very important" or "not important at all."[9] Perhaps even more telling, these declines were quite sharp among those affiliated with conservative and mainline Protestant churches. Among conservative Protestants, the move from the teen years into emerging adulthood was marked by a 13 percent drop in those claiming that faith was "very or extremely important" in shaping daily life (down from 70 percent to 57 percent). Mainline Protestants saw an even greater decline of 16 percent during this transition (down from 49 percent to 33 percent). According to the Pew Forum on Religion and Public Life, the declining perceived importance of religion is also evident when comparing emerging adults with those in older groups. While 59 percent of those over the age of 30 see religion as "very important," 45 percent of those between the ages of 18 and 29 state the same. Even among the religiously affiliated, those over the age of 30 were 9 percent more likely to see religion as "very important" than religiously affiliated emerging adults.[10]

Despite these moderate changes in belief and in the subjective sense of religion's importance, scholars across the board agree that Christian *practices and institutional participation* are far more likely to decline even when beliefs remain intact. In addition to widely publicized declines in church attendance, to be discussed in detail in chapter 4, a host of other spiritual disciplines become less prominent in emerging adults' lives. Looking at professing Christians, the NSYR identified declines between Christian adolescence and emerging adulthood in the frequency of daily prayer, Bible reading, Sabbath observance, religious singing, reading of devotional materials, and personal evangelism.[11] Among conservative Protestants, for example, a mere 10 percent in this age group read the Scriptures daily, down from 16 percent in adolescence.[12] Comparing emerging adults to their elders, the Pew Forum found that 34 percent of religiously affiliated emerging adults read Scripture weekly, compared to 41 percent of those age 30 and above. Similarly, 58 percent of religious emerging adults pray daily, while 66 percent of those 30 and over do the same. Another independent study found that, while 46 percent of older, religious adults take part in devotional practices, only 33 percent of religious emerging adults do the same.[13] The erosion of Christian beliefs, therefore, is coupled with a similar erosion of Christian behaviors. Smith estimates that about 50 percent of emerging adults remain stable in their faith commitments and practice while 40 percent decline and 10 percent increase in commitment, leading him to assert, "Emerging adults are, on most sociological measures, the least religious adults in the United States today."[14]

Yet there is a psychological component to this as well. In light of these figures, it is perhaps not surprising that a growing number of emerging adult Protestants, on a very personal level, feel distant from God. In a recent study, only 35 percent of conservative Protestants in this age group indicated that they felt "extremely or very close" to God, down from 48 percent among teenagers in this same group. Mainline Protestants experienced an even larger decline. While 40 percent of mainline teenagers felt "extremely or very close" to God, only 22 percent of emerging adults felt the same. Such statistics are important because they reveal not only a decline in religious belief and practice but also a waning subjective sense of God's presence in their lives. Speaking of the comprehensive cognitive, behavioral, and affective declines in these years, Smith concludes, "Some or even many American youth go into something of a religious slump during these years."[15]

Interestingly, while such data reveal troubling declines in measures of faith during emerging adulthood, other research presents a far more positive picture of spiritual interest among members of this age group. A number of studies seem to indicate that spirituality is on the rise among emerging adults. In an ongoing analysis of the spirituality of collegians, for example, the Higher Education Research Institute (HERI) at UCLA discovered that students across diverse institutions have "very high levels of spiritual interest" and desire to spend ample time "exploring the meaning and purpose of life." According to this research, four out of five students claim that they "have an interest in spirituality" and that they "believe in the sacredness of life" while two out of three state that "my spirituality is a source of joy."[16] Fifty-eight percent indicated that integrating spirituality into their lives is "very important" or "essential."[17] In addition, this research seems to indicate that increasing numbers of college students are engaged in a "spiritual quest," a broader search for meaning, purpose, and inner peace.[18] While women generally rate higher in spiritual interest than men in these areas, these studies seem to point to a generalized intensification of spiritual awareness during this stage of life.[19]

The explosion of spiritual interest, such authors suggest, is a result of many age-specific events. Separation from parents, in and of itself, can spark spiritual reflection since emerging adults gain a deeper sense of responsibility for their own lives and spiritual commitments.[20] In addition, as Alyssa Bryant and Helen Astin have discussed, the new experiences and challenges of emerging adulthood also foster spiritual awareness.[21] Many are confronted for the first time with worldviews and lifestyles different from their own, sparking questions about truth. Others, faced with vocational decisions, begin reflecting on their purposes and contributions in the world. Some lose parents or grandparents, heightening reflections on eternity. Collegiate exposure to national and global issues awakens concerns for justice and equity. Some even argue that changes in the brain during emerging adulthood—including synaptic pruning and continued myelination in the prefrontal cortex—enhance the physiological possibility of deep spiritual reflection and interior processing.[22] While many of these researchers would concur that measures of religious practice and church involvement decline during these years, they would argue that this simply represents a revised and perhaps evolving perspective on faith. Many speak of this generation of emerging adults as "spiritual but not religious," caring more effectively for their interior lives even as they eschew doctrinal creeds and formal participation in religious practices.[23]

Yet while such analyses reveal a purported uptick in spiritual interest, optimistic generalizations can be misleading. Estimates are often inflated because the ever-broadening definition of "spirituality" used by social scientists makes it almost inevitable that they will find heightened spiritual interest among emerging adults.[24] Since definitions of spirituality are generally quite vague—more akin to caring about one's "inner, subjective life," finding life meaning, and cultivating a greater sense of "connectedness to one another and to the world around us"—emerging adult interest in spirituality may not indicate much more than a growing self-awareness and exposure to new ways of thinking.[25] There is very little in these definitions that would tether spirituality to any personal conviction or commitment, much less an external faith-based narrative. As sociologist Tim Clydesdale points out,

> Asking incoming American college freshmen whether they "have an interest
> in spirituality" is like asking a soldier in a trench whether he has an interest

in world peace or an arguing spouse whether she has an interest in honest and loving communication. To learn that most agree should not surprise us in the slightest. The critical questions are whether indicating interest in religious and spiritual life, world peace, or loving communication makes a difference in present activities and long-range goals, and to what extent.[26]

Furthermore, accounts of widespread spiritual interest seem to be exaggerated. Sociologists do acknowledge that emerging adults are the age group most likely to speak of spirituality apart from religious involvement, but they claim that only a small minority of emerging adults fit the "spiritual but not religious" mold.[27] Among members of the broader population, one study estimates that 10 percent may qualify as "spiritual but not religious."[28] Smith suggests that 15 percent of all emerging adults are spiritually "open," meaning that they are "not personally very committed to a religious faith but are nonetheless receptive to and at least mildly interested in some spiritual or religious matters."[29] Another 15 percent qualify as "committed traditionalists," finding spiritual meaning and purpose in a formal commitment to a specific faith.[30] The majority of emerging adults, however, view both spiritual and religious matters as of marginal importance in their lives.[31] Smith's assessment is important: "So yes, some emerging adults, including students in college, are interested in spirituality. But for a good number of them, that simply means doing traditional religion. And for another chunk of them, that means they simply do not want to say that they are positively not interested in spirituality. Yet others may say whatever about matters spiritual but in fact are simply too distracted by other affairs to care very much."[32]

Smith's final statement here is important because it demonstrates that most emerging adults are characterized not by religious hostility but rather by a growing apathy and indifference to the life of faith. In their recent survey of 1,200 emerging adults between the ages of 20 and 30, Thom Rainer and Jess Rainer found that only 13 percent considered any type of spirituality to be important in their lives.[33] Similarly, Smith found that emerging adults were largely unconcerned about religion. Since matters of faith are considered "not a big deal" and "not something of central importance," such topics rarely come up in conversations with friends.[34] In fact, he notes, religion has

a status on the relevance structures or priority lists of most emerging adults that is similar to, say, the oil refinery industry. Of course, people know it is there, and it is important in some removed or distant way. Most people are glad someone is out there taking care of that business. But you really don't have to think much about it or personally get involved in it, unless it happens to be a personal interest. Religion for the most part is just something in the background.[35]

Overall, then, emerging adults are not antagonistic toward the Christian faith. For most, it would seem, faith is something "neither hot nor cold"—a tasteless product that has been pushed to the periphery of life.[36] Before we construct a positive approach to emerging adult spiritual formation, we must identify some of the reasons for this malaise.

The Sources of Spiritual Decline

The marginalization of spiritual formation among emerging adults is of course a function of many variables, but a few stand out as central to this age group. First, there are a host of new distractions emerging at this time of life that can easily de-center faith commitments. Because emerging adults are often living independently for the first time, there are a number of new life skills required in their attempt to "stand on their own two feet."[37] While tasks such as setting up bank accounts, paying bills, registering for classes, studying for exams, writing research papers, learning to get along with roommates, and preparing for job interviews may seem fairly commonplace to older adults, emerging adults can find them quite overwhelming. Though the cultivation of the spiritual life may still remain important in a theoretical sense, these other tasks can appear more urgent on a daily basis. In addition, since completion of these tasks often generates immediate feedback and both financial and psychological (identity-related) rewards, it is easy to see why they might rise to higher levels on the emerging adult priority scale. As one study summarizes, "Emerging adulthood brings with it a host of responsibilities (e.g., work, school) and opportunities (e.g., increased autonomy) that simply and subtly crowd out religious participation."[38]

In his analysis of younger emerging adults in the year after high school graduation, Clydesdale largely confirms this perspective. Most of these individuals, he suggests, spend the bulk of their time and energy on "daily life management," juggling personal relationships, personal gratifications, and personal economics. In such a context, he suggests, faith commitments are placed in a "lockbox," stowed away for safekeeping until later in life. These emerging adults may maintain their religious beliefs, but they are unlikely to cultivate personal faith practices if these interfere with their other life concerns. As he notes, "Teens view religious faith and practice as largely irrelevant to this stage in their life cycle. Religion is something they did as 'kids' and something they will probably do again as 'adults.' But, for now, teens tune out religion—at the very moment when they make decisions that can affect the rest of their lives and during the very time when they are individually establishing patterns of everyday living."[39] Referring back to the Higher Education Research Institute study, he notes, "I do concur that most teens are on a quest during their first year out, but that quest is to successfully navigate interpersonal relationships and manage everyday life (like eating, working, attending class, doing laundry, and having a little fun). Religious and spiritual identities are peripheral to that quest and stowed in an identity lockbox for a later point in the life cycle."[40] Because religion does not seem applicable to the all-consuming flow of daily life, faith is set to the side and rarely engaged, critically examined, or applied to the decisions and practices of life. According to Clydesdale, faith is neither "abandoned" nor "pursued," but rather "safely stowed."[41]

The distractions of emerging adult "tasks" are easily matched by the concomitant distractions of "fun." At this time of life, entertainment options abound and permit easy access. During those hours not taken up with jobs, schoolwork, or other life tasks, there are ample opportunities for play via video games, television, movies, parties, concerts, and sporting events. Since these events are often reserved for weekend evenings, as Smith suggests, they certainly detract from the opportunity to take part in weekend church activities. In addition, since the church is often opposed to some of the entertainment options preferred by emerging adults—especially those involving drinking and parties—it is quite common for emerging adults to simply decrease (or privatize) their religious commitments so as to limit the felt discontinuities between faith and lifestyle.

In fact, lifestyle choices at this age seem to be closely related to the decline in faith commitment. Such choices can have multiple faith-eroding results. Some emerging adults will compartmentalize their lives, continuing religious participation in their "Christian life" even while living contrary to their beliefs in other venues. For others, moral choices will move them to redefine Christianity in order to bring it in line with their chosen behaviors. For still others, Christianity will be put on the shelf with the intent that it may be reclaimed once the fun is over. And, of course, others will abandon the faith altogether because it seems to interfere with new ways of living. As Dietrich Bonhoeffer suggests, disobedience can actually obscure Christ and dull spiritual sensitivity.[42] There is, in other words, a moral component to Christian commitment that poses particular challenges in the "anything goes" culture of emerging adulthood.

Emerging adult lifestyles can also present challenges to the attentiveness required for spiritual formation. Sleeping habits tend to be quite poor at this time of life, leading to a host of difficulties in sustaining focus.[43] In addition, emerging adults are perpetually distracted by internet browsing and social networking, now present everywhere and at all times on laptops, tablets, and cell phones. Managing their friendships and other relationships through social networking has become a "24/7 life activity," a daily project that is always beckoning for their attention (and producing guilt if neglected). Nicholas Carr has demonstrated that the internet shapes the brain in ways that promote distractedness and inhibit depth of focus and concentration.[44] Because of the constant flow of sensory stimuli, hyperlinks, and intruding messages from the outside, the brain increasingly becomes habituated to perpetual skimming and browsing. Smith concurs: "All of these relationship-managing activities and private communication distractions seem to make it difficult for emerging adults to pursue tasks that require full concentration or patient dedication."[45]

To borrow Steven Covey's language, it seems that emerging adulthood is often consumed with matters that are "urgent and important" and "urgent, but not important."[46] Such tasks have deadlines, and they offer immediate rewards for their completion (or punishments if not completed). They also tend to provide a sense of growing adult identity, competence, and personal validation. Because many of these tasks are new, they also take longer than they will at a later time of life. It is easy to see why some who are overwhelmed with these activities retreat to the "not urgent, not important" forms of entertainment that are readily available.[47] It is quite common for emerging adults to solidify "work hard–play hard" rhythms in which they give full time to their responsibilities during the day and then use evenings and weekends to "blow off steam." Such rhythms leave little room for the dimensions of life "that are not urgent, but are important," including those related to the spiritual life.[48]

For many emerging adults, this perspective is actually linked to their own subjective impression of the uniqueness of this life stage. With a clear sense that the typical adult responsibilities of marriage, parenting, and a stable career are coming, many view the emerging adult years as a time to have fun and explore all life has to offer. The twenties, for many, provide a limited window of full freedom prior to the responsibilities required once one "settles down." As Smith notes, "Rather than being settled, most of them understand themselves to be in a phase of life that is free, fluid, tentative, experimental, and relatively unbound. They want to enjoy it while it lasts. . . . They want to acquire independence and the ability to stand on their own two feet. But most of them also do not want full adulthood to come too quickly."[49] Because of this, deep investment in spiritual formation appears to detract from the ability to live life to the full. The opportunity costs are just too high. Many therefore feel that intentional spiritual development can be put off until later and picked up as a task when they are no longer free to pursue their own interests unencumbered by other responsibilities. At that point, after they have gotten all of the fun and life experience out of their systems, they will assume traditional adult roles, including participation in a local church and attentiveness to the life of faith. For now, however, the twenties are unofficially labeled as "my time."

The disruptions characterizing this fluid and exploratory time of life are also critical forces working against faith commitments. The sheer scope of change in emerging adulthood often serves to disrupt the spiritual rhythms and continuity of the high school years. Rates of moving to a new residence reach their peak in the early twenties. Living situations (and roommates) change with great frequency. In addition, the average college student changes his or her major (and therefore potential career direction) three times during the undergraduate years. Furthermore, the average emerging adult in America holds seven to eight different jobs between the ages of 18 and 30, following a circuitous path to career satisfaction. Coupled with the ins and outs of friendships and romantic relationships, it is little wonder that psychologist Jeffrey Arnett calls this time of life as the "age of instability."[50]

While transitions can be beneficial in many individuals' lives, life disruptions tend to correlate negatively with strong religious commitment. As habits and routines are broken in the midst of transition, it often takes great effort to reestablish healthy spiritual patterns in these new settings. Finding a new church home, for example, can seem like a monumental task, especially if one is not sure he or she will be staying in an area for an extended period of time. On a smaller scale, spiritual practices, such as prayer, Bible study, fasting, solitude, and silence, can also drop off in the midst of transitions. New schedules often shake established habits. The stability of previous mentoring relationships (parents, youth pastors, etc.) gives way to an ever-shifting assortment of adult influences. New living arrangements mean accommodating new roommates and their particular life patterns (or lack thereof!). Importantly, the rapid and incessant changes characterizing emerging adulthood can have the psychological effect of discouraging any formation of life patterns, habits, and rituals. In other words, the effort needed to establish spiritual rhythms, congregational investment, and other practices may not appear worthwhile when emerging adults anticipate yet another impending transition in the near future. Many reason that it is fruitless to establish meaningful spiritual patterns until a later time when their lives will (presumably) be characterized by greater stability. When all of life seems "temporary," it is daunting to generate a way of life characterized by the faithful routines of the spiritual life.

In addition, as Smith indicates, these disruptions in housing and career also connect emerging adults to new social networks with people who may expose them to new (and potentially less spiritual) life patterns. For those growing up in Christian homes, the move to a new setting—college or career—will likely expand the range of contacts to include those with more diverse backgrounds, beliefs, and moral standards. In such new contexts, the sense of what is "normal" or "acceptable" can rapidly change as one is socialized into a new and ever-widening sphere.[51] The need to secure quick friendships in a new setting can easily lead to less discriminating choices. In addition, because of the increased depth of friendships at this time of life, linked now more than ever to the sharing of opinions and worldviews, these new relationships hold tremendous sway over emerging adults' shifting perspectives and orientations in the world. Whereas parents may have been able to constrain spheres of influence during the teen years, the world certainly opens up during emerging adulthood to include a far greater diversity of thought and practice. Those without strong foundations can quickly find themselves swept away.[52]

One caveat is important here, however. While disruptions seem to challenge the cultivation of faith, college is not as "disruptive" as some might think. Christians often blame colleges for the faith declines of emerging adults, assuming that the combination of liberal teaching, the loss of parental oversight, and the loose moral culture of the campus creates a perfect storm hastening the demise of strong faith. It is true that many scholars over the years have indicated that college serves as a ripe setting for the dissolution—or at least the liberalization—of faith.[53] However, while this may have been true for the baby boomer generation, more recent research reveals that those not attending college are actually more likely to experience a faith decline. Far more students indicate that their faith was strengthened rather than weakened during their college years, despite the fact that religious practices uniformly decline in these settings.[54] Even the practical involvement in religious activities declines less for those in college than for those who have never attended. While 64 percent of those enrolled in four-year higher-education institutions curtail their church attendance, 76 percent of emerging adults who never enrolled in college do the same. Regular church attendance among college students has been higher than noncollege attendees at least since the 1980s. In addition, while 13 percent of traditional college students renounce all religious affiliation during these years, 20 percent of those not enrolled in college do the same.[55]

While some of the collegiate spiritual "advantage" may have to do with expanding ministries on campuses, it may also, ironically, demonstrate students' lack of intentional intellectual engagement. Studies have shown that fewer students in recent years state that they are attending college in order to gain a "meaningful philosophy of life." Far more are now attending so that they can "be very well off financially."[56] Defined as "practical credentialists" rather than "intellectual explorers," they are less apt to be lured away by godless philosophies than they are to breeze through the college experience with little intentional reflection on faith.[57] The search for a marketable degree generally means finding courses that will provide the best "applicable" training with a minimal investment of thought and reflection.[58] "Religious faith," these researchers argue, "is rarely seen as something that could either influence or be influenced by the educational process."[59] In addition, since many do not have a strong theological background when entering college, they likely fail to identify antagonistic perspectives when they arise. While college may liberalize social and political positions and cultural values, the classroom doesn't appear to be a major barrier to faith. Thus, while there is a decline in religious involvement from the teenage years to the years of emerging adulthood, it does not appear, on the whole, that college is a significant factor in the slump. "Simply put," state sociologists Mark Regnerus and Jeremy Uecker, "higher education is not the enemy of religiosity."[60]

While these various factors all contribute to a diminished emphasis on spiritual formation, it is also true that this malaise may be a function of the type of faith embraced during the teen and emerging adult years. In other words, the forms of faith adopted in these years often have little natural connection to an ongoing process of spiritual formation. As Smith has posited, the majority posture among emerging adults still appears to be what he has termed "Moralistic Therapeutic Deism," otherwise known as "divinely underwritten personal happiness and interpersonal niceness."[61] Those influenced by Moralistic Therapeutic Deism view God as a distant creator who desires humans to be nice and fair to one another and who intervenes in human experience only when called on to bestow blessings or resolve problems. The purpose of life is happiness, self-fulfillment, and a degree of goodness sufficient to earn entrance to heaven.

From the moralistic angle, as Arnett and others have expressed, most emerging adults equate religious belief with some version of the Golden Rule, treating others as you would like to be treated.[62] Churches, accordingly, are defined as "elementary schools of morals," institutions dedicated to instilling a generalized ethical code while also urging belief in the God who established it. Christian faith, in this sense, has little to do with embracing a particular narrative of God's redemptive action in the world or of cultivating an individual and corporate identity with the people of God. It is instead an insipid call to niceness, to living as well-behaved citizens in this world (with a potential hope of heaven after death). While Smith's research is focused on a broad cross section of emerging adults, it is clear that this position describes many who would self-identify as believing Christians as well. Kara Powell and her colleagues recently discovered that many college juniors who were youth group graduates, when asked to define what it means to "be a Christian," stated that the faith's central characteristic was "loving others." Thirty-five percent did not even mention Jesus in their answer.[63]

This kind of perspective makes it challenging to articulate a continued need for spiritual investment beyond the teenage years. If all of the moral "life lessons" are learned in one's childhood, then emerging adulthood constitutes a kind of "graduation"—teenagers have already learned all that they need to know. By the time they reach their twenties, therefore, they can live on the basis of moral intuition, basic principles of Christian goodness etched in their minds through teaching in their youth. Aside from the need for periodic reminders, the only reason to reengage Christianity comes when it is time to inculcate these same principles in their children. These beliefs (believing in God, believing we should be nice to others, and believing we should be happy) certainly affirm emerging adults' identities as mainstream Americans because they represent core American values, after all. Such a civil religion, however, does not facilitate any continued movement in the direction of spiritual formation.

Importantly, this perspective means that many emerging adults see the actual content and stories of the Christian faith to be relatively unimportant in the ways they live out their spiritual lives. Since a healthy moral framework is all that matters (and since emerging adults seem to believe that right and wrong are easily determined), the distinct theological perspectives offered by different denominations or traditions are viewed as trivial minutia reserved for obscurantists or religious professionals. The stories of the Bible and the doctrinal content of the faith are therefore just meaningless husks enfolding the pure kernel of morality—the common principles of goodness at their cores. Like many of their school subjects, religious content is merely to be learned, affirmed, and stored away. As Smith helpfully suggests, "Most emerging adults have religious beliefs. . . . But those religious ideas are for the most part abstract agreements that have been mentally checked off and filed away. They are not what emerging adults organize their lives around. They do not particularly drive the majority's priorities, commitments, values, and goals. These have much more to do with jobs, friends, fun, and financial security." In short, "Religious beliefs are cognitive assents, not life drivers."[64]

The "therapeutic" side of this emerging adult faith also sets up barriers to ongoing spiritual formation. In these years, faith is often perceived as a lifestyle-enhancing appliance, a means of making a better life and meeting one's needs. God, in this sense, is still primarily viewed as what Smith called in an earlier book a "combination Divine Butler and Cosmic Therapist," on call and waiting to supply things that will enhance personal happiness.[65] Such a perspective creates a number of challenges. First, faith itself can be viewed as merely a tool of personal happiness. If it is true that within Moralistic Therapeutic Deism "the central goal of life is to be happy and to feel good about oneself," the potential for self-worship is quite high. What is even more dangerous here is that emerging adults can be swayed to use God as the currency needed to purchase personal idols.[66] They can begin to think that they want God in their lives so that they can get a good job with a good income, find a great spouse, be free from depression, and have someone around to help solve their problems. They come to the place where, as Larry Crabb puts it, they "see Christ as a savior from pain, not from sin; as a responsive benefactor rather than a Holy Lord."[67]

Ultimately, this leads to a path in which happiness becomes far more important than an unwavering and sacrificial submission to God and his kingdom. Moralistic Therapeutic Deism is a religion that promises personal assistance in making life better while making few if any demands on emerging adults in terms of identity, lifestyle, and purpose. Whether the desire is for more material possessions, better relationships, or heightened academic and vocational prestige, the key is that their loves have been turned away from God's kingdom (and particularly away from him) and toward the created kingdoms of this world. As Smith puts it, "Promoting an instrumentalist legitimation of religious faith may be effective in attracting adherents in the short and medium run. But it certainly comes at a long-term religious cost: faith and practice become redefined as instrumental therapeutic mechanisms to achieve personal goals that are probably not themselves formed by the religious traditions."[68] This therapeutic vision often means that the individual can determine which parts of the faith to keep or discard, ultimately crafting a God in his or her own image. Instead of placing oneself within an established religious framework, many now view religion as a "symbolic toolbox," a collection of ideas and practices from which they can select the components that "work" best.[69] Therefore, many emerging adults are not formed by the Christian faith into the image of Christ but are rather forming a faith that will shape them into their own image of happiness.

The therapeutic mind-set may also serve as one reason many in this age group leave the faith during these years. If emerging adults grew up thinking that Christianity was designed to secure blessings, life disappointments may cause them to discern that faith is an inadequate tool along these lines. If the Christian life was expected to eliminate doubts and to secure a good career, financial success, and a happy family, then failure in these areas may be enough to indicate that Jesus "didn't work." If Christian friends or spouses or leaders fail them, they may convince themselves that Christianity's promises ring hollow and that they instead better seek their own path to true happiness, healing, and fulfillment. Expectations formed earlier in life obviously set the stage for such disappointment, but it is often in emerging adulthood that the supposed pragmatic benefits of Christianity may unravel, leading to disillusionment and detachment from the faith.

Finally, when linked with the "deistic" aspect of this faith, Moralistic Thera-peutic Deism removes the sense of a personal God with whom one is related in the process of spiritual formation. If God is simply an absentee landlord over the universe without active involvement in people's lives, spiritual for-mation becomes nothing more than a personal project of self-improvement, lacking both the relational connection to God and the divine empowerment of the Holy Spirit in the process. More likely, Christianity becomes a religion concerned chiefly with obedience to biblical principles that can be used to carve out a better life. Obedience to biblical principles is obviously a good thing, but it can also be done without a personal, relational connection with the living God. If we possess the advice manual for how to live a good life, spiritual formation is simply a matter of adherence to the principles rather than genuine transformation. In the name of Christianity, we fall into the same pattern as the Pharisees, to whom Jesus stated clearly: "You study the Scriptures diligently because you think that in them you have eternal life. These are the very Scriptures that testify about me, yet you refuse to come to me to have life" (John 5:39–40).

It is important to recognize that the faith exemplified in the lives of emerg-ing adults is not merely an imposed mutation of the Christian faith result-ing from external, life stage, or generational challenges. Instead, as Kenda Creasy Dean has indicated, emerging adults are in many ways a reflection of the recent perspectives and priorities of our churches.[70] In our attempt to remain relevant and to compete with broader cultural forms, we have often neglected the hard work of teaching, shepherding, and mentoring students in the context of true Christian discipleship, serving instead as purveyors of cheap grace, the cult of niceness, and a God (butler?) who exists merely to meet felt needs. As Smith has insightfully suggested, the Moralistic Therapeu-tic Deism of emerging adulthood in many ways demonstrates the "cultural triumph of liberal Protestantism."[71] The core doctrinal values of Protestant liberalism—democratic sensitivities, the centrality of ethical action, pluralistic tolerance, a distant God, and resistance to rigid theological conviction—de-scribe well the key features of contemporary emerging adult faith even among self-described conservatives. Because these ideals have become so much a part of the American cultural and religious mainstream, they are readily imbibed into emerging adults' Christian framework.

At the same time, conservative Protestantism can also be implicated in forg-ing aspects of this tepid religious vision. Embedded in the broader American cultural context, the evangelical emphasis on personal faith, removed from the dictates of confessional authority, can evolve into the autonomous sub-jectivism of emerging adult faith. Emphases on piety and holiness—with an attendant lack of theological rigor—can be reduced to moralism that sees faith as important only in its pragmatic influence on life conduct. The therapeutic mind-set has certainly been strong within evangelical and charismatic contexts as well, placing firm emphasis on God's blessings in both this world and the next. While conservatives may see Moralistic Therapeutic Deism as an enemy, it is all too often an enemy that is nurtured "within the camp." In the end, we must at least entertain the idea that this anemic version of Christianity is arising not only because the din of the world has dulled emerging adults' hearing but also because they have been listening so well to the diluted faith we profess.

In addition, conservative Protestant emerging adults may fail to pursue spiritual formation because of the historical trajectory of the faith. As Jeffrey Greenman suggests, the strengths of evangelicalism can also serve as spiritual formation "weaknesses" if they are not carefully tethered to the fullness of the faith. Evangelical biblicism, while extremely helpful in maintaining a solid foundation of faith and practice, can also lead to an inappropriate rationalism or a false denigration of traditional spiritual practices. Evangelical crucicentrism (cross-centeredness), while anchoring us helpfully to the message of the gospel, can become skewed if it leads to antinomianism (a sense that grace frees us from moral law) or neglects the Holy Spirit's role in transformation. Evangelical activism, while providing a tremendous push in the direction of service and mission, may blind us to the need for contemplative practices such as prayer, solitude, and silence.[72] While these indeed represent what Smith terms "cultural mutations" of evangelicalism, they are easily identifiable patterns in many congregations, schools, and ministries around the country.[73]

Finally, evangelical soteriology (the doctrine of salvation) can fail to generate incentives toward spiritual formation. Many emerging adults may feel that their spiritual health is ensured simply by virtue of having "accepted Christ" and prayed a prayer for salvation and the forgiveness of sins. As Dallas Willard has suggested, however, when all of the emphasis is placed on a single "decision" for Christ, some may not even see the need for formation as long as the heavenly account has been settled. The language of salvation therefore loses its natural connection to the language of sanctification and spiritual formation. The truth of justification, Willard notes, must always be accompanied by the joint reality of spiritual regeneration, the reality that the soul has been renewed and reborn.[74] In other words, not only has the soul been saved but a new kind of life has also been birthed within the individual, a life "hidden with Christ in God" (Col. 3:3) that is to be developed and nurtured. As those who "participate in the divine nature" (2 Pet. 1:4), that life is designed to develop and grow, from glory to glory. We must find ways to help emerging adults connect their concepts of salvation and spiritual formation, of justification and sanctification, and of grace for salvation and grace for transformation. Spiritual formation is not an optional add-on to salvation for advanced saints but a logical consequence of the reborn soul that has found its true home.

The combination of the cultural, age-based, and theological challenges mentioned here makes it clear that emerging adulthood represents challenging soil in which to plant. As in the parable of the sower, some seed will fall along the path because emerging adulthood is not envisioned as an appropriate time of life to engage spiritual issues. Some will be choked out by the lure of wealth and the distracting cares of this world, so new and overwhelming at this time of life. And some will also remain shallow, the fruit of a tepid form of "nice" Christianity that cannot withstand life's hardships and persecution. In many ways, this context has produced exactly what C. S. Lewis described in the quotation opening this chapter, the attempt "to keep personal happiness as our great aim in life, and yet at the same time be 'good.'" True Christian spiritual formation is quite literally impossible in such a context. We must develop a posture of formation that attends to both the external challenges posed by cultural shifts and the internal theological challenges posed by false gospels and the imposter religion of Moralistic Therapeutic Deism. In the end, we must help emerging adults catch a vision for true spiritual maturation, one that is rooted in the gospel and penetrates to the depths of the heart, rather than mere external observance. As Lewis reminds us, change must go "deeper than the surface." To produce a spiritual crop, the emerging adults in our midst "must be ploughed up and re-sown."[75]

2 | Spiritual Formation

Reversing Moralistic Therapeutic Deism

And now we begin to see what it is that the New Testament is always talking about. It talks about Christians "being born again"; it talks about them "putting on Christ"; about Christ "being formed in us"; about our coming to "have the mind of Christ." Put right out of your head the idea that these are only fancy ways of saying that Christians are to read what Christ said and try to carry it out—as a man may read what Plato or Marx said and try to carry it out. They mean something much more than that. They mean that a real Person, Christ, here and now, in that very room where you are saying your prayers, is doing things to you. It is not a question of a good man who died two thousand years ago. It is a living Man, still as much a man as you, and still as much God as He was when He created the world, really coming and interfering with your very self; killing the old natural self in you and replacing it with the kind of self He has. At first, only for moments. Then for longer periods. Finally, if all goes well, turning you permanently into a different sort of thing; into a new little Christ, a being which, in its own small way, has the same kind of life as God; which shares in His power, joy, knowledge and eternity.

C. S. Lewis[1]

While the personal, cultural, and theological barriers to spiritual formation are daunting, they should not cause us to lose heart. If anything, such challenges simply remind us that we must be active and intentional in our work with emerging adults, thinking hard about the ways in which their lives are structured and shaped by these forces. Despite the spiritual hurdles, emerging adulthood actually provides exciting opportunities to engage twentysomethings in a journey that will kindle and sustain their adult faith development. If we are to facilitate Christian discipleship during these years, however, we must provide a formational vision that moves beyond Moralistic Therapeutic Deism to embrace the fullness of the abundant life Christ came to bring. Confronting this imposter religion at each of its three levels, emerging adult spiritual formation must reshape their loves, urge them to costly sacrifice, and call them to a life "with Christ" in which they are daily transformed by the work of the Holy Spirit.

Beyond Moralism: Shaping the Heart and Its Loves

As noted previously, many emerging adult Christians view spiritual growth as an enhancement of moral behavior, an attempt to act more in keeping with the image of the "nice" Christian. When the focus is placed on emerging adult morality and behavior (including poor decisions), however, it is easy to fall into the trap referred to by Dallas Willard as "sin management," the attempt to control individual behaviors through vigorous willpower.[2] Sin management tends to emphasize "sins" rather than "sin" and behavioral symptoms rather than the underlying sources of disease. If we think in terms of a polluted stream, the moralistic approach to spiritual formation is often akin to working on water-purifying projects in the tributaries rather than addressing the origins of the contamination further upstream. To use another image, we seek to destroy a malicious computer program by removing its desktop icon rather than the program itself. In both cases, the underlying core issues remain. The stream will continue to pour its filth into the tributaries. The program will continue to perform its unseen work in the computer's circuitry. Scripture provides many pictures of this inadequate formational vision. Matthew 23, for example, refers to the Pharisees' tendency to clean the outside of the cup and dish while "inside they are full of greed and self-indulgence" (Matt. 23:25). It speaks of them as "whitewashed tombs" (Matt. 23:27) in which a clean outside obscures the decay within.

When ministers seek to eradicate certain behavioral patterns in emerging adults' lives, they often fail to attend to the root issues at play. Therefore, ministry to members of this age group tends to amount to little more than what Paul David Tripp has termed "fruit stapling."[3] Leaders desire to replace rotting apples (behavioral and lifestyle problems) by "stapling on" new "fruit," practices of behavioral compliance. All the time, they ignore the root (heart) issues that are producing these problems in the first place. The new "fruit" may be shiny and attractive, but without spiritual renewal at the heart level, new behaviors will remain artificial and lifeless, shriveling up over time due to lack of nourishment from the root system. Therefore, while leaders may be able to see short-term improvements in behavior, these changes will not last because they are externally imposed rather than naturally flowing from a renewed root system. As Tripp suggests, "If the heart doesn't change, the person's words and behavior may change temporarily because of external pressure or incentive. But when the pressure or incentive is removed, the changes will disappear. . . . There is an undeniable root and fruit connection between our heart and our behavior."[4] Eventually, the true heart will be revealed.

In many ways, this is really about the ultimate loves that control emerging adults' hearts. As philosopher James K. A. Smith contends, we are "lovers" at our core, people whose lives are oriented by our ultimate longings and desires, by what we worship. While we may think that emerging adults are shaped only by their thoughts and beliefs, it is likely more accurate anthropologically to see that they are shaped by loves. These loves, Smith contends, are always aimed toward certain ends—visions of human flourishing that capture our thoughts and imaginations. As teleological beings, whatever picture of flourishing we embrace beckons us to live into this vision and to "start to look like citizens who inhabit the world that we picture as the good life."[5] We pursue, in other words, some vision of "the kingdom" that drives us to think, feel, and act in particular ways. The heart, of course, can be oriented in many directions— emerging adults have many different "kingdoms" to which their hearts are drawn and their lives oriented. Ultimately, however, their lives will be directed by the kingdoms that they love—by the directions of their ultimate worship. It is little wonder, therefore, that Proverbs 4:23 urges, "Above all else, guard your heart, for it is the wellspring of life."

Sin is always idolatry, exchanging the proper worship of the Creator for the worship of created things (Rom. 1:21–25). It is always adultery, the heart straying from its first love and giving the love God deserves to other kingdoms (Hosea 2:2; Rev. 2:4).[6] Sin is always, as Augustine indicated, a disordering of our loves.[7] Good things become elevated to the level of ultimate things, skewing life priorities and allegiances in ways that move us away from our created purpose. As Smith comments, "At the heart of our being is a kind of love pump that can never be turned off—not even by sin or the Fall; rather the effect of sin on our love pump is to knock it off kilter, misdirecting it and getting it aimed at the wrong things."[8] Sin is always life, as Paul would put it, "according to the flesh," with a core passion devoted to something besides the true King. True life in Christ is life "according to the Spirit," located "in Christ" so that all activities and desires are oriented around this one consuming passion.[9] The function of the Christian heart, Willard suggests, is to "organize our life as a whole, and, indeed, to organize it around God."[10]

Furthermore, twentysomethings are susceptible not only to the worship of *false* kingdoms but also to the worship of *many* kingdoms. Mass consumerism thrives on this multiplicity, attempting to keep people in a state of perpetual adolescence so as to kindle longing and fuel the "desire-based economy."[11] Emerging adults must recognize at this crucial stage that they cannot simply seek God's kingdom as one component of their multifaceted lives. The loving heart for God can be led astray, but it can also be crowded out and brought on to level ground with other sources of worship, leaving little space for divine hunger and thirst. As Matthew 6:24 reminds us, "No one can serve two masters." Instead, emerging adults are called on to "seek first his kingdom and his righteousness" (Matt. 6:33) and to participate in all of their other activities—school, job hunting, and relationships—as means of seeking that kingdom. The Christian life is not about balance but about single-mindedness, developing the undivided heart that is completely loyal to him (Jer. 32:39; Ezek. 11:19). As Søren Kierkegaard famously noted, "Purity of heart is to will one thing."[12]

It is this centrality of the heart—and the many competing kingdoms—that makes emerging adulthood such a potent time for intentional spiritual formation. When emerging adults leave home for college or work, their hearts are often exposed in new ways. Some experience a time of rebellion or moral laxity. Removed from the context of parental oversight, they capitalize on their new freedom by engaging in activities or lifestyles previously restricted. In reality, this is not often indicative of an overnight "change of heart." Instead, these behaviors often reveal the true character of a heart that was previously held in check by environmental constraints. The new setting is not typically the cause of the problem but rather the context in which the true heart is revealed. Formerly restrained by the dams of church and home, the river of the heart is now allowed to overflow its boundaries and stream into new terrain. While obviously this is not a desirable outcome, it does provide an unparalleled opportunity for ministry that attends to the deep places of the heart. When the environmental props are removed, there is an opportunity to deal honestly with root issues that were previously obscured by convention and fear of punishment. Like the younger brother in the story of the prodigal son, leaving home for "wild living" (Luke 15:13) may very well open the door to a recognition of the need for the heart-transforming grace of God.

At the same time, other emerging adults may stay "close to home" even when they leave the nest. They may continue to obey parental admonitions, ascribe to familial beliefs, attend church, and participate in ministries. Yet ministers, mentors, and parents should not assume that such compliance ensures positive spiritual formation. External conformity can mask hearts that actually seek human approval, consumer pleasures, prestige, or any number of other idols. This situation is more subtle, more insidious, because it can remain hidden from leaders who take comfort in exemplary external observance. It can even provide comfort for the emerging adult who assumes that the boundary markers of religious participation signify spiritual safety. Like the older brother in the story of the prodigal son, emerging adults can remain close to the Father and yet worship something else in their hearts, honoring God with their lips while their hearts are far from him (Isa. 29:13). As Timothy Keller has suggested, the two brothers in the story of the prodigal son both suffer from the same basic condition: they love something else more than the father. They want his benefits more than they want him. They have elevated some kingdom above his in their hearts.[13]

One of our central tasks, therefore, is to help emerging adults detect the idols in their hearts, to do the hard work of identifying competing sources of worship. Because the heart is "deceitful above all things" (Jer. 17:9), this work is quite challenging. Spiritual disciplines—to be discussed later in the chapter—provide experiential means for locating idols. In addition, however, there are some key indicators that might help us begin to see these false gods. As Keller suggests, a look at emerging adults' use of time and money might provide some initial clues. "Your money," he suggests, "flows most effortlessly toward your heart's greatest love."[14] Emerging adults can also look at their thought lives and daydreams. When they have no other pressing concerns, where do their thoughts instinctively turn? To some consumer good they desire? To a plan for personal success? To food or entertainment? The unconscious and often impulsive direction of their thoughts can provide a helpful diagnostic as to the heart's true loves. Finally, as Keller suggests, their uncontrollable emotions often reveal the heart's greatest aspirations. Explosive anger, fear, and despair can indicate that something or someone has taken on inappropriate importance in their lives. These things have often become so deeply attached to personhood and identity that they make people go to great lengths to secure them and elicit deep negative emotions when they remain elusive. Similarly, effusive happiness may indicate a deep source of pleasure in some person or object that exceeds proper boundaries. We must help emerging adults begin to see these false gods for what they truly are.[15]

Once these false gods have been identified, the fight against idolatry can commence in earnest. Much of the rhetoric of resistance to sin in our churches is rooted in a "just say no" mentality. Emerging adults are compelled to exercise willpower to avoid engaging in negative activities or life patterns. There is, of course, an important place for this. The individual struggling with alcohol or drugs should, through an exercise of will, eliminate these substances from a home or apartment even if the desire to consume is still present. The individual struggling with pornography should place filters on the computer and set up the accountability structures necessary to resist temptation. Yet there must be more. Paul told those in the church at Colossae that their restrictions, "Do not handle, Do not taste, Do not touch," had "an appearance of wisdom in promoting self-made religion and asceticism and severity to the body," but he also indicated that "they are of no value in stopping the indulgence of the flesh" (Col. 2:21, 23 ESV).

The real power, alternatively, comes as emerging adults embrace a vision of the beauty of Christ and his kingdom and therefore see divine truth as far more compelling than the temptations of this world. As Keller suggests, "Idols cannot simply be removed. They must be replaced. If you only try to uproot them, they grow back; but they can be supplanted."[16] With regard to lust, for example, John Piper notes that willful regard for the prohibitions of Scripture will rarely be sufficient to combat this powerful impulse. Instead, he notes, we must "fight fire with fire," battling lust's pleasures with God's pleasures so that the "little flicker" of lust's enjoyment can be swallowed up "in the conflagration of holy satisfaction." "When we 'make a covenant with our eyes,' like Job did (Job 31:1)," he notes, "our aim is not merely to avoid something erotic, but also to gain something excellent."[17]

The key here is that we must hold before emerging adults a captivating picture of the beauty of Christ and his promises. Temptations are powerful in part because they promise happiness, joy, and personal satisfaction in very immediate and tangible ways. Emerging adults will have a hard time saying "no" to such fleeting pleasures without the offer of a more compelling "yes" to something far greater. The problem, of course, is the ignorance of (and lack of consistent interaction with) the beauty of God and the precious promises of his Word (1 Pet. 1:14). As C. S. Lewis's oft-quoted saying from *The Weight of Glory* puts it, "We are half-hearted creatures, fooling about with drink and sex and ambition when infinite joy is offered to us, like the ignorant child who wants to go on making mud pies in a slum because he cannot imagine what is meant by the offer of a holiday at the sea. We are far too easily pleased."[18]

Perhaps an illustration might express this more clearly. About eight years ago, my (David's) family celebrated the Fourth of July by joining neighbors and friends for a cookout. My wife was pregnant at the time, and her craving was steak. Attempting to be a good husband, I went out to a grocery store and bought a nice steak for the celebration. While I was happily grilling, one of my neighbors arrived with a steak of his own. I slid my steak over to make room for his, and he began to unwrap from white paper the largest, most beautiful steak I had ever seen, at least an inch thicker than mine and a much deeper red. As he put it next to mine, I felt immediately that my very manhood was compromised. My steak looked thin and pale next to this incredible specimen. My grocery store steak no longer looked mouthwatering. Now it just looked pitiful. He had gotten his steak, not from the grocery store, but from a meat market. He let me taste a bite, and I was in awe.

Later it struck me—and don't press this analogy too far—that the grocery store steak represented the idols of life. These things look beautiful and satisfying, but only when we are shown something truly good do they begin to look like the pitiful things they truly are. They lose their allure when set beside the radiance of the "better steak" of God's character and promises. When we find ways to celebrate and meditate on God's goodness, when we "taste and see that the LORD is good" (Ps. 34:8), these other idols pale in comparison. We grow content with the "grocery store steaks" of the world because we don't realize there is something so much greater. The best cure for idolatry, therefore, is not only to "just say no" to that steak but to "say yes" to something much better. The cure for idolatry, in other words, is not only willpower but also worship.

We must, therefore, counter the lies of the enemy with truth, not only the commandments against sin, but also the countless appeals to the beauty of the gospel and the great rewards—chiefly God himself—promised to those who believe. The goal would be something like we see in the description of Moses in Hebrews 11, who "chose to be mistreated along with the people of God rather than to enjoy the fleeting pleasures of sin" (v. 25). The reason he was able to resist sinful temptations and choose to identify with the people of God was that he "regarded disgrace for the sake of Christ as of greater value than the treasures of Egypt, because he was looking ahead to his reward" (v. 26). Because he "saw him who is invisible" (v. 27), Moses actually considered worldly disgrace as more beautiful than the earthly treasures of Egypt. His perception of reality—his worldview, if you will—was completely altered by knowledge of and experiential interaction with the living God. Likewise, emerging adults must be confronted with a compelling picture of God and his kingdom so that they begin to recognize the deceit of sin and the fact that at God's "right hand are pleasures forevermore" (Ps. 16:11 NKJV).

To move in this direction, we must first seek to help emerging adults fall in love (or more deeply in love) with our beautiful God and his kingdom. But herein lies the question asked so eloquently by Willard: "How do we help people love what is lovely?" Since he resonates with Thomas Aquinas's sense that "love is born of an earnest consideration of the object loved," Willard's response is that we "bring the lovely thing—in this case, God—before the disciple as fully and forcibly as possible, putting our best effort into it."[19] Solid and compelling biblical teaching on the beauty of God's character and his precious promises is therefore absolutely essential. As Richard Foster suggests, "The mind conforms to the order of what it concentrates upon. The heart conforms to the beauty of what it gazes upon."[20] Our prayer for emerging adults struggling with idolatry must parallel Paul's plea in Ephesians 1:18–19, "I pray that the eyes of your heart may be enlightened in order that you may know the hope to which he has called you, the riches of his glorious inheritance in his holy people, and his incomparably great power for us who believe."

What this means is that pastors, teachers, and mentors must teach with creativity, imagination, and narrative power. The Word, of course, possesses its own inherent power to inspire, convict, and train in righteousness (2 Tim. 3:16). Yet we are also called to speak and live in such a way as to "make the teaching about God our Savior attractive" to all (Titus 2:10). As Sarah Arthur contends, we must be not only journalists but also "bards" that capture emerging adults' imaginations with the beauty and passion of the gospel.[21] Marketers certainly understand this, spending millions of dollars on captivating images and pictures of "the good life" rather than simply "instructing" potential buyers on the features of their products. As Smith notes, "the marketing industry is operating with a better, more creational, more incarnational, more holistic anthropology than much of the (evangelical) church."[22] Marketers recognize that we are embodied creatures and that the way to our hearts is not only through our heads but also through our imaginations, the pictures and stories of human flourishing that draw in our desires and passions—our loves. Emerging adults can certainly be learning all of the nuances of a Christian worldview while at the same time surrendering their hearts to the alluring cultural sirens of our day. If we are finding emerging adults too much at home in this world, we must question whether we have neglected to provide them with a compelling picture of the "city with foundations, whose architect and builder is God" (Heb. 11:10).

This does not, of course, mean that everything we share will be immediately joyful or attractive. In fact, the flaw of the "therapeutic" dimension of Moralistic Therapeutic Deism is found precisely here in its tendency to extract only those aspects of the biblical narrative that seem to promise happiness and personal benefit. The charge to emerging adults must be a call to costly discipleship, taking up the cross. Far from offering therapeutic happiness, we invite emerging adults to offer their bodies as living sacrifices, dying daily to self as sacred offerings to the God who gave himself up for them. As we will see, however, the call to sacrifice is simply another dimension of the soul-aching worship of the loving heart.

Beyond Therapy: Costly Formation for the Glory of God

Today's emerging adults are an optimistic lot, rejecting any sense of regret about the past and looking with unmitigated enthusiasm toward a hopeful future.[23] Yet the messages of John the Baptist and Jesus were both grounded in the initiating call, "Repent, for the kingdom of heaven has come near" (Matt. 3:2). True growth in Christian faith cannot occur without an underlying understanding that the soul is utterly incapacitated without God's prevenient and restoring grace. More and more, however, emerging adults appear uncomfortable with language that addresses sin or evil within the soul, preferring to speak of brokenness or woundedness inflicted by others. "People do not mind being sick or bogged down with problems or even weak," Dietrich Bonhoeffer once suggested, "but under no condition do they want to be sinners."[24] Growing up in a therapeutic culture anchored by self-absorption and self-esteem (as Cornelius Plantinga puts it, thinking much "*about* herself" and much "*of* herself"), the thought that we are radically sinful and in utter need of God's grace certainly goes against the cultural grain.[25] Yet as John Calvin asserts, "No one can embrace the grace of the gospel without betaking himself from the errors of his past life into the right way, and applying his whole effort to the practice of repentance."[26]

For most emerging adults—and maybe for most of us in general—sin is often viewed as a set of discrete acts, individual failures in specific situations. As philosopher Arthur Holmes once suggested in light of his own interaction with collegians, "Sin has been atomized in the popular mind into a collection of particular thoughts and deeds: the typical college student thinks of sin and righteousness as specific behaviors flagged by do's and don'ts, rather than as a pervasive condition of the heart, a question of moral identity."[27] An important precursor to the work of formation—and in many ways the first step of the process itself—is therefore to foster within emerging adults a sense of their radical need for the gospel of Christ. James Wilhoit reminds us, "When we perceive the true depth of our sin instead of merely being embarrassed over individual sins, we are prompted to seek the grace that can heal."[28] The invitation to the spiritual life is for those who are hungry and thirsty, broken and needy (Isa. 55).

Along with this, it is clear that the call to discipleship among Jesus's followers always begins with an invitation to consider the cost of such allegiance.

There is no sense in Scripture that faith is a consumer product designed to meet personal needs or slake personal thirsts. Well-intentioned definitions of spirituality focus on self-development and self-actualization. The clear call of Scripture, alternatively, is to self-denial, to the process of taking up the cross and following him (Matt. 16:24). For emerging adults raised in our therapeutic cultural mind-set, the call to self-denial will often appear overly morbid and negative—a blight on the project of self-realization.[29] Yet here is the paradox of Christian discipleship. While emerging adulthood is often characterized as the stage of life in which individuals "find themselves," Jesus notes that "whoever finds their life will lose it, and whoever loses their life for my sake will find it" (Matt. 10:39). Only the kernel of wheat that "falls to the ground and dies" will ultimately multiply and bear fruit (John 12:24).

Emerging adults, perhaps more than any other age group, are confronted in very concrete ways with the cost of discipleship to Jesus. Entering into an apprenticeship with him at this life stage may very well mean sacrificing a potentially lucrative career and a home in the suburbs in favor of one that is given to caring for the downtrodden. It may mean the delay of premarital sexual experience or the loss of friends who choose different paths. It may mean devoting part of one's newly acquired financial resources to the local church rather than to a new consumer good. As we see in the parable of the hidden treasure and the parable of the pearl of great price in Matthew 13, there is certainly a call to do what Jesus requires in Luke 14:33: "those of you who do not give up everything you have cannot be my disciples." The man who discovers the treasure and the merchant who finds the pearl are both required to "sell everything" in their single-minded pursuits of the prizes they seek. This can be a great challenge to those who, for the first time in their lives perhaps, have something (or someone) to lose.

Moralistic Therapeutic Deism, on the other hand, is not costly. Its appeal to niceness and to a God who can provide personal happiness actually requires very little of its adherents. At best, it can lead emerging adults to live sacrificially, perhaps giving up some time to help a friend or giving up some money to assist the poor. True Christian faith, however, is not about living sacrificially. Instead, Romans 12:1 calls each follower of Christ to be a "living sacrifice." Living sacrificially means that emerging adults are able to retain control over their lives, selecting the areas they wish to turn over to God and retaining those they wish to keep for themselves. Alternatively, being a living sacrifice involves much more, as Lewis reminds:

> Christ says, "Give me All. I don't want so much of your time and so much of your money and so much of your work: I want You. I have not come to torment

your natural self, but to kill it. No half-measures are any good. I don't want to cut off a branch here and a branch there, I want to have the whole tree down. I don't want to drill the tooth, or crown it, or stop it, but to have it out. Hand over the whole natural self, all the desires which you think innocent as well as the ones you think wicked—the whole outfit. I will give you a new self instead. In fact, I will give you Myself: my own will shall become yours."[30]

Emerging adulthood often sets the tone for this lifelong task.

But another truth is equally important. Moralistic Therapeutic Deism may cost little, but it also promises little: a bit of kindness in the world, freedom to do what you want, and a distant deity who may occasionally provide some blessings. True Christianity, however costly, promises far more. Emerging adults must understand that discipleship to Christ is costly, but they must also be confronted with the beauty of Jesus and his kingdom in such a way that they count the cost and find that the benefits far outweigh any earthly consequences. This is what Bonhoeffer referred to as the "costly grace" of God—costly because it "costs a man his life," but grace filled because it "gives a man the only true life."[31] As Lewis remarked in his own inimitable style, "You have noticed, I expect, that Christ Himself sometimes describes the Christian way as very hard, sometimes as very easy. He says, 'Take up your Cross'—in other words, it is like going to be beaten to death in a concentration camp. Next minute he says, 'My yoke is easy and my burden light.' He means both."[32]

Scripture provides us with pictures of two paths that may be taken by emerging adults along these lines. In Jesus's day, one young adult with great potential, when faced with the cost of discipleship, considered the price too high. The "rich young ruler," as he is often labeled, is also asked to "sell everything" in order to gain "treasure in heaven" by following Jesus (Mark 10:21). He "went away sad," the text tells us, "because he had great wealth" (10:22). He saw his own riches as more beautiful than the person of Christ and heavenly treasure. The cost, in this sense, was not deemed worthwhile. Many of the religious leaders, similarly, had hearts that were motivated by the earthly "treasure" of religious reputation. They gave, prayed, and fasted, Matthew 6 reminds us, in order to be seen and admired by people. Jesus's chilling description of these people is that they had "received their reward in full" (Matt. 6:2, 5, 16). They did get a reward: earthly reputation. But this is all that they got—they lost a treasure in heaven that is inestimably greater. They preferred to store up treasures on earth, and the location of that treasure also signified the location of their hearts (Matt. 6:21). In John 6, many people who heard Jesus speak counted the cost and determined that following Jesus was not worth it. "This is a hard teaching," they said. "Who can accept it?" (John 6:60).

Others, however, see the beauty of the prize in such a way that they are willing to count the cost and pursue the kingdom. In Matthew 13, one does not get the impression that the individuals pursuing the treasure and the pearl do so with either hesitation or reservation. They have seen the beauty of the prize and are therefore more than willing to part with other earthly possessions to acquire it. Peter, speaking for all true disciples, gave the alternative reply: "Lord, to whom shall we go? You have the words of eternal life. We have come to believe and to know that you are the Holy One of God" (John 6:68–69). These people counted the cost, and they concluded that it was really minimal in light of the beauty of Jesus and his kingdom. As hard as it may have been to relinquish attachments to earthly treasures, they began to recognize that the cost of nondiscipleship was even greater. Only those who see the beauty of the true reward—Jesus himself—will be willing to value the cost of discipleship to him.[33]

Here we see a very practical implication for emerging adults related to the way they perceive the "costly" commands of Scripture. When those in this age group hear the biblical commands prohibiting premarital sexual activity or encouraging honoring one's parents, these are likely to present themselves as arbitrary and burdensome restrictions on personal freedom. However, the biblical witness is clear in noting that God's commandments, while costly in one sense, are given for the purpose of providing a pathway to true life and flourishing. Far from arbitrary, they are designed for our good, establishing boundaries and crafting pathways to spiritual abundance, fruitfulness, and the fulfillment of the purposes for which we were created. As God himself states in Isaiah 48:17–18, "I am the Lord your God, who teaches you what is best for you, who directs you in the way you should go. If only you had paid attention to my commands, your peace would have been like a river, your righteousness like the waves of the sea." God's challenging commands, in other words, represent an invitation to the good life. His will for us is indeed "good, pleasing and perfect" (Rom. 12:2).[34]

Believing this, however, often requires that emerging adults live "by faith, not by sight" (2 Cor. 5:7). In other words, they need to believe, sometimes in the face of seeming evidence to the contrary, that God's ways do produce the abundant life. When others around them seem to be doing "just fine" while either ignoring or flouting God's commands, counting the cost can appear fruitless—even miserable. To communicate the importance of this, leaders must help emerging adults gain a different perspective, one tethered to a longer-range understanding of the time lines of their lives.

The issue of time, in fact, is central to the way in which we must understand spiritual formation in emerging adulthood. As mentioned previously, one of the barriers to formation at this life stage is the tendency to see this time of life as a time of freedom and exploration before "settling down." In addition, many emerging adults believe that their current actions have little impact on their long-term prospects. As Christian Smith reported, "The assumption seems to be 'Whatever happened in my early twenties stays in my early twenties,' and the memories and behavioral consequences will never haunt them down the road."[35] Many emerging adults assume that they will be able to flip a switch when they reach marriage and parenthood, leaving behind youthful passions to become "sober, faithful, and responsible adults."[36] For collegians, this is often stated as a desire for spiritual maturity "once college is completed." For others, it might be stated as growth "once I am married" or "once I have children." Spiritual formation, in other words, appears to be something relegated to the future.

The problem with this perspective is that it fails to take into account the reality of what educator John Dewey once called the "experiential continuum."[37] According to Dewey, no experience lives unto itself. Instead, every experience builds on previous experiences and also lays a foundation for subsequent experiences. Emerging adults often fool themselves into thinking that "some day," in five or ten years perhaps, they will simply be able to become the man or woman of God that they dream about. While God can obviously effect miraculous and instantaneous transformations, however, the more common pattern is to begin practicing a desired path in the present, knowing that the continual patterns developed will create habits and eventually emerge as full-blown "ways of life" in the future. Envisioning a godly future can be a very helpful and productive activity, but if it is not accompanied by an equal passion to enter into the kinds of experiences that will produce this kind of future, it can become a means of perpetual delay. In their youth, emerging adults may feel that they have an infinite amount of time out in front of them, a reality that diminishes the importance of the present and enhances the sense that one's choices can always be amended later on. The only way in which one will grow in maturity "in the future," however, is through initiating a costly process in the present that provides room for the Holy Spirit to do this transformative work.

Our job, therefore, is to help emerging adults gain a "harvest" perspective regarding the life choices made during this era. The Galatians 6 principle of sowing and reaping indicates that what is sown (to the Spirit or to the flesh) will also be reaped at some point in the life of the believer and into eternity. This passage begins with a clear call: "Do not be deceived" (Gal. 6:7). The potential for deception here is clearly related to the span of time between the sowing and the reaping. Sowing to the flesh does not always produce its negative fruit quickly, and so an emerging adult may be deceived into thinking that indulgence in youthful passions has little impact on future faithfulness or formation. The lack of visible decline, however, cannot mask the subtle decay that is gradually reshaping the heart in negative ways. Just because the fleshly seed lies dormant for a time does not mean it has lost its capacity to poison the soil.

The problem with the idea that the twenties are a time to get youthful passions worked out of their systems is that engagement in these passions tends to do the exact opposite—it works these things *into* their systems in ways that will be challenging to extricate later on. As medical doctor Jeffrey Satinover comments, "Sin, in short, not only represents a simple momentary failure of the will but progressively weakens and undermines the will, eventually destroying it altogether. . . . Yet it is also true that with each successive step we progressively lose the ability to turn around, and yet are unaware of this worsening, insidious moral incapacitation."[38] According to Satinover, habitual patterns produce real physiological changes in the brain, forming grooves in neural pathways that facilitate repetition. "Over time," he notes, "the choices we make fall into ever more predictable patterns because the pattern of choices tends to be self-reinforcing. As we practice certain behaviors, they become easier and easier, and we become 'better and better' at them. As they become easier, we grow more and more likely to choose them. The more we choose them, the more deeply embedded they become, and so on. What starts out as relatively free becomes ever less so as time goes on."[39] Emerging adults often think of this decade of life as an Etch A Sketch in which they can construct drawings and simply "shake to erase" when they are done. What they don't often recognize is that each drawing leaves a trace that becomes more evident and more permanent over time.

It is important to remember, however, that this "harvest deception" cuts both ways. Just as sowing to the flesh might not bear immediate negative fruit, sowing to the Spirit may also fail to show immediate positive results. The potential deception here is to think that sowing to the Spirit has little effect and is therefore unimportant. This is part of the reason why living "by faith, not by sight" is so important. In a world of instant gratification and a desire for instant feedback, the slow and patient cultivation of the soul can seem both unnecessary and restraining. Spiritual practices may not possess the same sense of pragmatic benefit as studying for an exam or working hard at the job to receive a promotion. Emerging adults have simply not lived enough of life to see the ways in which spiritual formation often bears gradual fruit over the course of years and decades. It may take older mentors both to exemplify this and to encourage emerging adults that the path is worthwhile, to commend what Eugene Peterson has termed "a long obedience in the same direction."[40]

Emerging adulthood therefore becomes an important time for developing spiritual "tendencies," strong dispositions (virtues and vices) that gradually engrave the character in ways that are difficult to change.[41] Philosopher Rebecca DeYoung compares this to a winter sledding party in which a group of people carve out a path in "freshly fallen snow." While the first group will move slowly through the thick snow, each progressive group will pack it down further, producing a groove that makes it easier and more natural to follow. Soon, it becomes difficult to steer the sled outside of this well-worn path. "Habits," likewise, "incline us swiftly, smoothly, and reliably toward certain types of action."[42] The key is to encourage emerging adults to engage formation not "someday" but "today" so that they will not "be hardened by sin's deceitfulness" (Heb. 3:13).

Emerging adults, therefore, must begin to understand the power of every mundane moment in shaping their future destinies. Many have been conditioned to expect spiritual formation to develop within the context of sporadic "mountaintop" experiences. For those growing up in the church, they can look back at Christian camps, youth group retreats, conferences, missions trips, and service projects as the spiritual milestones of their lives and the central agents of transformation. While such experiences can indeed spark tremendous growth, the reliance on such experiences can be a barrier to emerging adult spiritual formation. Because they attach spiritual growth to these events, they can hold very low expectations for growth potential in the mundane, everyday moments or the weekly rhythms of local congregational life. As Lewis notes, however,

> Every time you make a choice you are turning the central part of you, the part of you that chooses, into something a little different from what it was before. And taking your life as a whole, with all your innumerable choices, all your life long you are slowly turning this central thing either into a heavenly creature or into a hellish creature: either into a creature that is in harmony with God, and with other creatures, and with itself, or else into one that is in a state of war and hatred with God, and with its fellow-creatures, and with itself. . . . Each of us at each moment is progressing to one state or the other.[43]

Emerging adults must hear the message that spiritual growth happens not only in dramatic events of short duration but also in the ordinary activities, practices, and interactions of daily life.

In other words, we need to foster the expectation among emerging adults that life is to be lived "with Christ," bearing spiritual fruit because they are *abiding* with him. Contrary to the prevalent deistic notion of a remote God who intervenes only to solve problems and bestow blessings, Christianity is marked by a life "hidden with Christ in God" (Col. 3:3) in which Christ "dwells" in the heart through faith (Eph. 3:17). It is not compliance with the rules of a distant deity, but "Christ in you, the hope of glory" (Col. 1:27), serving a God "who works in you, both to will and to work for his good pleasure" (Phil. 2:13 ESV). Emerging adults must be given a vision of life that moves beyond a contractual relationship with an absentee God. They must begin to embrace the possibility of a true apprenticeship, a "life with God" that allows them the privilege of participating in the divine nature (2 Pet. 1:4). To do this, however, they must begin to think about the practices that govern their lives.

Beyond Deism: Practicing the Presence of God

While compelling pictures of Jesus and his kingdom are essential for penetrating emerging adults' hearts, it is clear that spiritual formation must also address the practices that govern their lives. The desires of the heart are often inscribed in their beings as habits—virtues or vices that have become so identified with them that they become automatic and second-nature tendencies in their day-to-day activities. By the time individuals have reached emerging adulthood, many of these habits have become deeply ingrained, resulting in lifestyle patterns that either move them toward or away from the priorities of the kingdom. Because actions often bypass careful reflection, emerging adults are usually attempting to "deal with" these habits after they have already been lived out in practice.

Interestingly, this suggests that spiritual formation must attend to the body. As Willard reminds us, the body is the very place where wrong habits reside and where new kingdom habits must be cultivated. The body, in other words, is the locus of the automatic responses to life situations that often dictate the ways in which emerging adults live in the world. Spiritual formation, therefore, must attend not only to the communication of biblical and theological truth but also to the "enfleshed" aspects of emerging adult life. As Willard proposes, "Very little of our being lies under the direction of our conscious minds, and very little of our actions runs from our thoughts and consciously chosen intentions. Our mind on its own is an extremely feeble instrument, whose power over life we constantly tend to exaggerate. We are incarnate beings in our very nature, and we live from our bodies. If we are to be transformed, the body must be transformed, and that is not accomplished by talking at it."[44]

Thus, we need to help emerging adults become more aware of both the ways in which their present bodily practices are shaping their loves and the ways in which intentional bodily practices might facilitate spiritual formation. This will involve, perhaps first, an awareness and analysis of present practices in order to determine the *telos* (purpose) to which they are aimed and the loves they are producing. Emerging adults should be taught to ask repeatedly the question posed by James K. A. Smith: "Just what kind of person is this habit or practice trying to produce, and to what end is such a practice aimed?"[45] It may be helpful for emerging adults to consider their daily routines—time schedules, work routines, eating, shopping, online habits, entertainment consumption, and so on—as ritualistic practices that are aiming their loves in particular directions by shaping unconscious habits of thought, feeling, and practice. This will be true both for those practices that are largely mundane (i.e., stopping by Starbucks before work each day) and for those that are more intentional (i.e., having a daily quiet time). Some practices, on the one hand, must be identified as deforming in that they shape loves in directions antithetical to the kingdom of God. Christian practices, on the other hand, can be identified as formational (in the sense that they are directed toward a growing love for and obedience to Christ) and counterformational (in the sense that they seek to oppose the deforming aspects of cultural liturgies that adulterously lure their loves in unhealthy directions).

Part of this important work will be to help emerging adults grow in their capacities for cultural critique. The media they consume, the institutions they join, and the activities in which they engage all carry with them implicit (or explicit) visions of the good life, pictures of "kingdoms" that represent ultimate goods. In reality, many of these places and practices are "serving up" false gospels, alternative versions of sin, redemption, and eschatological hope. Shopping centers (whether physical or online) may present sin in terms of material lack, redemption in terms of consumer purchases, and eschatological hope in terms of a life surrounded with all of the goods one wants (and always more than one's neighbor). The gym, likewise, might portray sin in terms of flab, redemption in terms of exercise, and eschatological hope in terms of the perfect body desired (and envied) by all. "We need to recognize," Smith suggests, "that these practices are not neutral or benign, but rather intentionally loaded to form us into certain kinds of people—to unwittingly make us disciples of rival kings and patriotic citizens of rival kingdoms."[46] How might emerging adults cultivate active resistance to the allure of these false kingdoms? In addition, how might they engage in formational and counterformational practices that will foreground different kingdom visions more in keeping with the gospel?

The answers to such questions highlight the critical importance of the classical spiritual disciplines in emerging adult life. Far from the deistic attempt to exercise willpower for spiritual growth, the disciplines represent a kind of "active receiving." We can do nothing to bring about our own spiritual transformation—this is all of the Spirit (Ezek. 36). At the same time, we cannot simply avoid all effort and wait passively for the Spirit to work. Rather, as Richard Foster has suggested, "The disciplines allow us to place ourselves before God so that He can transform us. . . . By themselves the Spiritual Disciplines can do nothing; they can only get us to the place where something can be done. They are God's means of grace."[47]

As Willard has indicated, spiritual disciplines can be divided into two main camps: disciplines of abstinence and disciplines of engagement.[48] Disciplines associated with abstinence, or detachment, include such practices as fasting, solitude, silence, celibacy, secrecy, sacrifice, and frugality, while those associated with engagement, or attachment, include study, worship, celebration, service, prayer, fellowship, confession, and submission. Disciplines of abstinence are generally devoted to the process of disrupting our "automatic thoughts, feelings, and actions" that pull us away from kingdom life, while the disciplines of engagement open us to the work of the Holy Spirit and connect us in powerful ways to kingdom realities and God's grace.[49] The spiritual disciplines are designed, therefore, to "help us withdraw from total dependence on the merely human or natural . . . and to depend also on the ultimate reality, which is God and His kingdom."[50]

Disciplines of Abstinence

Disciplines of abstinence, which generally involve abstaining from some normal and legitimate desires, serve many important purposes in the process of emerging adult spiritual formation. These disciplines all represent forms of fasting: fasting from food (traditional fasting), from fellowship and activity (solitude and silence), from sexual gratifications (celibacy), from human approval (secrecy), from comfort (sacrifice), and from material things (frugality). Such disciplines exercise their power by exposing idols. When all cravings are satisfied, it is very difficult to recognize the desires that actually rule the heart. Augustine once commented that true self-knowledge is only possible through an "experimental and not merely verbal self-interrogation."[51] In other words, these practices can enable emerging adults to test their own hearts to determine their true loyalties. Fasting may alert them to their worship of food, secrecy their reliance on affirmation, frugality their confidence in material possessions. These practices can reveal for emerging adults their true sources of strength, comfort, and contentment.

While such practices facilitate the process of detecting idols, however, they also open up pathways to enhance the worship and enjoyment of God. It is difficult for emerging adults to maximize enjoyment of Christ when they are continually satiated by the things of this world. Disciplines of abstinence, therefore, provide a form of intentional detachment from the habitual patterns of life in order to open up spaces for reflection, listening, and connection with God. They express dissatisfaction with this world and a desire to be satisfied with Christ. He is the bread of life (more than food), the most intimate companion (more than friend or spouse), the ultimate prize (more than material possessions), and the primary source of approval (more than the acclaim of people). Fasting leads to feasting on him. Solitude and silence open ears to hear his voice. Secrecy leads to seeking his "well done." Though they may be challenging to practice, it is important that we describe these disciplines of abstinence as gracious invitations to a life with Christ—the "abundant life" he came to offer.

While all of the disciplines of abstinence are extremely valuable, some seem especially poignant for those in the emerging adult years. Solitude and silence, for example, can serve as powerful agents of personal formation in the midst of the frenetic pace of daily life. In terms of uncovering the idols of the heart, solitude reveals the way in which emerging adults rely on words to provide meaning, significance, and a sense of identity in their lives. Identity, in other words, is wrapped up almost completely in what they say (or text) and what others say (or post) about them. They use words as tools of impression management, adjusting others' opinions of them by setting forth a verbal depiction of the way they wish to be seen. They also depend on others to speak words that give a sense of affirmation and validation. This is especially true among emerging adults who are desperately seeking to solidify an identity and to gain the affirmation of the gatekeepers in their lives. Social networking sites, such as Facebook and Twitter, accentuate this posture, creating spaces in which they are ultra-attuned to others' feedback. In solitude, however, they come face-to-face with their true identities, their inner-directed character as opposed to their other-directed personality.[52] There is no one but God to tell them who they really are at the core. There is no image management, only the voice of the One who knows them completely. "We are silent at the beginning of the day because God should have the first word," Bonhoeffer notes, "and we are silent before going to sleep because the last word also belongs to God."[53]

Furthermore, solitude and silence can help emerging adults break free from the illusion that they are defined by their productivity and accomplishments. It is quite common for emerging adults to derive a sense of worth from achievements, from a sense of growing competence and efficacy in the world as they "prove themselves." Whether striving for grades in college or promotions at work, performance becomes the measure of adult aptitude and a powerful source of self-understanding. However, silence and solitude remind them that God loves them as his children without reference to their accomplishments. His opinion of them is not rooted in fruitful labor or success. Furthermore, confronting the temptation of self-importance, silence and solitude remind them that the world does not rest on their shoulders, that their work is not needed to make the world run. In silence they relinquish control and recognize their own limited role in a world that is governed and sustained by God himself. In other words, silence and solitude can also be tools of humility, furnishing a renewed sense of utter dependence on God for everything that they are and for everything that they do.

Finally, silence and solitude not only reveal emerging adults' hearts but also detach them temporarily from habitual patterns so as to open them up to the work of the Holy Spirit. As noted, emerging adults are often lulled into spiritual complacency by the distractions and disruptions of their lives, placing their souls in a "lockbox" while they attend to the more pressing matters of their lives.[54] Busyness preserves the heart as a locked tomb. As Kierkegaard notes, "For this press of busyness is like a charm. And it is sad to observe how its power swells, how it reaches out seeking always to lay hold of ever-younger victims so that childhood or youth are scarcely allowed the quiet and the retirement in which the Eternal may unfold a divine growth."[55] Silence and solitude provide space for prayerful listening, a space in which they grow attentive to the still small voice that is so often drowned out by the competing voices around them. It is here, as Foster suggests, that they can put themselves in a position to "hear the divine Whisper better."[56] If emerging adults desire to combat the relentless cultural messages that elevate other kingdoms, they cannot afford to miss out on the space provided by solitude, in which they are liberated to listen to another voice.

Secrecy—fasting from others' approval—also becomes significant at this stage of life. Emerging adulthood often serves as the period of time in which the desire for approval reaches its apex. In such a context, one's own competence and character are frequently evaluated—by teachers, employers, prospective mates, and others. There is a tendency to grow dependent on others' approval, controlled by external opinions. In secrecy, the emerging adult takes part in some form of work or service for another without the recipient knowing the identity of the giver. Much like the directive in Matthew 6 to pray in one's closet, to fast with face glowing, and to give without the left hand knowing what the right hand is doing, the call of secrecy is to live out one's faith without the need for human approval. Secrecy alerts the emerging adult heart to the subtle idol of pride, providing a vivid picture of how much one relies on such affirmation as the chief motivation for activity. In addition, it provides a unique opportunity to look to God for commendation, learning to appeal reflexively to his Word rather than the evaluative voices of others. In the end, we desire that emerging adults recognize their need for an "audience of One," elevating the divine evaluation that comes in his voice.

As a final discipline of abstinence, fasting can be a very critical ally in spiritual transformation. As with the other disciplines, one of the key roles of fasting is to wake emerging adults up to the idols that control them. When they deny themselves some normal pleasure—food, computers, or shopping— they begin to recognize how much they rely on those things for comfort and joy. If they are having a bad day, what is the go-to source of solace? Where do they turn to secure a sense of peace and well-being? Fasting will often reveal these realities in stark fashion, opening their eyes to powerful idols. As Piper contends, "This is one way fasting serves all of our acts of love to God. It keeps the preferring faculty on alert and sharp. It does not let the issue rest. It forces us to ask repeatedly: do I really hunger for God? Do I miss him? Do I long for him? Or have I begun to be content with his gifts? Christian fasting is a test to see what desires control us. What are our bottom-line passions?"[57] Furthermore, like solitude and silence, fasting creates space for reflection on God and his kingdom. Just as busyness crowds out the still small voice of the Good Shepherd, food, computers, television, and cell phones can saturate the spiritual landscape of emerging adults' souls, dulling their sensitivities to the things of God. As Piper continues, "If you don't feel strong desires for the manifestation of the glory of God, it is not because you have drunk deeply and are satisfied. It is because you have nibbled so long at the table of the world. Your soul is stuffed with small things, and there is no room for the great."[58] Fasting, by removing these elements even for a short time, can become a means of shifting their gaze to the food that will not perish.

Disciplines of Engagement

Such disciplines of abstinence pave the way for disciplines of engagement. When our automatic responses against the kingdom begin to be broken and when some of our attachments to other kingdoms are severed, room is provided for the soul to reconnect more effectively with God and his kingdom resources. Of course, the chief discipline of engagement comes in the broad and deep encounter with God's Word. The broad study of Scripture is one of the primary ways in which emerging adults can internalize the narrative of God's work in the world and begin to see themselves as characters in the larger story that he is weaving through all of history. As they begin to digest the larger story line of the Bible—to see the wonder of creation, the painful fall of humanity, and God's relentless pursuit of his people culminating in the life, death, and resurrection of Jesus—the Holy Spirit can begin to renarrate their perspectives. Instead of finding themselves in a story consisting of personal development, financial and relational success, and eventual death, they begin to see themselves within a much larger story of God fulfilling his kingdom purposes throughout eternal life for his glory.

Yet this broad overview must also be accompanied by a deep engagement with Scripture. For many emerging adults, the manner of reading Scripture militates against this kind of penetration. For those who have been raised in academic environments in which they are acclimatized to read for quick information gathering, skimming for main points, and extracting key principles, such postures of reading typically remain the norm. Texts are engaged in a subject-object relationship, and metaphors of conquering and mastery are used to describe Bible study, "checking off" a daily quiet time or "achieving" a goal of six chapters a day. Scripture is viewed strictly as material to be mined and employed for personal use. As Jeffrey Greenman suggests, Bible study can easily devolve into "an information-oriented rationalism wherein the Bible is 'word processed' in a mechanical way, rather than being absorbed or digested in a more transformational manner."[59]

Both because of the distractions of our culture and the purely informational patterns of our reading, distinct postures and practices may help emerging adults encounter Scripture in a more transformational manner. We must help them approach the Word with postures of submission, humility, and receptivity, approaching Scripture as a subject-subject interaction with the living and speaking God. Helpful here is M. Robert Mulholland's adapted version of the ancient monastic practice of *lectio divina*. He recommends a series of six progressive steps in "spiritual reading" of the text: (1) *silencio*, (2) *lectio*, (3) *meditatio*, (4) *oratio*, (5) *contemplatio*, and (6) *incarnatio*. In *silencio*, the reader comes to the Bible with a submissive posture, marked by a readiness to receive and a fixed resolution to submit to its authority in all things. In what Mulholland calls an "informational-functional culture," such a step is necessary as a means of avoiding a purely rational and evaluative stance. *Lectio* is constituted by a slow reading of the text, "chewing" on the words and perhaps memorizing them until they become part of one's being. Careful study of the Word, *meditatio*, comes next, marked by observation, interpretation, and contextual understanding. Lest this be purely informational, however, this step is always followed by *oratio*, a response to God in light of the text. Usually marked by prayer or journaling, this is a dialogical stage in which the emerging adult can share the feelings and questions aroused by the text with God himself. Speaking to the Lord is then followed by listening (*contemplatio*), yielding control and waiting upon God with openness to hear what he may be impressing on the reader. Finally, there can be a move to practice (*incarnatio*), confessing sin, claiming promises, embracing truth, obeying commands, and ultimately worshiping the true living Word.[60] In all of this, we help emerging adults fulfill Paul's admonition to the Colossians: "Let the word of Christ dwell in you richly" (3:16).

Though seldom practiced by emerging adults, singing can also be important here. As James K. A. Smith reminds us, singing entails full-bodied action that calls on many aspects of our embodied selves to enter into acts of worship. Emerging adults hardly need to be convinced that music has a way of instilling itself within the very fiber of our beings, creating strong emotional connections that reach the heart quickly. Songs have a way of remaining with us, creating strong associations of memory to particular moments in time and reminding us of their themes as we hum them throughout the day. If hymns are included, these songs also connect us to the traditions of the past and provide a memorable language within which to interpret experiences. While some Christian music does little more than reinforce the cultural scripts of Moralistic Therapeutic Deism, there is much that provides a language of resistance to these themes and that also instills a firm sense of identity as the people of God. Again, we understand this well with regard to earthly citizenship. Patriotic songs are often viewed as powerful means of instilling loyalty, allegiance, and a sense of national pride. This is no less the case for our heavenly citizenship, where music can serve as a powerful means of imparting a deep emotional resonance with the ideals of the kingdom. Is it any wonder that Paul implores the members of the church of Colossae to sing "psalms and hymns and spiritual songs, with thankfulness in your hearts to God" (Col. 3:16)?

Confession also serves as a critical, though challenging, discipline of engagement. Christian Smith comments that emerging adults live with "no regrets" about past actions or decisions, protecting the "sacred" sense of self against any accusation of failure or flaw.[61] Reflecting doubts about a central orienting moral compass, such self-preservation also indicates the importance of a positive self-generated image of competence and goodness. In such a context, confession becomes more important than ever. It attacks pride, the root of all sin, and therefore provides a pathway toward humble submission to God's redemptive work. In fact, as Dietrich Bonhoeffer notes, it is in confession that the believer joins in the cross-shaped reality of true discipleship, dying (in humiliation) to oneself and rising to newness of life and the reality of forgiveness.[62] The act of verbalizing one's sin to another also reveals the ugliness of that sin. In other words, the very act of articulating sin can break through the internal rationalizations that often blunt perceptions of sin's gravity. While sin thrives in isolation, confession provides a setting in which emerging adults may become known, exposing sin so that it may be healed (James 5:16).

As a discipline of engagement, therefore, confession can connect emerging adults to the reality of kingdom life. It opens them to the beauty and joy of forgiveness, something often doubted in the absence of verbal proclamation. In addition, the accountability that comes from this act provides a venue in which to experience the sanctifying help found within the body of Christ. Finally, confession restores the true nature of the Christian community. As Bonhoeffer suggests, Christians are often tempted to live as the "devout," sinless followers of Christ.[63] Yet true Christian community is a collection of sinners saved by grace, drawn together at the foot of the cross as redeemed sinners. While many would agree with this, the practical omission of confession creates a setting in which the true basis and identity of Christian community is neglected. At a time of life when so much emphasis is placed upon success, competence, and independence, confession provides a powerful reminder of personal and corporate identity in Christ.

Many more disciplines of engagement will be described in the chapters to follow, but it is important to remember—contra deism—that these practices are spiritually formative not only because they are aimed at a kingdom vision of the good life but because they actually engage us with the Holy Spirit, the presence of God himself. There is always a tendency to see spiritual disciplines as pathways to a predictable result of spiritual growth and formation. If emerging adults practice secrecy, they presume, they will grow more humble and less prideful. If they serve others, they will grow less self-focused and gain a love for the downtrodden. These may very well be results of such actions, but they must recognize that disciplines are merely ways in which they offer themselves (their bodies) to the Lord with open hands, asking him to do in them what he will. Many emerging adults grow increasingly discouraged if the disciplines do not furnish an expected result in quick fashion, but they must recognize that God will take these offerings and shape their lives according to his purposes, sometimes in ways that they would never have expected (even in ways they would not have wanted!). As Mulholland reminds us, "A genuine spiritual discipline is a discipline of loving obedience offered to God with no strings attached. We put no conditions on it. We put no time limits on it. We add no expectations of how we want God to change us through it. We simply offer the discipline to God, and keep on offering it for as long as God wants us to keep on."[64] The goal of spiritual formation, therefore, is not a certain result but rather the development of a "with God" life, abiding in him as his apprentices.[65]

Ultimately, these disciplines should always bring emerging adults back to the gospel. Entering into these disciplines reveals the dark corners of the heart, exposing idols and deep-seated desires that lead them astray. Far from producing a path to continual improvement in which they are getting better day after day, the disciplines often produce a deeper recognition of the gaping chasm between God's holiness and their sinfulness. Practicing the disciplines almost always brings them back to a recognition that they are weak, fragile, and undisciplined, dreading the very things that can bring them life. Emerging adults practicing such disciplines often perceive themselves to be in spiritual decline because they see and feel more of their sin. For those expecting the disciplines to help them "do better" and "feel better," this can be a jarring experience. However, as we guide and mentor them through these emotions, we must help them to see that these practices are designed to turn their hearts back to the cross. The growing recognition of sin and weakness, in other words, is meant to lead them to despair of their own attempts at self-improvement and to puncture their pride and self-righteousness so that they are thrown upon the grace of God. Such practices bring them back to the realization that they are not only saved by grace but must also live on the grace of God anchored by the cross. In short, they provide means by which emerging adults can be continually reevangelized by the gospel.

In the end, emerging adult spiritual formation is not a process of therapeutic personal improvement as much as a process of reorienting the heart's affections, counting the cost of discipleship, and abiding with Christ in all of life. "Finally, if all goes well," Lewis notes, the Spirit will be turning them "permanently into a different sort of thing; into a new little Christ, a being which, in its own small way, has the same kind of life as God; which shares in His power, joy, knowledge and eternity."[66] Such a process will result in far more than a domesticated sense of "goodness." Instead, it will radically transform personal identity, corporate identity, vocational purpose, character, and relationships. To these factors we now turn.

3 | Identity

Internalization, Refusal, and Engagement

> The transition to adulthood today is more complex, disjointed, and confusing
> than in past decades. . . . These steps through and to schooling, the first real job,
> marriage, and parenthood are simply less well organized and coherent today
> than they were in generations past. These transitions are often accompanied
> by large doses of transience, confusion, anxiety, self-obsession, melodrama,
> conflict, disappointment, and sometimes emotional devastation.
>
> Christian Smith[1]

In 1960, Milton Bradley developed the board game LIFE. Fashioned after a
game developed on a checkerboard a hundred years earlier, LIFE was now
adapted to reflect the typical way people moved through the life span in the
post–World War II era.[2] As a cultural product, LIFE helpfully foregrounds
important cultural scripts and implicit perspectives on identity formation. For
example, the game does not begin at birth as one might expect from a game
called "LIFE." Instead, the game begins with the movement toward adult
life. Hence, with the first spin of the wheel, players must decide whether they
should (1) enter college and assume $40,000 in promissory notes, gaining
three career choices and the hope of a better salary, or (2) forego the college

experience and move directly into the life course with only one chance to pull an adequate salary from a deck of nine possible cards.

The beginning of the game underscores the reality that one's place in society is not determined, as it had been in the past, by ascribed status related to family name, gender, race, or parental socioeconomic status.[3] Unbound from traditional roles on the family farm in a community-based society and unconstrained by cultural roles obligating one to remain close to family, people now have the option of bettering their position in life by making individual decisions to attend college and choose a career (such an emphasis, of course, masks significant gaps in educational and career opportunities for women and racial/ethnic minorities).[4] Once this choice of college and career is made in the game of LIFE, it structures the family income and largely defines vocational identity for the rest of the life course.

After rounding the first bend toward adulthood, the pathways suddenly come back together and become uniform. The events along the journey become carefully sequenced. Within a turn or two, everyone stops at the church to get married. Once united, the player can potentially land on spaces that add pink and blue children (and that grant the player a "LIFE" card, suggesting that children are viewed as great benefits to the journey). Another spin of the wheel and the game now requires an additional event for all players—the purchase of a house. This is of course assumed possible because by this time one has passed several Pay Day spaces and accumulated several salaries. Like marriage, buying a house occurs in the young adult years and is regarded as a single occurrence. In the 1960s, the general societal pattern one could anticipate was for the nuclear family to occupy a geophysical space in the world for the remainder of LIFE. Ultimately, this scripted path would lead to a stable retirement at either Countryside Acres or, if one played exceptionally well, at Millionaire Acres.

Reflecting an American mid-twentieth-century consensus, this Milton Bradley world orders events in a way that makes cultural expectations clear and navigation through the life course relatively easy and coherent. Education is the requisite pathway to career; a career provides the foundation necessary for marriage; marriage precedes and is enjoined with childbearing. A normative pattern therefore establishes the shape of the good life. Few identity choices are required, and those that are establish a relatively stable place in society. Further, adherence to these cultural expectations affords a strong sense of cultural and familial belonging, requiring relatively little conscious deliberation to make the journey.[5]

Times have changed, however. In 2005, Milton Bradley produced a new edition of LIFE, and this particular version carried the subtitle *Twists and*

Turns. The game board no longer consists of a linear movement from young adulthood to retirement with transitional events sequenced in predetermined fashion. Instead, the LIFE game board now consists of four loops, and one must determine time and time again, in no particular order, which one to enter. *Earn it!*, *Learn it!*, *Live it!*, and *Love it!* are the declarative imperatives for these loops that now serve as the parameters for what it means to play the game of LIFE. Rather than the nine career cards and nine salary cards in the previous game, from which a player could at best choose among three, this version has twenty-four possible career cards open to every player as well as the possibility of attaining up to seven promotions within a given profession. Interestingly, the game is no longer played with paper money. Rather, each player is now issued a Visa game card that is zipped through a "Lifepod" monitor in the middle of the board, suggesting that LIFE has been restructured by a mass consumer mandate. Each player travels through the various loops of life, not as a family unit in an automobile game piece, but solo, scooting along on a skateboard unencumbered by a spouse or child. Marriage and child rearing are still optional but far less valued as integral to social personhood.[6] The object of the game, in case it is in doubt, is no longer a retirement spot at the end of the journey. Instead, the valuation of a player's life is determined relative to other players by sliding one's Visa card through the Lifepod at the end of the game and revealing how many "life points" have been earned through skillfully navigating life's loops.

Setting these game boards in contrast with one another provides a way of seeing why identity struggles have become more pronounced and prolonged among today's emerging adults. Consider how much more is required of an emerging adult psychologically when the range of alternatives seems endless, when there is no uniform conceptual itinerary to provide guidance, and when one travels with little collective support in navigating the life course. How precarious do choices become when the timing and sequencing of events—like finishing school, starting a career, getting married, buying a house, and having a baby—become decoupled? At an even more fundamental level, what happens when the game of LIFE is no longer perceived as a linear and teleological journey with others toward a final destination and is instead conceptualized as a series of loops traversed alone with little regard for its impact on others?

Important here is the extent to which identity formation has been individualized in American culture. Life events that were previously structured by social norms now require deliberate personal agency and decision making.[7] James Côté and Charles Levine help to clarify this reorganization of the life course by distinguishing social identity from personal identity.[8] Social identity is that part of our self-concept that we derive from membership in a social group, whether the group is defined by gender, nationality, religious origin, political ideology, social class, family, age, or profession.[9] Historically, cultural norms exercised considerable pressure on an individual to find identity by fitting into and sharing the values, beliefs, attitudes, role enactments, and expectations associated with a particular social mold. Thus, if you belonged to the class of "woman," your social identity was largely constituted and constrained by being a mother and a housewife, roles you would learn naturally by socialization in the family. If you were raised in a family of "farmers," you could identify the roles you would occupy in society by looking across the dinner table for a reference point in your father or mother. Alasdair McIntyre explains the power of social identity and how it contrasts with our contemporary model:

> The self is now thought of as lacking any necessary social identity, because the kind of social identity that it once enjoyed is no longer available; the self is now thought of as criterionless, because the kind of telos in terms of which it once judged and acted is no longer thought to be credible. . . . In many premodern, traditional societies it is through his or her membership in a variety of social groups that the individual identifies himself or herself and is identified by others. I am brother, cousin and grandson, member of this household, that village, this tribe. These are not characteristics that belong to human beings accidentally, to be stripped away in order to discover "the real me." They are part of my substance, defining partially at least and sometimes wholly my obligations and my duties. Individuals inherit a particular space within an interlocking set of social relationships; lacking that space, they are nobody, or at best a stranger or an outcast.[10]

In contemporary American culture, the potency of this social identity has progressively dissolved, replaced by a recurrent appeal to personal identity construction. Personhood has come to be experienced as a product created by personal choices or by participation in self-selected affinity groups.[11] Deeply biased toward independent self-construal, Americans claim the right to choose which duties and relationships oblige their allegiance and assert the right to reframe what any role requires according to self-expression.[12] If social identity has in fact diminished its role in conferring on someone a sense of self, it follows that a subjective sense of personal identity increases in importance. Côté and Levine argue that what many pundits have regarded as "postmodernity" may better be described as the reconstitution of the self's relation to society and the reordering of Western culture around a specific kind of individualization.[13] Stanley Grenz concluded that the "postmodern condition, therefore, entails the replacement of the stability and unity that characterized the self of the modern ideal with . . . the splintering of the self into multiple subjectivities."[14]

Côté and Levine comment that identity formation no longer consists of fitting one's brick into an already established blueprint; instead, individuals must engage in constructing the whole house.[15]

It is of little surprise, then, to hear Jeffrey Arnett report that "there has been a profound change in how young people view the meaning and value of becoming an adult."[16] The historical sociological markers assigning adult status—leaving home, finishing school, becoming financially independent, marriage, and child rearing—no longer become the defining characteristics of adulthood. Rather, the more subjective criteria of "becoming independent," "making my own decisions," and "supporting myself financially" now constitute the rites of passage into adulthood.[17] For those with a fund of familial support and sufficient financial resources, the process of maturation may indeed facilitate self-directed agency, making emerging adulthood a thrilling time of self-exploration and personal development. Given a moratorium from work and family responsibilities, a space is created that allows psychological deficiencies to be addressed and ego capacities to be developed that aid one in mastering social environments and making probable a thriving adulthood.[18] Others, however, enter these years ill equipped for the task of identity deliberation and without the financial, social, and familial support necessary to prepare for the possible life trajectories now available.[19]

Interestingly, the individualization of identity development tends to lead to one of two possible extremes: anxiety or apathy. While the task of self-creation may seem to liberate from the constraints of imposed categories, it also creates a recurring sense of pressure to create the best possible self. It inserts a deep sense of responsibility and culpability for one's emerging identity, producing an anxious sense that "I am not enough" and that "I must continue thinking ahead about how to do better." Côté contends that whereas the industrial revolution produced the "economic man" of that generation, contemporary society has created "psychological adulthood."[20] Foreseeing widespread problems with identity making in the future, Côté argues that the primary emotion haunting contemporary emerging adults in their struggle toward attaining "psychological adulthood" is not that of *guilt* (usually the targeted condition in most evangelical presentations of the gospel) but *anxiety*.

Such anxiety is clearly evident among emerging adults. Richard Kadison and Theresa Foy DiGeronimo document that in just over a decade, the percentage of students diagnosed with depression and suicidal ideation on one college campus more than doubled.[21] Likewise, the proportion of students taking stress-relieving medications rose from 10 to 25 percent. The top prescribed drug for college students today, they note, is not the birth control pill or acne medication but antidepressants. They also discovered that Adderall and Ritalin, drugs generally prescribed for attention deficit disorder, are often misused as brain steroids to artificially stimulate longer focus.[22] In other words, anxiety about fashioning a secure future internalizes the impulse to sacrifice your overall health for the sake of peak performance. When identity is perceived as a personal project of self-development, these high stakes drive some emerging adults to stress-filled achievement and others to failure-driven despair.

If anxiety marks one chronic condition of identity development in emerging adulthood, apathy may mark another. Helpful here is Côté's distinction between "developmental individualization" and "default individualization."[23] While developmental individualization involves a self-disciplined attempt to use the freedom of this stage to enhance the aptitudes and attitudes necessary for identity formation, default individualization is characterized by a passive acquiescence to a corporate society that offers a false sense of "individuality" via wardrobe selection, consumer purchases, body sculpting, and other forms of impression management.[24] By linking identity to consumer items such as clothing, cars, and phones, emerging adults often fail to recognize that they are "outsourcing" identity formation to the powerful moguls of corporate America. Succumbing to such manipulation creates the illusion of individuality while actually producing an ironic similarity to others who buy into the same trends.[25] In the end, default individualization neglects true identity formation in favor of a passive and mindless conformity to the whims of popular culture.

Whether moving in the direction of anxious striving or apathetic consumerism, the individualization of identity often supports extreme forms of both individualism and individuation within emerging adult culture. Orrin Klapp maintains that even when emerging adults strive for healthy developmental identity, the high value placed on individualism may yet contribute to a society of cultural narcissists who rarely make decisions on the basis of community flourishing.[26] When emerging adults grow accustomed to resolving identity challenges by asking, "What is best for me?" or "What will increase my marketability?" then consequently any concern for the common good, for what promotes healthy community, or for what serves the purposes of God in the world can easily be overlooked or jettisoned. Christian Smith reports that the governing outlook of nearly 91 percent of the young adults he interviewed was that of "liberal individualism."[27] Perceiving society as a "collection of autonomous individuals who are out to enjoy life," they rarely displayed any consciousness of altering one's own lifestyle for the sake of the common good or mobilizing for collective social or economic change.[28] Whether identity is defined in terms of self-improvement or impression management, it is still viewed by most emerging adults as an individual project.

Individuation (identity separation from parents) also tends to become extreme in this context. While differentiation from parents can represent a healthy process of independence and self-development, in an individualized culture it tends to take the form of a more radical rejection of parental influence. Many feel that their identity formation process requires opposition toward—or at best disregard for—the views and lifestyles of their parents, carving out a unique niche that is purely self-determined. Individuation can and should take place in the context of mutual admiration and support between parents and children, but in our culture this process seems to lead to a more dramatic separation.[29]

Freighted with the burden and blessing of personal choice and thrust into a world with few age-based social norms, how do emerging adults navigate their expanding spheres? How might adults in their world help them enter the process of identity formation in such a way as to develop a solid core of internalized conviction and faithfulness while also remaining tethered to helpful authorities and the community of faith? In the next section, we will discuss the "internalization" of convictions that often accompanies the emerging adult journey. Many of the beliefs and lifestyles assumed during childhood and youth are tried and tested in these years. Faced with new information, new life experiences, and new relational networks, some emerging adults revise earlier understandings. Others deepen their commitments to inherited ideals. In either case, this process in many ways shapes the contours of adult vision. Leaders must join emerging adults in this journey, providing support, challenge, and wisdom in the midst of the big questions that ultimately frame their chosen beliefs and lifestyles. While we want emerging adults to own their faith and identity commitments, this process must unfold within a mentoring context that provides a communal backdrop of nurture, encouragement, and truth.

Identity and Internalization: Forming Personal Convictions

Erik Erikson characterized the ego developmental task of young adulthood as *intimacy versus isolation*.[30] Linked closely with the adolescent crisis of *identity versus diffusion*, the young adult brings the consolidation of earlier identifications and resolutions (trust, autonomy, initiative) into a readiness to risk relationships of closeness to others. Identity that is ready for intimate engagement assumes a coherent self-structure comprising an "internal, self-constructed, dynamic organization of drives, abilities, beliefs and individual history, which is shaped by the child's navigation of normal crises or challenges at each stage of development."[31] In other words, by age 18, the child should know himself or herself well enough and have developed the necessary skills for intimate relationships. Arnett, however, reports that for many emerging adults such identity resolution is not occurring until at least the midtwenties. Arnett's research led him to conclude that the identity exploration Erikson regarded as characteristic of adolescence in the 1960s is now more commonly witnessed in emerging adulthood. The initial sense of identity gained in adolescence is better defined as "provisional." Such identity is rarely maintained once and for all but is instead tested and modified through further periods of exploration and commitment.[32]

Drawing on Erikson's model, James Marcia created a four-quadrant identity model defined by the axes of "commitment" and "exploration."[33] Commitment refers to the development of settled conviction about one's beliefs and ways of living. Exploration refers to an active questioning and testing of alternative beliefs and lifestyles or a deep evaluative reflection on one's own convictions and actions.[34] The measure of "commitment" can be low or high, and the measure of "exploration" can be low or high. Marcia labeled the resulting four quadrants *diffusion, foreclosure, moratorium,* and *achievement.* Individuals with few commitments and little desire for exploration were defined as "diffused," drifters with limited aspirations to explore alternatives or establish firm convictions.[35] "Foreclosed" individuals, on the other hand, possess strong commitments to certain beliefs or lifestyles but with little exploration of these ideals. Such people often uncritically accept the views of others, living on the basis of borrowed convictions instead of owned convictions. Individuals in "moratorium" actively explore ideas and lifestyles without having yet committed to them. They are testing and experimenting with these convictions in order to discern their adequacy for life but have not yet "landed." Finally, individuals who have "achieved" an identity, according to Marcia, have wrestled with and tested various belief or lifestyle options and made personal commitments to them, internalizing these ideals as their own.[36]

Emerging adults often begin this stage of life in foreclosure (strong commitment, little exploration) with a set of "borrowed" beliefs and lifestyles uncritically adopted from parents or other influential authorities. In this "authority-bound" posture, Sharon Parks suggests, "Knowing is inextricably bound up with the trusted authority," and there is an inherent desire to conform to others' expectations.[37] Similar to what sociologist David Riesman termed "other-directedness," this stance is generally characterized by a strong commitment to beliefs and behaviors that are assumed and unexamined.[38] If authority figures are Baptist and Republican, then emerging adults assume that they should embrace such positions as well. If authorities think the emerging adult should be a doctor, then there is little reason to question. However, authority-bound emerging adults may also demonstrate a reactionary "counter-dependence."[39]

They may seek to denigrate the beliefs or ways of living of their authority figures but fail to develop any new convictions of their own. In such a scenario, the convictions of the authorities, though rejected, are still the chief determinants of emerging adults' lives. In the authority-bound posture, emerging adults do not really explore various ideas or test presuppositions but merely adopt or reject others' perspectives and ways of living.

If emerging adults have borrowed traditional Christian beliefs and ways of living, it is appropriate to ask whether such foreclosed dependence is really such a bad thing. In other words, why encourage change if these individuals are maintaining orthodox doctrines and behaving in ways appropriate to the faith community? While such thoughts and actions are to be commended, there are also some liabilities to an identity that is completely "borrowed." This structure may work when emerging adults remain close to authority figures and the social context in which those beliefs were transmitted, but they can often be quite unsettled when venturing beyond the nest. They may achieve a sense of stability and security—even gratitude toward those who have shaped them—but fail to develop an established core of conviction that can stand the test of time and life experience. In addition, if the authority figures fall in some way, it is not uncommon for authority-bound individuals to "fall with them" or become so disillusioned that they are unable to sustain their own identity. Enmeshed with authority, these emerging adults place the weight of their convictions on these individuals rather than the underlying foundations of their beliefs or lives.

Challenges also arise when emerging adults are confronted by ideas and practices that conflict with those previously adopted. On the one hand, authority-bound emerging adults may simply reject any alternative view or distinct life pattern without consideration, demonstrating a closed-mindedness that avoids engagement with difference. They therefore lack the epistemological humility that would be open to dialogue with others who represent diverse perspectives. On the other hand, because their views are largely unexamined, they may actually be more prone to instability, tossed to and fro by every wind of doctrine set forth by the new authorities that emerge in their lives. This chameleon-like stance means that they simply accept the ideals of each new authority—professors, bosses, coaches, pastors, and others. They do not possess a solid core of self and tend to live life "by the poll" rather than by an internal gyroscope that provides a stable orientation regardless of context.[40]

Even more to the point, authority-bound living may result in the loss of the emerging adults' unique contributions to the world.[41] If they end up simply adopting or parroting the beliefs and practices of their authorities, they may fail to engage their specific and God-given gifts, passions, convictions, and personalities. They may, in other words, conform to others' expectations without asking what God would have them do. In this sense, it is worthwhile to ask whether they might lose some of the prophetic power—the rethinking and reimagining—that comes with each new generation. If they are simply adopting what has come before, conforming their lives to preexisting models, they may resist the creative work of cultural renewal.

If these issues exist, how can the process of internalization be encouraged? First, factors that tend to promote authority-bound ways of living must be identified. Often foreclosure (strong commitment, little exploration) is the default position in part because it is easier, providing a black-and-white world in which emerging adults know exactly where they stand. They do not have to face doubts or questions, and they typically earn the support of the authority figures who serve as academic, vocational, and spiritual gatekeepers in their lives. Many feel a sense of loyalty to these authorities. If they begin to question or reframe the beliefs or actions of these guides—especially parents—it can feel as if they are rejecting these individuals. Like Rapunzel in Disney's *Tangled*, emerging adults often betray considerable anxiety in questioning the opinions of parents or other authority figures. In the film, Rapunzel leaves her tower of safety against the will of her mother. In this funny (but realistic) scene, as she goes back and forth between, "This is so fun!" and "I am a horrible daughter—I'm going back," and between "I am never going back! Woo-hoo!" and "I am a despicable human being," Rapunzel embodies the tension that defines "moratorium" (high exploration, low commitment) for many emerging adults. When her companion, Flynn Rider, sarcastically notes that she appears "at war with herself," he captures quite accurately the stress and pressure of the internalization process. Emerging adults who choose to attend a church of a different denomination or embrace a different political orientation than their parents can feel as if they are betraying their upbringing and implicitly judging their parents' choices. Authority-bound postures alleviate such problems by avoiding such tensions altogether.

At times, foreclosed ways of life also result from environments that are either overly safe (no need to explore) or not safe enough (exploration is denigrated). Research studies indicate that homogenous environments are closely correlated with the perpetuation of authority-bound and foreclosed ways of being.[42] When everyone thinks and acts in a similar fashion, when things are "too safe," there is little incentive to develop personal convictions or to seek more adequate frameworks for thinking and living. Alternatively, in some familial, church, or educational settings, questioning itself is viewed in pejorative terms, either equated with backsliding or pathologized as immediate evidence of rebellion.[43] In these "nonsafe" environments, emerging adults are fearful of articulating questions, preferring instead to give the "right answers" even if doubts are swirling around in their minds. At times, leaders communicate to emerging adults that a "childlike faith" is one that never questions, never doubts, and never explores alternatives. With such powerful social cues, it is little wonder that many emerging adults choose to "toe the line" rather than explore new interpretations or ways of living out their faith.

In a related sense, many parents, teachers, and pastors operate within a "fixing" framework when guiding emerging adults in their faith journeys. When questions do arise, the tendency is to provide quick answers, shutting down any doubts and proposing immediate solutions to any problems. "Helicopter parents," by their very nature, hover over their children for the purpose of fixing any problems that may emerge after their children leave home.[44] The cell phone becomes a metaphorical umbilical cord in their lives, allowing parents to swoop in and save the day by ending their child's discomfort and restoring immediate equilibrium. It feels good to assume such a heroic role, giving the authority figure a sense of validation and power. However, as Daniel Heischman notes, such "trespassing" can sometimes do harm to the ultimate aim of transformation:

> As young people begin to incorporate influential adults into their lives, they need a space around themselves—I would call it a garden, where the ground can be fertilized and seeded. If the adult comes trespassing into that garden, nothing in the soil can really take root and flourish. . . . Adults who are mindful of the delicate but essential distance needed between young and old do indeed risk not knowing everything, not being there every time they are needed, not able to boast of that cherished notion of closeness, but they are allowing the garden to grow.[45]

Once barriers are identified, leaders can facilitate identity exploration and formation in a variety of ways, nurturing the emerging adult's still fragile voice. Melinda Denton and Lisa Pearce note that the internalization of faith increases when students feel understood and when freedom is granted to express their own views.[46] Leaders must ask "big enough" questions that invite emerging adults into the enduring conversations about God, faith, human nature, virtue, and destiny.[47] They must create safe places in which emerging adults are free to question and free to doubt, free to discuss competing ideals and their adequacy in light of biblical truth.[48] Rather than simply solving all of emerging adults' problems or answering all of their questions, leaders must ask questions, helping these nascent adults begin using their own voices to think through significant issues of faith and worldview. Asking "why" questions, in

fact, can be one of the most powerful means of facilitating ownership, helping emerging adults move beyond passive and assumed beliefs and assess the
adequacy of borrowed ideals.

Leaders can also guide and interpret emerging adults' interactions with "difference." For most emerging adults, this stage of life offers no lack of contact
with different individuals, cultures, and belief systems. Such encounters with
people who think and live differently have the potential to shape emerging
adults in many ways. First of all, these encounters highlight and clarify personal
perspectives. It is often difficult for emerging adults to see their own opinions,
presuppositions, and practices because these elements are part of the very air
they breathe. However, when emerging adults have the opportunity to hear
alternative perspectives or to visit another culture, they very quickly recognize
their own biases and proclivities. Picturing oneself from the vantage point of
the "other" facilitates true self-understanding.[49]

Second, exposure to difference also provides new possibilities to challenge
existing beliefs and behaviors. When introduced to new ideas, authors, exemplars (role models), or cultures, emerging adults enter "liminal spaces,"
domains where common assumptions and postures are challenged by unfamiliar surroundings. They often experience a kind of disequilibrium that
forces them either to dismiss these alternatives or to step back and reconsider
their own convictions. Such dissonance often prompts the probing of commitments that characterizes emerging adult identity formation.[50] This is why
experiences in new locations, such as mission trips, retreats, service projects,
and semesters abroad, can be such powerful stimuli for change. While they
cannot be depended on for long-term formation, detachment from the flow of
life and exposure to new settings do serve an important purpose of opening
the mind and soul to new ways of being.

It should be noted that this is not simply a matter of providing the emerging
adult with alternative perspectives and options, giving them a smorgasbord
of competing doctrines and perspectives and then asking them to choose
among the various "flavors." Some leaders feel that they need to resist describing their own convictions so as to avoid indoctrination. This is not the case.
While the development of a "new foreclosure" is certainly a possibility (the
emerging adult becomes committed to new convictions without doing much
exploring), the manner in which the leader shares convictions makes all the
difference. Leaders have an opportunity—even an obligation—to describe
various options in doctrine and practice but also to explain why they have
come to their own convictions. Emerging adults need to see how their mentors
have experienced the work of probing and testing commitment, visualizing
not only the answers their mentors have forged but the prayerful process they

have engaged in to arrive at their present locations. This does not mean that emerging adults will always come to the same convictions as their mentors, but the explanation provides both a means of proceeding and the hope that discerning answers can be found.

The image of an emerging adult leader, therefore, is something like a tour guide. An effective tour guide would never say to the aspiring traveler, "You don't have to go to all that trouble and take the trip. I've already gone, and you can simply look at my pictures." At the same time, the leader would be equally remiss to declare that he or she has decided not to accompany the traveler out of fear of imposition—"Here are your tickets, and I hope you enjoy yourself." Both flaws are common. Some feel that ministry entails the transmission of prepackaged information and experience. They shortcut the emerging adults' firsthand experience by assuming that the leaders' own experiences (their "pictures") can simply be given and incorporated into their lives. Such foreclosed teaching forgets, however, that the goal of the relationship is actually to open up spaces within which the emerging adult can encounter God, Scripture, and the world. Yet leaders do have something important to contribute. While they cannot "take the trip" for the emerging adult, they can and must point to the key locations where God is at work and where truth can be found, opening emerging adults' eyes so that they will themselves pursue lives of conviction and consequence.[51]

For this to happen, leaders must gain wisdom in providing "contingent responses."[52] Contingent responses begin by creating a context based on careful observations of an emerging adult's abilities, needs, and interests and then offering a response at a level just above their current capabilities. Educational specialists term this "scaffolding," offering just the right amount of support and challenge while demonstrating a willingness to withdraw the scaffold when students arrive at wise decision making on their own. If support is high and challenge low, the typical result will be complacency and stagnation, sapping the environment of a motivation to change. If support is low and challenge is high, conversely, the emerging adult may experience fatigue and burnout, a desire to retreat from dissonance into a shell of security or an attitude of "whatever." As psychologist Robert Kegan suggests,

> Environments that are weighted too heavily in the direction of challenge without adequate support are toxic; they promote defensiveness and constriction. Those weighted too heavily toward support without adequate challenge are ultimately boring; they promote devitalization. Both kinds of imbalance lead to withdrawal or dissociation from the context. In contrast, the balance of support and challenge leads to vital engagement.[53]

In the attempt to balance support and challenge, those who work with twentysomethings must not view these practices in terms of a "division of labor." Sometimes professors or pastors feel that their primary role is challenge, rocking the boat with new intellectual constructs that will force emerging adults to question the verities handed down by parents and former pastors. They may recognize the importance of support but see this as coming from other locations, perhaps viewing college residence life staff or close friends as those who will "pick up the pieces." If one introduces dissonance in emerging adults' lives, however, he/she should also demonstrate a willingness to walk through the journey of exploration with them. In addition, it is also true that the one offering the challenge is usually in the best position to provide support. Jesus challenged his disciples in many ways, yet he was also present (and promised the Holy Spirit) to support them as they wrestled through the implications of his teaching. Ideally, every emerging adult mentor should do the same.

This all requires a great deal of discernment. Leaders will need to discern whether an emerging adult is remaining in foreclosure in order to solidify beliefs and own this foundation or whether he or she is using this context as a means of "hiding," avoiding disequilibrium and challenge. The real issue in emerging adulthood is whether this authoritative stance will serve as a launching pad into explorations and convictional commitments or whether it will become a fixed and permanent posture that eliminates exploration, cultural engagement, and hospitality to "others." Leaders therefore will need to discern whether the individual is most adequately served by the supportive context of reinforced truth and like-minded community or by challenging encounters with other beliefs and individuals that prompt exploration and self-evaluation. Such issues of "readiness" can only be determined through much prayer, reliance on the Holy Spirit, and a growing understanding of the emerging adult's heart forged in relationship over time.

Furthermore, those who work with twentysomethings must be prepared for the risks inherent in internalization. In facilitating the process of moratorium (exploring, questioning, testing), mentors have no guarantee that the final commitments will conform to their desired results. In other words, emerging adults may enter a time of testing and exploration only to land in a belief or lifestyle "location" that the mentor sees as negative. Others who engage the exploration process of probing their commitments end up stuck within a perpetual process of questioning. They may seek answers to personal, political, or doctrinal questions, only to find that their questions unlock further questions that resist easy answers. If this process goes on for an extended period of time, "exploratory fatigue" may set in. Such emerging adults may opt for postures resembling identity diffusion (low commitment,

little exploration), a disengaged form of "drifting" free from both commitment and exploration.

For still others, perpetual questioning can itself become a fixed mode of
existence, "always learning but never able to come to a knowledge of the truth"
(2 Tim. 3:7).[54] David Horner helpfully distinguishes between logical doubt,
the proper testing of truth claims, and psychological doubt, a more pervasive
posture that questions everything without desired resolution.[55] While the former
can be helpfully coupled to active exploration, the latter often reflects either
the despairing cynicism of postmodern culture or an unwillingness to take a
stand. In comparing the two, Horner cites G. K. Chesterton who, commenting
on the so-called open-mindedness of H. G. Wells, noted, "I think he thought
that the object of opening the mind is simply opening the mind. Whereas I
am incurably convinced that the object of opening the mind, as of opening
the mouth, is to shut it again on something solid."[56]

For those who do arrive at settled commitments ("achievement"), arrogance
is another risk. While it is no doubt true that many authority-bound individuals
lack epistemological humility, we must also recognize the subtle pride that can
characterize those reaching convictional commitment. While authority-bound
individuals inappropriately elevate key authority figures, those in settled convictions can develop a contrasting problem—a denigration of the authority
figures from whom they are now distancing themselves.[57] This can take many
forms: "I have become so doctrinally sophisticated, and my authorities are
so simple in their faith"; or "I have become so spiritual, and they are just so
sinful"; or "I have become so broad in my understanding, and they are so narrow." Parents often bear the brunt of this when newly "enlightened" children
return from college. This can also happen within the context of the church.
Many theological students find it increasingly difficult to sit humbly under the
teaching of the Word because they have "achieved" commitment on certain
doctrinal issues and therefore scoff at the "uninformed" perspectives offered
by their church leaders.[58] Expanding knowledge and conviction, coupled with
limited life experience, can be a recipe for arrogance.

Leaders therefore must strike a healthy balance, helping emerging adults
develop their own voices while also helping them honor the parents and authority figures on whose foundation they are inevitably building. Even as they
may be adjusting inherited beliefs—even if they come to different conclu-
sions—the primary attitude toward past authorities should be one of gratitude
and indebtedness, thanksgiving for laying the groundwork on which they are
now creating new things. In other words, emerging adults must recognize that
their evolving identity is birthed not in opposition to but through the prior
influence of parents and other leaders. These inherited views are not just the

foils against which they craft new identities. Instead, they can be viewed as the foundations that make such a project possible. Mentors can help emerging adults recognize that this process of internalization is a lifelong process, one in which they enter into humble and receptive dialogue with these authorities. Sustained dialogue over time may or may not bring change to either side, but it will certainly eliminate the arrogant separation that can emerge in this period of individuation.

The goal of the internalization process, therefore, is not a rejection of authority. Many view identity formation as an attempt to move away from authority figures or communities in order to become independent. However, true Christian internalization does not promote rejection of authority as the goal in order to arrive at one's own way of thinking and living. Instead, internalization encourages the conscious choice of authorities to which one will submit and communities to which one will adhere, embracing a set of shared truths and values. The goal is not even the *changing* of authority-derived beliefs and behaviors. Emerging adults may come through the process of probing and exploration more convinced than ever about the veracity of received truth claims and lifestyles. The difference is that they now have *reasons* for their beliefs and chosen practices, reasons for finding them more adequate than alternative visions. They can face the diverse perspectives of our pluralistic world, standing firm in their convictions while also finding space to dialogue with difference. These internalized ideals are now etched on emerging adults' hearts and minds in a manner that will make the ideals more difficult to dislodge when the emerging adults find themselves in new locations. Such individuals may look very much the same, but there is a strength to them that has emerged from the questioning and testing—they have "set their hearts" in a way that will carry them forward into adult life.[59]

Identity and Culture: Refusal and Engagement

While the process of internalization is critical for identity development, leaders must also keep in mind that this process unfolds in the midst of cultures that also shape identity in significant ways. As participants in broader cultures and subcultures (families, schools, clubs, organizations, ministries, churches, etc.), emerging adults are shaped by the people and sociocultural systems surrounding them. Identity formation is therefore always a corporate, social process rather than an individual project of self-development. Those working with emerging adults must be keenly aware of culture's formational role, helping twentysomethings resist its deforming power while also making the most of its potential for positive identity development. To do this, they must guide emerging adults in processes of both refusal and engagement.

Identity and Refusal

The book of Daniel depicts the story of four young men (Daniel, Hananiah, Mishael, and Azariah) who by contemporary standards appear to be on the journey toward adulthood. The advances of their youth are now coming into fullness, evidenced by the description of their selection into the king's court: "young men without any physical defect, handsome, showing aptitude for every kind of learning, well informed, quick to understand, and qualified to serve" (Dan. 1:4). Like most emerging adults, these four young men are away from their homeland. They live as diasporic Jews in Babylon and are brought into contact with powerful leaders accustomed to holding young minds in their sway. Yet despite two worlds colliding, the transition to foreign soil seems initially favorable. All four have been admitted to a special, three-year training program in Babylon's best academy with tuition, room, and board all paid for! The curriculum is the predominant language of the day and the best literature found in Babylonian culture, aiming to fit them for distinguished roles in the king's high court after graduation. Daily amounts of food and wine are given to them as their staple, taken directly from the king's table, and each one is given a new name—Belteshazzar, Shadrach, Meshach, and Abednego—acclimatizing them to a natural following among the Babylonian rank and file. Despite being aliens in a foreign land, the future for these four young men appears bright.

However, Daniel has one objection; he does not want to "defile himself" with the royal food and wine (Dan. 1:8). To modern ears this seems like such a peculiar stand. Why be scrupulous over one's diet and potentially jeopardize the grand opportunity for upward mobility? The text itself makes clear the potential risk in refusing the king's good fare. If eating vegetables instead of kingly food and wine causes Daniel and company to look worse than the other young men, heads would roll (Dan. 1:10). So why even risk it? But Daniel is persistent and bargains with the chief officer for a ten-day vegetable test. The very fact that Daniel is shown such favor by the chief officer can only be attributed to the hidden way of God at work even in the hearts of those in kingdoms opposed to his purposes. Sure enough, at the end of ten days, Daniel, Shadrach, Meshach, and Abednego appear healthier and better nourished than any of those feasting on the royal cuisine.

But why is this detail central to the telling of this story, and how might it inform processes of identity formation today? Some commentators have suggested that Daniel was simply acting out of obedience to the Jewish dietary laws of his day. Others have surmised that there must have been an Israelite taboo against eating meat with the blood still left in it. Still others argue that it was prudent on Daniel's part to avoid the rich food the king was offering in order to promote a more healthy diet. Yet none of these seem to explain the weight given to what Sibley Towner calls Daniel's "magnificent refusal."[60] Towner instead follows Joyce Baldwin in locating the reason for Daniel's refusal. The word used in the first chapter of Daniel, translated as "rich" or "royal" food, occurs one other time in the book of Daniel (11:26). Here it implies that those who share the king's food enter into a covenantal relationship with him.[61] Baldwin suggests,

> It would seem that Daniel rejected this symbol of dependence on the king because he wished to be free to fulfill his primary obligations to the God he served. The defilement he feared was not so much a ritual as a moral defilement, arising from the subtle flattery of gifts and favors which entailed hidden implications of loyal support, however dubious the king's future policies might prove to be.[62]

Though we might remain uncertain about the precise motivation that prompted Daniel's refusal, this interpretation makes clear how it functioned in the lives of Daniel and his friends. To refuse the manner by which the king was currying favor set their identities in sharp contrast to other students in the Babylonian academy. Food and drink, the curriculum of Babylonian literature, the personalized tutoring given by Ashpenaz, and the giving of Babylonian names may have been gratuitous on the one hand; however, on the other hand, this was a complete and systematic process of identity formation designed to procure loyal vassals for the king. Separated from the customs of his Jewish homeland, captive to a culture where the social structures subtly pull one away from allegiance to Yahweh, and embedded in an academic setting where acculturation is rewarded, Daniel recognized his vulnerability. Without making it explicit, the king was attempting to reconstitute the identities of Daniel and his colleagues.

Seen in this light, Daniel's refusal was not simply a request for a change of diet but was akin to what E. Stanley Jones called a "decision that will decide all other decisions down the line—a master decision."[63] It is the refusal that daily established these four young men as a distinct group, grounding their identity as a people set apart. Had Daniel capitulated, says Towner, Daniel would have simply been "another man with a price."[64] Instead, this repudiation of identity-altering forces established the foundation for subsequent acts of refusal: Shadrach, Meshach, and Abednego refusing to bow down to the image of gold (Dan. 3) and Daniel refusing to eliminate his prayers despite the death sentence edict handed down from the king (Dan. 6). A fiery furnace and a den of lions were the potential risks, but this did not dissuade them from standing their ground. Strengthened by refusal, their identities were so fixed that even death was preferable to compromise: "But even if he [our God] does not [save us from the fiery furnace], we want you to know, Your Majesty, that we will not serve your gods or worship the image of gold you have set up" (Dan. 3:18).

Refusal of this kind was a defining characteristic of the early church as well. As D. H. Williams has suggested, conversion to the Christian faith was never simply a passive adherence to a new set of beliefs. Instead, it involved an active repudiation of competing sources of allegiance, rejecting pagan ideals and practices.[65] In a pluralistic culture (much like our own), early church leaders recognized that an assertion of belief could easily mask a syncretism that was simply adding Christian "ideas" to other idolatrous commitments. If Christian discipleship was to create new identities in Christ, the process would have to involve a rejection of other beliefs, lifestyles, and communities, discarding the baggage that could lead to double-mindedness. From the very beginning, Christianity was to be an exclusive faith, an identity formed in part by "excluding" all competing identifications.

What does such refusal mean for contemporary emerging adults also living in a pluralistic culture? North American society is far removed from a setting of kings and authoritarian structures of dominance and forced compliance. Yet, though more subtle in its allurement, the forces at play to restructure one's identity may be equally palpable on the college campus. Dallas Willard comments:

> Perhaps nowhere in the lifecourse are the pressures and values of culture more pressing or more formative than during the college years. Culture structures life, sometimes for good and sometimes for ill, in such ways that participating in it seems natural and even what is expected. On the college campus this often means binge drinking, becoming sexually active, choosing a career on the basis of its potential to provide wealth, crafting an identity that is primarily self-satisfying and autonomous. Legions are there who jump in unthinkingly, become trapped in a lifestyle that if they had the ability to distance themselves from it, they themselves would disown and despise.[66]

Removed from home, subjected to new behavioral norms, and introduced to new ways of thinking in a pluralistic context, identities can be gradually transformed by the "taken for granted" forces around them. Because collegians and other emerging adults live within cultures that foster competing identities, refusal will always be a necessary mechanism for identity preservation and formation. This may take the form of refusing the normalized "acceptable sins" of emerging adulthood: materialism, promiscuity, or other forms of immorality. It may take the form of refusing collegiate or graduate school teaching that contradicts biblical truth, actively opposing falsehood even if it means a decline in academic standing. It may take the form, as it did for Daniel, of refusing to relinquish Christian beliefs and practices even when others mock them. It may also entail a refusal of the "names" provided by others that serve as substitutes for one's primary identity in Christ.

It should be noted that refusal does not imply complete separatism. Daniel and his friends epitomize Christian identity for us not because they separated from participation in Babylonian culture but precisely because they crafted a path of biblical faithfulness and refusal while occupying prominent roles within it. They benefited from the educational culture they were thrust into, they placed their administrative acumen and spiritual gifts in the service of the royal court of a Babylonian king, but neither a lion's den nor a fiery furnace could unsettle what was "set" in their hearts. Daniel and his friends refused to permit the entry of identity-reforming forces, but they did not allow this refusal to thwart their roles as lights to the nations.[67]

Refusals almost always come with a cost. While these costs will likely pale in comparison to hungry lions and incinerating flames, the loss of friends, romantic attachments, popularity, and academic reputation are often felt acutely at this stage of life. Should emerging adults find themselves encountering compromises that blur their focus, that seek to co-opt them, or call them to forfeit their identity in the Lord, wholehearted devotion may compel them to pay whatever price necessary to resist bowing their hearts to those graven images. Without purposeful refusal, cultural messages can be subtly assimilated into the heart's core, redefining identity beneath conscious awareness until it begins to alter adult loyalties and allegiances. As mentioned in chapter 2, this is the cost of discipleship, saying "no" in order to say "yes" to something much greater. While others try to "name" them in ways that identify them with this world, they await something far greater: "I will write on them the name of my God and the name of the city of my God, the new Jerusalem, which is coming down out of heaven from my God; and I will also write on them my new name" (Rev. 3:12). This is the identity that will remain through all of eternity.

Identity and Engagement

Immediately following his description of the identity-deforming aspects of collegiate culture, Willard suggests, "It may well be that a Biblical worldview and community of truth are essential to liberate students from patterns of life, without which they almost inevitably find themselves susceptible to structuring their identifications."[68] Daniel's "magnificent refusal" was a critical aspect of his identity preservation and consolidation, yet this identity was obviously developed through an entrenched biblical worldview and through engagement in the communities of his youth. His identity was also sustained through "disciplines of engagement" (see chap. 2) that strengthened this identity in the midst of a foreign land (i.e., prayer). Surrounded by competing sources of identification, Daniel had to be purposeful in his attempts to bolster and reinforce his identification with the people of God. As emerging adults are surrounded by cultural forces competing for their allegiance, identity formation must include not only various forms of refusal but also an active engagement in an alternative culture—a "community of truth"—that forms them to see themselves and the world in a uniquely Christian way.

One means of understanding this is to examine the identity-shaping power of social groups. Tory Baucum, for example, uses encapsulation theory to understand "identity transforming organizations." Baucum's project is one of *ressourcement*—leveraging the Christian tradition for insights into how ministries can enhance identity formation today. Hence, he looks first to how ancient Christians used the catechumenate to disciple new believers into faith. Seeking common processes and elements, he then turns to analyzing both early Methodist band societies (small discipleship groups) and the evangelistic fervor of the contemporary Alpha Movement.[69] Baucum is keen on acknowledging that God is the primary agent who acts in regenerating and sanctifying people, but he recognizes that faith is interpersonally mediated and hence inherently social. Encapsulation theory maintains that people generally change through a process of socialization within a group setting. To say this another way, identity formation and consolidation is almost always fostered by settings in which communal relationships and practices shape meaning systems and plausibility structures, strengthening commitment along the way.

Theorists hold that the identity-shaping power of encapsulation largely depends on how the group provides various commitment mechanisms to create a buffer *physically*, *socially*, and *ideologically* between the desired identity and other competing identities.[70] *Physical encapsulation* is marked by geographical separation and may be represented by religious retreats, drug rehabilitation centers, or some communities that cocoon members away from outside influences. *Social encapsulation* is the provision of friendship that fashions and consolidates identity via solidarity with a group. Sororities, fraternities, and communal organizations like Alcoholics Anonymous (AA) provide useful examples. *Ideological encapsulation* involves regular inculcation of key ideals and philosophies that ground the organization's vision. In AA, for example, members memorize the twelve steps as a way of maintaining an ideological orientation to a new identity.

Residential colleges often serve to shape identity through such mechanisms. Separated from home, students are physically encapsulated in new environments that separate them from former identifications. They are socially encapsulated in new monogenerational relational networks that are often quite exclusive in nature. Ideological encapsulation is more diffuse, but this time still represents years of learning that can imprint a long-lasting worldview. There may be no other time in the life course where these dimensions function so completely to alter one's identity.

Scriptural examples seem to validate the identity-forming power of encapsulation. When Jesus summoned his disciples to "follow me," a deep form of encapsulation ensued, involving every one of these dimensions. Physically, the disciples left their homes and their vocations for the missional journey of becoming "fishers of men" (Matt. 4:19). Socially, most all of their time was spent together as compatriots on a spiritual journey of following Jesus. Ideologically, the disciples were "encapsulated" as a small group and frequently taught the ethics of the kingdom of God. If we look further back, we see this within the Old Testament as well. Israel was fashioned in the physical encapsulation first of Goshen and then of the desert. Israel was organized socially around tribal kinship groups and commanded to "utterly destroy" the wicked nations that would entice them to compromise. Israel's identity was fashioned according to the ideological encapsulation of the Ten Commandments, the Deuteronomic law code, and the teaching of the law and prophets.

Christian colleges and other emerging adult ministries can capitalize on these identity-forming mechanisms. While complete encapsulation is never an option for a mission-oriented faith seeking to engage the world, the dynamics of a strong identity-forming community should be cultivated in order to form countercultural societies of kingdom citizens. Baucum explains the potency of such communities by turning to Lewis Rambo's identification of four components in the "matrix of transformation": *relationships*, *rituals*, *rhetoric*, and *roles*.[71]

First, in each of the faith cultures Baucum analyzed, identity transformation involved a *relational* process, bonding individuals to the Christian community as well as to Christian meaning. The catechumenate initiated one into a network of sponsors and other converts. Methodist band societies operated from the basis that holiness was best engendered via accountable discipleship within small groups. The Alpha Movement invites six to twelve participants to engage in evangelistic friendships in settings of trust and transparency.

Theologically, an encapsulation model is built on the conviction that a believer's relationship with Christ is never simply an I-Thou encounter but is fundamentally a We-Thou relation. Emerging adult ministries must recognize that identity is shaped through the cultivation of strong relationships with others who share common commitments. Time spent with these others makes one's faith seem more plausible and also emboldens devotion over time.[72] As with Daniel, relationships also strengthen resolve when refusals of cultural identifications are required.

Second, Baucum regards *rituals* as important features of identity-transforming organizations because they script ways of being and belonging, thereby assisting the participant to embody and enact a new identity.[73] Repeated actions strengthen identifications and serve as continual reminders of the focus of faith, helping to resist tendencies toward ideological drift. The physicality of ritual practices also helps to inculcate truths more deeply, moving beyond cognitive affirmation to embodied practice. In each of the faith cultures examined, meal rituals such as the Agape feast, the Lord's Supper, or table fellowship encoded social relationships, leveraging against segregation and inequality. In the same way that Jesus's table companionship—welcoming sinners to ally with his kingdom—became a symbolic center of his ministry, so did these faith cultures adopt this as a central, generous practice, leading to testimonies of experienced grace and deeper spiritual sharing. Rituals of corporate prayer, Bible reading, and song also marked these settings, cultivating common loyalties around a body of truth and the person of Christ.

In addition, emerging adult ministries may be able to construct "rites of passage" rituals that enable those in this age group to enter into adulthood in a purposeful way. Especially in our culture, where the typical social markers of adulthood are vanishing and where formal rites of passage do not exist, ministries and churches have a responsibility to help emerging adults own adult identities within communities of faith. While these do not need to include elaborate ceremonies, there should be some means of symbolically marking the transition from one status to another, leaving behind certain identifications and embracing new privileges and responsibilities. Marked by prayer, dedication, and communal promises of support, such experiences can serve as powerful markers to motivate and provide meaning for the adult Christian life.[74]

Third, *rhetoric* signifies the way that words function in teaching, song, and dialogue to interpret human experience and to shape the conceptual and emotional world to which the disciple is identified. In the early catechumenate, as well as in Wesley's Methodist preaching, special emphasis was given to the Sermon on the Mount with the intent to generate a new set of desires and affections. Christian colleges move students systematically through a curriculum, educationally mapping a degree that forms a coherent worldview. Legions are the schools and campus ministries that started with such a clear purpose in mind and yet succumbed to ideological and institutional drift. Essential to the task of forming emerging adults with a biblical worldview is establishing a clear mission and ethos, identifying a grounded theological vision of spiritual maturity.[75] This is the "decision that will decide all other decisions" raised to the institutional level, without which one can hardly expect emerging adults to appropriate such an identity for themselves.[76] Steve Chalke once said, "If you want to change someone, you must first tell a different story about who they are."[77] Surely, this was what held Daniel and his friends at the place of their commitment. Despite everything around them trying to renarrate their lives, their ears were tuned to a different story—the story of a nation called into existence to be a people set apart, a people of God's own choosing for the sake of the world. The college and emerging adult ministries that are transforming the identities of students are those that are being storied by the biblical narrative.

One key in this rhetorical emphasis is that identity must be fostered through articulation. It is absolutely critical for emerging adults to learn and to use the distinct language of Christianity: the creeds, the doctrines, and the biblical vocabulary that shape the contours of the faith community. Emerging adults are generally quite attuned to the language of the broader culture, but an absence of significant biblical and theological vocabulary will leave them woefully lacking when it comes to the task of seeing and constructing an alternate identity. "If we do not know the language of a community," Kenda Creasy Dean suggests, "we can neither see the world as that community sees it nor become a part of that community ourselves. But when a community's language becomes our own, we become members of that community and increasingly come to see the world and structure our own lives through the lenses of that language."[78] One must learn the language to fully enter a culture—to see the world in a way that native speakers see it. Adopting, memorizing, and utilizing a distinctly biblical vocabulary is the only way emerging adults will enter deeply enough to be able to resist the pervasive cultural slogans around them.

Fourth, identity scholars have long recognized that personal transformation often results from people taking on *roles* that help them experience new possibilities for the self.[79] In the catechumenate, lay teachers were appointed to nurture, protect, and join new converts in their quest for faith. Lay preachers and class leaders in the Wesleyan Methodist revival were given responsibility for supervising schools of holy living. The Alpha Movement seeks to help members carefully discern the gifts of the Spirit and instructs them to serve as small group table leaders, hospitality coordinators, and worship leaders. Campuses and ministries that ghetto-ize emerging adults into passive roles as learners or consumers will not cultivate strong identity in the next generation of Christian leaders. Instead, emerging adults must be entrusted with genuine responsibility to serve the ministry and mend the broken places of the world, trying on various roles while attending to the Spirit in discerning their gifts.[80]

Enacting such roles is particularly important in shaping Christ-centered identity. Encapsulation, when taken to an extreme, can lead to insularity, creating dependence on the enclave, devaluing the uniqueness of its members, and undermining ministry goals such as missional engagement and outreach. However, as Jesus's example demonstrates, strong identity formation can—and indeed must—be combined with outward-moving ministry. In chapter 5, we will see how Christian identity is irrevocably tied to the concept of vocation. When the identity being formed is shaped in the image of the One who gave his life for the world, it can be no other way.

Identity formation takes place in every phase of the life span, but it has particular poignancy in emerging adulthood, when the previous bulwarks of identity—families, schools, churches, and friends—may no longer be present. Pressures to individualize this process are rampant, but emerging adults need mentors and communities that will provide biblical guidance while also helping them internalize their beliefs and behaviors. Leaders need to help create communities of truth that will foster engagement in alternative Christ-centered cultures, fostering relationships, rituals, rhetoric, and roles that anchor emerging adults to Jesus and to the people of God. Emerging adults should live vigorously into these years, preparing well to participate at the highest levels in various academic, professional, and civic communities, yet they must also stay connected to identity-shaping faith cultures that can sustain and empower them to live as Christ-followers in these worlds. This will enable them to practice the art of refusal when necessary, and it will also provide them with a coherent and communally supported path to guide their journeys.

For in the end, identity is not simply a personal choice or achievement. While there is a need to internalize and own beliefs and convictions, Christian identity is always tied to a community of truth that bestows an identity—ultimately through baptism—of communal membership in the body of believers. In other words, identity in Christ is inextricably intertwined with participation in the church. The Christian journey of emerging adulthood does not take place on a skateboard, individually determining a personal path to fulfillment. It does not even take place in a single car with spouse and children in tow. The Christian vision of identity and LIFE depends far more on a collection of passengers, some single and some married, some young and some old, taking the journey together and depending on one another for support, strength, and direction. To this interdependent, church-shaped identity we now turn.

4 | Church

Forming an Ecclesiological Vision

The amazing thing about this pattern of support and socialization is that it all comes to a halt about the time a young person reaches the age of twenty-one or twenty-two. After providing significant institutional support for the developmental tasks that occurred before then, we provide almost nothing for the developmental tasks that are accomplished when people are in their twenties and thirties. And, since more of those tasks are happening later, this is a huge problem.

Robert Wuthnow[1]

In January 2012, Jefferson Bethke became a YouTube sensation with his spoken word poem, "Why I Hate Religion, But Love Jesus."[2] Viewed more than ten million times in the first four days on the site, Bethke put words to the thoughts and feelings of many emerging adults by focusing on the differences between "religion" and "Jesus." While Jesus stands for grace and freedom, he suggested, the false "man-made" religion of many churches is consumed with behavior modification, image management, and judgmental self-righteousness, akin to "spraying perfume on a casket." A few months later, *Newsweek* ran an Easter-week cover story with a similar theme, describing a decadent "Christianity in crisis" due to political involvement, pastoral and priestly scandals, and the travails of "get-rich evangelists."[3] Implying that the institutional church had completely distorted the pure teachings of Jesus, author Andrew Sullivan called for the resurrection of an unsullied personal faith equipped to provide depth and security for our "modern twittering souls."[4] The cover's subtitle provided the oft-repeated tagline of our current cultural moment: "Forget the Church, Follow Jesus."

Apparently, many emerging adults agree. Whether temporarily or permanently, church involvement declines significantly in these years. Some Christian leaders place the blame on emerging adults themselves, calling attention to their lack of commitment, individualism, and aversion toward institutions. Others find fault in local churches, either because of their general flaws or because of their failure to adopt programs and emphases of interest to emerging adults. While few agree on the sources of decline, the result is clear: a loss of corporate spiritual formation and guidance at the very time when key life decisions are made.

Emerging Adult Disengagement from the Church

A number of recent studies give us a fairly concrete picture of local church involvement among emerging adults. In terms of church attendance, Christian Smith maintains that about 30.9 percent of young emerging adults (age 18–23) attend religious services "regularly," meaning at least twice a month, 35.4 percent report never attending religious services, while the rest (about 34 percent) attend very sporadically (once a month or less).[5] All told, about 54.6 percent of emerging adults in this age group could be qualified as "nonattendees," participating in religious services just a few times a year or less.[6] According to 2001 census data, emerging adults make up 22 percent of the adult population of the United States, yet they constitute less than 10 percent of the total adult population in evangelical, mainline, and Catholic congregations.[7]

One helpful way of depicting these statistics is to compare church attendance in the teen years with attendance in the years following high school graduation. According to a 2007 survey of 18- to 30-year-olds, about 70 percent of Protestants who attended church regularly for at least a year in high school drop out for at least a year between the ages of 18 and 22.[8] The Barna group claims that 61 percent of those who were churched at one point during their teen years become spiritually disengaged in their twenties.[9] For college students, this change often occurs quickly. In her study of collegians' first year, Alyssa Bryant and her colleagues found that the number of students "frequently" attending church services dropped about 20 percent during the freshman year while the number attending "not at all" increased by 27 percent over this same time period.[10] Compared with 13- to 17-year-olds, Smith suggests, "regular" attendance among 18- to 23-year-olds drops by 24.7 percent while "nonattendance" increases by about 24.5 percent.[11] As David Kinnaman summarizes, "Most young people who were involved in a church as a teenager disengage from church life and often Christianity at some point during early adulthood, creating a deficit of young talent, energy, and leadership in many congregations."[12] The loss of emerging adults does indeed create a "black hole" in many congregations.[13]

While alarming, these statistics are often tempered with three caveats. First, many point out that these declines are not new. The overall percentage of emerging adults attending religious services, some scholars note, has actually remained fairly consistent over the past forty years.[14] Yet even if these declines have precedent, this does not tell the whole story. Statistics noting historical continuity often mask considerable distinctions between religious groups. For example, while evangelicals and black Protestants have witnessed slight increases in emerging adult attendance over time, mainline Protestants and Catholics have seen sharp declines. For example, Catholic emerging adult weekly attendance has declined from about 25 percent in 1970 to just under 15 percent in 2006. Mainline Protestant emerging adults have declined from nearly 15 percent in 1970 to under 10 percent in 2006.[15] For these groups, the trend is decidedly negative.

In addition, partly due to the more general aging of the population (the baby boomers in particular), most religious traditions are experiencing a decline in the relative proportion of twentysomethings in their congregations. While in the early 1970s about one in six mainline Protestants was in his or her twenties, now only about one in ten are within this age span. For black Protestants, the percentage of attendees between the ages of 20 and 29 has declined from 21 percent to 16 percent while Catholics have seen this number decline from 24 percent to 18 percent. Even among evangelicals, who are usually portrayed as more youthful than others, the proportion of church attendees between the ages of 20 and 29 has declined 6 percentage points since the 1970s. "While it is true that evangelical denominations are composed of almost as large a proportion of adults age 45 or younger now as a generation ago (49 percent versus 51 percent)," Robert Wuthnow notes, "the proportion of evangelicals in their twenties has dropped dramatically. When one speaks of young adult evangelicals, one is thus speaking of adults in their thirties and early forties to a greater extent now than was true in the 1970s."[16] Such statistics help explain perceptions of a gradually shrinking presence of emerging adults in local congregations.

Finally, as Wuthnow suggests, historical continuity also masks the fact that churches are increasingly attracting an unrepresentative group of emerging adults. While in the 1970s both attendees and nonattendees in this age group were typically married with children, now the typical attendee is married with children while the typical nonattendee is single without children. Churches, in other words, have the hardest time reaching unmarried singles in their twenties, a growing concern in this era of delayed marriages.[17]

A second caveat often mentioned is that declines in church participation do not always reflect a loss in the self-reported importance of personal faith. According to Jeffrey Arnett, while only 17 percent of emerging adults claim that their beliefs are "not at all important to them," 42 percent affirm that attending services is "not at all important" in their lives.[18] In Kinnaman's estimation, only about 11 percent of 18- to 29-year-olds grow up Christian and then "deconvert" entirely or convert to another faith. To put it in Kinnaman's language, there are far more "nomads" than "prodigals" among contemporary emerging adults, most separating from the local church rather than separating from the faith. "The dropout phenomenon," he notes, "is most accurately described as a generation of Christians who are disengaging from institutional forms of church. . . . Many young Christians—even as they express generally positive associations with Jesus Christ—are alienated from the institutional forms of faith in which they were raised."[19]

Yet despite this stated distinction between belief and practice, there is still cause for concern. According to Smith, many religious leaders hold to a common myth: that emerging adults retain an internal commitment to faith even as they decline in external religious participation. "The implication," he notes, "is often that what 'really' matters about religion—interior personal commitment—is in fact well established and secured during the emerging adult years, that it is only the external 'trappings' of religious practice that decline during this life phase."[20] He suggests, however, that this is not the case. Less than 7 percent of the emerging adult population analyzed in Smith's study maintained low levels of church attendance while sustaining high levels of internal faith commitment. On the flip side, less than 1 percent of the sample attended church regularly while lacking internal commitment. Smith's conclusion is clear: "For most emerging adults, strong religion comes in fairly coherent packages—they basically either have it internally and externally or they do not in either. Strong religion on the inside, when it exists, is, for the majority, accompanied by strong religion on the outside."[21]

A third and final caveat often mentioned is the notion that these declines are temporary. In other words, while losses are clear across the board in the early to midtwenties, data seem to indicate that somewhere between 30 and 60 percent will return in some capacity in their later twenties.[22] There are several variables, however, that make the "they'll come back" argument less persuasive within contemporary culture. Since marriage is often the key variable that reestablishes the link between emerging adults and religious congregations, delayed marriage means prolonged separation. In addition, sociologist Jonathan Hill maintains that detachment from religious institutions is also increasing among teenagers. Therefore, if the period of time separated from the church is beginning earlier and ending later, it is appropriate to question the ease of recommitment. "If young adults spend a long enough time outside the confines of the church developing meaningful networks of relationships and establishing career trajectories," Hill contends, "then they may be less likely to return even if they do marry and have children. Understanding the full implications of this extended period of disengagement appears to be the next step in understanding religion in early adulthood for the current generation."[23] While many speak of the driver's license to marriage license "hiatus" in church attendance, many now wonder whether this lengthy hiatus will become an exodus. The habits and inertia generated by a decade removed from church participation may be hard to overcome, especially if emerging adults are content with their life prospects. At least one study demonstrated that the greatest factor reducing adult church involvement was the amount of time separated from local churches. If this is true, it appears that absence often begets absence.[24]

Furthermore, even if up to half of emerging adults come back, they return as people irrevocably shaped by some of the most critical decisions of life. All caveats aside, most recognize the "black hole" as a significant problem, especially when we take into account the life-altering choices and patterns that characterize this period of time away from church influence. When one considers the magnitude of the issues, it is hard not to lament the loss of communal spiritual care and guidance in local congregations. These are decisions and patterns that will influence the rest of life, and most are determined through a haphazard network of friendships, family, and the media. Wuthnow describes these ramifications:

> It means that younger adults are having to invent their own ways of making decisions and seeking support for those decisions. Whereas dating and mate selection used to happen within the social milieu of the high school, congregation, or campus, it now occurs increasingly in bars, at parties, and through the Internet. Other major decisions, such as when to have children and how to raise them, or where to live and what kind of career to pursue, are also being made on an improvisational basis, largely without firm institutional grounding. It is little

wonder that social critics write about the problems associated with individualism. In the absence of any institutional sources of support and stability, young adults are forced to be individualistic. They have no other resources but themselves.[25]

Finally, it is also appropriate to ask about the ways in which returning emerging adults will interact with the church after many years away. After all of the time socialized into a set of personal and cultural patterns outside the local congregation, the returning church attendee will be challenged to see church as a central component of life.[26] "When and if young adults do return to churches," Kinnaman notes, "it is difficult to convince them that a passionate pursuit of Christ is anything more than a nice add-on to their cluttered lifestyles."[27] Furthermore, it will be challenging for these emerging adults to assume leadership roles within their congregations. Leadership often depends on continuity of participation, contextual knowledge, and the establishment of relational networks characterized by trust. Prolonged separation makes such involvement far more difficult.

In the end, these caveats do little to change the basic reality of our current situation. Even if these declines have historical precedent, even if some emerging adults retain internal commitment, and even if a fair number return at the end of emerging adulthood, the losses here are substantial, both for emerging adults and for the church. To address the black hole, we must consider the reasons why emerging adults tend to separate themselves from the church during these years. The barriers are indeed formidable, but they also help illuminate potential ways in which the church can reengage twentysomethings in the corporate life of faith.

The Sources of Disengagement

On one level, the causes of local church disengagement are as varied as the people who leave. It is important to keep in mind that every story is unique and significant, requiring the utmost personal attention and care. Yet there are certain disengagement patterns related to this particular age group that may provide helpful context for rethinking the role of the church in emerging adults' lives. As mentioned, some tend to place the blame on emerging adults while others focus more on failures within the churches. There is probably truth in both of these suggestions. Key developmental and generational characteristics tend to blunt the appeal of local churches to emerging adults, erecting significant hurdles to consistent involvement. At the same time, churches also "lose" emerging adults through their own failures. Whether pulled by the personal and cultural tendencies of this life stage or pushed by institutional flaws, these challenges reveal a complex web of variables that threaten the centrality of the church in emerging adults' lives.

Emerging Adult Factors

As mentioned in the first chapter, life disruptions in emerging adulthood often wreak havoc with patterns of religious practice. Those same disturbances that interfere with spiritual routines—moving, separating from family, and entering new relational networks—are perhaps even more potent in disrupting church commitment. For many adolescents, being part of a church-going family means they are expected to be involved in a church. However, when one leaves home, those external expectations quickly evaporate and create space for unprecedented self-definition. Frequent mobility makes it hard to put down roots and discourages the formation of attachments to a local congregation. Moving also produces other disruptions, such as attempting to find churches close to their new home, making decisions about which church to attend, and taking part in the difficult practice of joining an unfamiliar intergenerational group—many for the first time.[28]

Delayed marriage and parenting tend to be some of the most important factors associated with church declines. Looking at data between 1998 and 2002, Wuthnow found that almost all of the decline in church involvement among 21- to 45-year-olds since the 1970s has taken place among unmarried men and women. Married men in this age group are about twice as likely to attend church than those who are unmarried, and married women are also much more likely to attend than unmarried women. Those with more children are more likely to attend than those with fewer or no children. The reasons for this are likely diverse. Because women tend to be more religious in general, men are more likely to attend church once they are connected to a believing spouse. Marriage often entails settling down in a particular community, promoting church involvement. Furthermore, married couples may feel more at home in congregations since these institutions tend to focus a great deal on programs for couples and families.[29] All things considered, delayed marriage correlates strongly with declines in church attendance.

New life distractions also play a significant role. Learning how to live on one's own, as previously noted, requires a great deal of physical and emotional energy. Furthermore, new educational and work demands drive a strong pressure to succeed. Some jobs will require Sunday work and travel for young employees. In addition, church involvement can appear to detract from work that directly contributes to personal success. As one student put it, "I put less value in external factors like going to church and stuff, because it doesn't really seem that important to me to like lose sleep and go to church, because sleep is good for grades, and grades are good for what I'm going to do for the rest of my life."[30] Even "fun" distractions can threaten church participation. As Smith points out,

> Crucial with regard to religious community and practice in all of this are Friday and Saturday nights, the emerging adults' key times for recreational and social life. Most of the week is consumed with work and maybe school. The fun emerging adults believe they are supposed to be having usually centers on the evening and weekends, and especially weekend evenings. Even if one wanted to go to religious services, one has probably stayed up too late the night before to wake up, dress nicely, and head off to such a service in the morning.[31]

Linked with this pursuit of fun, many emerging adults feel that local churches will criticize their lifestyle choices, condemning actions and activities (e.g., drinking and premarital sexual activity) that are increasingly normalized within their social groups. Continued church participation, then, requires that emerging adults either resist these activities or find ways to compartmentalize "religious" activities from the rest of life. Because it is difficult to live with such incongruity and guilt, many simply eliminate the tension by steering clear of church doors. Studies have indeed demonstrated that declining church participation is often closely correlated with increases in social drinking, frequent partying, premarital sex, cohabitation, and interfaith marriage.[32] The relationship between lifestyle and church attendance is likely bidirectional— declining church commitment may also lead to behavioral change—but we must recognize that church declines are often coupled with real changes in emerging adult social patterns.

While many of these lifestyles are acquired in college, college by itself does not appear to be a significant factor in reducing church attendance. Of course, church attendance does decline during college. The Higher Education Research Institute found that the rate of "frequent" church attendance declines from 44 percent in high school to about 25 percent in college while the rate of nonattendance nearly doubles.[33] Overall, they found that nearly 40 percent of students decrease their church attendance while only 7 percent increase attendance. At the same time, it appears that attendance may be curtailed even more for those not attending college. A 2007 study tracing various sources of religious decline found that emerging adults not attending college were the most likely to decline while those achieving a bachelor's degree were the least likely to drop.[34] Other studies have described a net positive effect in long-term church involvement among those attending college.[35] In short, while attendance falls in the college-age years, it does not appear that college attendance itself is a significant factor in this decline.

For some emerging adults, however, collegiate religious involvements can diminish the perceived need for local church involvement. Students at Christian institutions often find that the combination of Bible classes, chapels, small groups, and campus-sponsored ministries provides all the spiritual nurture that they need. Such built-in programs can produce a sense of spiritual overload for those saturated with spiritual input throughout the week. For those attending secular institutions, parachurch campus ministries can also serve as alternatives to local church participation, providing easy access to teaching, worship, fellowship, and service. In both settings, furthermore, involvement in campus-based ministries can actually de-motivate church involvement in the postcollege years. In particular, the highly relational and hip, age-appropriate worship and teaching of these groups can make local intergenerational churches appear dull by comparison. Never able to recapture the energy and "buzz" of these earlier groups, some emerging adults simply give up on the institutional church.

In addition to these more mundane factors, the struggle for identity in emerging adulthood can also threaten church involvement. Since many emerging adults see this time of life as their opportunity to stand on their own and forge a unique identity independent of parents, the elimination of church attendance can present a clear means of differentiation. As Smith suggests, "For most of them, to attend religious services with their families of origin on a regular basis—holidays and special visits are exempt here—feels like being the old dependent child again, a role they feel they have outgrown. For some, even to attend services in another place at a religious congregation that is something like their parents' can feel the same way."[36] Some, to be sure, may exercise this impulse in muted fashion by choosing a denomination or church style distinct from their home church setting. Others, however, eliminate church attendance altogether in order to establish a clear personal identity.

The desire to stand on one's own can also be aimed more directly at the local church. While emerging adults often seek to differentiate themselves from parents, they may also see a need to make life decisions independently from church structures. As Arnett discovered,

> Just as it would be wrong in their eyes for them to accept wholesale the beliefs of their parents, so many of them view participation in religious institutions as an intolerable compromise of their individuality. Participating in a religious institution inherently means subscribing to a common set of beliefs, declaring

that you hold certain beliefs that other members of the institution also hold. To
the majority of emerging adults, this is anathema. They prefer to think of their
beliefs as unique, the product of their own individual questioning and exploring.[37]

Independence, it seems, is often perceived to be at odds with submission to
preexisting creeds and belief structures. Rather than accepting ready-made
beliefs, many emerging adults see it as both a right and an obligation to
construct their own religion, true to their emerging sense of self-definition.
Church, in this vein, is often associated with external conformity, unthinking obedience, and a posture of pleasing others rather than "authentically"
choosing for oneself. Since authenticity has become a kind of ethical mandate
in contemporary culture, submission to institutional norms can appear not
only spineless but also immoral.[38]

While we have indicated that such exploration (moratorium) is a critical
component of emerging adult identity formation, we also argued that this
process must be tethered to the community of faith through time and space.
Many emerging adults choose to cobble together their own personalized faith
in isolation, a "pastiche" uniquely designed to appeal to their sensitivities and
meet their needs.[39] This creates a ripe setting for a kind of "Starbucks Christianity" in which emerging adults can sift through faith options and choose
their own unique blend. If church is helpful, then by all means it can serve as
an aid to spiritual growth. If other options provide more insight, however, there
is no reason why they should not serve as substitutes. Emerging adults may
therefore miss out on the wisdom of historical traditions and contemporary
elders expanding and correcting their limited subjectivity.

In our "downloadable" world, many ask whether or not the local church is
really all that necessary. Emerging adults have access to Christian teaching on
television, through online sermons, and through Web-based Bible studies and
blogs. They can worship along with downloaded praise music. They have opportunities for fellowship with friends and through social networks. They can
engage in evangelism and social welfare work through numerous secular and
parachurch organizations devoted to missions and social justice. Such options
may be perceived as superior because of their flexibility, allowing for listening,
learning, worshiping, and serving at any time and in any location. Waking up
early and dressing for church can appear quite unnecessary in such a world.

Such realities also tend to promote church shopping and hopping. "Shopping" indicates that many take an extended period of time to look for a
congregation that will fit their style and meet their needs. "Hopping," on the
other hand, refers to the fact that increasing numbers of emerging adults move
from one congregation to another, failing to commit to a single local body

over the long haul.[40] Many who choose to get involved in church participate in multiple churches simultaneously, perhaps choosing to go to a worship service in one setting, a small group in another, and an outreach event at still another.[41] Much of this reflects the growing tendency to see faith as a personal quest rather than a grounded participation in a local body of believers. Defined by Wuthnow as a shift from a spirituality of "dwelling" to a spirituality of "seeking," this move centers the spiritual life in self-development rather than congregational commitment.[42] As the leader of one prominent young adult ministry noted, "Almost daily I am reminded that few of these young adults are interested in helping the established church work. For them, it is all about 'my journey,' what helps me get to where I need to be."[43]

The focus on personal journey is paralleled by a growing sense that faith is something internal rather than external and practiced. Church attendance and participation are thought to be far more susceptible to religious pretense and hypocrisy—a mere "going through the motions"—whereas personal belief is automatically deemed authentic and genuine, true to one's spiritual "core." In part, of course, this is more broadly related to the nature of Protestantism itself. Because Protestantism highlights the spiritual authority of the individual over and against church and tradition, many have viewed the local church as a helpful but peripheral agent of formation. Since the Reformation heralded the capacity of individuals to read Scripture for themselves and to go directly to God in prayer, some have viewed church involvement as unnecessary (and sometimes hurtful). For evangelicals, who stressed the primacy of conversion, personal heart religion emerged as the sine qua non (the essential ingredient) of "true Christianity." As a result, these groups speak much of salvation but little about adoption into the family of God. They speak much of being saved from sin but rarely of the importance of being saved into the communion of saints.

Not surprisingly, the emphasis on personal heart religion tends to promote the elevation of the "invisible" over the "visible" church. The invisible church, according to Wayne Grudem, "is the church as God sees it," those who have truly been regenerated and born again. The visible church, on the other hand, "is the church as Christians on earth see it," which will always include some unbelievers who profess true faith.[44] While this distinction has a long history and helpfully foregrounds the importance of true personal faith, for some it has implied that participation in the visible church is "soteriologically irrelevant" (irrelevant as far as salvation is concerned).[45] If the invisible heart is all that matters, the visible church only has relevance as a matter of pragmatic concern ("My children can be educated here") or personal preference ("I enjoy the worship and fellowship"). However, Scripture very clearly speaks of both the universal church (Heb. 12:23 speaks of the "church of the firstborn, whose names are written in heaven") and the local church, assuming that Christians will join the organized body of believers (1 Cor. 12; 1 Tim. 3). While the invisible and visible churches can be logically separated, they can never be divorced. They are two expressions of the same reality, one eternal and one temporal. As Dietrich Bonhoeffer suggests, "The Body of Christ takes up space on earth. The Body of Christ can only be a visible Body, or else it is not a Body at all."[46]

The bottom line is that the church has become a vestigial structure for many emerging adults, useful in the past but now more of an optional relic. It is less a life-sustaining and identity-bestowing community than an optional accessory for those who need such things. In light of these realities, it is perhaps not surprising that, when emerging adults were asked to register their agreement or disagreement with the statement, "For believers to be truly religious and spiritual, they need to be involved in a religious congregation," only 34 percent of conservative Protestants, 31 percent of black Protestants, and 16 percent of mainline Protestants registered agreement, and all three had declined since the teenage years.[47] As Smith summed up, "Clearly, personal involvement in actual religious communities is not for most of the emerging adults of any tradition examined here a necessary part of a life of faith."[48]

Church Factors

While emerging adult life patterns play a significant role in detaching emerging adults from religious congregations, negative perceptions of the church also serve to keep some away. Surveying 20- to 29-year-olds, Kinnaman found six key impressions fueling emerging adult alienation from the church. First, many see the church as overprotective and sheltered, maintaining a fortress mentality that denies both creative engagement with society and contact with the suffering of the world. Second, many see the church as shallow, teaching broad and trivial content that often seems irrelevant to present and future realities. Third, church is perceived as "anti-science," out of step with scientific advances and providing simplistic answers to complex scientific questions about such issues as creation and genetic engineering. Fourth, a fair number of Christian emerging adults claim that the church is repressive, maintaining outdated sexual standards and judging those who fail to measure up. Fifth, emerging adults see the church as exclusive, spurning interaction with those outside of the faith (including homosexuals and those of other faiths) and creating a judgmental culture of insider/outsider that opposes attitudes of tolerance.[49] Finally, Kinnaman found that many emerging adults leave the church because they feel unsafe expressing their doubts, fully one-third claiming that "I don't feel that I can ask my most pressing life questions in church."[50] When added to perceptions among emerging adult unbelievers that churches are too political, homophobic, racially intolerant, oppressive to females, hypocritical, and insensitive to the poor,[51] it is easy to see why Kinnaman titled his most recent book *You Lost Me*.

In addition to these thematic failures, we must also acknowledge the structural issue: a scarcity of leaders, programs, and activities for this age group. Emerging adults recognize that churches provide significant staff, facilities, and programs for children and adolescents. They also recognize that this pattern of support largely ends upon high school graduation, picked up again only when couples are ready to enter the "young marrieds group" and reinitiate the family-building process.[52] Many have experienced churches that seem to be geared to families, designing all sermons, programs, and classes for couples, parents, and children. Such a "focus on the family" can leave single members of this age group feeling abandoned, unappreciated, and transitional, devoid of a clear identity within the people of God.[53] Despite the changing nature of emerging adulthood, many churches plan ministries within the framework of a rapid and seamless transition from adolescence to young marriage. Classes for singles often assume this to be a transitional and short-term spouse-searching problem rather than an extended stage of the life span deserving focused attention.[54] Since marriage is delayed, many experience this neglect for a full decade of life.

Many pastors do not see emerging adults as potential contributors in congregational life. Families are considered stable and therefore likely to contribute to the church over the long haul. But emerging adults are mobile and transient, so they are easily overlooked. Some pastors and core members may even resist deep investment because emerging adults will likely attend only for a short period of time before moving to a new location. This is particularly true with regard to college students who, at best, are present only for a few years. As a result, emerging adults often feel that they are not taken seriously as potential contributors to congregational life, vision, and service. While schools and jobs are providing them with unprecedented levels of responsibility in a variety of leadership roles, churches still seem to treat them as "children," wholly dependent on the wisdom and experience of elder members. Many indicate that they are not viewed as capable adults until they are married with children. In short, emerging adults are not entrusted with significant responsibilities in the church, minimizing their sense of investment, ownership, and belonging in these settings.

In a developmental stage marked by idealism, emerging adults will see the church as anything but ideal. The church will be characterized by broken relationships, petty offenses, and hurt feelings. It will likely not reflect the desired diversity of races, ethnicities, and genders that will ultimately mark the gathering of every tribe, tongue, and nation before the throne. The quality of the music will likely be middling, maybe even cheesy. Personalities will be annoying. Teaching will at times appear inadequate. There will be insufficient time and attention given to issues of great importance: poverty, racism, environmentalism, the AIDS crisis, and many others. Church members, even pastors, will sin against them in word and deed.

Such failures should generate calls to repentance and change. The next section, in fact, will detail some key practices that might alleviate some of these problems. Yet even in the midst of these flaws, emerging adults must be careful that their idealism does not prevent commitment to a local body. Local churches have always been plagued by sin. As much as emerging adults want to idealize the early church as a pre-Constantinian exemplar of idyllic Christian community, local congregations in that era were far from ideal. One cannot read a book like 1 Corinthians with Paul's continual chastisement of disunity, immorality, elitism, and class division without coming face-to-face with the reality of sinful Christian community. Yes, emerging adults should desire that the church strive for its ideals. At the same time, they must reckon with the doctrine of human depravity and understand that church problems provide a never-ending context in which to cling to the cross with their sinful brothers and sisters.

Emerging adults must not, therefore, be so consumed by what Bonhoeffer calls the "wish dream" of ideal community that they are unable to acknowledge the gift of Christian community anchored by the cross. As he puts it,

> The man who fashions a visionary ideal of community demands that it be realized by God, by others, and by himself. He enters the community of Christians with his demands, sets up his own law, and judges the brethren and God Himself accordingly. . . . He acts as if he is the creator of the Christian community, as if his dream binds men together. When things do not go his way, he calls the effort a failure. When his ideal picture is destroyed, he sees the community going to smash. . . . Because God has already laid the only foundation of our fellowship, because God has bound us together in one body with other Christians in Jesus Christ, long before we entered into common life with them, we enter into that common life not as demanders but as thankful recipients.[55]

In other words, emerging adults must recognize sooner rather than later that the one thing that holds church members together is their common sinfulness and reliance on the blood of Christ. They will fail each other and they will fail the larger kingdom vision, but they will also be able to forgive (understanding their common frailty) and celebrate all of the good things that come through the Christian community (thanking God for the undeserved gift of the body). The church is not marked by its perfection but rather by its reconciling love, grace-laden forgiveness, and utter dependence on a Savior. It is this that reflects the power of the gospel of Jesus Christ.

Prospects for Emerging Adult Church Life

To reenvision the relationship between emerging adults and the church, we must recognize these various sources of disengagement. The church must attend to emerging adults' critiques, reconsidering the thematic and structural issues that alienate and marginalize the younger generation. At the same time, mentors must also challenge emerging adults to recognize their need for church involvement, looking beyond the self to submit to a local body of believers. It seems clear that most emerging adults lack an ecclesiological vision, a sense of why the local church might be an important—even a central—aspect of their lives. Yet communal formation through the local congregation can serve as one of the most powerful forces of spiritual growth in emerging adults' lives, countering many of the deforming beliefs, attitudes, and behaviors endemic to this stage, while forming them in ways that lead to mature adult faith.

In Acts 2:42–47, we are provided with a snapshot of the activities of the Spirit-birthed early church, a group of ragtag disciples who were nonetheless "devoted" to the apostles' teaching, to breaking bread in each others' homes, to prayer and praise, and to outreach. These key components of early church life—teaching (*didache*), fellowship (*koinonia*), worship (*leitourgia*), and outreach (*diakonia*)—constitute a kind of "curriculum" for the body, a holistic picture of the communal life of faith in the local congregation. In the following pages, we look at the importance of the local church for emerging adult formation by focusing on these central tasks. Careful attention to these areas will help address some of the church problems identified in the previous section while also calling emerging adults to commit to a local body in the midst of its flaws.[56]

Teaching (Didache)

While it is true that emerging adults can access downloaded sermons or tune in to churches on television, the systematic, weekly preaching and teaching of the local church is critical for spiritual formation. While they can pick up helpful piecemeal thoughts related to personal interests in many places, only in a local body will they receive a biblical and theological "curriculum,"

designed for the body with a particular scope and sequence. A Christian form
of self-education will often put emerging adults in touch with resources relevant
to their felt needs, but they really need broad teaching in "unchosen" areas
that expose them to the bigger picture of God's character, human nature, and
redemption history. Finding answers to felt needs can be helpful, but studying
the whole counsel of Scripture will often elicit an awareness of needs they
never knew they had. In addition, only in the church will they receive this
preaching from a pastor or leader who is teaching a particular congregation,
prayerfully aware of the specific needs, trials, and temptations of this group.
Preaching that is separate from context can still be helpful, of course, but
emerging adults can only receive teaching linked with particularities of time,
place, and personality when it is directed at a unique local body of Christ.

As mentioned, however, many emerging adults describe church teaching as
shallow and irrelevant, tied only weakly to their concerns and to the vexing
intellectual and ethical questions of life. Teaching, therefore, must be "deep."
The church must be willing to teach the whole counsel of Scripture and the particular doctrines of the faith. If many feel that churches are simply elementary
schools of morals, that perspective may reflect accurately on the church's anemic
curriculum. Churches must teach the "solid food" of the gospel, providing
theological depth to complement the academic depth emerging adults receive
in their classrooms. Many want to be challenged, and they are generally willing
to embrace mystery in areas that resist easy answers. Biblical illiteracy is high
among members of this generation, so teachers must not assume background
knowledge about the biblical narrative or basic Christian doctrine. It is only in
teaching the full story line of the Bible that emerging adults will gain a deeper
sense of redemption history, the story that should define their lives.

For this to happen, emerging adults must be taught the actual language and
stories of the Bible and the creeds, not just pious moral platitudes or contemporary glosses on biblical themes. In other words, we must teach in such a
way that we actually use biblical language rather than attempting to sanitize
the text by making it indistinguishable from the vocabulary of the broader
culture. In addition, we must give them opportunities to hear older adults
dialoguing with one another using the language of the faith.[57] They must see
it as part of normal conversations, as the language that colors everyday life
activities. Finally, we must also give emerging adults opportunities to practice
this, using the language of the Bible to describe and interpret their own lives
and the events surrounding them. Perhaps one of the most significant ways
this can happen is through provision for times of testimony. Emerging adults
should be given opportunities to describe the past and current work of God
in their lives, speaking with the language of faith about their own formation

and using the stories and characters of the Bible to draw comparisons and contrasts. In addition, they must be encouraged to verbally share their faith with those outside the church, recognizing that the sharing of faith is "effective in deepening your understanding of every good thing we share for the sake of Christ" (Philem. 6). As emerging adults are immersed and saturated in the Word of God and then use biblical language to share their faith and describe their everyday lives, they begin to live in a God-bathed world.

This biblical depth must be accompanied by appropriate breadth. Educational theorist Elliott Eisner coined the term "null curriculum" to describe that which is not taught, the content and experiences intentionally or unintentionally left out of the curriculum.[58] Churches, for example, often ignore awkward or controversial issues related to science, sexuality, alcohol, politics, environmental issues, and other religions. By avoiding such topics, however, the church is actually communicating that these issues are either unimportant or unrelated to Christian life and thinking. Such a null curriculum leaves many emerging adults ill prepared to face the questions that will loom large in adult life. It may also cause some to leave the church, recognizing that they are not getting answers to their questions. Pastors and leaders will not often be experts on such issues, of course, but they can offer forums for discussion, providing biblical wisdom on these topics while resisting easy, pat answers. Many emerging adults, especially those who attend college or graduate school, will be accustomed to engaging such issues on a regular basis, and they will be hungry for Christian insight on these concerns.[59]

To be truly transformative, such teaching must also be experiential, linking truth to life experience. In Kinnaman's research, about a quarter of the interviewees stated that church teaching was irrelevant to their careers and interests, failing to prepare them for "real life."[60] As John Dewey indicated, effective experiential education is rooted in the teacher's ability to facilitate interaction between the external content and the inner needs, desires, and purposes of the student.[61] This approach requires that teachers know their students, connecting truth to life situations. It also requires that teachers in the church provide opportunities for practicing the truth, both within and outside of the ministry. Many ministries have effectively used small groups as locations designed for applying truth, taking the principles communicated in larger group settings and assisting one another in personal and communal application. This does not mean that the emerging adult will simply apply certain principles to their lives. It means that they will have the opportunity to consider how their lives can be applied to the larger biblical story, investing themselves in God's larger kingdom purposes in light of what he has done, is doing, and will do in the future.

Finally, teaching must be empowering, providing emerging adults with an apprenticeship in the work of biblical and theological inquiry. In this light, it may be appropriate to recommend a paradigm shift in the way that churches think about emerging adult ministry. While many in the church look at teaching as the communication of life application principles, we may also want to consider this as a key time to develop emerging adults as theologians. In other words, instead of viewing them as passive consumers of religious teaching, leaders should foster opportunities to help emerging adults study and interpret the Bible and Christian doctrines, discussing key implications and thinking about connections to personal, social, and global issues. While the church is ordinarily thought of as a place to be fed, this shift would embrace the opportunity to equip emerging adults to engage the conversation across the centuries about the nature of God, self, and world. This is a critical time to initiate the adult process of lifelong learning that will prepare each as an individual who "correctly handles the word of truth" (2 Tim. 2:15).

Fellowship (Koinonia)

The development of strong biblical community is another key contribution of the church during the emerging adult years. While community can be found in many venues at this time of life, the local congregation provides a number of unique communal components that facilitate spiritual formation. Six seem especially critical. First, fellowship in local churches is important because it is unchosen. Emerging adults spend the majority of their time in self-chosen settings, selecting groups of friends that reflect their personalities and affinities. The growth of virtual communities makes this more and more likely since emerging adults can have absolute control over which people they choose to "friend" or "follow" online.[62] They can come and go from these communities, continually choosing their level of involvement to fit their needs. In the unchosen community of the local church, on the other hand, they can learn the true meaning of "love of neighbor," thrust into situations in which they must care for and learn from those who are quite unlike them in age, social status, or personality. Joining a local body entails a commitment to love a group of people who will be annoying, uncool, physically or mentally deficient, and broken. When communities are self-chosen, it can seem as if the Christian life is based on affinity. As Bonhoeffer argues, the path of "spiritual selection" generates settings in which people feel that the Christian community is held together by bonds of common interest, education, and spiritual maturity. In the local church, however, where emerging adults are surrounded by people of diverse ages, social statuses, and personalities, they can begin to see more clearly that it is the gospel—not human similarity—that serves as the irreducible bond of Christian fellowship.[63]

Participation in the local church, in this sense, can be a critical force for true Christian identity formation in emerging adulthood. It is in the church that they can begin to see that it is not skills, occupations, media habits, or athletic interests that form true identity—it is rather a communally bestowed "baptismal" identity as sinners saved by grace. While friendship clusters will often reinforce self-constructed identities, the local church will be a constant reminder of their corporately defined identity as members of the body of Christ. Combating the sense of self-definition that often attends development at this life stage, church participation foregrounds the reality that emerging adults are not only "becoming" someone but are also taking their place in a preexisting community that gives shape to their identities. It is, as Bonhoeffer would say, community "through and in Jesus Christ."[64]

Second, fellowship in local churches is important because it is intergenerational. College represents one of the most monogenerational periods of the life span, a space dominated by interactions with peers of similar age. The postcollege years, prior to marriage, often extend this generational homogeneity. The paucity of older saints leaves emerging adults bereft of the wisdom, experience, and modeling of those further along on the journey of faith. They need to hear the testimonies of those who have seen God's hand at work in both good and hard times, witnessing to God's faithfulness over the long haul. They need to receive biblical teaching from those who have wrestled for long years with the text and its application in the world around them. With the benefit of hindsight, older adults can often provide wisdom regarding fruitful and unfruitful life patterns. Older adults' very presence in local congregations provides models—both positive and negative—of Christian approaches to marriage, parenting, singleness, vocation, church leadership, and community involvement. Emerging adults can, by observation, begin to visualize life trajectories that lead to righteousness and peace and those that lead to quiet desperation. In short, older adults can be both guides to and exemplars of the adult faith journey.

Research also indicates that such intergenerational relationships greatly increase the likelihood of continued faith commitment after adolescence. In her research on factors promoting a lasting faith beyond high school, Kara Powell found that intergenerational worship was the closest thing to a "silver bullet" among high school seniors and college freshmen. Those who worshiped and interacted with older adult Christians were far more likely to continue their faith and church commitments into the college years.[65] Likewise, Wesley Black discovered that a relationship with nonparental adults within a congregation was a strong indicator of continued church involvement and participation.[66] These relationships appear to have a large impact on the continuity of emerging adult faith, helping bridge the gap between adolescence and adulthood.

Of course, attendance at a local church in no way guarantees such intergenerational contact. In many churches, college and young adult ministries are completely separated from the larger congregation. All too often, age-based segmentation limits cross-generational interactions related to Word and sacrament, creating parallel homogenous groupings where the only thing shared is a common parking lot. Churches are not immune from the creation of "lifestyle enclaves," defined by Robert Bellah as groups maintained by similar tastes and interests. Such groups, he notes, are "fundamentally segmental and celebrate the narcissism of similarity."[67] Scripture declares, "One generation commends your works to another; / they tell of your mighty acts" (Ps. 145:4), but the locations in which such teaching takes place are often few and far between. The vitality and idealism of the younger generation is detached from the wisdom and experience of the older generation, a separation that hurts both groups and blunts the power of the united church body for personal and cultural influence.

The vision of separate generational groupings is often appealing both to emerging adults and to the older adults within the congregation. For twenty-somethings, such segregation means that they can establish programs, music, and teaching in accordance with their values, generationally appropriate and free from the flaws they see in the older models. They can move in these new directions quickly, avoiding conflict with their elders over forms, styles, and themes. As Andy Crouch suggests, "As the experience of countless energetic and entrepreneurial young adults can attest, the ease, and the thrill, of starting something new 'for people like us' is mighty tempting when set next to the plodding rate of change in established, multi-generational organizations which seem unwilling to share power or reward initiative."[68] For older adults, segregation means that the new approaches championed by emerging adults can be implemented outside of their world, sealed off from their comfortable church patterns.

To avoid this trap, individuals on both sides of the generation gap must commit to the hard work of true fellowship. Older adults must be willing to engage the emerging adults around them, teaching but also humbly listening to and learning from the younger cohort. They must be willing to share power with emerging adults, giving them spaces to use their gifts and provide input for programming. Emerging adults, on the other hand, must also exhibit humility and patience, learning from the wisdom and experience of elders and exhibiting a willingness to compromise with older adults as they work for faithful change over time. As Kevin DeYoung and Greg Gilbert note, emerging adults must engage the church as "plodding visionaries," working with those above them to facilitate gradual reform.[69]

This may feel constraining to emerging adults since those with the greatest power will likely be older and more conservative. It may even feel like a betrayal of ideals, an unholy compromise with the static forces of tradition. However, we must help emerging adults see that this delay of instant gratification contributes to an even greater ideal. While they may not be able to see immediate implementation of their favored programs, the work together with older generations moves in the direction of an ecclesial ideal: hospitality, love of neighbor and stranger, and a local body caring for and submitting to one another, serving and listening despite differences of life stage. In a culture where young people are depicted as "in the know" and where older adults are often displayed as archaic buffoons past their prime, the church is a location in which emerging adults can demonstrate a humble posture of learning from their elders and in which older adults can display a humble posture of learning from and investment in the next generation. As Kinnaman notes, "The Christian community is one of the few places on earth where those who represent the full scope of human life, literally from the cradle to the grave, come together with a singular motive and mission."[70] Since such unity is something only God can do, intergenerational community can display the countercultural kingdom of God to a watching world.

College and young adult ministries can exist as intact units, of course, but emerging adults must somehow be connected to the larger intergenerational congregation. This can obviously happen in many ways. They can be encouraged to participate in the main church services in addition to the age-segregated ministries. They can join in church-wide service projects, working alongside those of different ages in kingdom labor. They can join intergenerational small groups that are based on geographical proximity rather than age-based affinity. They can serve on church committees, learning from older adults and using their gifts and fresh perspectives to make significant contributions. They can participate in leading worship, preferably with other age groups. They can invite members of older generations to attend their services, giving testimonies or leading small groups. College students and other emerging adults can be connected to families, and these families can have them over for meals and family events. It is also important that such relationships are maintained from the high school years. Kara Powell, for example, urges adult youth group volunteers to commit to a "4 + 1" leadership model, shepherding these youth for their four years of high school plus one year of college in order to maintain intergenerational influence in the critical first year away.[71] Such contacts will certainly help emerging adults sense that they are valued and that they are still integral members of the larger family of God.

Third, fellowship in local churches is important because emerging adults need authority and discipline. Though it will no doubt sound countercultural, it is only within the structure of an institutional church that emerging adults can place themselves under the authority of elders, pastors, and other leaders within local congregations. Emerging adults may desire to cobble together their own self-generated faith without any sense of accountability, but church authority and discipline provides boundaries of belief and practice that can protect emerging adults from their own tendencies to construct false gods in their own image.[72] Such a role, which can only come through church membership (as opposed to shopping and hopping), is especially important for emerging adults who are separated from parents and other authority figures. Church discipline provides a context within which they can affirm that they need others to safeguard them against the world, the flesh, and the devil. Not only does this develop a sense of humility, but it also is a tangible means of expressing one's desire to pursue truth and holiness more than independence and self-expression. The authority structures of the church provide a powerful reminder that there are authorities outside of the self and belief and behavioral standards outside of personal opinion.[73]

Fourth, fellowship in the local church is also important because of its embodied nature. The invisible church is indeed a reality, but embodied local churches provide powerful representations of what sociologist Peter Berger once called "plausibility structures."[74] Many emerging adults are living in school and work worlds that completely reject the plausibility of Christian beliefs and practices. Without weekly, embodied contact with a local body of believers affirming common doctrines and practices, emerging adults can begin to doubt the legitimacy of their worldviews and to wonder whether their own beliefs are simply absurd. As Berger notes, "To have a conversion experience is nothing much. The real thing is to be able to keep taking it seriously; to retain a sense of its plausibility. This is where the religious community comes in."[75] A local body of believers can be an important and powerful plausibility structure in emerging adults' lives, reminding them that they are neither crazy nor alone.

Fifth, fellowship in local churches is important because it provides a family for emerging adults at the very time in which they need such connections. Along these lines, the church must think hard about the role of unmarried emerging adults within the congregation. While the proportion of single twentysomethings within the population is rising, they are significantly underrepresented in most aspects of church life. Singles are much less likely than their married counterparts to attend services, to take part in Sunday school classes, to participate in small groups, and to give of their time and money to the church.[76] The reasons for this gap are diverse, but surely some relate to the church's exclusive emphasis on marriage and family. Churches often set forth a vision of the "American family dream," designating the middle-class home as the epitome of Christian faithfulness. Singles can feel invisible, out of place, or, even worse, like a problem needing to be fixed. We are quick to blame lack of church attendance on delayed marriage, but is it possible that the church has alienated singles by focusing exclusively on marriage and family as the context for the full life of faith? Leaders should be attentive to their use of family-dominated language and programming that seems to exclude or marginalize unmarried emerging adults. Rather than sectioning off singles in homogenous groupings, they can provide programming that includes singles and connects them with the larger body.

By enshrining the American family, we have perhaps lost the deeper sense of the church as "first family," the true centerpiece of family life within redemption history.[77] We are born single, most of us will die single, and there will be no marriage in heaven. Rather than assuming that marriage is the "correct" Christian option, perhaps it is better for the church to communicate that all are called to discipleship and that this calling can be fulfilled either in marriage or in singleness. There is room here for the church to bestow an identity on unmarried emerging adults that calls them to a relational and vocational commitment to the church, much as the language of celibacy has communicated through the centuries. Rather than picturing them in terms of lack ("singleness"), the church can portray this time of celibacy (whether chosen or not) as a vocation in which emerging adults are linked to the broader family and uniquely "concerned about the Lord's affairs" (1 Cor. 7:32). Far from a deficiency, singleness serves as a "visible testimony of Christ's sufficiency in the present age and the true inheritance yet to come."[78] As Marcy Hintz has pointed out, such language would "name the countercultural life to which singles are called. In doing so, we encourage more than just abstinence from sex. We bless the single vocation. We recall the church's history and remember our true family. We christen singles as called-out ones with familial gifts that amplify the church and her outward-looking mission."[79]

Sixth, fellowship in local churches is important because it can provide a place of love, support, and healing. The church must be a place of mending and restoring, bearing burdens in the midst of personal suffering. It must also be a safe place to confess and deal with issues of sin. Quite often, the church represents what Bonhoeffer called the "pious fellowship," a community of "good" people who try to set forth an image of perfection so as to maintain

membership among the pious. However, as he notes, such attempts only serve
to block the potential for a real community of grace:

> The final break-through to fellowship does not occur, because, though they
> have fellowship with one another as believers and as devout people, they do not
> have fellowship as the undevout, as sinners. The pious fellowship permits no
> one to be a sinner. So everybody must conceal his sin from himself and from the
> fellowship. We dare not be sinners. Many Christians are unthinkably horrified
> when a real sinner is suddenly discovered among the righteous. So we remain
> alone with our sin, living in lies and hypocrisy. The fact is that we are sinners![80]

Emerging adults are not drawn together by their piety but rather by the common fact that they are sinners saved by grace. When they conceal sin, therefore, they live in falsehood and hypocrisy, eschewing their true identities as
saved sinners in favor of pretend portraits of piety rooted in human achievement. Such falsehood destroys the possibility of a gospel-centered Christian
community. A true Christian church will be marked by continual confession,
furnishing corporate and private settings in which emerging adults can pull
back the curtains of their hearts and allow the penetrating grace of God to
begin his work of healing and transformation.

Worship (Leitourgia)

In addition to teaching and fellowship, the church must prompt and sustain
deep worship, providing ample opportunities for emerging adults to abide in
the presence of our supernatural God. Emerging adults are hungry for connection with the divine, something that transcends their earthly lives. Tired of
slick programs and image-based entertainment, many world-weary emerging
adults seek the mystery and awe of true spirituality.[81] They desire to be part of
something beyond themselves not only vertically but also horizontally, reflected
in a craving for connectedness with Christians through the centuries and
around the world. Many in this age group are attracted to liturgical worship
styles, in part because of a longing to transcend their limited contemporary
experience. To know that they are connected to past Christians provides a
sense of historical rootedness, an anchor for the soul amid the fluidity of the
modern world.

Through its liturgical structure, the church calls emerging adults to participate in practices that counter the destructive patterns that can evolve at this
time of life. As Craig Dykstra suggests, worship confronts the pathological
achievement-oriented lifestyle that is solidified in the early years of one's

career.[82] This performance-based treadmill establishes and engraves on the soul patterns of striving, manipulation, and image management that can last a lifetime. Church, of course, can become just another setting within which to enact and display the successful life. Yet the weekly call of the church to corporate confession, repentance, thanksgiving, and praise can break this pattern of self-destruction. It allows emerging adults to acknowledge failure and to stand before others as they truly are—as sinners. It also cuts at the root of the self-promoting posture of the achievement-oriented life, weekly proclaiming indebtedness to God for his grace, forgiveness, and unconditional love. Prayer and praise promote postures of humble receptivity, a continual recognition that they are not standing on their own but are rather sustained "by his powerful word" (Heb. 1:3). The weekly rhythm of corporate confession, repentance, thanksgiving, and praise is perhaps the best means of attacking these self-destructive patterns before they become etched within the soul.

Participation in the annual church calendar is also critical. As emerging adults take part in the rhythms of Lent and Easter, Advent and Christmas, they are immersed within a repeated chronology rooted in the narrative of redemption history. They will be reminded over and over again that they are not living for the present but are rather living with a backward gaze at the finished work of Christ and an eager expectation of an eschatological future with him. They will be reminded that they live between the already and the not yet, causing them to look back with thankfulness and to look forward to the hope of the resurrection. They are not simply introduced to moral principles but are instead incorporated into a story that establishes the scope of human history and therefore gives shape to their lives. Instead of viewing the twenties as "my time," these years are instead infused with the centrality of Christ as the defining axis upon which their lives revolve.[83]

Church sacraments do the same. Baptism serves as a reminder of new life in Christ and the resurrection power of the gospel. It can help emerging adults recognize that Christianity is not about "niceness" but rather about a transfer from one kingdom to another, a move from death to life. As a visible and embodied renunciation of the world, it serves to designate identity in Christ and a commitment to the kingdom life. Furthermore, baptism signifies the formation of a new family. In many churches, baptisms are accompanied by a verbal commitment among congregation members to nurture and care for the individual. Challenging the privatized and autonomous notion of the American nuclear family, baptism proclaims that the person is first and foremost identified as a member of the larger family of God. This is incredibly important for emerging adults who have recently separated from the immediate family to enter the wider world. Participation in the sacrament of baptism serves to experientially remind them that their identity is firm within the eternal family of believers even in their earthly transience.

The Eucharist also forms emerging adults in significant ways. The fact that this is a liturgical "practice"—requiring bodily engagement in the sights, smells, sounds, and tastes of the elements—means that the narrative story of salvation gets woven into the fabric of the heart's desires much more quickly. In addition, it serves as a regular reminder of God's great work in the past and future. "This do in remembrance of me" creates a pathway to remember God's faithfulness, and the fact that this is to be done "until He comes" serves to create a longing for his future return. This practice also requires reconciliation with one another. As a communal meal together, the Eucharist mandates interpersonal forgiveness not because the feelings have quieted or the hurts have been forgotten but because the blood of Jesus unites the body and covers over a multitude of sins. In the process of remembering the cross, the Eucharist literally "re-members" the community, rejoining those who were alienated by unifying them in Christ.[84] The communion meal is again a reminder of the centrality of the cross in creating the Christian community, thus bringing healing and restoration even in places where the feelings are still raw. We forgive, Scripture reminds us, because we have been forgiven (Col. 3:13).

Finally, worship can liberate emerging adult creativity, helping them use their God-given gifts and talents to ascribe praise and honor to the Lord. Music, poetry, writing, dance, drama, craftsmanship, and the visual arts can all be encouraged as means of displaying his beauty and calling attention to his character. Churches often fail to attract those with creative gifts, viewing these areas as antithetical to Christian culture.[85] Instead, they must promote these gifts as creative expressions of God's character that can be used in sanctified ways to reveal the inbreaking of God's kingdom in the world. Worship through the arts can redeem these creative faculties, restoring their original purpose of glorifying God and reflecting his creativity. At a time when many begin to recognize such gifts, churches can provide fertile settings for emerging adults to use these talents to glorify God rather than self.[86]

Outreach (Diakonia)

Finally, the church provides an important setting for service, engaging emerging adults in work that looks beyond themselves to the needs of others within and outside the congregation. As mentioned, churches frequently deny emerging adults opportunities to serve in the church, viewing them as too young, too inexperienced, or too transient to make a contribution. Yet emerging adults need others to recognize and develop their gifts, helping them locate areas in which they can serve the body. Service of this kind provides what situated learning theorists call "legitimate peripheral participation."[87] Emerging adults learn how to contribute to the church's mission as they use their gifts alongside others who are more experienced. Such apprenticeships are critical means of developing the necessary skills and confidence to sustain current and future ministry. As Sharon Parks suggests, "The religious community does not fulfill its role in the formation of young adult faith unless it can recognize the gifts of young adults, welcome their emerging competence, and give them power."[88]

Through service, the church immerses emerging adults in the trinitarian reality of the body of Christ. In 1 Corinthians 12:4–6, we read that individuals in the church have different gifts, different avenues of service, and different ways in which God chooses to work within them, yet all serve under the same Spirit, the same Lord, and the same God. The trinitarian language here is no accident. As the church lives out its diversity of gifting and its unity of belief, it properly reflects our trinitarian God, the very picture of diversity and unity within himself. Of course the universal, invisible church demonstrates this profoundly, but it is in local churches that this trinitarian reality is played out in concrete forms week after week. Emerging adults contribute their own gifts for the edification of the entire body, and they also humbly receive others' gifts as they seek to grow in Christlikeness. Receiving gifts may actually be more challenging as many emerging adults are attempting to stand on their own. Dependence, especially at this time of life, is associated with weakness and immaturity, especially if they are relying on others who appear inferior. Mutual ministry, however, combats the pervasive language of independence that attends the move into emerging adulthood, replacing it with the language of interdependent commitment to people with whom they can serve and be served, "joined and held together by every supporting ligament" (Eph. 4:16).

In addition to this church-based service, churches must also provide opportunities for service and justice beyond church walls. As Colleen Carroll discovered in her interviews with emerging adults, many Protestants growing up with an individualistic view of Christianity hit a "brick wall" in early adulthood, hungering for something beyond a focus on personal growth.[89] Rather than viewing service as an optional add-on to worship, fellowship, and learning, they recognize that it is essential to the action-oriented love of neighbor that characterizes true discipleship. Increasingly exposed to the injustices of the world through technology and media, emerging adults desire the church to leave behind its self-protective impulses and enter the pain of the world with the hope and healing of the gospel.[90] Such a vision may indeed provide a means of combating emerging adult perceptions of the church as a hidebound and sheltered institution that does little more than critique the surrounding culture.

Emerging adults need and want a church that is missional, a witness to the self-sacrificial love of God in the world. Just as Christ was sent into the world on a mission and sent the Spirit to the church to continue that mission, so the church, as the body of Christ and habitation of the Spirit, is sent into the world to proclaim and embody the message of the kingdom. The boundary-crossing impulse of the *missio Dei* implies that the church does not simply send people out on mission projects but exists by definition "on a mission," spread out into the world as ambassadors of the King. This represents a move from an "ecclesiocentric" to a "theocentric" vision of the church, shifting the focus from church activities to the members' participation in God's mission in the world.[91] The church "gathered" for preaching and fellowship must work hand in hand with the church "scattered," embarking on a mission to announce and demonstrate God's healing and redemptive grace in all areas of life and culture. While it invites others into the church because it wants them to experience the alternative kingdom community, it also disperses into the broader community to preach the gospel and live as salt and light. As Kenda Creasy Dean notes, if Christians are temples of the Holy Spirit, they will indeed be missional by their very nature. "An insular church is an oxymoron; churches 'on fire' with the Spirit cannot contain themselves, any more than a forest fire can stop itself from catching."[92]

Essential to this outreach focus is a clear link to emerging adults' work environments. The church does a wonderful job of focusing on family issues that define the core identity concerns of those married with children. However, churches often neglect the fact that vocational and work-related issues are central to emerging adults' sense of identity and personhood at this stage of life. As Kinnaman laments:

> Millions of Christ-following teens and young adults are interested in serving in mainstream professions, such as science, law, media, technology, education, law enforcement, military, the arts, business, marketing and advertising, health care, accounting, psychology, and dozens of others. Yet most receive little guidance from their church communities for how to connect these vocational dreams deeply with their faith in Christ. Despite years of church-based experiences and countless hours of Bible-centered teaching, millions of next-generation Christians have no idea that their faith connects to their life's work.[93]

The church must devote more attention to helping emerging adults think about how to use their gifts and talents to work for the kingdom beyond church walls.

Many churches focus only on the abilities that can serve the church, implicitly de-spiritualizing the "secular" vocations that most emerging adults pursue. If churches are to equip emerging adults for kingdom living, they must "go with them" into their jobs, shining the light of the gospel on their labor and helping them see how a kingdom vision can animate the nine-to-five aspects of their lives.

In the end, the church must rethink its missional role with emerging adults. Those who mute their investment in emerging adults because of their transience are generally thinking purely in terms of the contributions emerging adults can make in local congregational life, ignoring their broader missional power. Perhaps it would be helpful for churches, as Benson Hines has argued, to think of emerging adult ministry as missions work rather than in the more traditional terms of Christian education.[94] These emerging adults are generally poised at a critical juncture of life, honing gifts and talents and seeking guidance related to their potential place within God's kingdom purposes. The church, therefore, should see itself as a powerful missionary agency, training and sending emerging adults out into the world to work in various life callings as ambassadors of the gospel. Churches can be a remarkable force to mobilize a generation waiting to be launched into global kingdom service.

Embodied Witness: The Church as an Apologetic

In many ways, this ecclesiological vision accords with what Darrell Guder and his colleagues have defined as the central mission of the church: to represent the reign of God. They note that this representation takes place in two chief ways. First, the church is a "sign and foretaste" of God's reign, a community that displays God's rule and shalom through its love and unity as a peculiar people. When the church lives out loving intergenerational relationships, when it forges family bonds that embrace singles, and when it applies authentic, healing care to all, it serves as a foretaste of kingdom reality. Second, the church is also an "agent and instrument" of God's reign, actively promoting kingdom labor in the world. When the church participates in service and justice, responding with compassion to human need and equipping its members in their vocations, it serves such a role. When it sends forth its members to announce and proclaim the gospel of the kingdom—the good news—it also serves as an agent of the redemptive grace of the cross. "In this respect," Guder suggests, "the church is the preview community, the foretaste and harbinger of the coming reign of God."[95] The love and unity of believers in the church, demonstrated through teaching, fellowship, worship, and outreach, is one of the most potent means of demonstrating to the world the reality of God's character and presence.[96]

Admittedly, the preview is blurry and muted, a blemished picture of the future glory that is to come in the New Jerusalem. Those who say that we should "forget the church and follow Jesus" have their eyes trained squarely on this gap between present and future reality. Yes, the church is "in crisis." It always has been and will continue to be until Christ returns. Yet it is also the community of the redeemed, the gathering of those who depend on the finished atoning work of Christ for forgiveness, salvation, reconciliation, and hope. It is a place to learn how to love those who are different, to practice forgiveness, and to challenge and "spur one another on toward love and good deeds" (Heb. 10:24). The church, as Robert Webber pronounced, is "where the Spirit of God is forming a people who are the expression of God's redeeming work in the world. They are the people in whom the dwelling of God is forming a new creation."[97]

It is easy to stand back and criticize the flaws. Much more challenging is to join with this band of spiritual misfits—helping, teaching, bearing burdens, encouraging, confessing, correcting, forgiving, and praying—celebrating the grace of God in the community of the redeemed. Jefferson Bethke is right to critique false "man-made" religion,[98] but even more helpful is the perspective on the "God-made" church set forth by Christian hip hop artist Lecrae in his song "The Bride":

> You might see her actin' crazy
> Be patient with her though cause she still God's baby
> She the Church
> Before you diss her, get to know her
> Jesus got a thing for her and He died just to show her
> She the Church

Let us help emerging adults "get to know her," learning from and contributing to the messy but hope-filled story of the community of faith.

5 | Vocation

Purpose and Providence

To be in vocation means to grow in a grace-full fitting of our dance to the larger movement of the core plot. To be in vocation means to make creative contributions to the ongoing unfolding of the drama, in accordance with the vision and denouement intended by the playwright. To be in vocation means to develop the talents and gifts one has been given for the sake, and within the constraints, of enriching and moving the whole drama-dance toward the climactic fulfillment envisioned by the script. . . . The challenge and invitation that the Christian community has to offer late adolescents is that of shaping their young adult dream in terms of vocation.

James Fowler[1]

In his brilliant 2011 film *Hugo*, Martin Scorsese weaves the tale of an orphaned boy attempting to find answers regarding his father's death and a larger sense of meaning for his life. Hugo's father was a watchmaker, and the images of springs, gears, and sprockets emerge as powerful metaphors in his quest for purpose. "I'd imagine the whole world was one big machine," Hugo tells his friend Isabelle while standing on a clock tower surveying all of Paris. "Machines never come with any extra parts, you know. They always come with the exact amount they need. So I figured, if the entire world was

111

one big machine, I couldn't be an extra part. I had to be here for some reason." The orphan's boundless sense of hope, even in a seemingly hopeless situation, emerges from a deep quest to find his purpose—his vocation.

Yet Hugo also recognizes that many of the people in the film are completely missing this purposeful existence. The once-great filmmaker, Georges Méliès, has abandoned all sense of meaningful contribution in the world, leading Hugo to a profound lament: "Everything has a purpose, even machines. Clocks tell the time, trains take you places. They do what they're meant to do. . . . Maybe that's why broken machines make me so sad, they can't do what they're meant to do. Maybe it's the same with people. If you lose your purpose, it's like you're broken." The pervasiveness of such vocational "brokenness" leads Hugo to discover that his particular purpose—much like his father's—is to "fix things," to help people recover their sense of purpose and significance. His vocation, in other words, is to help others find their vocations, to bring all of the "parts" together so that they can harmoniously produce meaningful work in the world.

Hugo's vocation is also the vocation of those ministering with emerging adults. Like the orphan, we are called to help twentysomethings develop a broader sense of God's purposes and discern their particular areas of contribution within this grand plan. Vocation is an area that reflects and shapes an individual's views of God, people, culture, and life purpose. Vocation unearths tacit beliefs about how God guides and directs, about the roles of work and leisure in Christian discipleship, and about the location of one's identity and calling. It also serves as a foundational crucible for Christian character development, establishing habits and patterns that influence the individual, familial, and communal spheres of life. As we walk alongside emerging adults navigating vocational discernment, therefore, we must be attentive to the fact that this process represents far more than a search for gainful employment. It is also a formative locus for theological, spiritual, and social transformation.

If Christian vocational discernment involves a growing awareness of God's kingdom purposes and the capacity to select a unique calling within those purposes, then emerging adults must focus on both of these areas. With regard to the first, Christian Smith has suggested that emerging adults fail to cultivate a deep sense of purpose in their lives. "Emerging adults are determined to be free," Smith suggests. "But they do not know what is worth doing with their freedom. They work hard to stand on their own two feet. But they do not really know where they ought to go and why, once they are standing."[2] By defining adulthood in terms of freedom and independence, the sense of responsibility that marks true vocation is often neglected. In addition, compartmentalized visions of Christianity tend to narrow the kingdom vocational vision that might inspire real purpose in emerging adults. As Sharon Parks has expressed, those in this age group often miss out on the formation of "big enough" questions and dreams to guide their adult vocational lives.[3] Those who minister with emerging adults must expand these dreams beyond self-interest and help emerging adults embrace a comprehensive kingdom purpose that encompasses all of life.

With regard to the selection of a unique calling, we must also help emerging adults in the decision-making process that attends to the question, "What should I do with my life?" Because delayed adulthood prolongs decisions and highlights the proliferation of choices, choosing among vocational options can be a painful process. In addition, because many Christian emerging adults seek to discover God's will about their future vocations, the decision-making process is that much more challenging. What if they choose wrongly? What if they miss out on God's will for their lives? Because emerging adults desire to expand possibilities and yet find the will of God, their discernment process frequently leads to anxiety, paralysis, and a lack of vocational commitment and contentment. Those ministering with emerging adults must help them navigate their many choices and quests for the elusive "will of God" by shifting their gaze toward the providential hand of a loving God in their vocational lives.

This chapter will address these two challenges—pursuing a kingdom vocational purpose and discerning a unique vocational niche—and discuss the theological and practical means by which Christian leaders can foster a renewed vision of vocational faithfulness among emerging adults. While the cultural scripts for vocational living emphasize a constricted understanding of vocation and the continual expansion of options and possibilities, the Christian narrative points to a different posture: vocation rooted in *purpose* and *providence*.

The Challenge of Emerging Adult Vocational Purpose

There are a number of factors challenging a purposeful vocational vision among members of this age group. One factor relates to the way in which adulthood is defined in contemporary culture. As Jeffrey Arnett has argued, the perceived meaning of adulthood has changed dramatically over the past fifty years. Previously, adult status was linked to social markers such as marriage and parenting. These milestones showed that the young adult had gained a desire and an ability to take responsibility for others. In more recent years, however, achievement of adult status has been defined more in terms of taking responsibility for oneself, making independent decisions, and becoming financially independent.[4] These variables—more individualistic in nature and more psychological than sociological—point less to an ability to take responsibility for others (which is often held at bay for as long as possible) than to a growing sense of autonomy. "Becoming an adult today," Arnett comments, "means becoming self-sufficient, learning to stand alone as an independent person."[5] Rather than attaching adult status to a sense of "responsibility for" dependent others, adulthood is now linked more to a "freedom from" constraining others. In some ways, this shift has acted to sever the tight correlation between adulthood and other-directed vocation.[6]

The loss of vocational purpose also relates to the delay of adulthood. Many emerging adults maintain that they do not feel ready to invest vocationally in others or in God's kingdom purposes. Even those in their late twenties, many of them well educated, will admit that they still feel they should be on the receiving end of care and support rather than giving to others. In part, this may be a function of the stretching of the life span, leading emerging adults to see themselves still within the early stages of their earthly pilgrimage (and therefore still in need of support). Furthermore, extended schooling can result in a prolonged sense of passive receptivity, even a perceived lack of competence and expertise because they are "still learning." Many express the common idea that they cannot care for others when they have not yet learned how to care for themselves physically, socially, economically, and spiritually. In any case, delayed adulthood prevents not only "growing up" but also "leading down," short-circuiting a sense of responsibility for guiding, mentoring, and serving those coming up behind them. While humility is to be encouraged, this appears more as a generalized lack of confidence, manifested as a delayed readiness to invest in others and in the world at large. Many see emerging adulthood as a time in which to focus strictly on their own development. Vocation is for the future.

This perception has tended to create a self-focused vocational posture. While a degree of self-concern is critical for the developmental tasks of emerging adulthood, we suggest that the pendulum has swung too far, moving in the direction of self-absorption. Higher education is viewed as a passport to privilege, a means to growing as a "moneymaking machine."[7] In addition, surveys of emerging adults still find that most individuals choose jobs on the basis of personal fulfillment and the rewards of status.[8] Lacking a larger vocational vision, they tend to fill the void with default middle-class dreams, described by Smith as, "Get a good job, become financially secure, have a nice family, buy what you want, enjoy a few of the finer things in life, avoid the troubles of the world, retire with ease."[9] Consumed by their private lives, Smith relates, "their horizon is disappointingly parochial," aimed at little more than a comfortable existence and freedom from the pain of the world.[10] Frederick Buechner speaks about his own twenty-year-old self in these terms:

> Whatever my twenty-year-old self was, it was the pivot on which the circle of my life revolved. . . . And though I think I knew even then that finding that self and being that self and protecting and nurturing and enjoying that self was not the "everything" I called it in the poem, by and large it was everything that, to me, really mattered. . . . But to lose track of those depths to the extent that I was inclined to—to lose touch of the deep needs beyond our own needs and those of our closest friends; to lose track of the deep mystery beyond or at the heart of the mystery of our separate selves—is to lose track also of what our journey is a journey toward and of the sacredness and high adventure of our journey.[11]

Devoid of a larger purpose, many emerging adults make the self the vocational reference point, missing out on the "high adventure" furnished by attentiveness to God's kingdom purposes.

In addition to this self-focus, vocation among emerging adults is also constricted by compartmentalization, the loss of a holistic vocational vision. Since the industrial revolution and its separation of work and home, there has been a tendency to view culture as divided into separate spheres governed by disparate values. The public sphere, largely the province of work and politics, is presumed to be a domain anchored by secular ideals, bureaucratic rules, neutral facts, impersonal relationships, and a task orientation. On the other hand, the private sphere, the province of home and church, is a domain ruled by potentially sacred ideals, personal values, intimate relationships, and leisurely pursuits. Such a divide provides the cultural framework for a number of common dualisms: secular and sacred, facts and values, public and private, matter and spirit, work and leisure, and sometimes men (public sphere) and women (private sphere). Missing a comprehensive Christian narrative to weave through the spheres of life, emerging adults readily fall prey to such a split vision.[12]

Compartmentalization obviously affects many dimensions of the Christian life, but it has a potent influence on vocation. The work/leisure distinction, for example, has created a scenario in which vocation has been identified with the workplace alone (public sphere).[13] Equating vocation with a paid occupation can overvalue this sphere, producing tendencies toward workaholism.[14] In addition, such a perspective has the tendency to divest other activities of their meaning and importance in the life of the kingdom. When work is viewed as the exclusive venue of vocation, in other words, other spheres are automatically ascribed leisure status and treated accordingly. The home becomes a place to rest and enjoy the fruits of one's labor with fellow family members.

The church becomes a place to be "refreshed" or "recharged" and to enjoy fellowship with other like-minded families. The community becomes a domain in which we consume goods, services, and entertainment as an antidote to the stresses and strains of paid occupations (a consumer annex to the private sphere).

These purposes have their rightful place, to be sure. However, within such a vision the family is seldom viewed as the vocational setting in which one is discipling a spouse or children and seeking venues for hospitality and family ministry. Church is not envisioned as the vocational setting in which one does the "work" of worship and uses the gifts of the Spirit to serve others. The larger community is not pictured as a vocational setting in which emerging adults live as contributing citizens, praying for leaders and playing their role in seeking justice and peace. Referring to such spheres as "avocations" serves to drain these activities of their massive vocational significance in the kingdom of God.[15]

Compartmentalization also influences emerging adult conceptions of vocational hierarchies. For many in this age group, spiritual activities consist of those things that put people in direct contact with God and eternal souls (prayer, Bible reading, worship, preaching, evangelistic conversations) while secular activities consist of those things that put people in contact with the more mundane and physical realities of everyday life (daily labor, play, politics, institutional engagement, etc.). This perspective actually has a long history. In Greco-Roman and medieval cultures, for example, it was common to distinguish between contemplation and reflection on God and his Word (*vita contemplativa*) and various forms of active work and manual labor (*vita activa*). While most ascribed value and necessity to both arenas, it was clear that the contemplative life was privileged as of higher spiritual worth.[16] Since the contemplative life turned the gaze of the soul toward eternal things and the active life considered merely the temporal realities of earthly life, contemplation was viewed as the chief location for connection with the divine. Active labor, according to Aquinas and others, was beneficial only to the extent that it provided for life's necessities (and therefore opened up possibilities for godly contemplation) or because it financially supported those who spent their time in contemplation.[17] Those who worked in the church and those who lived the monastic life, therefore, were accorded respect as recipients of a true "calling" while others merely worked at their "jobs."

Lest we think we have advanced so far beyond this mentality, it is clear that remnants of this dualism remain. As emerging adults consider various jobs, they often imbibe the subtle message that vocational "calling" is reserved for those with explicitly religious careers. This can begin institutionally on the

Christian college campus with a sense that chapel and small groups represent the "sacred" aspects of college life while the classroom, laboratory, and library are all "secular" in nature.[18] Such a perspective can quickly degenerate into a spurious distinction between those who deal with eternal matters and those who deal with earthly, material realities—the "stuff" of temporal existence.[19] Along these lines, entire career hierarchies emerge with pastors and missionaries at the top; teachers, those who deal with intellectual work, and those in the helping professions in the middle; and businesspersons, politicians, and manual laborers at the bottom (because they are seemingly the least connected to eternal and spiritual matters).[20]

There are many negative ramifications of this sacred/secular divide. Such a mentality can engender a false pride in those preparing for explicitly Christian professions. It can also potentially lead some to choose such careers merely because of their supposed superiority on the spirituality scale. More often, however, this mentality leads many who pursue nonministry employment to feel that they lack a calling and that their jobs maintain "second-tier status" in the kingdom of God. The oft-heard designation of "full-time Christian service" applied to church and missionary occupations only fosters the vague suspicion among others that they are "part-time" servants of the Lord (and then only when they participate in church-oriented activities). We must always be attentive to the ways in which our churches and colleges shape emerging adults' understandings of which spheres are most important.

In addition, this sacred/secular divide colors the ways in which emerging adults try to link Christianity with their nonministry jobs. For many, the "spiritual purposes" of work are pictured in terms of purely contextual factors rather than the work itself. So work carries sacred weight only when it provides opportunities for evangelism among coworkers or when it provides financially so that they can do some volunteer church work "on the side." These are indeed important, but they tend to shift our gaze away from the inherent value of the work itself. The thought here is that spiritual work can only be accomplished in activities related to the private spheres of life: home, church, and personal conversations. The public sphere is then labeled either as neutral—irrelevant to spiritual matters—or, more harmfully, as irredeemable and automatically antithetical to Christian values.[21]

In the end, college and young adult ministries are not immune to the forces of self-focus and compartmentalization that blunt vocational purpose. When the focus of spiritual growth in such ministries is aimed exclusively at personal salvation and character development, it can quickly devolve into a Christianized form of self-actualization. This is where Moralistic Therapeutic Deism is most destructive. While the ideal of interpersonal "niceness" certainly possesses a social dimension, Moralistic Therapeutic Deism's real foundation is personal fulfillment and security. Consumer ministry models also cater to this theme, dispensing attractive religious products to those seeking a happy life with the hopes that they will return for more. Such ministries place great emphasis on what emerging adults have been saved "from" but very little on what they have been saved "for."[22] There are few references to Christian vocation—to our role as "salt" and "light"—within the therapeutic culture of consumer ministries (Matt. 5:13–14).

In addition, many ministries see themselves as compartmentalized "safe havens" to shelter students from the secular winds of the larger campus or culture. While individual discipleship within the private sphere is critical, college and young adult ministry organizations often miss out on broader issues of the public sphere: intellectual issues, social justice issues, environmental issues, and policy issues. If such concerns are seen as unrelated or even antithetical to the "spiritual" work of ministry, emerging adults will likely receive a split vocational vision. They are apt to separate faith from their career choices and the broader context of their public lives. In short, a compartmentalized view of the world is likely to produce a compartmentalized life.

To break these patterns, we must communicate to emerging adults a purpose that shifts the gaze away from self-focus and expands vocational scope to include every aspect of life and every sphere of culture. They need a kingdom vocational vision.

From Constricted to Comprehensive Vision: Purpose and Vocation

A kingdom vocational vision will begin with the recognition that one's life is always "for the sake of others."[23] In the Old Testament, the righteous, as Amy Sherman suggests, were those who viewed their spiritual and material resources not as a means of self-enrichment but rather as a vehicle for blessing others and advancing God's justice and shalom (Prov. 11:10).[24] God has lavished emerging adults with gifts, passions, and unique opportunities not for personal gain but for stewarding their vocational power for the common good. The freedom of emerging adulthood is not a freedom "from" constraints as much as a growing freedom to be self-giving "for" others. As Galatians 5:13 reminds us, "Do not use your freedom to indulge the flesh; rather, serve one another humbly in love." Freedom opens the door to vocation.

If Christian spiritual formation is a matter of being conformed to the image of Christ, whom Dietrich Bonhoeffer called the "man for others," it cannot rest with personal development alone.[25] Conformity to Jesus's image entails not only growing in Christlike character but also embracing a commitment to his mission to proclaim and demonstrate the kingdom in all areas of life. Jesus tells his disciples in John 20:21, "As the Father has sent me, I am sending you," not just into the local congregation for fun activities but into the dark places of the world to proclaim, embody, and actualize the life-changing power of the kingdom.[26] As "God's workmanship, created in Christ Jesus to do good works" (Eph. 2:10), emerging adults are growing in conformity to the One who crossed boundaries of heaven and earth to fulfill his calling. He gave himself—ultimately his very life—for others. Spiritual formation cannot truly be Christian unless it does the same.

Important here is Walter Brueggemann's assessment that a covenantal view of reality "transposes all identity questions into vocational questions."[27] The root of the term "vocation" actually comes from the Latin *vocare*, which means "to call." While the quest for identity is often undertaken as a project of self-definition, the covenant relationship with God means that emerging adults are irrevocably related to the One who has called them into being, taking on his purposes as their own. Therefore, as Brueggemann notes, "Identity for a person is given in the call of the other One. . . . Biblical faith asserts that being grounded in this other One who has purposes that are not our purposes characterizes our existence as missional, that is, as claimed for and defined by the One who gives us life. . . . Vocation means we are called by this One who in calling us to *be* calls us to *service*."[28] When we help emerging adults move beyond the identity question "Who am I?" to also embrace the larger question "Whose am I?," the vocational discernment process will shift. Emerging adults do not discover their identity and then pursue a calling consistent with that vision. Instead, they grow in their recognition that the One who has bestowed an identity upon them has also called them to his mission. Because we belong to God—we are "bought at a price" (1 Cor. 6:20)—we can affirm Brueggemann's definition of vocation: finding a "purpose for being in the world which is related to the purposes of God."[29]

This identity-laden "call" eliminates not only a self-focused perspective but also a compartmentalized vocational vision. Os Guinness helpfully reminds us that vocation must always include an emphasis on both the "primary" and the "secondary" calls of God.[30] Primary calling represents the call to God himself, to a recognition that our lives belong to him alone. Along these lines, "calling" refers to God's call to salvation, discipleship, and citizenship in the kingdom of God. The Old Testament speaks repeatedly of God's call upon the people of Israel. Jesus called the disciples to follow him, and the apostolic church became known as the *ecclesia*, the "called-out" ones. Thus, Christians are first of all "called" to repentance (Acts 2:38–39), "called" to be holy (1 Cor. 1:2), and "called" out of darkness (1 Pet. 2:9) and into peace (Col. 3:15). This is a Christian's primary vocation.

Secondary calling simply speaks to the reality that wherever we are and whatever we do, we are to live out our primary calling in every area of life. Therefore, while our primary call relates more to our identities as Christ followers, our secondary callings speak to the various "stations" (job, family, church, leisure activities, etc.) within which we live out this primary call to love God and neighbor. The order here is important. We can indeed speak of being called to medicine or to coaching or to politics but only in a derivative sense. These secondary callings are simply vehicles and expressions of the primary calling (what Douglas Schuurman calls a "refraction" of the primary call into various settings), and they lose their significance when detached from the primary calling of devotion to Christ.[31] Instead of dividing up spheres into "public and private" or "work and leisure," this is a single calling that infuses all spheres. As James Fowler puts it, "The shaping of vocation as a total response of the self to the address of God involves the orchestration of our leisure, our relationships, our work, our private life, our public life, and the resources we steward, so as to put it all at the disposal of God's purposes in the services of God and the neighbor."[32]

This comprehensive vocational vision has very practical ramifications when it comes to decisions about future jobs. Most emerging adults make career decisions on the basis of the job alone, choosing according to pay, status, and personal fulfillment. Even if they consider the job's spiritual contribution, however, very few think of this choice within the context of the larger constellation of "secondary callings." In other words, many fail to consider the impact of a particular job choice on the ability to disciple one's family members or to serve as a contributing church member. If a particular job derails one's ability to live the primary call in other aspects of life (family, church, community, etc.), it becomes decidedly antivocational. When it comes to the selection of a job, we should help emerging adults see that an occupation is simply one context within which they can pursue their larger vocational responsibilities. Emerging adults should be encouraged to think purposefully about their many roles, formulating goals that help them express vocational love for God and neighbor in these various contexts. The correct question to ask is not, "What will I do for a career?" but "What will I do with my life?"[33]

For emerging adults, this holistic calling can be fostered by resurrecting the Reformation vision of vocation. A reaction against medieval dualism, many of the Reformers eschewed the divide between "spiritual" and "secular" callings by recognizing that all tasks done "in faith" were equally spiritual in nature. William Tyndale stated that "there is no work better than any other to please God; to pour water, to wash dishes, to be a souter, or an apostle, all is one; to wash dishes and to preach is all one, as touching the deed, to please God."[34] If done out of obedience and gratitude to Christ, in other words, the work of the merchant and the peasant was as "spiritual" as that of the monk or priest. In his well-regarded work on Martin Luther's ethics, Paul Althaus commented that "since the Christian has received the meaning and value of his life through God's gracious act of justification, all tasks and works of life are equally important and holy because they have been assigned to him by God's direction. Everything that we do is secular. However, it all becomes holy when it is done in obedience to God's command and in the certainty that he will be pleased, that is, when it is done in faith."[35] Such a perspective can liberate emerging adults to ascribe spiritual worth to activities in all domains of life. As Timothy Keller notes, "No task is too small a vessel to hold the immense dignity of work given by God."[36]

However, it may take more than this. As Darrell Cosden has argued, the Reformation vision did not completely destroy the dualistic understanding of vocation but rather "relocated" it between heaven and earth.[37] While Luther did away with the distinction between the active and the contemplative life, he did not proclaim that earthly work had any eternal worth. The spiritual value, therefore, was derived from the attitude of obedient faith rather than the work itself. Along with a number of other authors, Cosden recently posited that a correct eschatological framework is also key to investing all vocations with spiritual purpose.[38] Using the logic of bodily resurrection and a belief that the earth will be transformed rather than annihilated, these authors argue that the re-created New Jerusalem will include redeemed and purified versions of the cultural goods that have been generated by human work in this life. If the "glory and honor of the nations" will be brought into the new heavens and the new earth (Rev. 21:26), there is at least some evidence for the survival (and perfection by God) of vocational fruits into eternity. Andy Crouch speaks of current human culture as the "furniture of heaven."[39] If this is true, he notes, we should be asking, "Are we creating and cultivating things that have a chance of furnishing the New Jerusalem? Will the cultural goods we devote our lives to—the food we cook and consume, the music we purchase and practice, the movies we watch and make, the enterprises we earn our paychecks from and invest our wealth in—be identified as the glory and honor of our cultural tradition?"[40] Cosden adds that this will likely not only include the products of work but also the "cumulative nature and impact of our work on this earth and on the whole of humanity."[41] Such a perspective can free emerging adults to see their "secular" work as both spiritual and eternal in value and destiny.

To live with this kind of eschatological vision means that we must help emerging adults vocationally account both for the "great commission" and the "cultural mandate." They are to be about the process of "making disciples of all nations," baptizing and teaching people to obey all that the Lord has commanded (Matt. 28:19–20). At the same time, they are to live out the cultural mandate that includes filling, forming, and caring for the earth in a way that addresses human needs and brings glory to God (Gen. 1:28). This is indeed a comprehensive calling that includes both public and private spheres, spirit and matter, souls and "stuff." The fullness of this dual vision—a comprehensive "kingdom vocation"—must be reclaimed, helping emerging adults cultivate a capacity for evangelism and justice, discipleship and culture making, responding to the cries of the heart and the groans of all creation. As Cornelius Plantinga puts it, "To be a responsible person is to find one's role in the building of shalom, the rewebbing of God, humanity, and all creation in justice, harmony, fulfillment, and delight. To be a responsible person is to find one's own role and then, funded by the grace of God, to fill this role and to delight in it."[42]

Practically speaking, how can we enable emerging adults to see the breadth of this perspective? In part, we must provide them with a picture of vocation that is "large enough" to encompass the kingdom vision of God. It seems clear, for example, that vocation should include participation in all of the relational domains that were perfect in creation, marred by the fall, and awaiting full restoration in the New Jerusalem. We should, in other words, help emerging adults see that the life of the kingdom has broken into the world through Jesus Christ and that they can live out a vocation that anticipates future reality in the here and now. In the broken relationships between people and God, they can seek "communion," the reconciliation of people to God through the gospel of Christ and the work of the Holy Spirit. They can seek to help people worship and abide with their Creator, growing in conformity to Christ. In the broken relationships between people and people, they can seek "community," working for healed friendships, marriages, and families, and race, class, and gender harmony. In the broken relationships between people and themselves, they can seek "character," helping people understand their sin and woundedness and the need for integrity, healing, and wholeness. Finally, in the broken relationships between humans and the rest of the created order, they can seek "cultivation," promoting environmental stewardship but also the cultivation of the earth to create new cultural goods that glorify God and serve others. In each of these dimensions—communion, community, character, and cultivation—emerging adults can be challenged to invest vocational energy, praying for and participating in areas where there have been breaches of God's perfect justice and shalom.[43]

Within each of these four domains, it may be helpful for emerging adults to think in terms of creative, sustaining, and restorative tasks. In other words, vocation will provide opportunities to create new things (works of art or music, meals, sermons, buildings, medical procedures), to sustain and refine existing cultural goods (perfecting musical scales, sustaining relationships or quality work procedures, preserving natural and cultural beauty), and to be an agent of God's healing, restorative power (in relationships, cultural systems, and areas of sin and brokenness). A pastor, for example, would be concerned with the birth of new families through marriage but also with the sustaining of healthy families and the mending of broken families. A politician might create economic legislation, seek to sustain effective policies, and use the power of office to restore justice to the oppressed. A teacher might create new learning experiences, nurture excellence in writing, and correct bullying patterns. As they assume such responsibilities, they can avoid both triumphalism and despair. As Plantinga comments,

> Christians have been put in a solid position where the reform of culture is concerned: we have been invited to live beyond triumphalism and despair, spending ourselves for a cause that we firmly believe will win in the end. So, on the one hand, we don't need to take responsibility for trying to fix everything. The earth is the Lord's, and he will save it. On the other hand, we may take responsibility for contributing what we uniquely have to contribute to the kingdom, joining with many others from across the world who are striving to be faithful, to add the work of their hands and minds to the eventual triumph of God.[44]

It should be noted that this broad calling also includes a very intentional and God-ordained need for rest. God rested from his work of filling and forming the earth (Gen. 2:1–3), and he calls emerging adults to reflect him in this way as well. Some may picture rest as necessary only as a means of preparing again for work. However, as Keller has suggested, God rested even without a need for renewal. Rest, in other words, is good in and of itself and not merely as a tool for increased productivity. Rest is not simply the absence of work but rather intentional time and space devoted to the worship of God and enjoyment of his gifts. It is, as Keller suggests, "joyful reception of the world and of ordinary life."[45]

As we guide emerging adults in grasping this expansive kingdom purpose, we are also helping them navigate the transition from adolescence to true adulthood. As Crouch has commented, adolescence is often a time of life consumed with cultural awareness and engagement. Teenagers often specialize in consuming culture and may begin gaining a capacity for cultural critique. However, an indicator of growing Christian adulthood is the ability to move beyond consumption and critique, embracing the call to responsible action by making new culture (creating), preserving current cultural goods handed down from previous generations (sustaining), and bringing healing to cultural products and forms that no longer reflect the divine pattern (restoring).[46] The very meaning of adulthood is linked to the ability to move beyond passive receiving and to see oneself as a contributing agent in the world. In other words, it is a time to begin moving past cultural fluency and toward adult cultural responsibility—toward vocation.

The search for a "purposeful" approach to vocational discernment responds directly to emerging adult self-focus. Using the images of salt and light, self-centeredness will lead some emerging adults to live blissfully within the decay and darkness of the world, blunting their distinctiveness so as to enjoy what life has to offer. Alternatively, other emerging adults will remain separate from the world's decay and darkness, still betraying a focus on self-fulfillment by seeking a comfortable life of spiritual retreat. In other words, they can desire to be either "in and of the world" or "not in or of the world." A Christian vocational purpose, however, does not permit either posture. By calling for an "in but not of the world" life, this vision clearly mandates a "faithful presence" in the world, eliminating both selfish pleasure and selfish retreat.[47] The decisions made here regarding vocation will go a long way toward directing emerging adults toward a life of self-fulfillment or one of responsible adult investment.

While such kingdom purpose must serve as a starting point for considering present and future plans, the actual process of vocational selection also requires more specific and personal direction. As we lead emerging adults to consider the many options in front of them, we must help them see the unique ways in which they can contribute to God's holistic purposes in the world. One of the essential paths to such clarity, it turns out, depends on emerging adults' ability to pay attention to God's providential hand in their lives.

The Challenge of Emerging Adult Vocational Selection

Once emerging adults are taught to think broadly about the scope of kingdom vocational purpose, they still must discern the best places to live this out. While the question "What should I do with my life?" has always been a central concern among members of this age group, a variety of factors have made this more challenging in the contemporary setting. Looking only at the "job" aspect of vocation, the changing nature of the life span has made job selection a more protracted experience. Either by choice or necessity, emerging adults frequently delay the post-undergraduate job transition and opt for extended years of higher education. In part, this is a simple reality of contemporary economics. Fifty years ago, a high school graduate was able to secure a relatively high-paying manufacturing job providing enough income to support a family. In the move to an information- and service-based economy, however, jobs with adequate pay now often require advanced education. Relative incomes have substantially declined for those lacking a college or graduate degree.[48] With parents increasingly willing to fund educational and life expenses, emerging adults often take advantage of extended schooling opportunities before entering the workforce.[49]

In addition, older marriage ages also influence vocational timing. Fifty years ago, most women worked only into their early twenties (if at all), the age at which many entered marriage and motherhood. Men also sought work at an early age to secure an income sufficient to support their early marriage and family. Now, however, with marriage and parenthood pushed into the late twenties, there is more time for emerging adults to search for a job capable of providing personal fulfillment, status, and a link to identity. Because of this relatively lengthy period in which one is free from the requirement to provide or care for a spouse and children, both men and women can delay vocational commitments for a longer period of time.[50] For these reasons, vocational selection often becomes a protracted, decade-long process of agonizing discernment.

In addition to these sociological factors, emerging adults may struggle psychologically because of the proliferation of choices available to them. While previous generations were not devoid of choices, options were often restricted to a constellation of jobs closely associated with their parents' occupations or to the few occupations considered appropriate for women. Occupational and social mobility was far from the norm, as jobs and apprenticeships were typically circumscribed within the narrow limits of family geography, economic status, and gender. In contemporary culture, by contrast, job selection often approximates choosing from a large smorgasbord of available options. A parent's career might signal one possibility, but children are typically raised to see vocational selection as a purely personal matter. Following in the footsteps of one's parents is often viewed as a cop-out, a decision to "settle" for less than one's unique potential.[51]

Choice can be intoxicating and liberating in part because it promises to expand the options of what emerging adults may do and what they may become. Dale Kuehne has termed our culture the "iWorld," a society that is "identifying and deconstructing every possible boundary in order to provide the broadest range of options in each individual's quest to understand who he or she is and wants to be." "The iWorld," he suggests, "seeks to not promote any particular choice; rather, it seeks to expand the available choices."[52] Psychologist Varda Konstam speaks of emerging adults as "maximizers," seeking always to verify that they have chosen the best option among all possibilities. Multiplying options, therefore, is viewed as the pathway to the best possible life.[53]

Yet because choice is so compelling, selection is quite painful. When the options are so numerous, every decision feels like a slamming of the door to other possibilities. In a world where choice is viewed as an unadulterated "good," a deep sense of loss often attends the decision-making process. Having choices is perceived as a blessing, but choosing is viewed as a curse because it eliminates options, requires commitment, and sets one on a single (read "narrow") path. Philosopher Robert Nozick points out that the challenge of emerging adulthood comes in part from the recognition that one will not be able to traverse every path that was deemed a possibility in the younger years. "Economists speak of the opportunity cost of something as the value of the best alternative forgone for it," he says. "For adults, strangely, the opportunity cost of our lives appears to us to be the value of all the foregone alternatives summed together, not merely of the best other one. When all the possibilities were yet still before us, it felt to us as if we would do them all."[54] The word for "decide" actually comes from the Latin *decider*, which means "to cut off." To emerging adults, vocational selection can indeed feel like an amputation, a restriction on the endless possibilities of their ever-expanding lives.

In such a context, selection is almost always attended by a longing backward glance. Once a decision is made, emerging adults can spend a great deal of time wondering what might have happened if they had chosen otherwise. When things are hard, they assume another choice might have provided unmitigated blessing. When things are good, they still wonder what might have been behind "door number two." Needless to say, this can furnish a challenging context within which to develop postures of contentment and commitment.

Finally, vocational selection is complicated by many emerging adults seeking a clear sign from God regarding what they should do. As Jerry Sittser has pointed out, many hold on to some version of the "conventional approach" to God's will:

> Convention teaches us that the will of God consists of a specific pathway we should follow into the future. God knows the pathway, and he has laid it out for us to follow. Our responsibility is to discover this pathway—God's plan for our lives. Unfortunately, it is not always obvious. If anything, it is often ambiguous.

We must figure out which of the many pathways we could follow is the one we should follow, the one God has planned for us. . . . If we choose rightly, we will experience his blessing and achieve success and happiness. If we choose wrongly, we may lose our way, miss God's will for our lives, and remain lost forever in an incomprehensible maze.[55]

While maintaining an admirable desire to submit one's own will to God's larger plan, such a perspective can create a kind of vocational paralysis. Many, for example, cannot decide on a vocation to pursue because they are waiting for a sign—a lightning bolt in the sky, a voice from above, or even a clear sense of inner peace. Others are paralyzed by fear of making the wrong choice. If a wrong decision may forever remove one from the will of God, it is easy to see why emerging adults may be reluctant to make any choice at all.

In the end, these sociological, psychological, and theological factors complicate the vocational selection process, making it both more protracted and more distressing. As we work with emerging adults, we must direct their attention to the fact that God created them in his providence to play a strategic role in his kingdom purposes, both in the present and in the future. He has wired them in unique ways and set them in unique times and places to reveal his glory through them. Emerging adults will need to make choices about life calling, but these choices reflect more than mere self-determination or searches for external signs of God's will. Instead, they will reflect a conscious recognition that their lives have been shaped by God with indicators of his loving care and guidance already "built in." They have to make choices, but the more fundamental reality is that they are chosen.

From Choosing to Being Chosen: Providence and Vocation

Before communicating a proper vision for vocational selection, a few key issues must be addressed. First, we must help emerging adults see the benefits of narrowing choices and of selecting a path. The constant multiplying of possibilities may be liberating, but it also tends to develop shallowness, a life that never fully invests in an area of labor with deep commitment. Importantly, then, we should help emerging adults recognize the positive aspects of the "narrowing" that takes place in vocational selection. Limits provide clear boundaries within which they can make significant contributions, particular corners of the universe in which to sow and reap. Boundaries provide a solid and consistent location for careful thought and fruitful labor, helping emerging adults avoid the scattered fragmentation of their gifts and passions. As

Brian Walsh and J. Richard Middleton have noted, "It is literally impossible to 'keep your options open' and live a life of any significance."[56] Decisions, while painful, establish the necessary landscape for vocational contribution.

Second, we can communicate to emerging adults that they do not need to figure out the "one plan" that God has for their future vocation. Emerging adults seeking God's will often picture him as hiding his will from them, purposely obscuring his good plan and forcing them to hope for the best with their choices. God does have a plan for emerging adults' lives, but it is not one that he promises to reveal ahead of time and not one that he sets up as a puzzle for them to figure out. With regard to "tomorrow," God commands only two things: do not worry about tomorrow (Matt. 6:34) and do not boast about tomorrow (Prov. 27:1; James 4:13–16). Both commands are rooted in the fact that God holds the future in his hands and wants us to rest in his daily care for us.

In addition, multiple options may all be "good" options. The revealed will of God is clear: to seek first the kingdom of God (Matt. 6:33), to pursue sanctification (1 Thess. 4:3), to act justly, love mercy, and walk humbly with God (Mic. 6:8), to be joyful always, pray continually, and give thanks in all circumstances (1 Thess. 5:16–18). Pursuing such things will always be the will of God, and these can often be lived out in many different vocations. John Wesley, preaching on discerning God's will, noted that

> the Scripture itself gives you a general rule, applicable to all particular cases: "The will of God is our sanctification." It is His will that we should be inwardly and outwardly holy; that we should be good, and do good, in every kind and in the highest degree whereof we are capable. Thus far we tread upon firm ground. This is as clear as the shining of the sun. In order, therefore, to know what is the will of God in a particular case, we have only to apply this general rule.[57]

In the end, whether they work in business or education, politics or the pastorate, their chosen career will always be less important than their devotion to God and neighbor in all areas of their lives.

Finally, emerging adults must be warned that their obsession with seeking out a future vocation may blind them to the God-given vocational opportunities that exist right before their eyes. In other words, they may spend so much energy focusing on the unclear path in front of them that they neglect the very clear teaching of Scripture regarding their present vocational responsibilities to love God and neighbor. This emphasis on present vocation is absolutely critical in work with collegians, seminarians, and graduate students. Many college students picture their experience in higher education as preparation for a future calling or vocation. Thus, they are taking classes in biology, education, or theology so that they can prepare for a medical, teaching, or ministry vocation upon graduation. However, a present-oriented perspective has the capacity to open students' eyes to their present vocation. When students begin to see that their role "as students" is a vocation in and of itself—that it possesses intrinsic vocational value—they can view their present studies, friendships, and campus activities with a new sense of meaning and significance. Many students confess guilt in spending so much time on their studies rather than in practical ministry. However, it is important to remind them that, for this period of life, studying represents a significant part of their vocational responsibility. "Called" to be a student, their reading, writing, painting, laboratory work, problem solving, and performing become the platforms on which they live out their primary calling as disciples of Christ. As they faithfully attend to this central calling in the present, they will be prepared to do the same in the future.

Of course, decisions still have to be made. Yet the cues for vocational selection should come not only from a choice of self-determination or by waiting for a sign from God but also from a growing awareness of the ways in which God has already been active in their lives to shape a vocational orientation. Instead of viewing vocational selection as a straightforward search for personal "fit," they must see instead that they have been "fitted" for God's purposes in the world. The providential vision of vocation reminds them that God has already been at work in their lives, bestowing gifts, developing passions, and providing opportunities and people to shape their vocational lives. As Lee Hardy suggests,

> It is not as if our abilities, concerns, and interests are just there, as accidents of nature, and then God has to intervene in some special way in order to make his will known to us in a completely unrelated manner. Rather, in making a career choice, we ought to take seriously the doctrine of divine providence: God himself gives us whatever legitimate abilities, concerns, and interests we in fact possess. These are his gifts, and for that very reason they can serve as indicators of his will for our lives. . . . Too often our search for God's will in our lives has been skewed by a highly secularized view of the world. We don't really believe that God is present and at work in the concrete events and circumstances of this world.[58]

Emerging adult vocational discernment, in other words, is not simply about making decisions for an unknown future. It is also about paying attention to the given aspects of their lives, viewing these as indicators of God's providential hand in their personal stories.

The emphasis on "givenness" highlights a number of providential guideposts that should take center stage in the discernment of vocational direction: gifts, passions, opportunities, and community. We will discuss each in turn. One of the most helpful guideposts in vocational selection is that of providential gifting. Recognizing that God gives gifts "just as he determines," a growing awareness of spiritual and natural gifts represents a means by which emerging adults can see how God, in his providence, has wired them for fruitful service in church and world (1 Cor. 12:11). In Paul's writings, gifting and calling seem closely related: "We have different gifts, according to the grace given to each of us. If your gift is prophesying, then prophesy in accordance with your faith; if it is serving, then serve; if it is teaching, then teach; if it is to encourage, then give encouragement; if it is giving, then give generously; if it is to lead, do it diligently; if it is to show mercy, do it cheerfully" (Rom. 12:6–8). If a person is gifted in a particular area, in other words, Paul recommends that those gifts be used in vocation, primarily in the church but by extension in the world as well. Likewise, 1 Peter 4:10 says, "Each of you should use whatever gift you have received to serve others, as faithful stewards of God's grace in its various forms." Gifts become a primary means by which emerging adults administer and dispense God's redemptive grace to the world around them. The presence and empowerment of the Holy Spirit is the vital source of vocational strength. The "manifestation of the Spirit," Paul tells us, "is given for the common good" (1 Cor. 12:7).

The flip side is also true—emerging adults are not generally called to those vocations for which they have no apparent gifting. Vocational selection, therefore, requires not only a proper assessment of gifts but also a willingness to acknowledge providential limits. It is important to note that such discernment should not be built solely on presumed adequacy or inadequacy along these lines. Without actual life experience, a sense of inferiority or superiority can provide false pictures of actual gifts in untested areas. While many emerging adults chafe at the idea that they cannot be "anything they want to be," this again is a providential gift of God and a reminder that they live within what Fowler calls an "ecology of giftedness," contributing to others with their gifts even as they receive the contributions of others' strengths. "In vocation," he notes, "we can experience our *limits* as gracious, even as we can experience our gifts as gracious."[59]

When helping emerging adults consider their gifts, there are a few caveats to keep in mind. God does not always call people to specific vocations in line with their giftings. We see a clear discrepancy between gift and vocation, for example, in the calling of Moses. When God calls Moses to speak to Pharaoh, Moses uses his lack of giftedness as a potential reason why he should not undertake this mission: "Pardon your servant, Lord. I have never been eloquent, neither in the past nor since you have spoken to your servant. I am slow of speech and tongue." God's response is straightforward: "Who gave human beings their mouths? Who makes them deaf or mute? Who gives them sight or makes them blind? Is it not I, the LORD? Now go; I will help you speak and will teach you what to say" (Exod. 4:10–12). For Moses, God issues a calling independently from gifting.

Such an account should not be taken as normative (it reflects an exceptional moment in biblical history), but it does point to an important reality. It is unlikely that someone would be called to do something for which they are unqualified. The unlikeliness, however, should not close us off from the reality that God can call us whenever and to whatever he would like. Thus, emerging adults should approach decision making with open hands and also hold loosely the vocation they find themselves in, recognizing that they should be available for God to move at his discretion. As Karl Barth acknowledged,

> In relation to the personal presuppositions which he himself brings, the action of man must be one which always and in all directions is open, eager to learn, capable of modification, perpetually ready, in obedience to the exclusively sovereign command of God, to allow itself to be oriented afresh and in very different ways from those which might have seemed possible and necessary on the basis of man's own idea of his ability and capacity.[60]

While gifting provides crucial information, this should not close out the possibility that God will gift emerging adults in new ways for new tasks to which he calls them.

Finally, it is important to keep in mind that a discernment of gifts should never be used to absolve emerging adults from a sense of responsibility for areas related to God's revealed will. An apparent lack of gifting in evangelism, for example, should not serve to limit participation in this essential work. The absence of an encouragement gift does not somehow free them from the responsibility to "encourage one another and build each other up" (1 Thess. 5:11). While some are uniquely gifted in these areas for the good of the church, every Christian is commanded to pursue obedience in these domains. Highlighting the primary call, gifts should never be a cop-out to avoid the clear commands of God.

In addition to gifting, passion is a second providential guidepost along the way. One of the most frequently cited quotations regarding Christian vocation is Buechner's expression that "the place God calls you to is the place where your deep gladness and the world's deep hunger meet."[61] While the "world's deep hunger" speaks to the various needs that exist in our world, "deep glad-ness" addresses the God-given passions that drive vocational awareness. Many emerging adults, for example, possess a deep internal motivation to work among a particular group of people (elementary school students or refugees) or in a particular place (China or the inner city). Others possess a passion for particular issues or causes (racism, the AIDS crisis, or marital harmony). For such individuals, there is often a deep sense that they have to do something in this area. Perhaps a better way of stating this is in the double negative—they "can't not" engage vocationally with these people, places, or issues.[62]

Life experiences and exemplars are often the providential means of birth-ing such passions. Emerging adults may take a mission trip only to find that they feel pulled in the direction of overseas missions or development work. Others might find that, through participating in a campus ministry, they feel a growing desire for full-time vocational ministry. Some might find that painful (or positive) experiences in high school propel them to assume roles as high school teachers or that a particularly powerful teacher generated a passion to influence lives in the classroom. Quite often, emerging adults develop pas-sions as they see others active in vocation, determining that they would love to engage in that same activity or carry on the legacy of chosen mentors.[63]

As with gifts, however, there are important qualifications to this emphasis on passion. First, desires are not always trustworthy. Passions for material comfort, for human approval, and for prestige are obviously not reliable in-dicators of vocational selection. We should, therefore, always be praying for the Lord to open their eyes to false or misdirected desires that can derail them. In addition, as Parker Palmer has noted, true passions can at times be buried underneath a pile of imposed desires.[64] Emerging adults can develop certain passions, in other words, that are nothing more than the assimilated expec-tations of others. Because of the desire to please, emerging adults often fall into what sociologist David Riesman has called the "other-directed" life, one that is more about living up to what others think they should be than actually discerning the unique ways God has wired them.[65] A student who feels he or she wants to be a doctor, for example, may discover in time that this dream was purely the expectation of parents or teachers. Emerging adulthood has the potential to become a time of proper individuation in which there is a growing recognition that one's "derived" passion is either unfulfilling or cuts against the grain of one's developing sense of calling. Such imposed passions must be acknowledged before the path of true self-understanding can begin.

Finally, we must not take this to mean that such work will be easy. There will be tasks in any vocation that don't elicit immediate exuberance: relational conflicts with coworkers, dirty diapers, irascible clients, nutrient-depleted soil, issues without easy answers. All work since the fall includes "thorns and thistles," pain and hardship. God may indeed call emerging adults to be in situations that involve deep suffering and pain. Vocation will not always bring happiness, but true passion will often find joy even in the struggle. In this sense, emerging adults should not consider the ease or difficulty of a certain path as a clear indicator of God's will. True passion emerges from a deep sense of God-given motivation rather than from the changing rhythms of circumstance. Perhaps a better cue might be the persistence of passion even in the midst of hardship and challenge. This indeed is where passion can show its true strength.

A third guidepost relates to providential opportunities. At times, these opportunities come from roles rooted in family or friendship ties. In their "given" positions as sons and daughters, brothers and sisters, aunts, uncles, cousins, friends, and neighbors, many providential vocations will arise, often related to familial hardships. At other times, opportunities will arise (or not) in the form of open and closed doors, revealing areas in which the emerging adult may or may not seek a vocation. In still other cases, local or global events related to an emerging adult's particular place and time in history may reveal needs that call him or her into vocational action. Emerging adults tend to place emphasis on chosen vocations, likely because these activities reflect self-determination. From a Christian perspective, however, they should recognize these opportunities as provisions of a loving God, laden with vocational potential.

As emerging adults consider providential opportunities, however, there are cautions. Not every need is a call. Not every global crisis or empty nursery position has their name on it. When every need seems like a call, emerging adults can often respond out of a sense of guilt rather than joyful obedience. They can lose the ability to say "no," and serve begrudgingly. They can adopt a messiah complex and forget that they are only one small part of a larger Christian community. There will always be more needs than can be filled, and therefore they should cultivate an ability to rest in the contribution they can make. The rhetoric of open and closed doors can also be fraught with uncertainty. Speaking of open doors can be a good thing, demonstrating that they see the providential hand of God in daily life experiences. It can also provide rationalization for selfish desires. Similarly, closed doors may simply speak to laziness or to attempts to escape the costliness of discipleship. Furthermore, a closed door does not always mean that one should give up on a presumed desire or call. It is certainly possible that a closed door will later open or that continued persistence will pay off in securing a certain vocation.

As emerging adults reflect on their providential gifts, passions, and opportunities, all discernment should take place within a communal context, affirmed and modified by the people God has providentially placed in their lives—this is the fourth guidepost. Many emerging adults entertain "calls" to ministry and other occupations with little counsel from church leaders, family members, or friends. Such a reality provides clear evidence of the individualism of their isolated lives. Often those who are friends, parents, teachers, mentors, and pastors can help them see areas of gifting and limitation in ways that are less clear through their subjective eyes. Emerging adults can be quite self-deceptive at times, estimating themselves too highly or too lowly. It can therefore be helpful to seek wise counsel from those who know them best. Do others see them possessing the gifts necessary for a particular vocation? Do others see the calling fitting well with their passions? Do others see them flourishing or floundering in such a role? Most calls should be "mediated" calls, channeled through the communal voice of the body of Christ.

As we minister with emerging adults, the recognition of God's providential hand can be a powerful force for spiritual formation. This orientation strikes at the heart of two of the most common vocational vices: pride and envy. It is so easy for emerging adults to see their gifts as self-generated traits to be cultivated for self-promoting ends. They can take great pride in their newly discovered competencies, basking in the glory of ascribed praise. As Brueggemann has suggested, we all face the modern temptation to "self-groundedness," the belief that "our life springs from us, that we generate our own power and vitality, and that within us can be found the sources of wholeness and well-being."[66] On the other hand, vocational discernment can also become a context within which emerging adults cultivate a spirit of envy toward those who seem more gifted or better equipped. In other words, some may begin to feel compromised by others' gifts, passions, and opportunities, seeing their own vocational lives chiefly in terms of "lack."

In contrast to these vices of pride and envy, the sense of God's providential hand generates instead a posture of "grateful stewardship." This posture reminds them that everything they have is from God, that his grace alone brings them the gifts, passions, opportunities, and communities that shape their vocational vision. It reminds them that God does not gift them and send them forth into vocation because of their inherent worthiness but because of his grace and love. Grateful stewardship, therefore, cuts at the root of pride. Instead of feeling worthy of the call, they fall to their knees in humble gratitude, eager to serve as stewards of these gracious gifts. Like Isaiah, the response to these undeserved gifts is a vocational passion to join his mission in the world: "Here am I. Send me!" (Isa. 6:8). Grateful stewardship of God's gifts is indeed the answer to the postmodern posture of self-expressive choice.

The sense of God's providential hand also cuts at the root of envy. Emerging adults can begin to see that God has apportioned gifts, passions, opportunities, and communities to each person as he wishes, stemming from his love for each one of them and from his purposes in the world (1 Cor. 12). When they see themselves as grateful stewards, there is no sense that another's gifts compromise their own worth. Instead, they can celebrate others' gifts, passions, and opportunities, recognizing that these are actually God's providential means of fulfilling their ultimate purpose: the glory of God and the spread of the kingdom. As Fowler suggests, "God has called each of us, with our unique range of gifts and our unique patterns of limits, and calls us to a vocational adventure that is distinct from that of anyone else. We do not need to establish it in competition with others. . . . In vocation we are augmented by others' talents rather than being diminished or threatened by them."[67]

In all of this, it is helpful to recognize that the discernment of God's providential hand should be pursued within the balance of the *vita activa* and *vita contemplativa*—the active and contemplative lives. Much of this discernment takes place in the midst of active obedient living rather than in isolation or through a written assessment. While spiritual gifts tests and inventories are often helpful tools of self-discernment, there is no substitute for stepping into certain tasks and seeing how God chooses to work. An awareness of gifts and passions is generally a growing and evolving awareness, emerging through experimentation as one steps out in faith. Quite often, the very process of vocational experimentation will teach emerging adults realities about themselves, about God, and about the vocation itself that they would never have known otherwise. God's guidance often takes place not in passive searching for signs but rather as they actively obey his revealed will in everyday life.

Yet the activism of providential discernment must also take place within a contemplative and prayerful context anchored by a posture of humble listening. Sometimes our fascination with vocational testing, spiritual gifts inventories, and personality tests can actually lead us to neglect prayerful listening. In our Western, scientific culture, in other words, we can view vocational selection as a straightforward process of matching assessed gifts with available positions. Yet the very foundation of vocational commitment is that it emerges as a response to God's loving call. As Laurent Daloz has suggested, the Latin roots of both "vocation" and "commitment" imply a response to an external summons, a received call and a commissioned task. "Both," he notes, "imply relationship rather than an individualistic choice."[68]

It may very well be true that the absence of a clear voice simply indicates that any vocational choice is fine, provided they are pursuing Christ and his kingdom. Yet emerging adults should not neglect the possibility that a speaking, loving, relational God desires to interact with them personally. The reason so many of the great "heroes of the faith" entered times of decision making with extended periods of prayer and fasting is precisely because they desired to hear from God. It is of course true that we cannot make Moses and Paul exemplars of how every Christian will receive a call from the Lord; these were extraordinary moments in biblical history. Yet we often seem to fall to the opposite extreme of discounting the possibility of a special call altogether.

Emerging adults cannot and should not demand such experiences or avoid all decisions because they are "waiting for a voice." God may be providing space for them to use their own decision-making power in accordance with godly principles. But they also should not carry on smugly with a sense that they always know exactly what to do. Paul was frequently directed and redirected by the Holy Spirit during his missionary journeys, vocational pathways opened and closed by the Spirit's intervention (Acts 16:6-10). Perhaps the best approach, therefore, is to make choices that honor their gifts, passions, opportunities, the wisdom of others, and the greatest commandments to love God and neighbor while also cultivating receptive eyes and ears to hear the forceful or still small voice of God. Vocation will always be from God (providence) and for God (purpose), but it must also be with God (prayer).

As we guide emerging adults in their vocational quests, therefore, purpose and providence become two central domains for countering flawed cultural constructs. Both are critical. Emerging adults are quite capable of turning their gaze on God's providential hand into a project of self-fulfillment. They are capable of using their gifts to elevate productivity and reputation. They are capable of pursuing their own passions to seek personal meaning and a sense of enjoyment. Because of this tendency, we cannot allow them to stop with the discernment of God's providential hand. While "paying attention" is absolutely essential as a means of discerning their paths, they must consider these themes only in relation to God's larger purposes in the world. Likewise, purpose without a sense of God's providential hand can become skewed. If they seek to actively pursue a comprehensive vision of the gospel and yet lack a clear sense of God's prior leading and gifts of grace, they are likely to become arrogant and self-sufficient, obeying the secondary but not the primary calling of God. Grateful stewardship is replaced with prideful striving. The combination of purpose and providence reminds us that Jesus's disciples are to carry on his kingdom mission, all the time recognizing that "apart from me you can do nothing" (John 15:5).

In the end, we are well served by Crouch's observation that vocation is often discovered at the intersection of "grace" and "cross." Grace represents the places where we see God's providential hand in our lives and work. The cross represents the world's broken places, domains crying out for the healing and redemptive power of the gospel. As Crouch suggests, "So where are we called to create culture? At the intersection of grace and cross. Where do we find our work and play bearing awe-inspiring fruit—and at the same time find ourselves able to identify with Christ on the cross? That intersection is where we are called to dig into the dirt, cultivate and create."[69] Grace (providence) without the cross can lead to self-absorption. Cross (purpose) without grace can lead to an empty activism rooted in personal willpower. Purpose and providence are both needed for a truly Christian vocational vision among emerging adults.

The Creator of the world has revealed his purposes and providentially created each emerging adult with gifts, passions, opportunities, and communities so that they may participate in his plan. As Hugo believed about himself and the world, all are here for a reason; there are no extra parts.

6 | Morality

Training the Dispositions of the Soul

We say we want renewal of character in our day but we don't really know what we ask for. . . . We want character but without unyielding conviction; we want strong morality but without the emotional burden of guilt or shame; we want virtue but without particular moral justifications that invariably offend; we want good without having to name evil; we want decency without the authority to insist upon it; we want moral community without any limitations to personal freedom. In short, we want what we cannot possibly have on the terms that we want it.

James Davison Hunter[1]

American emerging adults are a people deprived, a generation that has been failed, when it comes to moral formation. They have had withheld from them something that every person deserves to have a chance to learn: how to think, speak, and act well on matters of good and bad, right and wrong. . . . They do not adequately know the moral landscape of the real world that they inhabit. . . . They need some better moral maps and better-equipped guides to show them the way around.

Christian Smith[2]

Jordan grew up Catholic, but by his emerging adult years he no longer identified himself as having any religious affiliation. Within the past two years, he separated from one live-in girlfriend and was now cohabiting with his fiancée. Jordan lived according to a belief he referenced as "the full circle," an implicit conviction of reciprocity governing the world. If he did the right thing, God, or the forces at play in the world, would brings things to balance. Here is one narrative from an interview with Jordan:

> IBM [the company for which Jordan works] does their employee thing, charitable thing. We take food into God's Pantry (a charitable organization that distributes food and clothing to the needy). . . . Last Thanksgiving I was driving to work and listening to the radio. It was before Thanksgiving . . . they were saying that they were really short on turkeys. We were at work and we went to lunch and we were coming back from lunch. I told Holly, "Let's go to the store and buy some turkeys. Let's go buy God's Pantry some turkeys." . . . We went and bought eight or ten turkeys and dropped them off at God's Pantry.
>
> This is the full circle thing I was telling you about. . . . I went up to my parents' house for Thanksgiving. . . . I'm coming back home and it's raining about nine o'clock and I'm coming off the bypass . . . we're merging in traffic and there's this lady. It was raining and she was an old lady and she had no business being on the freeway . . . I was in her blind spot and she was probably going 45 miles an hour. She came over right and I smacked right into the back of her. I hit the corner and went spinning across I-75 at 65 miles an hour. If it hadn't been raining the Jeep would have flipped God knows how many times across that interstate. I did two 360s from the right hand all the way to the emergency lane on the left hand side. . . . I was coming through and I don't know how I missed other cars coming through there. . . . I had no idea how he missed me. I ended up stopping, stalled, facing oncoming traffic on I-75 and I didn't touch a thing. Nobody hit me; I didn't hit them. I hit her initially, but I was able to get the Jeep started and get off the road and everything was fine. I was thinking, "I used up all my turkeys, and I need to go buy some more." That is one of those things that I think; chances are maybe it's luck, maybe it's not. That's a full circle thing.

Jordan's story is noteworthy because it resonates with what others have reported from similar interviews. Christian Smith characterized emerging adults as "morally adrift," lacking consistency and coherence in their moral choices.[3] Jordan gropes to find the right framework for interpreting what has happened to him. Was his near-fatal accident simply chance? Or is there some force (karma perhaps) at work in the world that holds the balance between good and evil?[4] He does not offer language or an ideological system that compels him toward good. Morality is instead based in consequentialism, determined more by observing the effects of actual living than by processes of thought occurring in advance of a chosen behavior. What appears at first glance to be altruistic is in the end driven more by an individualistic need to build up enough credit in one's moral bank account to ensure immunity from harm.

The impulse to care for others comes from an anticipation of generalized reciprocity rather than a principled responsibility to seek the common good.[5]

But how might Jordan have arrived at this point? What accounts for his cultural construction of morality and the implicit values that shape his moral behavior? In earlier chapters, we provided a look at how twentysomethings have come to regard independence and self-creation as central tasks of emerging adulthood. We begin this chapter by suggesting that these factors have also shifted the value base for morality, rendering moral individualism the default position undergirding the emerging adult character.

Emerging Adults and Moral Individualism

Historically, shifts in American character education have altered the ways in which we think about morality in contemporary society. Through the work of common school leaders in the nineteenth century, progressive educators in the early twentieth century, and psychologists in the later twentieth century, the very meaning of character has been radically transformed. In broad strokes, up until the early nineteenth century, character was chiefly defined as adherence to the convictions of particular religious traditions. Rooted in a belief in the objective and external moral authority of God and his Word, conformity to his character and purposes represented the pinnacle of morality. In the nineteenth century, this began to shift a bit as public schools initiated plans for moral education marked by a more generic and inclusive form of character, a kind of middle-class civil religion anchored by pan-Protestant American ideals.[6] To develop a nonsectarian morality, character was no longer connected to a specific narrative or doctrinal foundation but rather to natural and universal moral laws that all could agree on. By the twentieth century, many liberal progressives had further removed moral education from religious sanctions, rejecting moral absolutes altogether. They tended to view moral development in terms of a democratic process, highlighting the ability to adapt and adjust to changing circumstances and social needs.[7]

This relativizing of morality found its ultimate expression in the psychological emphases of the later twentieth century. As David Wells and many others have argued, fewer leaders spoke in terms of "virtue" and "character," replacing these terms with references to "values" and "personality."[8] Values spoke more to personal preferences, divorced from any kind of external reference point. Rooted in emotivism, many began to believe that moral decisions were a matter of likes and dislikes, personal inclinations rather than rights and wrongs. Thus, the values clarification movement popularized in schools in the 1960s and 1970s emphasized commitment to personal ideals, whatever they might be, rather than adherence to a set of moral norms outside of the self. Morality was defined chiefly in terms of personal happiness and the therapeutic value of self-actualization rather than self-restraint. Much of this produced a kind of expressive individualism where the ultimate value was a freedom to express and live by one's own opinions and preferences. Detached from duty and obligation to external codes or communities, character emerged as a process of self-construction.

The focus on personality, as Warren Susman contends, entailed a move from solid character traits, such as honor and courage, to traits such as attractiveness and magnetism.[9] Drawing from the consumer mind-set of the salesperson, these traits were less about an unchanging inner character and more about the constantly evolving ways in which others perceived the individual. In such a setting, Wells suggests, individuals struggle less with guilt than with shame.[10] Guilt implies failure to conform to God's standards described in his revelatory Word. Shame, on the other hand, implies failure to meet others' expectations, a continually shifting standard based on social context. While the moral life formerly involved both, Wells argues that guilt has been minimized by the dissolution of an external moral order that is given rather than self-created. The irony here, of course, is that the desire to live authentically by one's own preferences is attended by a strong desire to form a persona acceptable to one's peers. Everyone is "true to themselves," but that self begins to look remarkably uniform, typically authorized by the consumer and media industries.[11]

Moral individualism is also related to the "thinning" of the communal moral fabric in emerging adulthood. Removed from family and home contexts, many rely on higher education institutions to fill the moral void. Yet while early colleges did sponsor moral education through Bible studies, codes of conduct, moral philosophy courses, and faculty modeling and mentoring, much of this has been discarded since the early twentieth century. Stemming from the adoption of German models of specialization and professionalization, faculty members are seldom chosen for their moral character. Separating facts and values, concern for morality is typically relocated to the co-curriculum and marginalized from the larger purposes of these institutions. Many institutions uphold a scientific ideal of "value-free" education, claiming moral neutrality in the unbiased search for truth and thereby divorcing intellect from character.[12] Universities teach professional ethics to keep graduates out of legal hassles and to uphold the respectability of their professions, but Dallas Willard maintains that "there is in fact no body of moral knowledge now operative in the institutions of knowledge in our culture."[13] It takes little imagination, and perhaps even less recent national historical memory, to consider the societal impact of highly educated leaders who have voided any sense of an internal moral compass.

Roy Baumeister and Mark Muraven argue that when identity was socially ascribed (i.e., formed by the expectations of others and implicit in social roles), tradition and culture functioned to ensure a natural, consensual morality that was subjectively experienced as objective fact.[14] Traditional virtues, culturally ingrained, lent positive value to certain ways of doing things. As emerging adults began orchestrating their lives to align with these proximal values, persuasive moral criteria aided everyday decision making and endowed life with personal meaning. Conversely, if emerging adults chose to ignore these social mores (e.g., moving in with one's girlfriend or boyfriend, succumbing to substance abuse, cheating on an exam, dressing provocatively), they would feel a public sense of disapproval. Indeed, for most of our nation's history, moral axioms constituted a sort of social contract that both safeguarded against rampant self-indulgence and established a sense of moral coherence in one's life.

As society gradually restructured around the preeminent values of individuality and freedom, however, these cultural shifts initiated a profound revision of the moral order.[15] Rather than morality serving as it has historically to curb self-interest, it now became realigned in such a way as to sanction and promote self-interest. Gratification of felt needs now seems justifiable because, after all, it is one's "right to choose." Consider the conventional belief that almost anything is regarded as sexually permissible as long as it is between "consenting adults." If one *chooses* to participate, what right does anyone else have to suggest that it is wrong? Or note the argument that is typically evoked in debates surrounding standards of decency in the media. Inevitably, an argument is made for a person's right to free speech. Unrestrained expression is legitimated on the basis of a presumably convincing argument: "If you don't like it, you don't have to watch it; *the choice is yours.*" Smith calculates that six out of ten of the emerging adults interviewed regarded morality as "a personal choice; entirely a matter of individual decision."[16]

Moral individualism of this kind creates a ripe context for three other "postures": moral intuitionism, a self-focused moral consequentialism, and moral privatization. Moral intuitionism refers to the fact that many emerging adults "believe that they know what is right and wrong by attending to the subjective feelings or intuitions that they sense within themselves."[17] When facing difficult moral decisions, most emerging adults say that they appeal chiefly to personal happiness or "feeling good" as the final court of appeal.[18] David Kinnaman found that emerging adults are "significantly more likely than older adults to say they do whatever feels comfortable or whatever causes the least amount of conflict."[19] Others depend on a sense of subjective peace, trusting internal feelings over any kind of external or social standards. The criteria for evaluating any kind of moral action, therefore, are found solely within the self.[20]

Moral consequentialism, on the other hand, refers to the fact that morals should be judged on the basis of their end results rather than any prior standard. While the evaluation of those "end results" may vary based on moral perspective, most emerging adults seem to judge on the basis of personal benefit or loss. As long as an action does not hurt other individuals (larger groups appear not to count), all moral decisions are based on positive personal outcomes. Many, it appears, even feel that rules may be broken without remorse as long as this results in personal advantage without pain to others.[21]

Finally, moral privatization speaks to the fact that many emerging adults feel that they should neither judge others nor be judged by others in matters of morality. As Smith found, most feel that they should never suggest a course of moral action to another. Since all are "self-directed choosers," each person has a right to be free from external suggestion.[22] Perhaps not surprisingly, judgment itself is often viewed as immoral, violating personal boundaries by foisting one's own moral opinion on another. Therefore, there is deep resistance to judging others for any moral claims or actions since each person is sovereign over his or her own moral boundaries.[23] These three postures—moral intuitionism, moral consequentialism, and moral privatization—define the "good" as anything that feels right to me, benefits me, and is determined by me. Such are the contours of a pervasive moral individualism.

These moral postures provide challenges for parents, Christian colleges and ministries working with emerging adults. The theological convictions of leaders compel them to transmit morals and practices through preaching, teaching, mandatory chapel attendance, ethos statements, and strict ethical standards. Yet many emerging adults feel a cultural mandate to explore, to resist the pronouncements of others as judgmentalism, to avoid moralizing, to keep options open, and to adopt their own moral perspectives without being told what to believe or do.[24] Christian parents face the tension when they must determine how far an emerging adult child should be allowed to explore within or beyond a homegrown morality and propriety. Should they force compliance or permit more freedom regarding issues such as appropriate dress, choices in music, dating partners, college and church choices, and living arrangments. Colleges and universities face the tension when making decisions on educational mission and community boundaries. Should they impose restrictive moral codes or allow more freedom in personal lifestyle decisions? Those ministering to emerging adults face the tension when they encounter individuals who raise questions about the tacit moral beliefs and practices of their youth. Are doubts indicative of growth toward intrinsic moral and religious convictions or of first steps toward dissent and abandonment of faith? How can leaders sustain the reality of moral authority while also honoring the emerging adult need for personal ownership of moral beliefs and actions?

Moral development theories provide one angle of vision. Typically, these theories begin with the view that the emerging adult experience builds on earlier stages of familial and parochial influence by exposing a young adult to a variety of experiences, worldviews and lifestyles, and moral dilemmas eventuating in a greater owning of beliefs and practices that are self-chosen (autonomy). Under the compulsion to take responsibility for their own lives, emerging adults move beyond conventional morality, away from "identification with" as a modus operandi, and toward becoming independent thinkers and moral philosophers.

Lawrence Kohlberg's moral development scheme, for example, elevates autonomous reasoning as representing advancement to a place where one grows through and beyond forms of moral judgment primarily on the basis of what solicits punishment—stage 1, what produces rewards that serve self-interest—stage 2, what meets the expectations for goodness of one's primary social group—stage 3, or what is dictated by law—stage 4. Rather, one becomes free in stage 5 to take into account many perspectives, locating the self as a legitimate voice within this council and then joining with others to fashion a social contract that promotes a just society. In the highest stage of moral functioning, stage 6, philosophical reasoning produces universal principles of justice that transcend concern for one's own group and emerge from a concern for the dignity and well-being of all people. Kohlberg envisioned this as a developmental move from preconventional (stages 1 and 2) to conventional (stages 3 and 4) to postconventional (stages 5 and 6) morality. Postconventional thinking is championed because it enables one to understand that what is established by custom or by authority figures is not always what is most realistic, authentic, or just.[25] Kohlberg's theory provides a useful heuristic for distinguishing various patterns of moral reasoning and providing a conceptual itinerary for moral growth.

Also influential here is William Perry's 1970 theory of ethical and intellectual development during the college years. Perry suggested that most students entered Harvard as *dualists*, perceiving the world in terms of moral absolutes with few gray areas. To the dualists, beliefs are derived from authority figures without conscious reflection. However, when dualists recognize that credible authority figures (such as parents and professors) disagree on some issues, cognitive dissonance occurs that results in a posture of *multiplicity*, a sense that everyone is entitled to their own opinions. They begin to think that absolutes are the exception rather than the rule. Authorities no longer hold the answers but are groping for truth along with the rest of the world. With time, Perry proposed that many students move from this stage to *relativism*, recognizing that opinions vary in quality and must be evaluated on the basis of evidence. Truth is relative to what each discipline or academic circle has come to believe and has to be evaluated on the basis of data. This epistemological shift, as depicted by Perry, can be quite disequilibrating to students and consequently can lead to a variety of outcomes: (1) pausing and plateauing, (2) retreating back to dualism with fundamentalist vigor, (3) escaping to academic disciplines that avoid multiplicity, (4) submerging into a subculture, or (5) reevaluating their own position toward an evolving commitment within a relativistic worldview.[26]

Decades ago, Ronald Duska and Mariellen Whelan offered the following (lengthy) illustration that attempted to capture in narrative expression the processes these theories were explaining:

> Imagine an isolated society completely surrounded by mountains, such that virtually no contact occurs with the outside world. Assume that such a group is organized according to a system of rules and taboos, each re-enforced with sanctions, either natural or conventional. Suppose further that one of the rules requires members of the tribe to attend a weekly ritual at a specified period of time and that the tribe also believes (with no established basis in fact) that not attending the ritual makes a member infectious to the other members, and thus they ostracize such an offender from the group for a period of a month. However, being a tribal society there has never been a way to verify the existence of the mysterious infectious powers. Now, suppose one of the members of the tribe violates the taboo, is indeed ostracized. While being temporarily expelled from the community, he climbs up the mountain and discovers a path to another valley whereby he encounters a new tribe with practices he has never seen before. They require no mandatory attendance at rituals and after welcoming him in, do not end up being infected by him. Furthermore, this tribe performs practices which were forbidden in his originating tribe, and they outlaw practices which were considered perfectly normal where he came from.
>
> Now, asks the developmentalist, if this wandering nomad left his own valley absolutely convinced that the rules of his tribe were universal, that is, were the best rules for society (and why should he not assume that, since he had encountered no other sets of rules?), what would this experience do to him? Wouldn't it make him aware of the fact that not everything he thought to be absolute or "the law" was necessarily the law? He would be exposed to other ways of doing things—other ways that did not lead to chaos. Might he then become skeptical of the correctness of his own tribe's rules? Might he not also become skeptical of the correctness of the foreign tribe's rules? Wouldn't he now be driven to wonder what is the best or ideal way of behaving and believing? The magical hold

that his picture of the proper order of things had over him would now become broken (unless, of course, he came to view these strange people as monsters).

Suppose further, that after his time of expulsion from his own tribe is completed, that this nomad decides to leave this new valley to return home and enlighten his people as to their wrongheadedness in some matters. On his return journey he took yet a different passage and encountered another tribe with yet different practices and rules. If this wanderer were bright enough and tolerant enough, would he not begin to view the rules of each society as relative to the beliefs and needs of that society? Would not a relativism begin to develop?

Finally, consider what might occur when he returns to his native tribe, exuberant that he has marvels to relate. Eagerly he tells the authorities that some of their practices are obsolete (or "old school" in common parlance), that there are better ways of doing some things, and that some practices they have been engaging in are actually detrimental to growth. How would such a declaration be accepted by the tribal chiefs or by the authorities who were the interpreters of the received law which was assumed absolute for all tribes everywhere? He would, needless to say, probably be punished as a harmful maverick. But what happens internally to him? Intellectually he may well become disillusioned about beliefs he previously held sacred. Further, since he is now alienated from the tribe because of these beliefs, he no longer feels the same emotional attachment to the group and becomes isolated. He needs society, he loves his home, but he is cut off from it because of his intellectual and moral awakening. He sees his tribe's rule no longer as special or sovereign, but as ranging alongside the rules of every other tribe, no longer providing him comfort and intellectual assurance that he is on the right way. He must think for himself, for there is no one to guide him. Having been forced out of the contentment of certitude and ease of practice in the rules of the community, he has nowhere to turn for comfort and solace except inward, having to figure out for himself what mores to follow.[27]

This type of paradigm has been both appreciated and held suspect by those in the faith community.[28] Such narratives and schematics provide important psychological insight into common processes that emerging adults experience in the transition away from family and in exposure to cultural diversity, offering strategic pedagogical insight in the formation of moral reasoning. As we discussed in chapter 3, this is an important phase of identity formation. However, there are cautions here. For example, such schemes can create the impression among emerging adults that a high regard for the authority of Scripture, teachings of the church, cultural sages, or family customs relegates them to positions of moral immaturity. If the telos of development is aimed at autonomy alone, faith orientations that call for submission to external authorities are often excluded.[29] As their early moralistic frameworks collide with other belief systems, many emerging adults will intellectually scrutinize their early frameworks and question their rigidity, legalism, certainty, and exclusivism. Change no doubt will occur, but movement into or through a period of "postconventional morality" (Kohlberg) or "unqualified relativism" (Perry) may suggest a more complete unmooring from their childhood moral framework than is actually experienced or desired.

If we regard the wandering nomad as the normative journey of emerging adulthood, we are likely to respond passively when faith practices are jettisoned, morality is disregarded, sexual explorations are engaged, and adults get rebuffed in the quest for independence. "After all," some might say, "this is what young adults are supposed to do when they are in college." But what if the appropriate metaphor for an emerging adult's journey is not "separate to educate," casting the nomad out of intergenerational community into a solitary pilgrimage? What if our model for developing emerging adult morality begins with a trinitarian view of personhood that sees individuation coexisting with a supportive community?[30] What if we awakened to the reality that moral shaping in the emerging adult years depends on social arrangements and a shared moral order that give plausibility to the moral life?

Important here is Smith's distinction between (1) a subjective embracing of objectively true moral claims, and (2) a belief that moral claims have a status of truth because they are subjectively embraced.[31] The first of these ideas is rooted in moral realism, the belief that objective moral truths exist independent of the self. The second moves in the direction of moral relativism, anchored by the assertion that "people believing something to be morally true is *what makes it* morally true."[32] The first—subjective moral realism—is grounded in the presupposition that objective moral truth exists but recognizes the importance of processes by which an individual comes to appropriate and internalize these truths as morally binding. The second— subjective moral relativism—dismisses objective truth and regards morality as personally constructed. In subjective moral realism, individuation, increased agency, perspective taking, and critical thought may all occur, but they do so as one gains a better apprehension of objective reality.[33] In moral relativism, these same processes generally occur by discarding childhood moorings and by customizing one's moral values much the way one stylizes a Facebook page, according to personal preference.[34]

To promote a subjective moral realism, a delicate balance is required. So-cial science research confirms that excessive control, demandingness, strict enforcement of rules, and unilateral discipline may correlate with compliance of behavior but produce little intrinsic motivation for morality. Conversely, passivity, permissiveness, and indifference correlate with a lack of self-reliance, lower exploratory behavior, and diminished self-control.[35] Locating a middle ground between these extremes, Diana Baumrind's framework of parenting styles describes what constitutes an optimum context for moral formation. Baumrind defines "authoritarian" posturing as demanding but not responsive and "permissive" posturing as responsive but not demanding. Balancing the two, "authoritative" posturing is both responsive and demanding.[36] Morally authoritative communities are created and sustained by a shared vision of what is good and by providing subsequent generations with both warmth and support in pursuit of that good.[37] The communities are defined more by a covenant based on a corporate authoritative vision than by control based on arbitrary rules. Implicit in studies that use the authoritative concept for promoting prosocial outcomes is the realization that moral formation is best forged not by *control* of behavior but by *closeness* of relationship around a set of shared values.[38]

As N. T. Wright has argued, however, our culture has produced a fragmented moral climate in which we vacillate back and forth between permissiveness and authoritarianism, freedom and law. We prize the ability to give people freedom to do what they want. Recognizing that unlimited freedom can be abused, however, we also escalate the formation of rules and laws that will restrain the negative aspects of this freedom. Interestingly, as Wright argues, this tends to generate a culture that defines morality in one of two ways. Some define morality as authenticity, doing whatever one wants and following the heart, being true to oneself. Harkening back to such sources as the nineteenth-century romantic movement, early twentieth-century existentialism, and emotivist impulses that root morality in preferences, this perspective falls directly in line with the emerging adult moral individualism and relativism outlined above. Others, alternatively, see morality as following the rules, behaving in ways that conform to the standards of the law. Rooted in legalism, this perspective highlights external actions and moral boundary markers, the dos and don'ts often imposed by parents, teachers, and ministry leaders. The therapeutic and moralistic aspects of emerging adult faith fit very nicely with these two mentalities.[39]

Both, however, miss out on the fullness of the character transformation promised in Scripture. A completely rule-based morality will never suffice. Rules, for one, can never cover every single situation and circumstance. Following the rules may work in certain cases, but what happens when one encounters a scenario not covered by any rule? There is a certain amount of improvisation necessary in the moral life, and we need a form of character development that will prepare emerging adults to respond well in the thousands of situations that are not covered by simple rules. Rules can legislate behavior but they are unable, in and of themselves, to transform the inner life. Adherence to rules can easily cloak a wicked, idolatrous heart. In addition, as John Coe has argued, even rule following represents a form of moral individualism, seeking good in the power of the self and "hiding" from God through attempts to seek goodness through personal resolve rather than the cross and personal transformation by the power of the Spirit.[40]

As opposed to rule following, character refers to something engraved into an object and thus is more akin to "the pattern of thinking and acting which runs right through someone, so that wherever you cut into them (as it were), you see the same person through and through."[41] True character formation, therefore, involves inner transformation in such a manner that the individual not only does the right things but "is right." The hope is that emerging adults will indeed obey God's rules, not simply out of a sense of external compulsion but out of a transformed character that is beginning to delight in the freedom of obedience.

The freedom of "following one's heart," however, is also problematic because the heart can be both desperately wicked and hard to evaluate. Authenticity provides no guarantee of moral excellence. There is something right about the impulse to be true to oneself (as opposed to a robotic adherence to rules), but only if that self is being conformed to the image of Christ and his standards. As Wright notes, freedom is not a right but a hard-won gift, the result of the effort and personal cost of character formation through the work of the Holy Spirit. We want to see emerging adults who can be virtuous naturally, but this "second nature" character can only come through submission to what feels at first like an unnatural process of moral formation involving both the joy and pain of transforming grace. As Wright summarizes,

> This transformation will mean that we do indeed "keep the rules"—though not out of a sense of externally imposed "duty," but out of the character that has been formed within us. And it will mean that we do indeed "follow our hearts" and "live authentically"—but only when, with that transformed character fully operative . . . the hard work up front bears fruit in spontaneous decisions and actions that reflect what has been formed deep within.[42]

Authoritative moral formation will resist both an authoritarian, rule-based mentality and a permissiveness that leaves emerging adults to their own autonomous moral lives. Instead, it proposes to provide authoritative guidance and support to twentysomethings in their growing personal commitments to shared objective values anchored by the biblical narrative. More than securing good behavior, character formation requires the deep engraving of the heart that comes through inner transformation, the development of a virtuous life.

The Shape of Virtue in Emerging Adulthood

Nikki Tousley and Brad Kallenberg recently proposed a three-fold definition of "virtues" that establishes helpful guidelines for how we might approach the process of emerging adult moral formation:

> Virtues are (1) habituated dispositions involving both an affective desire for the good and the skill to both discern and act accordingly; (2) learned through practice within a tradition (i.e., a historical community with a rich account of the "good"); and (3) directed toward this tradition's particular conception of the good (making virtues teleological).[43]

While many cognitive developmentalists focus chiefly on moral reasoning, the first part of this definition emphasizes that character involves cognitive, affective, and behavioral aspects of human life.[44] As Jay Wood has suggested, people who have the virtue of "compassion" would, first of all, be able to discern specific needs within their sphere of influence. They would also feel emotions that arouse deep sympathy for those who are suffering. In addition, they would act appropriately to ease the pain of those in hardship. All three of these domains are essential to the formation of virtuous dispositions. As Wood suggests, "Virtues . . . paradigmatically dispose us to think and feel and act in ways that contribute to ours and others' flourishing."[45] Even when virtuous individuals are not in situations that require them to act, they are still inclined to think, feel, and act virtuously because this is who they are at a very deep level.

By suggesting that virtues are dispositions aimed at certain ends that must be cultivated through practice, Tousley and Kallenberg provide a window into how we might foster moral formation in emerging adults' lives.[46] Following directly from such a definition, Wright suggests that any worthy approach to character development must account for three "steps": (1) aiming at the right goal—developing an appropriate telos or view of human flourishing, (2) figuring out the character strengths and virtues that can best contribute to that goal, and (3) determining how to foster these virtues so that they become deeply rooted and habitual over time.[47] These steps ensure that character formation will move beyond both the whims of personal choice and mere adherence to laws and rules. Instead, from a Christian point of view, the development of virtue draws on the purposes of the divine narrative and sees virtue as a set of habitual dispositions necessary to fulfill one's role in this larger story. As Wright notes, "For a start, [virtue] is a call not to specific acts of behavior but to a type of character. For another, it is a call to see oneself as having a role to play within a story, a story where there is one supreme

Character whose life is to be followed. And that Character seems to have his eye on a goal, and to be shaping his own life, and those of his followers, in relation to that goal."[48]

As leaders work with emerging adults, then, they must provide a moral telos—a vision of the divine purposes that set the stage for the moral life. This really makes moral formation a matter of cultivating wisdom. The Hebrew word that translates "wisdom" carries the meaning of "firm, fixed, or that which restrains." Attaining wisdom is therefore a process of acquiring a unified, well-ordered moral and spiritual life that aligns with the fixed realities and ends—the moral arc—built into the universe. As creation reflects the image of the moral God by which it was created, so will the "wise" seek to orient life according to the teleological structure of the world.[49] Alternatively, the "fool" will either deny this structure, refuse to live within its boundaries, or simply ignore opportunities to acknowledge and learn about its configuration.[50] Moral formation is therefore a formation in wisdom that conforms to the teleological shape of the world.[51]

The aim of such formation is human flourishing, but this entails far more than the Aristotelian vision of "happiness," or *eudaimonia*. Instead, as Wright suggests, the Christian telos anticipates a future eschatological hope in which we will be priests and rulers in the new heavens and new earth (Exod. 19:4–6; 1 Pet. 2:5, 9; Rom. 5:17). Looking forward to those roles, we recognize that in Jesus's life, death, and resurrection, this future life has already broken into our world. Following Jesus and empowered by the Holy Spirit, we therefore assume the twin vocational tasks of kingly mission and priestly worship. As kings (subregents), we reflect God's righteous purposes into the world, stewarding the created order in such a way as to reflect his rule. As priests, we "bring the loyalty and praise of that creation for its creator into love, speech, and conscious obedience."[52] Human flourishing thus has a teleological focus, directing us to lives marked by mission and worship, roles that last throughout earthly life and into eternity. Becoming virtuous as a Christian, therefore, means becoming the kind of people for whom this dual role is becoming "second nature."

Such a telos should determine which virtues are highlighted and which vices assiduously avoided. Aristotle focused on the so-called cardinal virtues of courage, justice, prudence, and temperance, but preparation for present and future roles as rulers and priests demands a bit more. In practicing now what we will be in the God-given New Jerusalem (and in a real sense already available in Christ), we must help emerging adults live into the virtues mentioned in various parts of Scripture. The Sermon on the Mount mentions humility, meekness, mercy, purity, and peacemaking (Matt. 5:3–10). Colossians mentions compassion, kindness, humility, gentleness, patience, forgiveness, and (above all) love (3:12–14). First Corinthians speaks of the distinctly Christian virtues of faith, hope, and love (13:13). The fruit of the Spirit in Galatians is defined by the qualities of love, joy, peace, patience, kindness, goodness, faithfulness, gentleness, and self-control (5:22–23).

Aristotle had little regard for many of these virtues—especially humility—but they are critically important in light of the kingdom telos of forming emerging adults as rulers and priests for kingdom citizenship. For rulers, those taking part in God's mission in the world, they cultivate postures of submission, stewardship, gracious care, and loving compassion toward those served. Virtues such as faith, hope, and patience also reflect an abiding sense that God is in control of the outcomes of this mission. For priests, these virtues ground the experience of worship as an expression of humble gratitude. They also support the prayer-filled intercessory role that emerging adults play in the lives of others. In both roles (rulers and priests), these less flashy ideals show that virtue is designed, by its very nature, to "point away from itself, and outward to God in worship and the world in mission."[53] When such virtues are connected to the broader telos, they are not arbitrary rules of goodness but rather significant qualities of life that fit us for our place within the divine narrative.

Such a teleological perspective, for example, highlights and clarifies the importance of emerging adult moral purity and holiness. Many twentysomethings question the importance of this virtue. Kinnaman's research seems to reveal that born-again Christians between the ages of 23 and 41 have much lower standards of personal purity than those in older generations.[54] Holiness can seem arbitrary and unnecessary when they wish to focus instead on the need to make a difference in the world or to fight for social justice. This must again, however, be seen in relation to the larger telos. Wright remarks that holiness provides a path to kingly ruling though on a small scale: "If they are to take redemptive responsibility for the whole of creation, they must now take responsibility for that one bit of creation over which they have the most obvious control—their own bodies."[55] In addition, since their bodies are offerings of worship (Rom. 12:1) and temples of the Holy Spirit (1 Cor. 6:19–20), holiness represents a critical means of performing their priestly roles.

Even more importantly, Scripture often connects purity to mission, indicating that holiness is a means of shining God's light into a dark world. This is why Paul calls on the Philippians to be "blameless and pure, 'children of God without fault in a warped and crooked generation.' Then you will shine among them like stars in the sky" (Phil. 2:15). Purity is not a path to personal pride and separatism but a means by which emerging adults can offer themselves to serve as cleansed vessels—God's lights to the world. As Wright suggests, "The call to holiness comes precisely because it is as genuine human beings that we will be able to sum up the praises of creation, and as genuine human beings that we will be able to bring God's justice, freedom, beauty, peace, and above all rescuing love to the world."[56] It is a call to be set apart from the world for the sake of the world and for worship. We need to move away from the old fundamentalist/modernist divide between those personally pure and socially irrelevant and those socially active and unconcerned with personal morality. In light of our telos, both are necessary and indeed intrinsically intertwined.

This eschatological vision also provides a strong rationale for the so-called intellectual virtues: teachableness, love of truth, honesty, reverence, tenacity, attentiveness, persistence, precision, and creativity, to name a few.[57] Christian academic learning requires a focus on such virtues, stressing the importance of moral formation in the acquisition and utilization of knowledge. Again, these anchor emerging adults' kingly mission and heighten their capacity for priestly worship. Priestly intellectual virtue can be seen, for example, in the case of reverence. "The fear of the LORD is the beginning of knowledge," declares the writer of Proverbs (1:7). Reverence is the response of the soul to that which has awe-filling power and goodness. To revere is to admit complete dependence on Christ, recognizing that one is neither the creator of the universe nor the sustainer of life. Reverence, therefore, requires a posturing of the mind and soul toward gratitude and receptivity in the vocation of learning, a sense that learning provides a window into the character and purposes of the sovereign God. It also considers education itself as an act of worship, an offering of the mind to Christ, and a growing capacity to see and highlight God's glory in both special and general revelation.

Also important here is the motivation of learning. One's passion for knowledge can be motivated by *curiosity*, what premodern Western Christians called *curiositas*. In their understanding, curiosity was an "appetite for the ownership of new knowledge," a desire for mastery and possession of something not yet known.[58] In pursuing the inquisitive drive to discover what is inside the wrapped box, the human genome, the marvels of space, or the intricate functioning of the human mind, knowledge can quickly become an end in itself, something to be conquered. One's passion for knowledge can also be motivated by *control*—the attempt to exercise mastery and gain power over the forces of nature, over ourselves, or over each other. However, the desire for control can "carry us toward ends we want to renounce."[59] Writing a couple of decades ago, Parker Palmer reflected on the producers of the atomic bomb who, feeling the irresistible urge to release the seemingly illimitable power of the knowledge that now lay in their minds, only paused to ask what their work had become on the day after Hiroshima.[60]

As alternatives to these vices, there are virtuous motivations for learning that embrace the Christian telos of worship and mission. Medieval Christians contrasted the vicious *curiositas* with *studiositas*, or studiousness. Rather than seeking possession, the studious person seeks participation, interacting with knowledge lovingly as a gift. "The curious," Paul Griffiths notes, "inhabit a world of objects, which can be sequestered and possessed; the studious inhabit a world of gifts, given things, which can be known by participation, but which, because of their very natures can never be possessed."[61] The moral posture of studiousness, therefore, is a loving, participatory relationship with the gift of knowledge, ultimately leading emerging adults to worship the Giver. The other key motivation is compassion. As Palmer notes, compassion aims not at exploitation, not at making a name for oneself, not at securing a passport to privilege. Rather, its aims are missional: mending the world, creating hospitable community, and binding us to each other and the world in love. "Curiosity and control," writes Palmer, "create a knowledge that distances us from each other and the world, allowing us to use what we know as a plaything and to play the game with our own self-serving rules. But a knowledge of love will implicate us in the web of life . . . it will call us to involvement, mutuality, accountability."[62] Paul was stunningly contemporary when he wrote that "knowledge puffs up while love builds up" (1 Cor. 8:1). Students who are compelled to pursue excellence in their coursework because education expands their capacity to worship and serve are qualitatively different from those who seek education for a chance at prestige or control.

The focus on virtue has the potential to reshape much of the current emerging adult moral landscape. In contrast with moral individualism, Christian virtue is focused not on personal self-interest but on the good of others and the glory of God. In contrast to a self-evident moral intuitionism, virtues require a purposeful cultivation and training of desire. Happiness and a sense of peace are no sure guides to moral excellence. Instead, virtue upheld by moral realism requires coordination with an external moral order outside of the self. In contrast with self-directed moral consequentialism that looks at results, virtue focuses more on the character of the person, the inner dispositions that produce external actions. In contrast with many of the theories of moral development that ask, "What are we to do?" when faced with moral dilemmas, virtues focus on training character, asking, "What kind of people ought we to be?" In Christian virtue ethics, the end conditions the means, so moral behavior is shaped not by a telos of personal freedom but by an ultimate vision of kingdom citizenship. Hence writes John, "Everyone who has this hope in him purifies himself, just as he is pure" (1 John 3:3).

Critical here is that these virtues are both gifts of God's grace and qualities in need of cultivation. The emphasis on "blessedness" in the Sermon on the Mount highlights the fact that these virtues are *given* by the gracious hand of God. The Sermon begins not with imperatives that impose "shoulds" upon people, the kind of religious diatribes resisted by most emerging adults. Rather, nine indicative statements are made, declaring that the reign of God is fully offered to all, even to moral failures. One gains these virtues not through intellect or will but by being open and receptive to unmerited favor. Unable to keep the commands of the law, we need the law written on our hearts (Jer. 31:33). We need the Spirit to "move [us] to follow [his] decrees and be careful to keep [his] laws" (Ezek. 36:27). The recipients of such grace and empowerment are blessed indeed.

Yet it is also clear that virtue formation requires effort. We may live by the Spirit, but we must also "keep in step" with the Spirit (Gal. 5:25). We are called to "take off" the old self and "put on" the new self, active verbs for virtue development. Proverbs says that wisdom must be sought by "making your ear attentive" and "inclining your heart" (2:2 ESV), also suggesting that youth must "seek it like silver" and "search for it as for hidden treasures" (2:4 ESV). It also seems clear that virtues can decline through neglect; they are weakened or lost as time erodes moral convictions, feelings, and actions.[63] As with spiritual formation, the call here is to repeatedly put oneself in a position where the Holy Spirit can transform the heart and renew the mind, practicing the virtues until they become habitual and ingrained, increasingly "natural" responses to life's circumstances. In the following section, we will mention just a few of the means by which this character formation process can be facilitated in the lives of emerging adults.

Pathways to Emerging Adult Moral Maturity

While there are many fruitful resources for facilitating moral formation in emerging adults' lives, we wish to briefly highlight five that seem essential to the lifelong process of virtue development: stories, exemplars, practices, communities, and conscience catalysts. A first critical element in the practice of moral formation is engagement with stories. We must surround twentysomethings with stories, most prominently the story of Scripture but also other stories that demonstrate lived character in context. Stories—including great works of literature, history, and film—can furnish the moral imagination with examples of virtuous (and immoral) living, tracing the sources and consequences of such lives. Study of the biblical story will provide not only key moral ideals and principles but also the larger story within which all of these virtues make sense. It seems likely that one of the key reasons many Christians abandon adolescent moral codes in emerging adulthood is that their moral identities were not rooted within the divine story. Without a coherent redemptive story to explain these ideals, moral commands can appear as legalistic codes devoid of purpose. As Stanley Hauerwas suggests, "The development of character involves more than adherence to principles for their own sake; rather, it demands that we acquire a narrative that gives us the skill to fit what we do and do not do into a coherent account sufficient to claim our life as our own."[64] The moral instruction to forgive, or to show love to the foreigner, or to show justice for the poor all take on different meanings when we locate ourselves as people ransomed from our own sins, strangers to God's holiness and yet included in his economy of grace. If not linked to the broader story and their place within it, such morals can be easily abandoned when emerging adults leave home. As Alasdair MacIntyre suggests, "I can only answer the question, 'What am I to do?' if I can answer the prior question, 'Of what story or stories do I find myself a part?' . . . Deprive children of stories and you leave them unscripted, anxious stutterers in their actions as in their words."[65] Emerging adults must be called to Christian moral living not only because it is what they should do but also because it is who they are and where they are going. Stories remind them of this reality.

Second, moral exemplars (role models) are necessary for emerging adults to form a concrete picture of the moral life. The biblical authors used such a technique repeatedly. Paul implored the Philippians to model certain aspects of their character after himself but also after such leaders as Timothy and Epaphroditus (Phil. 2:19–30; 3:17; 4:9). James called attention to Elijah as a model of prayerfulness (James 5:17–18). The author of Hebrews obviously called attention to the faith-filled lives of many of the former saints, "a great cloud of witnesses" capable of motivating action. In addition, the letter's recipients were encouraged to look at their leaders, to consider the outcomes of their lives, and to imitate their faith (Heb. 13:7). In addition, Scripture does not shy away from using negative moral examples as warnings of what to avoid—Esau and Lot's wife come to mind (Heb. 12:16; Luke 17:32). Such lives provide vivid illustrations of the paths to moral degradation. We will discuss personal modeling more in the chapter about mentoring, but it is important to note that emerging adults need moral exemplars who can show them how to live out the virtues in daily life experience, providing historical, literary, and real-world case studies of human flourishing (and decay) for their consideration. This can come through written or verbal testimony, but it happens best through regular contact with role models who can demonstrate virtuous thinking, feeling, and acting in the midst of real-life circumstances. As Hauerwas and Thomas Shaffer remind us,

> Our claim is this: Not only does hope employ and give the basis for certain skills, but it is a skill. It is a skill which one learns. We do not learn to lay bricks without guidance from masters; neither do we learn how to hope without guidance from masters. . . . If the moral life is inseparable from the life of wisdom, then, in spite of modern philosophy's attempt to secure an independent status for "morality," our moral lives as lived continue to depend on the existence of masters.[66]

Third, moral formation is absolutely dependent on repeated practices that inculcate virtuous habits. Every moral community develops particular rituals and practices that highlight the virtues of that tradition.[67] While the Holy Spirit is ultimately responsible for transformation, character must be learned through practice and habituation, reinforcing virtuous thoughts, feelings, and actions repeatedly until they become second nature over time. Some practices, such as Bible study, sitting under weekly preaching, and singing, will remind emerging adults of the larger telos, helping them to remember who they are and where they are going. Others will give them time and opportunity to practice the virtues. Prayer, for example, serves as a practice that can train emerging adults in faith, hope, and love as well as open doors for patience, humility, and peace. Practices of giving similarly inculcate virtues of love, faith, hope, humility, kindness, and compassion. Corporate confession reinforces postures of humility, meekness, and self-control. Regular practices of service strengthen virtues of humility, kindness, faithfulness, and compassion. These kinds of practices are disciplined ways of living toward the ultimate telos, developing virtues that, through repetition, become instinctual ways of thinking, feeling, and living.[68]

A fourth critical element of moral formation is the social context of community. Most of the virtues are communal virtues, dispositions that must be lived out among others. As mentioned previously, a moral community provides a powerful means of establishing a shared teleological and practical vision within which emerging adults can live and learn.[69] Friendships, therefore, become key locations for virtue formation. As Arthur Holmes indicates, "Consider that good friendship requires unselfishness, loyalty, sympathy, habitual consideration of another's needs; it contributes the wisdom and experience of others, common goals for moral development, emotional support in cultivating needed habits, the conscience of an alter ego to prod one's own. . . . A friend's values are next in importance to my own."[70] On the other hand,

Proverbs warns the reader, "Do not make friends with a hot-tempered person, / do not associate with one easily angered, / or you may learn their ways / and get yourself ensnared" (22:24–25). With regard to emerging adult virtue, it is indeed true that "the righteous choose their friends carefully, / but the way of the wicked leads them astray" (12:26).

Finally, conscience catalysts—discussions, experiences, and events that trigger moral awareness—can be important means of linking virtue with real-world experience.[71] Some of this can arise through simple teaching and discussions related to moral issues, social concerns, or portrayals of ethical quandaries in books and movies. Alternatively, consciousness-raising experiences can be a potent means of developing conscience. Ministry experiences in settings marked by poverty and homelessness can sensitize students to needs by giving emerging adults firsthand contact with people struggling in these circumstances. David White argues persuasively that without active experiments that engage students with the physical, political, and social problems of contemporary society, faith easily becomes co-opted by our lifestyles and shaped by cultural forces that simply maintain class status.[72] Developing partnerships in cross-cultural missions, assigning class projects that address particular social issues, reading texts by international authors, structuring service projects to underdeveloped parts of the city—all have transformative power to develop empathy and a concern for justice in the lives of emerging adults. When supplemented with discussion, such encounters can arouse cognitive, affective, and behavioral compassion within emerging adults who are often exposed to such needs only through the safe and distant filters of television and the internet. A missional moral formation requires that emerging adults learn to care and to take responsibility—this can only come through the development of a strong conscience.

These five components of character formation were all exemplified in the ministry of Jesus with his disciples. His moral instructions were couched in the context of the story of redemption and his own life, death, and resurrection. He exemplified virtue as the perfect model of the fully human life. He demonstrated and led his disciples into practices of prayer, service, hospitality, and ministry so that they would be continually connected to and dependent on God and the kingdom life. Through failure and success, blessing and betrayal, in community the apostles helped each other to be faithful to the moral call and to persist through the pain of the crucifixion. Jesus repeatedly brought his disciples into situations where they could minister among the poor, the sick, and the grieving, raising their consciousness of spiritual, physical, and emotional need. Without question, Jesus's discipleship method was a holistic curriculum of moral formation.

This kind of morally authoritative community is needed now more than ever. Smith's quote at the beginning of the chapter describes emerging adults, like Jordan, as a "people deprived," devoid of the training necessary to equip them for consistent moral living. Smith suggests that twentysomethings need "maps" and "guides" to outline the moral landscape and provide direction for lives of character.[73] For parents, professors, pastors, and ministry leaders, this is an absolute necessity in our world. As we, in our homes, schools, churches, and ministries, inculcate emerging adults into moral traditions populated with stories, moral exemplars, practices, communities, and conscience catalysts, we invite them into a shared world that frees them from the self-absorption of moral individualism. Moving beyond the freedom that ultimately enslaves, they can begin to develop a true moral freedom, born of the inner transformation that makes virtue both understandable and habitual. To facilitate this movement, we must help them see the telos that shapes their actions, the virtues that support these larger ends, and the divine and human resources that exist to form them for a flourishing and virtuous Christian life.

7 | Sexuality

Forming a Sexual Ethic

Our society is filled with people for whom the sexual relationship is one where body meets body but where person fails to meet person; where the immediate need for sexual gratification is satisfied but where the deeper need for companionship and understanding is left untouched. The result is that the relationship leads not to fulfillment but to a half-conscious sense of incompleteness, of inner loneliness, which is so much the sickness of our time. The desire to know another person's nakedness is really the desire to know . . . to know and to be known, not just sexually but as a total human being. It is the desire for a relationship where each gives not just of one's own body but of one's own self, body and spirit both, for the other's gladness.

Frederick Buechner[1]

(Chris) was curious how my friends Dana Taylor and Kary Reid would open an undergraduate class discussion on sexuality. They had been teaching sexuality classes and practicing marriage and family counseling for decades, so I anticipated a creative and engaging class. It was Dana who began the address to the class. Requesting a show of hands, she asked, "How many of you have been sexual today?"

Like most of the students sitting around me, the question immediately got my attention. What did Dana mean by this question? What was she driving at? After an awkward pause, a few students seemed to catch on. Dana was not asking a question about their recent erotic thoughts or behaviors but was asking a deeper question about whether they had come to recognize and own the gift of being created as sexual beings.[2] Finally, after what felt like an eternity, a few brave souls raised their hands, willing to admit that they had been sexual that day.

Pedagogically, the question served us well. In the opening minutes of class, we had inwardly come to own our sexual selves even as we felt again the culturally ambiguous messages that accompany sexuality. For emerging adults, those cultural messages are indeed powerful and pervasive, inculcated by peers, the media, celebrities, and social institutions. In this chapter, we want to explore the changing nature of romantic relationships in contemporary culture, tracing the evolution of current patterns. We then describe the outlines of a relational sexual ethic framed by an understanding of Paul's approach to these issues in 1 Corinthians. In the midst of the confusing cacophony of voices competing for emerging adults' attention, leaders in churches, on college campuses, and in other ministry settings have an awesome opportunity to furnish countercultural biblical wisdom on relationships and sexuality as they walk alongside those under their care.[3]

A Brief History of Romantic Love in America

Present approaches to relationship formation differ markedly from those of previous eras. In the nineteenth century and into the early 1900s, the common courtship practice was one of "calling."[4] Prompted by an invitation, a young man paid a visit to a young woman's home. As part of the custom, the young man was introduced to the woman's family. This was a critical moment because the family functioned to monitor, regulate, and approve or disapprove of the relationship.[5] Some time was typically structured for the couple to be together, perhaps in the family parlor. The purpose of "calling" was to engage in conversation and to partake of refreshments the young woman and/or her mother had prepared. To call on a young woman implied serious intent to marry, providing clarity about the relationship's status to the couple, to the family, and to those in the broader social network. Physical contact was limited both because of social expectations and because of the close proximity of family members. Victorian ideals of purity and chastity certainly bolstered these conventions, but they also promoted a double standard. Many supposed that men, on the one hand, had sexual needs requiring expression, making it permissible for them to visit a brothel. "Proper" women, on the other hand, were to keep themselves pure for marriage.[6] Virginity was regarded as the woman's "jewel" that she would bestow on her beloved on their wedding night.[7] Premarital sexuality, therefore, was atypical and judged harshly by the general public.

The roaring twenties ushered in a new standard, located not in "calling" but in "dating." The arrival of the automobile altered the geography, and therefore the social context, of relationship formation. No longer confined to the family parlor, couples could "go out" of the home to restaurants, theaters, dance halls, or church socials. Removed from the watchful eyes of parents, a "dating" couple experienced a great deal of unencumbered freedom. Though premarital sex was still uncommon, passionate kissing and intimate contact in the "rumble seat" of the car breached the strict taboos of chastity before marriage and positioned physical intimacy as central to a relationship.[8] Dating freed young women from the surveillance of parents but made them more dependent on men to initiate a date and more vulnerable to demands for sexual favors in exchange for money spent on food and entertainment. By the 1920s, sexual expression between men and women was deemed more acceptable, commensurate to the perceived level of commitment. "Permissiveness with affection" assumed that intimate affairs needed the protection of trust that could only be ensured within a fully committed relationship headed for marriage.[9]

While these trends largely continued from the 1920s to the 1960s, two notable changes altered the contexts of such dating practices. First, the median age for marriage actually declined during this period, from 24.6 to 22.8 for men and from 21.2 to 20.3 for women.[10] As Jeffrey Arnett proposes, this likely meant that dating "became more serious at an earlier age," leading many to seek engagement during high school (after "going steady") and marriage soon after graduation.[11] Second, with the large increase in college attendance after World War II, college campuses became important settings for dating and finding a mate. Initially, college officials were expected to act in loco parentis ("in the place of a parent") by enforcing curfews, prohibiting co-ed living arrangements, and ensuring that women kept their dorm room doors open if a man was visiting. However, such standards loosened a bit during this period, providing an unprecedented freedom for those now far removed from home. By midcentury, about 40 percent of collegians reported having sex at least once.[12]

Social and sexual revolutions in the 1960s and 1970s undermined a number of traditional relational norms. The publication of the Kinsey reports (that described human sexual behavior based on thousands of interviews), Hugh Hefner's launching of *Playboy*, and the widespread availability of birth control allowed more sexual permissiveness. Customary male-initiated patterns of dating came to be regarded as sexist, and prohibitions against premarital sex were regarded as restrictive and antiquated. The birth control pill separated sexuality from childbearing, eliminating the physical consequences that had supported a natural connection between marriage and sexual relationships. "Permissiveness without affection" supported the idea that sex could be a recreational activity, no longer requiring personal commitment and often void of authentic intimacy.[13] By the mid-1970s, 75 percent of college students reported having sex, a 35 percent increase from twenty-five years earlier. "Serial monogamy"—a series of love relationships—became the new idealized pattern, and the typical age for marriage began a gradual ascent that continues to this day.[14]

In the current age, emerging adult dating has morphed in significant ways. Serial monogamy has evolved into a "hookup" culture. This phrase refers to a variety of different behaviors—anything from "hanging out" to "making out" to sexual activity.[15] Often beginning at parties or in bars and frequently fueled by alcohol ("liquid courage"), hookup culture generally favors single encounters with little or no commitment for further relationship. Friendships may turn into "friends with benefits," involving physical intimacy but devoid of any romantic context or future trajectory.[16] Colleges have obviously created settings ripe for such interactions by eliminating curfews, allowing for co-ed dorms and floors, and turning a blind eye to the steady flow of alcohol on campus. As many authors have suggested, such configurations disproportionately harm women, who not only risk pregnancy but also subject themselves to male advances with little emotional or relational return. On college campuses, some have spoken of the female "walk of shame," the morning journey back to their dorm or apartment after a liaison that will likely lead nowhere.[17]

Hookup culture still supports the double standard. Parental messages to sons in college often include appeals to exploration and pleasure, whereas messages to daughters center on restrictions, protective issues, and the negative consequences of promiscuity.[18] Men are given all the power positions and women carry the burden of constantly balancing how to be appropriately sexy as defined by their subculture without turning easy or slutty.[19] Paradoxically, the more culture promotes a liberated sexuality of easy access, the more it seems to create imbalances of power between genders. To further complicate things, women and men often view acts of intimacy quite differently. Women are more likely to connect sex with emotional commitment and feel a greater sense of betrayal when an intimate connection turns out to be short-lived. On the contrary, some men regard sexual conquests as boosts to self-esteem and may never intend long-term commitment. Derek Kreager and Jeremy Staff found that a greater number of sexual partners diminishes a woman's acceptance among her female friends. To the contrary, a young man's popularity within his peer group tends to increase along with the number of sexual partners.[20]

Mark Regnerus and Jeremy Uecker clarify this historical shift using a theory of sexual economics.[21] Though supported by much more than we can elaborate here, they contend that the "cost" and "exchange value" of sex is negotiated between partners both interpersonally and socially. Though inequitable, the woman is typically the one determining when to consent to male desire (in the language of economics, men have a high demand for sex, and so women get to set the price).[22] Since marriage historically was the chief "location" for men to find sexual fulfillment and relational care, women were able to establish a higher price for sexuality, demanding relational stability and financial security in return. Today, however, the availability of pornography, birth control, and social media relationships have all "cheapened" the price of sex.[23] In the current emerging adult sexual economy, it appears that it is not terribly difficult to come by "free" sex—sex requiring little relational commitment or sustained faithfulness from men. Free sex diminishes the incentive for working at romance or intimacy. Sex becomes "associational" rather than "relational."[24]

These trends obviously generate new patterns when compared to the practices of previous eras. Vestiges of previous decades remain in traditional adolescent customs of homecoming dances and proms and in the conventional practice of fathers "giving the bride away."[25] Some elements of social regulation resurface with a contemporary twist, such as the purity pledge or purity ring designed to vouchsafe a woman's virginity prior to marriage. Yet while "calling" and "dating" were aimed at marriage (and fun), "hooking up" is aimed purely at fun of a more explicitly sexual nature. While former relationship formation provided clarity about a couple's status, Christian Smith notes that current opposite-sex relationships are often "amorphous."[26] Young adults have difficulty naming and distinguishing between different types of romantic relationships, creating confusion in defining interactions and commitment levels. Yet despite all of this, it is important to note that emerging adults still seem to yearn for an eventual lifelong, monogamous relationship. Arnett reports that most emerging adults come to desire the stability and comfort of a long-term relationship with a person who seems to fit them just right—the proverbial "soul mate."[27]

The way this search unfolds, however, is also changing. The delay of first marriage is one of the most significant factors influencing relationship formation in our current era. Ninety percent of Americans still get married, but the average marriage age is nearly 28 for men and 26 for women with age 30 constituting a sort of hypothetical finishing line for "settling down."[28] Women perhaps feel a bit more pressure to marry by this time because they are cognizant of their biological clock and are fearful that choices may be markedly reduced after age 30 as men seek "younger models."[29] Men, however, seem quite willing to wait for longer periods of time, especially if they are already involved in a sexual relationship. Regardless, this delay means that many college students are not really thinking much about marriage during their college years, viewing a committed relationship as something that is still off in a distant future. As Arnett attests, emerging adults are frequently "meandering toward marriage."[30]

There are many reasons for such delays, some objective and some more subjective. Economic changes have created a context in which more education is needed to secure desired jobs. This tends to delay the financial security often desired before beginning a marriage. Women in particular may feel less of a need to marry young. With more education (women outnumber men in colleges and universities and often equal or outnumber them in graduate programs) and greater career opportunities, women are less dependent on marriage for financial and social status.[31] While the biological clock is a reality, reproductive technology also secures options for later childbearing that previous generations of women did not have. The widespread availability of birth control and the cultural tolerance for premarital sexual activity means that individuals no longer need to get married to enjoy a sexual relationship.

Subjective factors are also at play. Many have grown up in the shadow of divorce and are wary of commitments in general. They want to take extra time to be sure that a relationship will work, attempting to avoid the pain of past experiences. Some simply avoid marriage because they still desire freedom to explore, travel, experience life on their own, and develop a strong personal identity. As the common description of marriage as a "ball and chain" would imply, this commitment is often viewed as the end of the carefree possibilities of emerging adult life. Finally, the very meaning of marriage has changed within an emerging adult culture marked by individualistic pursuits.[32] As Andrew Cherlin has remarked, marriage is now "less of a social role and more of an individual achievement—a symbol of successful self-development."[33] Many emerging adults see marriage not as part of the pathway to adult maturity but as the culmination of that pathway, a relationship to engage once their individual achievements are in hand. "Most young Americans no longer think of marriage as a formative institution," notes Regnerus, "but rather as the institution they enter once they think they are fully formed."[34] If viewed this way, marriage is often delayed until personal dreams have been fulfilled. Marriage is often seen as the final lynchpin of that success. "It has become," Cherlin suggests, "the ultimate merit badge—the marriage badge."[35]

It also seems apparent that there is an overriding pessimism about the institution of marriage among contemporary emerging adults. Despite evidence to the contrary, many seem to think that most married people are unhappy in their relationships. Such a perspective can arise from multiple sources: divorce statistics, personal relationships with those who are struggling, the media, and so on. However, it may also be a function of the changing understanding of the meaning of marriage. In past centuries, as Timothy Keller has pointed out, marriage was often viewed as a God-ordained social contract, designed to reflect God's purposes for the good of the world.[36] In the current era, marriage is more often defined in terms of finding a "soul mate," a person who will assist in the development of individual satisfaction and fulfillment. According to Barbara Dafoe Whitehead and David Popenoe, the soul mate is portrayed chiefly in two ways: someone who can offer peak sexual fulfillment and someone who displays a "willingness to take them as they are and not change them."[37] Obviously, this vision generates unrealistic expectations that can never be fulfilled. This kind of idealism can both prime individuals for a protracted search for "the one" and promote a quick divorce if the new spouse fails to meet these exacting standards.

While marriage is often delayed, this does not mean that emerging adults have stopped living together within the context of romantic relationships. Studies have reported that somewhere between half and two-thirds of emerging adults live with a romantic partner before marriage, creating what is arguably the most significant shift in family demographics in the past century.[38] Living together out of wedlock—typically termed "cohabitation"—is less often stigmatized than in the past, representing a crisis in confidence over the institution of marriage. The percentages of both men and women that eventually marry have also been on the decline. In 1987, the number of cohabiters who eventually married was 57 percent, but by 2004 that number was already down to 40 percent. Not only do the majority of young adults cohabit before marriage, but they also have children; nearly half of all out-of-wedlock births are linked to cohabiting mothers.[39] About 40 percent of all children in America are expected to spend some time in a cohabiting household during their growing-up years. Cohabitation therefore affects the lives of some two million children, creating what some regard as America's most serious social issue.[40]

Couples cohabit for a variety of reasons. Some confide that they cohabit for love, companionship, sexual exclusivity, finances, ambivalence, loneliness, or even peer pressure. Considering the variety of these motivations, Jack Balswick and Judith Balswick pose an intriguing question: "Is cohabitation an alternative to being married or an alternative to being single?"[41] Are cohabiters primarily seeking companionship and avoiding loneliness, in essence numbing the pain of singleness with sex, never intending to move into a committed relationship? Or is cohabitation a prelude to marriage? The Balswicks cite studies that suggest four different categories of cohabiters, each representing a different relationship to marriage. "Premarital cohabiters" anticipate an eventual marriage. "Uncommitted cohabiters" seek sexual privileges without formalized contracts. "Semi-cohabiters" maintain two houses for appearance and periods of separation but generally stay with each other. "Committed cohabiters" stay together but are biased against traditional marriage and never intend to have a public service.[42]

Some cohabiting couples may end up marrying on account of relationship inertia, regardless of whether there is a good relational fit.[43] Whenever a couple cohabits, they inevitably build constraints that make leaving the relationship more difficult. Comingled resources, sharing a lease, pregnancy, the perception of few alternatives to the current partner, and the difficult process of terminating the relationship compel couples to *slide* toward marriage. However, despite the intermingling of lives, there is nothing inherent in the process that necessarily increases levels of commitment or dedication. Research is discovering that a majority of cohabiting couples start living together via a "non-deliberative and incremental process" that involves little *deciding*.[44] Rather, after seeing each other for several months, a partner stays overnight. This becomes increasingly regular, more and more belongings are left at the partner's residence, and the couple drifts into living together but with ambiguity about the future of the relationship.

For many emerging adults, the avoidance of marriage is often motivated by fear. Having witnessed pain from their parents' and/or others' bad marriage or divorce, they desperately want to avoid making the same mistake. So, they buy into a cultural myth that cohabitation provides a "test-drive" of the relationship, which will allow them to (1) separate and avoid the difficulty of divorce if the relationship is not satisfactory, or (2) ride the relational inertia toward marriage.[45] Neither has proved to be a very effective strategy. Cohabitation is disconnected from the covenantal idea of love and marriage, where commitment and permanence give the security and safety one needs to be fully vulnerable to a partner. People begin withholding themselves from a relationship (while still sharing their bodies) in case it does not work out. They pass sexual thresholds without securing the corresponding level of trust. According to some studies, in about 70 percent of cases the tentativeness at the outset of cohabitation proves to be a self-fulfilling prophecy.[46] Cohabiting couples have less interaction, more disagreements, exhibit a greater likelihood of instability, and have a 50 percent higher hazard rate of divorcing after marriage than couples that had not cohabited.[47] As one might anticipate, cohabiting with previous partners prior to marriage likewise has a marked negative influence on the marriage and increases the likelihood of a couple experiencing infidelity in their marriage.[48]

All of this obviously points to an increasingly sexualized emerging adult culture. The average age of first intercourse (evangelical Protestants included) hovers at around 16, meaning that many will have sexual experience even before entering the emerging adult years.[49] Regnerus and Uecker conclude from their extensive studies that about 84 percent of Americans between the ages of 18 and 23 have had sex.[50] By some estimates, this percentage may top 90 percent by age 24.[51] Regarding this as "premarital sex" is now a bit of a misnomer since most sexual activity is not experienced with a partner that eventually becomes one's spouse.[52] The *Chicago Tribune*, in December 2009, reported that one in four teens says they have "sexted" a nude picture of themselves, and about a third admitted to having asked someone to send a nude picture to them.[53] The enigmatic phrase "friends with benefits" captures the curious relationship between friendship and sexuality, with 15 percent of females and 27 percent of males reporting an experience of sexual intercourse in a non-romantic relationship.[54] Statistics also verify the predictably sexual nature of typical emerging adult relationships. According to estimates, only 6 percent of 18- to 23-year-olds are currently in a dating relationship and not sexually involved.[55] Sex and dating, it appears, are nearly inseparable.

The prevalence of sexual activity and the normalizing of casual sexual encounters for emerging adults create quite a dilemma for emerging adults serious about their faith. Smith surmises that emerging adults have three choices: (1) they can choose to reject heavy partying and premarital sex—usually by belonging to a religious subculture or evangelical college or church community that encourages abstinence outside of marriage, (2) they can compartmentalize their lives so that partying and sex are partitioned off from religious activities in a way that borders on denial, or (3) they can live with the cognitive dissonance of being committed to two incompatibilities.[56] The following anecdote from one of Smith's interviewees captures the dilemma and frequent acquiescence experienced by many collegians:

> I always did believe what I do now [about not having sex before marriage], but I just thought, whatever. Whatever I wanted I just went for. I saw the importance of waiting but I kind of just went with how I felt and what I wanted. . . . I was feeling guilty, feeling dirty and "easy," all of those things. . . . But I was hard-headed. I should have just listened to people but [I didn't]. I have a lot of regrets.[57]

Sadly, this is not an isolated case. Robert Wuthnow points out that evangelical Protestants are the most likely to assert that premarital sex is always wrong (about 42 percent at the end of the twentieth century). However, profession and practice are not the same. According to his research, 69 percent of unmarried evangelicals (age 21–45) admitted to having sex with at least one partner during the past year. One study estimated that about 30 percent of unmarried evangelical women (age 18–29) have experienced a pregnancy. While many of the stated beliefs against sex outside of marriage remain unchanged among evangelicals, practices have not followed suit. Whatever the causes, we must acknowledge that this is an issue for emerging adults both inside and outside the church.[58]

Various media forms exacerbate cultural norms along these lines. Perhaps most importantly, internet pornography has escalated as a critical emerging adult problem.[59] While access to pornographic materials was challenging in previous generations—often requiring one to purchase materials in public settings—the internet has reduced the threshold to a simple click in the privacy of one's own home. According to recent statistics, 86 percent of male college students view pornography at least once per month. Among the broader emerging adult population, one scholar estimates that about half of all men in this age group view pornography weekly and about 20 percent daily.[60] More and more seem to view this as an acceptable practice. One study revealed that among emerging adults, 67 percent of men and 49 percent of women see pornography use as acceptable.[61] Another study found that only 18 percent felt "embarrassed" and 24 percent "guilty" about their pornography use.[62] Christian emerging adult men obviously feel more guilt about these practices, but the power of normalization should not be underestimated. Repeated pornography use among male emerging adults has been linked with alcohol and drug use, depression, low self-esteem, and both sexual promiscuity and violence. It also has the tendency to separate the physical from the emotional/relational aspects of sexual intimacy, leading to compartmentalized patterns that can continue within marriage. For women, the prevalence of this practice among men can often lead to body image problems, anxiety, and relational discord.[63]

Other media sources also shape sexual norms. One source noted that 9 out of 10 prime-time television sitcoms contain sexual material. Although rating systems are in place, these often provide little guidance regarding the quantity of provocative content. Magazines and billboards attract viewers through sexual images that are hard to avoid. Advertisements on otherwise acceptable websites can lure emerging adults into temptation without willful intent. The assumed social scripts that come through media outlets and friends both shape and reflect common practice. A steady diet of prime-time television communicates that long-term exclusive relationships are boring and inferior to serial encounters with new acquaintances. It communicates the "boys will be boys" philosophy that depicts men ruled by hormones with women playing along so as to secure desired relationships. It communicates a belief that sex doesn't mean anything, that it is just a common and expected activity in any relationship that is progressing in positive ways. It normalizes the "obscenity, foolish talk or course joking" (Eph. 5:4) that pervades emerging adult speech patterns. Is it any wonder that emerging adults' expectations begin to mirror these realities?

Perceptions molded by the media can be very important in shaping behavior. Studies have shown that most college students greatly overestimate the number of people having sex on the campus, leading them to feel isolated and unusual if they are not active themselves. The National College Health Association survey of over 29,000 college students in 2002 found that students assumed that only 2 percent of their peers were sexually inactive when in reality 24 percent of the peer group reported themselves to be sexually inactive. Likewise, students estimated that about 85 percent of their peers have had two or more sexual partners when the actual report data revealed the percentage to be 28 percent.[64] The pressure many feel to include sex in their relationships may indeed come from inaccurate perceptions of widespread sexual activity.

In the midst of all of these factors, emerging adults experience devastating breakups and significant relational grief. In a survey conducted at Case Western Reserve, 93 percent of both male and female students reported being spurned by someone they adored, and 95 percent reported rejecting someone who was deeply in love with them.[65] Seventy percent of emerging adults reflect in hindsight that their first intercourse took place when they were too young. Drawn in by curiosity, they discovered themselves too immature to appreciate the significance of what they were doing.[66] Precocious sexual activity is associated with lower academic performance, emotional turmoil, depression, and weakened attachment to others.[67] Many are forced to deal with even weightier issues such as sexually transmitted diseases, pregnancy scares, actual pregnancies, abortions, and adoptions. Such experiences, which again seem to disproportionately affect women, reveal what Smith describes as the "shadow side of sexual liberation."[68] The exhilaration of sexual freedom, in other words, is often attended with hurt, brokenness, and loss. As Smith concludes, "Not far beneath the surface of happy, liberated emerging adult sexual adventure and pleasure lies a world of hurt, insecurity, confusion, inequality, shame, and regret."[69]

Emerging adults need a broader perspective on these issues. Leaders of all stripes—pastors, professors, student development staff, and parents—are poised to provide a relational and sexual ethic for emerging adults growing up in the midst of deep cultural confusion about these issues. Leaders must provide a compelling and winsome portrait of relationships and sexuality that is grounded in the gospel. In the midst of this pain and anguish, emerging adults need a different picture of these concerns, one that is tied to the larger narrative of Christian faithfulness. While the culture has embraced a relational vision that is viewed in terms of self-fulfillment and freedom, a Christian vision highlights a self-giving posture rooted in covenant fidelity.

First Corinthians and an Emerging Adult Sexual Ethic

Ancient Corinth was likely the wealthiest and most cosmopolitan city in Greece. Built as a colony of Rome, it was a commercial and capital center. The most prominent physical feature of the city was a steep mount rising to a height of 1,800 feet. Atop this summit sat the temple of Aphrodite, a symbolic representation of the licentious impulse that no doubt found dominance in the hearts and minds of the city's inhabitants.

As Keller has noted, ancient Greek philosophy offered two opposing viewpoints regarding sexual expression in relationships. One position, which he calls "sexual realism," provided easy justification for indulgence: "I have the right to do anything" (1 Cor. 6:12). The material world and all that belonged to it were regarded as temporary and relatively unimportant in comparison with the eternal soul. Hence, what people did with their bodies was not nearly as important as what they did with their souls. Since sex was nothing more than a bodily appetite akin to eating or sleeping, one could engage in such activity whenever the need arose: "Food for the stomach and the stomach for food" (1 Cor. 6:13). A second school of thought, "sexual Platonism," arrived at the opposite conclusion. Rooted in a dualism that viewed the body as housing the lower "animal nature," encasing the more noble and rational soul, it regarded sex as inherently defiling, tinged with evil and good only for procreation: "It is good for a man not to have sexual relations with a woman" (1 Cor. 7:1). Consequently, this position promoted a practice of strict abstinence for those who wanted to remain virtuous, sanctioning sexual activity only as a necessary evil for producing children.[70]

The parallels to contemporary life can hardly be missed. Convinced that sex is a bodily appetite or even a biological necessity, emerging adult culture promotes "sexual realism," presupposing that casual sexual experiences, even sex between nonromantic partners, are natural and inconsequential. Some go as far as to imply that abstinence does damage to this essential need. To counterbalance such indulgence, religious leaders many times align themselves with "sexual Platonism." Their message often pathologizes sex as inherently evil, posturing Christianity as a faith bent on quenching sexual desire. Even more frequently, faith communities remain silent, implicitly conveying disapproval for this "inappropriate" topic. It is little wonder that David Kinnaman found that Christian emerging adults are often caught in a bind. They see the church as overly repressive and joyless when it comes to sexuality, yet they are equally dissatisfied with the permissiveness of their peers. Sex is either evil and dirty or unbridled and indulged at will.[71]

Donna Freitas has documented these opposing ideals on college campuses.[72] She discovered that, on the one hand, evangelical campuses often promote a purity culture that postures romantic allurements as potentially deadly to one's spiritual life and hence encourages fear of, or dissociation from, sexuality in the service of restraint. On the other hand, "spiritual universities" (named as such because students often regard themselves as spiritual without being religious) promote a hookup culture that fosters dissonance between Christian beliefs and typical sexual behavior.[73] Sex at "spiritual universities" is defined as normative for collegians, and religion that pushes against consensual sex easily becomes regarded as irrelevant or antiquated. Therefore, the options for emerging adults seem to reside as polar opposites—free sex without concern for the soul, or care for the soul that rejects sexuality as evil or ignores it altogether.

The Christian vision provides a third way. In contrast to "sexual Platonism," Christianity proclaims the goodness of our embodied and sexual natures. Both Jesus's incarnation and the promise of bodily resurrection reinforce the goodness of embodiment, both now and in the future. Likewise, Scripture proclaims the goodness of sexual intimacy when pursued in God-honoring ways within a marriage relationship. The Song of Solomon is filled with celebrations of bodily, sexual pleasure. In contrast to "sexual realism," however, Scripture is equally clear that sexual appetites can be misused, diverting the heart toward idolatry. First Thessalonians notes, "Each of you should learn to control your own body in a way that is holy and honorable, not in passionate lust like the pagans, who do not know God" (4:4–5). Sex is neither defiled nor a neutral appetite but rather a good gift that can be distorted when engaged outside of its stated intentions.

Emerging adults need to understand that they are created in God's image as relational and sexual beings and that this is "very good." Reflecting a trinitarian God means that they are relational by their very natures, and thus "it is not good for the man to be alone" (Gen. 2:18). They are created with a desire to know and be known, partially now and fully in glory (1 Cor. 13:12). Not only are they created inherently relational but also inherently sexual: "God created mankind in his own image, / in the image of God he created them; / male and female he created them" (Gen. 1:27). Emerging adults are created not only as generic "people" but as male and female with distinct anatomies and physiologies. Their sexuality should remind them that they are not meant to be alone, and it also should awaken them to their "good" need for relationships with others.

Relational and sexual brokenness, therefore, emerges from the fact that we pursue these "good" realities in ways that go against their created designs. As Stanton Jones reminds us, sexual intercourse has "objective meaning" and is not defined by its ends or by what we bring to it. Therefore, the only way in which we can approach healthy relationships is by conforming our own thoughts and actions to the objective truths that anchor these realities.[74] One of those realities is that sexual intimacy is designed by God to be a picture of both his nature and the union he shares with his people. Sex, Keller notes, reflects "the joyous self-giving and pleasure of love within the life of the Trinity."[75] It is wonderful because it "mirrors the joy of relationship in the Trinity and because it points to the eternal ecstasy of soul that we will have in heaven in our loving relationships with God and one another (Prov. 5:18–20; Deut. 24:5)."[76] Adam and Eve were created "in his own image" as male and female to display the beauty of relational oneness. One-flesh union is therefore an expression of God's very nature, depicting the fullness of sharing and intimacy present within God himself. At the same time, it is also a portrait of Christ's relationship with the church (Eph. 5:24–32). Sexual intimacy is meant to portray the covenant love of Christ for his people, his "single-minded connection and devotion to his bride."[77] As Lisa McMinn notes, "Faithfulness, permanence, and the welcoming and nurturing of children born of their parents' sexual union teach us about God as lover and life-giver."[78] It points to God's great covenant faithfulness to his people and ultimately foreshadows the wedding supper of the Lamb when this union will be fulfilled (Rev. 19:7).

While we may point to all of the human reasons for avoiding sex outside of marriage, therefore, this divine vision must undergird all recommendations. God's marriage covenant with his people serves as the model for emerging adult relationships. God describes his relationship with his people as a marriage marked by exclusivity, permanence, and complete faithfulness, marking the outlines of proper relational intimacy. Marva Dawn notes that we can always utilize God's covenant faithfulness as a rubric for our own relational purity: "The sexual lives of God's people, therefore, are always judged by this question: Are we symbolizing God's fidelity or imitating Israel's faithlessness?"[79]

Part of this fidelity comes as we "flee from sexual immorality" (1 Cor. 6:18). The connotation here refers to any sex outside of the bonds of marriage: premarital sex, pornographic use of others, and adultery within marriage. Why was this so important? Paul recognizes the power of sexual intimacy by noting, "The two will become one flesh" (1 Cor. 6:16). The "one-flesh" union, argues Keller, is about so much more than the act of sexual intercourse. "Flesh" here refers to embodied personhood so that sex implies the giving of oneself to the other in a complete and exclusive way (much as Christ does for the church). Uniting with another in a one-flesh union intends whole-life sharing.[80] Physical oneness therefore requires whole-life oneness that expresses a desire to bring pleasure to one's spouse in every area of life. Sex outside of marriage attempts to give the body without giving the whole self, a sure path to frustration divorced from God's design. One cannot remain independent and take part in this act of self-donation without significant consequences.

The command "You shall not commit adultery" (Exod. 20:14), therefore, clearly signals the exclusive boundaries designed to protect sexual and whole-life oneness within the womb of marital faithfulness. For those who are not yet married, the idea of future covenant marital faithfulness can provide guidance for present actions.[81] It is possible that the emerging adult and partner will one day be married either to each other or to other individuals. Therefore, the couple can think together about what it might mean to guard that future covenant relationship even now. In addition, a dating relationship provides a setting in which they can practice in the present what will be true in their future marriage, a habituation in the virtues that will be needed for a lifetime of faithful sexual intimacy. Even if they end up single, they are practicing covenant faithfulness in their relationship with God, resisting the idolatry of sexual expression and remaining faithful to their first love (Rev. 2:4).

Such commitments make sense of Jesus's later description of the adultery of the heart. Jesus states, "You have heard that it was said, 'You shall not commit adultery.' But I tell you that anyone who looks at a woman lustfully has already committed adultery with her in his heart" (Matt. 5:27–28). Jesus's words here call us back not only to commands against literal adultery but also to Job's declaration, "I have made a covenant with my eyes not to look lustfully at a young woman" (Job 31:1). He is not condemning here any recognition of attractiveness in another person but rather a lustful intent to desire another person, seeking to create opportunities to use others (or their images) for sexual gratification.[82] Lust is a completely self-centered activity, marked by the objectification of the other rather than the whole-life, self-giving oneness of true sexuality. Since sexuality is both relational and covenantal, it exists for one person to bless the other. Therefore, sexuality that treats the other as a tool of personal pleasure or an object to be "used" is rejecting God's created design.

While these forms of relational adultery and fornication tear at the fabric of human oneness and distort the picture of God's character, they also create pathways to idolatry and adultery against God. Centuries ago, Augustine coined his now famous dictum, "Oh God, you have created us for yourself and our hearts are restless until they find their rest in Thee."[83] Implicit in this statement was his understanding of disordered love.[84] Augustine posited that humans seek happiness by their very constitution as incomplete beings. In their finitude, they search for what will bring them completeness and naturally go beyond themselves to fasten their affections on objects of love. These affections could be directed to physical objects, to other persons, or toward oneself. Augustine believed that all things were created good by God so that all of these objects of love would provide some measure of satisfaction and happiness. Nothing was evil in itself. Evil was defined as the absence of, or distortion of, some good.

The problem for humanity, then, came not from loving, nor in the objects of love, but in the manner in which humans attach themselves to these objects and the expectations they bring to them in terms of desired happiness. Satisfaction or happiness is procured whenever an object contains within itself a sufficient quantity to fulfill or satisfy the need that was brought to it.[85] Hence, when one is hungry and consumes an amount of food commensurate to this need, happiness ensues. Objects of art, however, seem to offer something more qualitative, something that meets a need for the aesthetic and beautiful. Clearly one cannot exchange these objects and assume that a great painting can meet a person's physical hunger.

Similarly, a need for companionship cannot ultimately be met by eating chocolate because chocolate does not contain within itself the ingredients of human personality. Chocolate may be a legitimate object of love, but dissatisfaction will result if individuals expect more from it than it can provide. In the same way that things cannot substitute for persons, persons cannot substitute for God. Hence, loving God becomes the indispensable requirement for happiness.[86] Augustine maintains that we will only be able to love another person properly if we love God first. If we do not seek primary satisfaction in him, we inevitably expect to derive from human love or sexual expression what only God can provide.[87] Human loves provide some measure of satisfaction as human relationships too were created good and for our happiness. If we bring a God-shaped need and attach it to another person, however, it may at first elate us, but we will eventually discover that it does not contain within itself the capacity to meet our deepest needs. Love has become disordered. As C. S. Lewis comments,

> St. John's saying that God is love has long been balanced in my mind against the remark of a modern author (M. Denis de Rougemont) that "love ceases to be a demon only when he ceases to be a god;" which of course can be re-stated

in the form "begins to be a demon the moment he begins to be a god." This balance seems to me an indispensable safeguard. If we ignore it the truth that God is love may slyly come to mean for us the converse, that love is God. . . . We may give our human loves the unconditional allegiance which we owe only to God. Then they become gods: then they become demons. Then they will destroy us, and also destroy themselves. For natural loves that are allowed to become gods do not remain loves. They are still called so, but can become in fact complicated forms of hatred.[88]

It is only when all human loves are subordinated to and in the service of love for God that they become properly ordered and yield satisfaction. As McMinn writes, "When we acknowledge that our yearnings will never be fully satisfied, we can welcome God into our disappointment and then turn toward the abundance yet available through the temporal blessings of relationships, knowing they were never intended to completely satisfy our longings."[89]

What is true with others can also be true with ourselves. Self-love is also affirmed in the Scriptures, "Love the Lord your God . . . [and] your neighbor as yourself" (Mark 12:30–31), but disordered self-love turns into pride and self-sufficiency, either determining that the self needs nothing outside of itself for happiness or using other people and objects merely as tools of self-fulfillment. While intense romantic relationships may be susceptible to the idolatry of the partner, emerging adult hookup culture is likely more vulnerable to the idolatry of self-love. Eventually, the infinite need meets the finitude of the self. So, the first step toward sexual integrity is always one of first addressing the hunger of the heart to be loved and known deeply without reservation. If there is no recognition of the primary need for God, the hungers of the heart can turn to more destructive, overindulgent, or compulsive behaviors.

Such a perspective is implicit in Paul's proclamation, "I will not be mastered by anything" (1 Cor. 6:12). For too many emerging adults, sexual indulgence leads to sexual addiction. In the progression of an addiction, a distinction can often be made between an infrequent, episodic, casual, and moderate behavior and a compulsive behavior that preoccupies one's thoughts and to which one turns frequently to feel a certain way, numb pain, or overcome social insecurities. Paul urges one to ask, is anything gaining mastery over me? Many who are caught in the throes of chat rooms, masturbation, pornography, sexting, or other addictive patterns begin ordering life to protect the indulgence, intensifying the binge by thinking about it throughout the day, sometimes even becoming ritualistic in the way they enter the experience.[90] Far from "free," such individuals often find themselves unable to control their thoughts and behaviors, living under the compulsion of patterns and habits that have become thoroughly woven into the fabric of their lives. They will find it difficult to extricate themselves from such patterns even if they get married.

Because of the seriousness of these issues and the high value given to Christian sexuality, Scripture speaks of the need to confront sexual immorality with vigor. Right after addressing the adultery of the eyes and heart, Jesus warns the crowd, "If your right eye causes you to stumble, gouge it out and throw it away" (Matt. 5:29). Elsewhere, we are called upon to "flee from sexual immorality" (1 Cor. 6:18). Such passages speak to the necessary radical nature of resistance. While not wanting to fall into legalism, we must also help emerging adults avoid the kinds of situations and settings that heighten opportunities for immorality. In a relationship, this might mean setting appropriate physical boundaries and boundaries regarding time alone. It might mean keeping a closer eye on the kinds of television shows, movies, and websites viewed, recognizing that such sources can gradually desensitize them to immoralities and create new perceptions of "normal" relational and sexual activity. And then there will be times to "flee." St. Benedict threw himself into a briar patch when confronted with lustful thoughts; while we are not calling on emerging adults to do the same, we must help them find "escape routes" through which they can flee temptation when it arises.

Helpful here is Dallas Willard's application of his well-known "Vision—Intention—Means" model to the specific case of pornography.[91] Speaking to men, Willard indicates that a man struggling with pornography use has a "vision" of women as objects capable of stimulating sexual desire. He may also see his own body as a "source and means to pleasure."[92] This must be replaced with a vision of women as sisters created in God's image for his glory with infinite worth and eternal destiny. It must be replaced, as indicated above, with a vision of the beauty of sexuality within the covenant bonds of marriage. The individual must also come to terms with the fact that he has decided ("intention") to use pornography for sexual gratification and has "not decided not to be there."[93] Recognition of this kind may then lead to a new intention to avoid sinful lust.

Yet willpower alone will not suffice. When it comes to the "means" of avoidance, Willard suggests four things. First, since "desire overpowers the will by obsessing the mind," he indicates that we must teach emerging adults about the degrading aspects of pornography, the ways in which it exploits women for financial gain.[94] In Paul's writings (1 Cor. 8:9–13), love for one's brother or sister is a higher principle than exercising one's personal freedom or insisting on one's right of conscience. Thus, emerging adults need to see how viewing pornography supports an industry connected with human trafficking and the selling of young girls. This "bigger picture" can be an effective means of creating a resistance to this evil. Second, he recommends accountability to others in confession, prayer, and mutual support, finding individuals who will ask the hard questions and help in times of temptation or failure. Third, he urges "resolute avoidance" by working to make sure that pornography is out of reach.[95] This would involve recognition of situations and locations in which one is particularly susceptible to such temptations, and it may mean the elimination (or filtering) of devices that make pornography easy to access. Fourth, true victory will be impossible without forming the heart and mind in new ways through spiritual disciplines that can connect the individual to kingdom reality. In other words, he suggests practicing spiritual disciplines like solitude, silence, study, fasting, and worship "that are not focused upon the avoidance of pornography, but upon the healthy fulfillment of your life under God in the dramatic goodness of God's world with others you love and serve."[96] Because "pornography involvement is a sure indicator of the impoverishment of life," reconnecting to all that is good (Phil. 4:8) will be a central way for emerging adults to move in a new direction, to form new desires that make these others appear repulsive in nature.[97]

Willard's last recommendation reminds us that Paul's admonitions are not simply a matter of prohibitions but also a matter of cultivating positive virtues that aim one's sexual life in the direction of the covenantal vision previously described. Several virtues have risen to the fore in recent discussions of relationships and sexuality. Abstinence is a common prohibition often set forth as the Christian ideal in sex education programs (e.g., "Just Say No," "True Love Waits," and school-based abstinence programs). Abstinence indeed names the required posture of avoidance toward sexual activity outside of a marriage relationship. In naming what to avoid, however, it does little to name what can be affirmed. It postures Christianity against prevailing culture but often stops with God's "say-so" without expressing in a convincing way *why* God placed prohibitions on sexual immorality. Furthermore, if taken as a solitary response, abstinence tends to focus primary attention on avoiding sexual behavior while seeming to focus little on the shaping of imagination, desire, and emotion. Can't one claim to be sexually abstinent while regularly viewing pornography, having flirtatious conversations, engaging in illicit texting, or living in a relationship marked by "technical virginity"?

Similarly, purity often surfaces in sermons and talks aimed at sexual integrity. Purity has good biblical precedent, recognizing that the "pure in heart" are "blessed" (Matt. 5:8). It casts the searchlight deeper than abstinence, bringing the inner motivations and imaginations of the heart to light and calling for inner cleansing. But purity, when held as the ultimate virtue, may be perceived by some as discounting them from the only possible pathway to righteousness. Purity pledges or the giving of a purity ring may be helpful, extending righteous living for some and delaying sexual activity for others, but studies substantiate that many break their pledges. When innocence is lost and purity forfeited, it can seem that nothing is left for them. They may, in fact, distance themselves from Christian community, indulging immorality because it is already "too late."[98] Some have suggested that they can be "re-virginalized" in Christ and thus argue that upholding purity as the virtuous ideal still works. Others prefer to locate purity in the finished work of Christ and the hope of final redemption.[99] Despite the consequences that may arise in this life, they are still new creations in Christ and pure in his sight.

Lauren Winner and Dawn Eden propose chastity as a virtue. Chastity also probes deeper than abstinence, focuses beyond behavior, and retains its claims on believers even after becoming married. Winner defines chastity as a "spiritual discipline that moves us beyond the mere absence of sex to the conforming of one's body to the arc of the gospel."[100] The challenging thing about promoting chastity as a sexual virtue is its unfortunate historical use in early Western theological tradition. Clifford Stevens traces this heritage and sets it in contrast with its parallel use in Eastern theological tradition.[101] In the West, chastity emerged from what Stevens called an anthropological pessimism that associated the "flesh" with sinful sexual tendencies. Sex was permitted only for procreation, the Song of Solomon was interpreted only as allegory, and chastity conveyed apathy (literally "without passion") toward sexuality, foregrounding only temperance and abstinence. Though short-lived and infrequent, chastity belts conveyed the fear of wanton sexuality and over-protective measures that this posturing toward the body sometimes produced. In the East, writes Stevens, the body was instead associated with the "flesh" of the incarnation.[102] Children were the fruit of sacramental love between man and woman that imaged the overflowing abundance of the Trinity, the Song of Solomon was interpreted as an exaltation of sexual love, and chastity took on the connotation of joy and pride in bodily living. So, chastity may indeed be a virtue to promote, but this requires reinvigorating the term with substantive biblical teaching to overcome the latent anthropological pessimism that may still freight the term.

Wendy Shalit has promoted modesty as an alternative to superficial allure.[103] Shalit's book is helpful because it is written in a spirit of what can be promoted through the pursuit of virtue. Modesty is infused not with notions that seem prudish but respectful of oneself and honoring of relationships. It values not only one's own purity but the purity of those observing as well. Modesty, however, typically places the burden of virtue almost entirely on women. Furthermore, focusing primarily on what is attractive without being seductive, modesty can elevate the opposite sex rather than God as the primary reference point in one's decision making.

What seems to be needed is not setting these virtues in competition with one another but rather regarding them as complementary. Abstinence recognizes that there is a moral rectitude in the heart of God that will not cater to our desires and hence sometimes says "no" to what we think would satisfy. Purity paints an image of coming clean and holds out the hope that a pure heart can be maintained or restored through Christ. Chastity requires practices and habits that dispose us to be people of godly character. Modesty calls for an orientation of respect, boundaries, and protection that recognizes the vulnerabilities of others. Virtues offer much more than prohibitions on sexual behavior, pointing to positive aspects of being that an emerging adult is choosing when resisting sexual temptation.

In the end, however, the appropriateness of these particular virtues must be determined by the telos or normative vision of good toward which they are moving. Abstinence, for example, is often commended to emerging adults because it paves the way for an even greater sexual experience in marriage, free from the baggage of previous encounters. If this really is the ultimate telos— "great marital sex"—what does this mean for those who will never marry? Will they still have a reason to "hold out"? What about those struggling with homosexual attraction? In addition, such a telos can reinforce the idea that marriage will fulfill all of their deepest longings and serve as the ultimate prize for self-control. Even more fundamentally, such a rationale seems to endorse the very self-centered and individualistic moral culture that we desire to combat. As Christine Gardner indicates, the rhetoric of abstinence can "present a limited and distorted view that marriage is all about self-fulfilling sex. . . . Although purity may be a God-centered approach to abstinence in that purity is described as a lifestyle standard created by God, the underlying reason offered for pursuing purity is that it is a lifestyle that is most beneficial (and pleasurable) to the individual."[104] Such a posture can easily locate the "happily-ever-after" in this life.

Even modesty can be communicated in this way. Gardner discovered that many describe modesty as a way for women to gain power and control over men. Since men are most tempted by what is "yet to be seen," female modesty forces the man to invest more deeply in the relationship to get what he "really wants."[105] While immodesty gives the power over to men to do as they please without effort, modesty is a way to retain the control and attract the best candidate. If one acts (and dresses) like a princess, this will attract a true prince. Marriage, in other words, is the reward for modesty.

When tied instead to the big picture of covenant fidelity to God and a present or future spouse, these virtues aim at something beyond personal benefit. As a result of baptism, Paul argues, a believer's body has become part of the body of Christ and therefore part of his bride. This marriage, therefore, must exclude all other unions that are incompatible with covenant fidelity (1 Cor. 12). The avoidance of idolatry and adultery becomes a means of drawing closer to our first love. It becomes rooted not in a personal payoff in the near future but in a clear belief in the goodness of God's commands whether or not they result in what is perceived as personal benefit in this life. Present behavior becomes conditioned by what we believe about our ultimate future. For the Christian, hope in the final wedding banquet—when Christ the bridegroom returns—compels his bride, the church, to keep herself pure and faithful until that day.

This lofty reality, then, should also lead emerging adults to recognize that their bodies and relationships are missional. For Paul, a Christian's use of the body was not only a personal issue but a witness to the surrounding world. One can no longer claim that "what I do in private is none of your business," or that "it's my body and I should have the right to do with it as I please," or "what happens in mutual consent with a partner has no bearing beyond the relationship." Paul argues that the gross immorality of one person (a man having relations with his father's wife in 1 Cor. 5) exemplified the separation of morality from spirituality that would inevitably be detrimental to both. Paul's indignation over the sexual immorality in Corinth flowed from the realization that the church would fail to be purifying leaven to the rest of the world, growing into disrepute, and losing the spiritual and moral identity to attract people away from the surrounding decadent culture. The body is a temple of the Holy Spirit (6:19), a member of Christ himself (6:15), and therefore a chief means by which we show off God to a watching world. "You are not your own," Paul states, "you were bought at a price. Therefore honor God with your bodies" (6:19–20). In singleness, dating, or marriage, sexuality becomes a means by which we worship God, revealing his glorious nature and plan to the world.

For fifty miles along Interstate 40 near Knoxville, provocative road signs solicit customers to an adult superstore. When the highway finally loops by the store, passersby are also confronted with an imposing sixty-foot white metal cross that stands on the lot next to the store. Years ago Orrin Klapp wrote that people are forever attempting to create and hunt for symbols that give meaning and identity to the self.[106] However, symbols can become disturbed to the extent that they no longer provide reliable reference points for bestowing identity on people.[107] Both the cross and the superstore have been interpreted in a myriad of ways, often creating the impression of mutual antagonism between Christianity and sexuality. In this chapter, we hope we have offered a view where emerging adults could stand at the foot of that cross and raise a hand in gratitude, declaring, "Thanks be to God, we have been sexual today."

8 | Relationships

Pitfalls and Pathways

When it (love) comes, will it come without warning
Just as I'm picking my nose?
Will it knock on my door in the morning,
Or tread in the bus on my toes?
Will it come like a change in the weather?
Will its greeting be courteous or rough?
Will it alter my life altogether?
O tell me the truth about love.

W. H. Auden[1]

In the 2006 romantic comedy *Failure to Launch*, Matthew McConaughey played the part of Tripp, a thirtysomething adult who invites his date to spend the night. At an inopportune moment, Bradshaw, Tripp's dad, walks in on the couple in bed together. Indicative of the permissive parenting style that must have allowed for such an arrangement, Bradshaw's only response in exiting the room is, "You two have a good time together." Tripp's date, however, shocked by the sudden intrusion, says, "You still live with your parents?" Tripp smugly replies with the acknowledgment and question that frames the plot of the movie, "Is that a problem?"

As sexual mores continue to shift for emerging adults and as culture encourages and enables exploration of any and every kind, Tripp's question, asked with a sort of anticipatory indulgent triumphalism, echoes in many conversations. The challenges and changes described in the previous chapter call for those who come alongside emerging adults to practice a great deal of discernment. The task is not an easy one because with the diversification of the life course and a multiplicity of options available at every turn, what may be prescriptive and provide security for one emerging adult may feel restrictive and imposing to another.

A key task for those in emerging adult ministry is developing a deep capacity to understand the divergent chords of a young person's life however jumbled the melody may currently sound. Emerging adults welcome into their lives those who honor their journeys of desire and who listen as they recount the murky waters in which they swim. They will confide in those who they believe have walked in their shoes and shared their heartaches, who surround them with understanding and acceptance, and who offer guidance and challenge in the context of support.[2] But they will often conceal their lives and avoid those who live by easy moralisms either because they perceive these leaders as having rarely contended with conflicting passions or because they assume these leaders do not want to deal with the emerging adults' lives of elation, fear, uncertainty, or shame.[3] Emerging adults learn at an early age to keep feelings and experiences hidden from parents and other adults; therefore, they are left with peers and popular culture to direct their journeys.

If leaders desire emerging adults to grow as people of relational and sexual virtue, we must discern helpful means by which they can grow in these ways. In this chapter, we will explore three approaches: helping emerging adults trace past influences on their ideals, helping them discern the proper paths of relational formation, and helping them think through the connections between physical intimacy and relational intimacy at this stage of life.

Tracing the Past: Creating a Relational and Sexual Autobiography

Attachment Theory and Relationships

One significant way in which leaders can assist emerging adults is by helping them trace the influence of past experiences and interactions on their present approaches to relationships and sexuality. In trying to figure out relational turmoil, social scientists have sought ways to understand the antecedents of healthy relationships. Early family and peer relationships both show relatively strong correlation with the quality of intimacy experienced in adult relationships and yield important clues to support emerging adults in their eagerness to form meaningful and sustainable marriages and families. In providing the following overview of correlations, we are not defining deterministic outcomes but identifying established correlations that can be changed by God's transforming grace.

Erik Erikson, in his eight-stage construction of the lifecycle, named the developmental task of young adulthood as "intimacy versus isolation."[4] Erikson predicted that the quality of intimacy one experiences in the adult years largely hinges on the resolution of previous developmental tasks. With successful navigation through the adolescent identity crises, a well-integrated personality naturally grows toward psychological intimacy—a readiness to risk self in relations of closeness to others. Conversely, when identity has not been solidified, pseudo-intimacy and enmeshment are likely to occur.[5] One partner pushes away from the other to avoid a sense of encroachment or entrapment; another partner emotionally clings to the relationship, overly depending on validation from the partner and relinquishing aspects of personhood in fear of abandonment.

John Bowlby's work on attachment styles has provided important insights into how early formative experiences shape patterns of relating in adulthood.[6] Bowlby hypothesized that an attachment bond is created between an infant and a primary caregiver that provides the child both a sense of security and a safe haven from which to explore.[7] Through many cumulative interactions, cognitive and affective appraisals emerge that establish expectations about the availability and responsiveness of a child's primary caregiver. As these patterns of relating acquire representational meaning, an individual naturally constructs an *internal working model*.[8] As the internal working model organizes memory, knowledge, experiences, and facts into a coherent whole, it then begins directing and influencing future evaluations and interpretations of others' actions. A person's internal working model filters self-perception such as the degree to which one sees himself or herself as worthy of love, care, and protection. It also creates a perceptual grid whereby the intentions of others are interpreted.[9]

A *secure* attachment bond is formed when a child experiences a primary caregiver as dependable and psychologically available. These children feel their attempts to achieve closeness met with security, so they quite naturally come to see *themselves* as friendly, good-natured, and likeable. Consequentially, their attachment bond disposes them to assume others are well intentioned, reliable, and trustworthy. Such a representational model predicts that individuals will enter adult relationships with a minimum of frustration, anxiety, and fear.

They should find relative ease in getting close to a significant other and find it comfortable to depend on someone else or have others depend on them.[10]

On the contrary, when a child's attempts to find security are ignored or rejected, a primary caregiver comes to be regarded as untrustworthy, distant, and unsupportive. Children within this home environment shift attention away from the caregiver to minimize stress and avoid dependent relationships. In more extreme cases, children may learn to deny emotion altogether or protect themselves through emotional withdrawal.[11] In this *avoidant* pattern of relating, children come to view themselves as suspicious, aloof, or skeptical and view others as generally unreliable. As adults, their internal monitoring system may sound an internal alarm when a relationship reaches emotional intimacy, catapulting them toward emotional and behavioral withdrawal.[12]

When a caregiver is inconsistent, a child's feelings may become a mixture of affection, protest, and anger. A child internalizes a self-perception of being misunderstood, tentative, and underappreciated. Suspicious that others are unwilling and/or unable to commit to a relationship, they worry that others don't really love them or will abandon them. Children in this context may come to exaggerate their emotions in attempts to regain attention while at the same time worrying that hurt will ensue if they become vulnerable. Their representational model functions in such a way that it heightens fear, anxiety, and possibly anger whenever there is relational stress.[13] Consequently, they often try to secure partner commitment through nagging, groveling, cajoling, or demanding persistent reassurances to quiet their anxiety.

Many children of divorce discover a sleeper effect from the separation they experienced from one or both parents.[14] Fearing the abandonment that marked their childhood, children of divorce often feel increased anxiety whenever there is conflict with their partners. Such fear may cause them to avoid disagreeable parts of a relationship, or demand a desired response, or conceal certain parts of the self they deem undesirable. Christopher Lasch writes that with the instability of family, children growing up today learn "a protective shallowness, a fear of binding commitments, a willingness to pull up roots whenever the need arises, a dislike of depending on anyone, an incapacity for loyalty or gratitude."[15] With divorce so prevalent in our culture, many emerging adults enter relationships with such postures, often oblivious to the ways in which these lingering perceptions influence interpersonal interactions.

Attachment theorists hold that subsequent relationships may serve to challenge and modify internal representations of the self and other. Authorities in one's social context can serve as reparative parental figures providing surrogate relational experiences that were absent during childhood.[16] In these exchanges, emerging adults experience a different and broadened way of relating that fosters a heightened awareness of the discrepancy between a new relational reality and the deficient emotional environment of the past. When this occurs, a recasting of one's internal working model is made possible. Those ministering to emerging adults have an enormous opportunity to provide an auxiliary secure base by providing genuine interest in the person, reliable availability, and/or a safe place to uncover family secrets and surface internalized messages from past attachment experiences.[17] Importantly, this may involve joint mourning not only of actual losses but of deeply desired family relationships that were never fully experienced. Childhood wounds are held differently when resentment and anger can be transformed into healthy sadness and grief. In working with emerging adults, leaders can begin to grasp the nature of governing images, trace their origins, and seek to understand what has propelled a person to see the world, others, and themselves the way they do. This may not eliminate the pain or fully resolve the past. What it can do, however, is open emerging adults to the importance of becoming "conscious" of themselves and the subtexts influencing their relational formation, broadening their capacity to bring positive affect to new relationships.[18]

In addition to research on parental influences, studies have also analyzed the influence of peers and friendships on romantic relationships. Unlike family relations in early childhood, friendships are voluntary, mutually acknowledged, and typically egalitarian, causing some to argue that they are more akin to romantic relationships than the hierarchical patterns found in parent-child interactions.[19] In this view, friends function as interaction prototypes, providing important testing grounds for experiencing and managing emotions. According to recent research, the quality of same-gender friendships does predict romantic relationship quality in early adulthood.[20] Emerging adult ministries therefore have a vital role to play in teaching and modeling relationships built on truthfulness, emotional integrity, promise keeping, gratitude, appropriate boundaries, and hospitality.[21] As leaders help students manage roommate conflicts or navigate relational issues with difficult people in their small groups, students enter rich training grounds for healthy dating and marriage relationships. Solid friendships grow the capacity to achieve intimacy. Conversely, negative experiences of peer rejection can produce what some have named the "rejection sensitivity syndrome," making it difficult to feel positive emotions even when good things happen.[22] Such attitudes then often transfer to future romantic relationships as well.[23]

Importantly, what attachment theorists name on the horizontal plane of relationships has its corollary on the vertical plane of spirituality. As people begin to share life in the fellowship of the Trinity, a change begins to occur, sometimes dramatically and sometimes a little bit at a time. People gaze into the face of a God who was wounded for them, who suffered death to grant them mercy and draw them to himself, whose unconditional covenantal love abides, and in whose eternal presence is found security and joy. When this occurs, real transformation begins and one's representational images shift.[24] Finding God to be trustworthy, unfailing, consistent, and always present, emerging adults' internal working models can be renewed. As their sense of self becomes secure in him, they can find freedom from the incessant need to seek validation from others. Key focal images shift so that they can begin loving unconditionally, out of a sense of fullness, rather than taking part in recurring patterns of demand and withdrawal. Such transformation does not eliminate the desire or even the need for lifelong companionship, but it does recognize that the most crucial hungers of the human heart are met in God and not in romantic intimacy. When God is allowed to order our loves—when he becomes the ultimate source of security and satisfaction—we are freed from placing unrealistic expectations on a romantic partner. We can love out of the overflow of God's love, extending ourselves for others without compromising personal joy.[25]

Programs that episodically address marriage preparation, therefore, often fail to provide a holistic relational curriculum for emerging adults. Ministries should help students look at past family and peer relationships to better account for their approach to relationships in the present. Such an analysis can embolden them to understand their strengths and weaknesses and to seek healing in areas of brokenness so that they can enter new relationships with freedom and self-understanding. Ministries can also emphasize healthy relationships between leaders and emerging adults, setting examples of wholeness that can reframe their internal working models. Teaching on God's unconditional covenantal love will also be a critical means of forging a "secure" attachment that will never fail, providing a strong foundation from which to relate to others.

Tracing the Contours of Sexual Identity

Similarly, because early developmental stages interact with familial and cultural messages to form emerging adult sexual identities, retracing the past can also be instrumental in assessing sexual trajectories in emerging adults' lives. Judith Balswick and Jack Balswick characterize sexuality as comprising four primary dimensions:

- Natal sex—the physical and biological features present at birth that are generally used to determine whether a newborn is male or female;
- Sexual identity (or sexual self-concept)—the view individuals have of themselves as sexual people;

- Sexual orientation—the direction of one's erotic attraction;
- Gender or gender role—attitudes and interests, stereotypes and behavioral expectations as defined by a particular culture.[26]

The Balswicks believe that when there is good congruence between these four dimensions, sexual identity and gender are clear. However, it is not uncommon, especially during the formative years of emerging adulthood, for some inconsistency between these four dimensions to surface, creating issues of gender and sexual confusion and anxiety. Individuals may feel shame over the bodies they inhabit (natal sex) that fail in their mind (sexual identity) to capture the attention of potential partners. Individuals may feel that the constraints imposed on them by familial or religious expectations (gender role)—such as the belief that girls should not be too assertive or that boys should not show an emotional side—invalidate their own perceived preferences or temperament (sexual identity). Sometimes, a person may find conflictual, inner vulnerabilities, insecurities, or attractions (sexual orientation) that become pronounced when cultural expectations (gender role) encourage accenting one's sexual prowess and power toward the opposite sex.

With increased self-understanding and awareness of one's sexual history, an emerging adult is better equipped to understand the ways in which these aspects of sexuality have been shaped over time. They can also begin to understand particular views and temptations, therefore developing an intentional posture toward integrity, wholeness, and sanctification. The following are questions emerging adults might consider in owning their sexual histories and sifting through the various voices that have "told" them who they are as sexually embodied beings.

- What understanding do you have about your earliest attitudes and memories regarding your sexuality? Are birth stories told by the family that indicate the kind of attachment bonds that formed in your early days?
- In the early years when children are naturally curious about their bodies and engage in playful exploration, what memories do you have of parents/guardians providing affirming acceptance or shaming restrictions on you? What sense of sexual self did you get from your dad? Your mom? Your siblings or other family members? Were boundaries that respect growing independence and privacy respected, or were family members intrusive and violating?
- When the school years gradually exposed you to socializing agencies broader than your family and friendship network, what influences did these have on the way you were formed sexually? What familial and cultural

portrayals did you encounter of what it means to be a woman/man and how to regard and relate to the opposite sex?

- Which voices shaped your understanding of sexuality in the teenage years? What feelings did you come to associate with the arrival of puberty and the realization that you could now generate new life?

- What story does the media tell about sexuality? How are women/men portrayed in popular videos, movies, songs, and magazines? What roles do they play? What body types seem to be excluded from the media? What social visions of adulthood are valued in the media, and what does it suggest one needs to do to be fashionable?

- As an emerging adult exploring a variety of new roles in life, how does being a sexual person, sharing emotions, or feeling confident enter into the interpersonal and intrapersonal space that you inhabit with the opposite sex? As you trace your own history of sexual and gender formation, what accounts for the way you currently engage in personal and intimate interactions? If you have been sexually active, what vulnerabilities did you encounter from and after the experience? Were there defense mechanisms at play by which you hoped to protect yourself from getting hurt either then or in the future?

As emerging adults begin to establish a deeper understanding of their relational and sexual histories, they can more effectively discern the sources of the challenges they face in these areas. Perhaps parental relationships have left them uncertain and anxious about romantic interactions, giving them false internal working models that must be healed through new representational images of God's unconditional love. Perhaps their culturally informed visions of sexuality are diametrically opposed to the covenantal images of one-flesh union provided in Scripture. They may again need clear counsel on the larger meaning of sexuality and instruction in the virtues and focal images that place sexual relations in the context of the larger Christian narrative. Even if their previous experiences have been healthy, however, emerging adults will need guidance in navigating the new relational terrain that now exists. Singleness, dating, calls for early marriage, and cohabitation provide a number of options for emerging adults, and leaders must be prepared to provide wisdom for those seeking direction in these areas.

The Shape of Relationship Formation

Marriage is still the assumed trajectory of most emerging adults in America. Among Christian emerging adults, this is especially the case. In our society, however, we miss how revolutionary and liberating Paul's message was for those who were single. Despite the social stigma attached to singleness in that day, Paul presented both fidelity in marriage and chaste singleness as viable ways in which to display the glory of God to a watching world. Christine Colon and Bonnie Field observe that marriage metaphors are almost exclusively used to express the intimacy of God's love, inadvertently communicating that singles somehow miss out on the best that God has designed.[27] Yet singleness testifies to the all-sufficient relationship with God that supersedes all human relationships. Celibacy subverts the cultural script that sex cannot be restrained without doing damage to oneself. In doing so, singles provide a countercultural witness that our deepest needs are met in God rather than in physical intimacy, and they witness to the eschatological reality that in the afterlife none are "given to marriage." Celibacy can point to the reality that a fulfilling human sexuality does not depend on sexual intercourse. Debunking the false bifurcation that singles are forced to choose between unharnessed abandon and suppression of sexuality, Colon and Field note that sexuality is ultimately defined more by a desire to connect to others and to give oneself to others in love and care.[28] "The drive to bond with others in community," Lisa McMinn writes, "is an expression of our fundamental sexuality, a sexuality that goes deeper than body parts, potential roles in reproduction, and genital acts."[29]

Therefore, while marriage highlights God's exclusive covenantal relationship, singleness gives expression to "God's all-inclusive love that invites everyone to participate."[30] It foregrounds the church as the "first family," the primary setting in which identity and community resides. In this light, singleness also demonstrates the location of ultimate hope. As Stanley Hauerwas has pointed out, the most significant sacrifice of the single person is not living without sex but living without children. "There can be no more radical act than this, as it is the clearest institutional expression that one's future is not guaranteed by the family, but by the church."[31] Singleness is not to be valued solely because it provides more time and space for ministry but also because it is a clear picture of a life marked by Christian hope that transcends the temporal borders of this life. It behooves those who work with emerging adults to regard as beneficial not only journeys toward marriage but also faithful lives of celibacy (by choice, chance, or circumstance).

So while a married couple practices fidelity as a way to display the reality of divine love, singles, wrestling with sexual desires, consider how self-restraint witnesses to the cross of Jesus and an eschatological hope in an ultimate marriage to Christ. Embracing their sexuality, they draw near to others in loving and caring relationships within the body of Christ, using their gifts to serve and nurture others. Critical in teaching emerging adults is to constantly hold before them these images of telos, helping them see themselves in the story of God's mission in the world, helping them access and experience the abundance of life made possible through the cross and the power of the Spirit, and inclining them to locate their treasures in heaven. In short, we want to encourage them to "fix [their] eyes . . . on what is unseen" (2 Cor. 4:18) and therefore develop "the conviction of things not seen" (Heb. 11:1 ESV).[32]

And what about dating? Can such relationships serve as healthy pathways to marriage? If God can meet the deepest hungers of the heart, and if casual romantic relationships often create hurt and brokenness, perhaps we should encourage emerging adults to "kiss dating goodbye."[33] The reasoning for this proposal, made most prominent by Joshua Harris, is generally built on several arguments. The purpose of dating, some argue, is to find a marriage partner, so unless you are ready to make a lifelong commitment to another person, you should not date. Others note that dating implies "giving one's heart away" to another, inevitably leading to intimacy and the development of strong bonds. Since intimacy apart from commitment to marriage violates biblical principles, dating hence leads us to sin against each other. Still others contend that dating may actually be committing idolatry, looking to another person rather than God as the means of personal fulfillment. Since the heart is deceitful and cannot be trusted, many argue, the safest way to pursue opposite-sex relationships is through friendship and group activities that do not blur the line of intimacy.

There are aspects of this approach that we think are commendable, and we appreciate that it is generating a long overdue conversation in Christian circles. We share the motivation to create an alternative to casual physical intimacy, and we find wisdom in discouraging emotional entanglements that outstrip one's readiness to commit in a relationship. When one has been sexually active, avoiding dating for a season is especially wise. We also find value in encouraging platonic friendship as the basis for romantic relationship development. Group activities in public spaces can safeguard relationships and create a positive setting for building cross-gendered relationships.

However, when students enter the emerging adult years, we think there are ways to reshape relationship formation that do not require jettisoning dating altogether. Dating itself does not violate biblical principles. There are multiple descriptions in Scripture of finding a spouse, none of which are sanctioned as prescriptive. We would encourage young adults to seek wisdom from elders who can share how they formed relationships of integrity and loyalty, and we would encourage elders to give space to emerging adults to discover new and faithful ways to pursue romance.

The elimination of dating may actually skip an important element in the relationship-formation process. Joseph Myers borrowed from Edward T. Hall the heuristic of four different kinds of space that characterize the types of disclosure and belonging that occur in relationships.[34] Myers's focus is primarily on small groups and how we transition between spaces in group formation, but the schema he adopts from Hall may have clarifying value for dating as well. Hall noted four types of interpersonal space: public, social, personal, and intimate. When people are in public space together, a minimum of twelve feet separates them. "Relating" is composed of sharing a common external experience, generally without the sharing of personal information. Social spaces typically operate with about four to twelve feet between people, providing locations in which small snapshots are shared to find common ground for communication. When people enter personal space, the distance between them shrinks to a range between eighteen inches and four feet. Private information may be shared and designated for safekeeping. In the most intimate spaces, eighteen inches or less, private feelings, thoughts, and experiences are shared.[35] If we abandon dating as a viable option, the progression through these spaces may seem awkward. Friendships fit well within public and social spaces, allowing for the inclusion of many others. But where would one locate dating? Dating as characterized above becomes equated with intimate space, that territory one should only enter when there appears to be an exclusive relationship leading to marriage. With friendship and dating located within these domains, personal space—a transition between the social and the intimate—disappears.

Perhaps we are just battling semantics, but we think important things can be learned in sharing personal space, and that it can be done without precocious intimacy. The ability to take initiative, learn self-disclosure, share appropriate vulnerability, keep boundaries, grow in self-awareness, and even manage emotions through a breakup are important skills that will surface on many fronts across the life course. Simply from a social science perspective, it would seem beneficial for emerging adults to gain as much knowledge about themselves and prospective spouses as possible while avoiding premature entanglements. We can't ignore the evidence that many personal relationships turn sexual in our culture today, and so safeguards would obviously be essential. Structuring events that provide favorable ways for unmarried people to get to know each other personally, while finding ways to protect against premature intimacy, is an ongoing but important challenge.

As emerging adults consider entering into romantic relationships, leaders can guide them to consider healthy patterns. They can encourage emerging adults to seek out those who are appealing at all levels. Physical attraction is often highlighted in our culture, but we can encourage them to be looking also for an attractive character, spiritual depth, an others-focused heart, compatible passions and goals, and spiritual gifts. While a return to courting is often impractical in our mobile society, we might recover certain helpful aspects such as the priority of conversation and assessing character over time. We can encourage interaction with both sets of parents as they consider the bonding together of two families. We can also encourage the involvement of the broader Christian community of the church. Many Christian emerging adults pursue relationships without any input from pastors and other church members. Such guidance is critical, especially if they can seek out married couples to share their experience and wisdom. Relationship formation, to the degree possible, should always take place within the context of community.

Online dating sites have both pros and cons in this regard. Finding a match online may actually enhance the gradual and conversational process that is often absent in today's hookup culture, restoring attentiveness to character preceding physical intimacy. However, it has the downside of potentially creating a false identity, creating a persona from strengths while eliminating potential weaknesses. When a couple does not share a physical space, it can be challenging to really know each other "in context" rather than in abstraction. When we see a live person in an embodied context, we can see the ways in which body, soul, mind, and emotions work together to produce a comprehensive picture of the person. When viewed online, even if all of these components are described, their artificial separation may provide a false picture. The online location may also foreground physical appearance as this is often the first filter that is used in the selection process.

Some have argued that we need to encourage early marriage among emerging adults to eliminate the trials and risks of such dating relationships. Mark Regnerus, for example, contends that sexual immorality has become such a rampant issue in part because of delayed marriage.[36] When the time between sexual maturity and marriage stretches out to fifteen years or more, he notes that it may be unreasonable to expect sexual purity. We move outside of God's reproductive designs by pushing marriage outside the normal range of women's fertility and both men's and women's sexual peaks and therefore pay the price in sexual brokenness. A helpful aspect of this argument is that it shines the spotlight on our true priorities. Many couples may be ready for marriage and yet delay this commitment only because they desire to wait until they can establish a high standard of living. Such a perspective may need to be challenged because it elevates material gain to inappropriate levels and may indeed make relational and physical purity more difficult. In addition, a long season of single living in a Generation Me world can make the self-giving posture of marital commitment more difficult. Waiting too long for marriage in order to "find oneself" and explore all possibilities can produce patterns that are challenging to eradicate when living with another. Marriage does not need to be a merit badge for achievement of full personal development but instead can serve as an important formative institution.

The push for earlier marriages also raises an important point: a Christian approach to relationship formation will recognize that effective partnerships leading to marriage involve not only personalities but also practices.[37] Delayed marriage can be the result of the prioritization of a perfect "fit," the soul mate that is the ideal complement to the self. While it is important to recognize personality similarities and differences and to seek a good "fit" in a relationship, marriage is ultimately rooted more powerfully in practices that sustain covenant faithfulness over the long haul. Hauerwas has suggested that "you always marry the wrong person."[38] If love is rooted only in "chemistry" rather than practices of covenantal commitment, it will be a shaky foundation on which to build for a lifetime. Personalities will change and physical attractiveness will wane, but commitment to practices of communication, prayer, conflict resolution, and forgiveness establish the bedrock of marital faithfulness.

At the same time, we must be wary of assuming early marriage to be a cure-all. First of all, many advocates of early marriage seem to imply that a chaste relationship is impossible if a couple fails to marry until their mid-to-late twenties. While this is no doubt a challenge, such a perspective seems to ignore the real possibility of self-control that is a fruit of the Holy Spirit in a person's life. And while some do indeed delay marriage for the wrong reasons, it is also true that some couples need more time to mature, to get to know each other, and to discern God's direction in their relationship. We certainly do not want to urge couples to marry for sexual intimacy if they are not grounded appropriately and holistically in other ways.

The normalizing of cohabitation provides another challenge. Imperative for leaders is to communicate to emerging adults the covenantal breach implicit in extramarital sexual activity, replacing cultural expectations with a clear picture of the divine meaning of sexual intimacy. They can also point to mounting evidence that debunks the commonly held myth that cohabitation lowers the risk of a failed relationship. Cohabiting couples are actually more likely than noncohabiting couples to get divorced if they eventually marry. Further, cohabitation may increase constraints that create relational inertia before goodness of fit is realistically determined.[39] Other ways of testing compatibility and relationship satisfaction can be offered that leave fewer skid marks on the soul if the relationship is terminated. For example, leaders might host seminars on love, sex, and dating; provide good literature for a couple to process together; invite a marriage therapist to speak; and encourage couples to experience one another in a variety of ministry and social contexts together.

Ministry leaders may have to determine how they will respond to cohabiting couples within the ministry. It may be helpful to first state regret for the cultural messages on which their relationship was founded and the inability of the church to have shaped a different and more appealing ethic that might have better supported their relational formation to this point. Leaders can share with them what Christian marriage looks like—the concepts of covenant, marriage vows, and love that is built on reflecting God's nature to a spouse. They can talk with the couple about the significance of taking these vows before a faith community that can nurture in them the focal images that sustain a good marriage. They can explain that a wedding with vows provides a means for the couple to make expectations about their relationship explicit and public, something most likely lacking in their cohabitation. They can also describe the boundary lines of Christian sexual intimacy within marriage, noting the seriousness of sexual sin and the need for Christians to witness to the world the eternal love of God. If the couple is willing, the relationship can be moved toward marriage. Alternatively, they may need to separate for a time to work on the commitments involved in a long-term marriage relationship, avoiding sexual intimacy as they seek to develop a true whole-person union.

The Trajectory of Healthy Physical Intimacy

Physical intimacy within a dating relationship also raises a number of questions. Many emerging adults struggle to determine concrete physical boundaries in relationships, puzzling over which lines can be crossed and which need to remain firm. They struggle with frustration and guilt when self-imposed lines are crossed or when each partner desires to maintain different standards. How might we provide guidance to those who are struggling with these issues without creating legalistic structures that create artificial boundaries?

The social sciences provide interesting perspectives along these lines. Desmond Morris, a British zoologist and famous human behaviorist, documented the "complex sequence of gradually increasing intimacies" that characterize healthy progress for a human couple.[40] Written over forty years ago, this book remains in circulation because of Morris's keen observations Morris made. Significant to our consideration is that Morris regarded attainment of each successive stage as constituting a new threshold of trust for a couple. Consequently, though his descriptors emphasize physical intimacies, they lend themselves well to parallel emotional and spiritual movements in a relationship. In this regard, the language of "threshold" is especially salient. Threshold can be used to name that point in the stimulation of a nerve that begins to produce a physiological response. Hence, once a stimulus exceeds a threshold, it almost certainly elicits particular sensations and begins producing a given effect. Likewise, the term "threshold" is used in marking boundaries. To cross a threshold indicates that one has passed through or entered into a new space. This is helpful language in sexual decision making because it helps us realize the interconnectedness of the sexual, emotional, and spiritual dimensions of our sense of self. Each step forward physically in a relationship involves permitting a partner to cross an emotional and spiritual threshold, entering increasingly personal and interior chambers. Morris names twelve steps in the sequence.[41] Each step, when it is reflective of processes that build deepening trust in the relationship, produces a strong bond. In the following summary, we name Morris's observations, adding to them our thoughts of what accompanies these physical markers in the emotional and spiritual domains.

1. Eye to Body—Morris notes the recurring mental grading processes that occur instantaneously as we scale someone from extremely attractive to extremely repulsive. Based entirely on visual information (gender, size, shape, age, coloring, status, mood) ascertained from a distance (today we might add from a digital photo), there is no trust that forms from this initial "social" contact. Donald Joy notes that this is not a sexual look but a snapshot image that often imprints on a person's memory the first time he or she remembers seeing the other and experiencing that "wow" moment.[42] One of the dangers of overexposure to pornography is that it almost inevitably sexualizes the first glance of a potential partner, trending toward predatorial regard only for body type rather than fuller dimensions of a person. Though a potential partner may be entirely unaware of a threshold being crossed, the awakening of potential love marks the beginning of the bonding sequence.

2. Eye to Eye—Morris comments that "while we view others, they view us. From time to time this means that our eyes meet."[43] Typically locking eyes with a stranger compels us to look away, the acknowledgment that further staring constitutes an act of invasion. If the other is recognized as an acquaintance, mutual greetings and gestures follow.[44] As the eyes are the windows to the soul, much information may be assessed between two people in a moment of mutual recognition when eyes see into each other. Such moments create high levels of self-consciousness because the eyes search for clues of reciprocal awareness or interest. When it is perceived favorably, a threshold of mutuality is entertained, compelling a move toward the next stage. Conversely, when individuals cannot look each other in the eyes, it is a good indication of trouble in relational harmony.

Morris could not have anticipated the digital revolution that is fostering new ways of introduction. Some have argued that the danger of computer-mediated communication is that many of the visual social cues (that Morris is here pointing to as important input) are missing from one's initial evaluation. Indeed, one survey found that 81 percent of respondents admitted to misrepresenting their height, weight, or age on their profile page.[45] Others, however, argue that cues are available in such things as one's email address, the formality of language, and the spelling and grammar one uses. Some anecdotal evidence argues that fewer visual cues are more than compensated for by the digital communication that ensues. Couples introducing themselves online, by necessity, ask more questions and offer more intimate responses in getting to know one another.[46]

3. Voice to Voice—Historically, vocal contact signaled the moment when most couples report that they first "met," but this may not be the case with partners who communicate first through technology. Although initial talk is usually trivial, small talk enables verbal cues to be assessed in addition to visual cues. Dialect, tone of voice, accent, and use of vocabulary supply new information to the brain. It is through calculated conversation that people look for what is common between them and by which people "test" whether they desire this relationship to move from public to personal space. When verbal exchanges or digital communiqués prove unattractive, either party can retreat from the relationship with relative ease and a polite dismissal. When communication is sustained, a new threshold ensues as the verbal exchanges then begin disclosing personal moods. Often in contemporary hookup culture, this step is rushed through on the way to premature physical intimacy. Physical touch, created to evoke physiological effect, convinces one of the "rightness" of the relationship before deeper issues of compatibility become part of the conversation.

4. Hand to Hand—Morris notes that these early stages (1–3) can occur instantaneously or over a period of months.[47] This is also true of stage four. Hand-to-hand touching can occur quickly with an introductory handshake. It can be delayed if there is a shy partner or postponed longer by necessity if a pair is interacting through a Web-based matchmaking service and geographically separated. Without the formal handshake, Morris observes that the first actual body contact may then occur disguised as an act of support or assistance (e.g., to keep from falling on a slippery surface). This safe touch conveys little of the emotional state of the couple and allows either partner to withdraw without causing hurt to the other.[48] Nonetheless, it initiates a behavior sequence that both are usually aware of and signals that another threshold is being approached. Prolonged hand holding serves as a public statement that individuals now wish to be known as a couple. This has its equivalent in changing one's status on Facebook. Running parallel to open

and mutual declarations of feelings, hand-to-hand touching typically signifies that this is now a mutually exclusive relationship grounded in personal space.

5. Arm to Shoulder—Physical contact down the side of the body represents for Morris a threshold beyond the hesitant characteristic of the last stage.[49] Bodies are now in close contact with each other but in a posture that publically conveys something between close friendship and love. This formation, historically seen even among sports teams that "huddle," symbolizes a low-level embrace of shared purpose and ownership.[50]

6. Arm to Waist—Pulling one closer together becomes symbolic of deepening trust and a statement, says Morris, of amorous intimacy. This is a posture men typically do not share with other men despite close friendship.[51] When fidelity has been well established, a natural reciprocal disclosure of one's life history and the confiding of one's future dreams naturally occurs. Critical at this point is discerning whether one's partner supports a personal vision of who he or she wants to become, important dialogue that can be preempted if a couple's primary way of relating is "making out."

Joy wisely encourages couples to spend ample amounts of time in a slow, celebrative cultivation of these first six steps in order to avoid foreclosing the bonding process.[52] Group activities and pairing up in public places avoid the premature privacy that too often creates the context where physical intimacy outruns secure and trustworthy bonding. For this reason, we favor long courtships and encourage couples to experience each other in a variety of social contexts and in a variety of roles as opposed to simply watching movies or other activities that require little conversation or exploration of mutual interests.

When these early stages are skipped or rushed (often initiated by a more experienced partner wanting to return to the level of intimacy of a previous relationship), a defective bond forms, and anxiety is introduced in the relationship.[53] Within two years, even sexuality can seem empty because it is devoid of bringing the fullness of one's personhood into a shared partnership. Mistrust can run deep, and self-respect can diminish when personal boundaries have been violated. Further, because the physical act of sexual playfulness is designed to accompany whole-life oneness, one cannot exit a relationship that has gone beyond stage six without feeling that a part of oneself has been ripped asunder.[54] "Friends with benefits," "hooking up," "cuddle parties," mutual masturbation, phone sex, and other attempts at deriving sexual or emotional gratification without honoring this natural process of trust building and pair bonding are probable avenues to either a broken or closed heart.

7. Mouth to Mouth—More than a peck on the cheek that acknowledges an appreciated good time, the couple now turns face-to-face in progressively intimate steps. Prolonged mouth-to-mouth kissing, especially combined with

full frontal embrace, crosses the threshold of physiological arousal for both the man and woman.[55] Whatever hesitancy there may have been in earlier steps is usually diffused, symbolic of past secrets and histories being shared. Typically, there is now ease in being with each other as vulnerabilities are shared. Such full disclosure may seem a small step physiologically, but its presence or absence at this stage psychologically and spiritually is telling.

8. Hand to Head—It is perhaps unanticipated to find Morris putting this step here in the sequencing of physical intimacy, but considering that our head is one of the most vulnerable parts of our body, we are naturally protective of who touches it. To allow one's hair to be stroked or the lines of one's face to be traced represents adoration, an admiration and studying of the body. Metaphorically, the warrior sets aside psychological and physical armor, allowing another close enough to place life in another's hand. It takes little to imagine the locks of Samson's head being stroked by Delilah as she coaxes him into uttering the secrets of his strength.[56]

9. Hand to Body—The hands now explore the partner's body, commonly culminating with the male manipulating the female's breasts. Morris notes that for many females, reaching this threshold emits a temporary halt.[57] Intuitively, further movement results in increasing difficulty and frustration unless the sequence can continue to completion. Therefore, such exploration is reserved for covenant marriage within the context of the whole-life sharing of one-flesh union.

10. Mouth to Breast—The threshold Morris sees operative here is the movement to strict privacy.[58] Although stage nine may be included here, this stage involves exposure of the female breast that meets with public disapproval in most Western countries. At a lover's breast, a person revisits the dependency of being a baby. Joy suggests that the gesture marks the male transfer of the bond with one's mother to the beloved.[59]

Neuroscience also provides intriguing insight that raises the stakes of these final stages even higher. Fisher found that romantic love is associated with elevated activities of central dopamine and decreased activity of central serotonin. Both of these hormones are positively associated with the firing of sexual desire. What this suggests is that the chemical interactions surrounding sexual arousal naturally trigger the sensation of falling in love. Hence, emerging adults who may be intending a casual sexual encounter with no intention of romantic involvement may find themselves inadvertently triggering the brain system for attachment, leading to "complex, unanticipated emotional entanglements with psychologically and socially unsuitable mating partners."[60]

11. Hand to Genital—As the hand explores the partner's body, it inevitably reaches the genital region, first caressing, then simulating the rhythm of

intercourse.[61] Here the intent is clearly toward intercourse though numerous couples will justify orgasm in a variety of ways to claim technical virginity. Regnerus and Jeremy Uecker, for example, report that oral sex is now common within the repertoire of emerging adults. Its prevalence as foreplay is likely connected to the perception in many young adults' minds that oral sex does not constitute "having sex."[62]

12. Genital to Genital—Morris notes that the final consummation of the one-flesh union for a female virgin physiologically represents the first irreversible act.[63] The hymen is ruptured and with it the possibility of a second irreversible act, pregnancy. When the twelve-step sequence has been navigated properly, each stage will have brought a couple together physically, emotionally, and spiritually. With each intimate threshold crossed, trust is deepened, opening couples to a full experience of oneness and safeguarding the raising of children that may result.

There are, no doubt, variations in this chronological sequencing, some that might be culturally or even ethnically specific, others that might result from religious values, and still others that might be specific to personal preferences.[64] Morris argues, however, that the general sequencing is relatively universal, tied to the anatomy and physiology of being human and necessary for establishing lasting bonds of attachment. We believe that whenever a physiological threshold is passed that does not procure an equally significant advance in the emotional attachment and mutual trust of a couple, the biblical ideal of oneness begins to diminish. The quality of intimacy experienced by the couple at the end of the sequence is diminished by the faulty process that preceded it. Yet sexual freedom, experienced by so many in emerging adult culture and encouraged by the media, rushes to the later genital stages, uncoupling them from the culminating expression of a marital one-flesh union. Inevitably, when maximum physical intimacy is sought with minimum bonding, a compensatory activity sets in. Rather than cherishing the partner or deepening trust, focus often turns to maximizing the physical intensity of the encounter (note the huge economic markets created by pharmaceutical companies that reinforce this focus). In sharp contrast, when the powerful bond of attachment is well formed, the early steps of the sequence retain symbolic meaning and pleasure for the couple. What comes to count is the quality of the sexual behavior in recurring celebration of their shared life rather than its intensity or frequency. All of this provides empirical support for biblical prescriptions regarding the location of sexual intimacy within the protected sphere of covenant marriage.

"I have the right to do anything," writes Paul, "but not everything is beneficial" (1 Cor. 6:12; 10:23). Emerging adults may not find particulars in the Scriptures detailing what kind of touch is permissible in the flowering of a relationship or when to enter an intimate relationship, but they can ask, "Is this beneficial to our relationship, my communion with the Lord, stewardship of schoolwork, and our connections within the community, to pair off and relate physically in this fashion at this point in our relationship?" Emerging adults may desire rules, but we must encourage them to seek God's guidance and to seek biblical grounding in the nature of covenant fidelity. A sexual conscience can be shaped by a deeper awareness of the story that shapes our sexual lives and by the broader sense of communal hope that elicits virtuous practices. "Rather than asking ourselves how far is too far," Colon and Field suggest, "perhaps we should ask ourselves if we are merely following (or trying to circumvent) a set of rules, or if we are demonstrating our humble response to God's faithfulness in how we live our lives."[65]

"Is that a problem?" In a culture of tolerance where anything goes, this question highlights the maze that emerging adults must navigate on the path to relational wholeness. In the end, leaders and mentors can help provide them with relational paths that are attentive to their pasts, are purposeful in the present, and look forward both to their future relationships and to the ultimate eschatological future in which they will enjoy perfect relationships with others and spiritual union with their Savior. As the final chapter will demonstrate, helping emerging adults turn their gazes purposefully to the past, present, and future is the unique role of a spiritual mentor in all areas of life.

9 | Mentoring

Past, Present, and Future

> Remember your Creator in the days of your youth.
>
> Ecclesiastes 12:1

Without question, emerging adulthood acts as a "hinge" moment in many individuals' lives. Caught in the "liminal space" between adolescence and adulthood, these years represent a pivot point for the soul. In this moment of transition, a variety of unhelpful postures can emerge. Some emerging adults cling to the past, retaining childhood identifications and shrinking back from God's expanding vision for their present and future lives. Some seek to live only for the present moment, ignoring personal history and resisting a future-oriented picture of adult faithfulness. Still others focus all of their concern on the future, working toward an adult dream while ignoring God's work in their past and present experiences. Ultimately, each of these postures represents a failure of emerging adult vision, a perceptual "blind spot" that limits a comprehensive view of life in Christ.

Effective mentoring requires a keen awareness of the postures necessary at the hinge. At this "in between" juncture, mentors must help emerging adults open their eyes to God's work in their lives and in the world through attentiveness to the past, present, and future. Mentors can guide emerging adults to look back and consider the past works of God in Scripture, in history, and in their own lives, solidifying a deep sense of his faithfulness and provision. Mentors can guide emerging adults to look at the present and develop attentiveness to God's work around them and in their own souls. Mentors can guide emerging adults to look forward and envision future faithfulness, forming commitments and lifestyles that will endure over the long haul. At this hinge moment, in other words, mentors can facilitate postures of remembering, attentiveness, and envisioning that allow the divine Mentor to infuse and transform emerging adults' past, present, and future stories. Even more to the point, they can help emerging adults connect their stories to the past, present, and future story of God. Viewed correctly, mentoring provides an opportunity to help emerging adults see all of life with spiritual eyes, to remember their Creator in the days of their youth (Eccles. 12:1).

The Challenges of Mentoring in Emerging Adulthood

There are a number of factors that make emerging adulthood a period ripe for mentoring. As previously indicated, emerging adults are beginning a time of life in which they move beyond passively receiving others' commitments and start to develop their own convictions, ideals, and voices. There is no sense in which this "dissolution and recomposition of meaning" marks a complete independence.[1] Guidance is still desperately needed, but it is a guidance that is dialogical and mutual rather than unidirectional. It is (in this sense) accurate to say that emerging adults are seeking mentors rather than heroes. They do not need someone who will overwhelm them with unquestioned expertise as much as a faithful mentor who will facilitate the development, nurture, and, at times, correction, of their growing faith, relationship, and vocational commitments.

Furthermore, the emerging adult years generate a number of new stressors, particularly for those in higher education. In their book, *College of the Overwhelmed*, Richard Kadison and Theresa Foy DiGeronimo describe the numerous challenges that plague American college students on a daily basis. Financial pressures are ubiquitous and often linger for students throughout their undergraduate and graduate school careers.[2] Academic stress is also on the rise, leading many to become depressed and anxious as they sacrifice sleep, friendships, proper eating, and exercise so that they can devote more time to studying. For many emerging adults, the academic, athletic, social, and religious venues that once structured life and identity quickly disappear, leaving them devoid of a sense of rootedness in their new environments. Many find that their high school "glory days" as star athletes, school leaders, or musicians no longer apply in this new setting, surrounded by thousands of qualified peers. For some, especially the high achievers, this can be a disillusioning time, raising significant questions about their unique contributions.[3]

Specific groups face unique challenges. Members of ethnic and racial minority groups often face both subtle and overt forms of discrimination on campus, compounded by the loneliness of exclusion and "difference." International students face issues of culture shock, lengthy separation from family, and learning style and language issues on top of the other challenges of college life. Women often fear for their safety, particularly in the sexually exploitative campus culture. At times, they also face unique challenges in the classroom, experiencing what some scholars have called a "chilly climate" of stereotyping, false expectations, and devaluation. The prominence of eating disorders among female collegians also speaks to the body image stress at this stage of life. It is little wonder that collegiate counseling centers have witnessed surges in caseloads over the past ten years.[4]

Amid these larger concerns, emerging adulthood is also frequently characterized by spiritual struggle. In their research on this area, Alyssa Bryant and Helen Astin found that spiritual struggle is most prominent among members of minority religious groups, females, those attending religious colleges, those majoring in psychology, and those who face experiences in college that "challenge, disorient, and introduce students to new and unfamiliar worldviews."[5] As students are confronted with unique perspectives and lifestyles that conflict with cherished beliefs, they are faced with new decisions about what to believe and how to live. Struggle of this kind can of course be very good, but it would be wrong to assume it always leads to spiritual formation. As Bryant and Astin contend, "Another possibility: spiritual struggle might not, in the end, result in growth; rather, it might hinder development if one is locked into maladaptive ways of conceiving and responding to the existential questions life poses."[6] In the midst of such confusion, mentors can serve both as guides across treacherous terrain and as worthy exemplars who have traversed the land and emerged whole on the other side.

Despite these needs, the cultural context of emerging adulthood has made mentoring more challenging than ever. Perhaps the most significant barrier to mentoring is the structural separation of emerging adults from the older adults around them. For example, cultural constraints often stifle the mentoring role of parents. Some of this begins in adolescence.[7] The proliferation of youth activities places great strains on parents' ability to have meaningful interaction with adolescent children. Parents are often relegated to roles as chauffeurs, and the home becomes little more than a boarding house for food and shelter. The loss of common family meals often means the elimination of the one location fostering adult-child conversation in a shared time and place. The widespread availability of entertainment in the home also tends to isolate family members from one another even when they do occupy common space. Furthermore, instead of working alongside parents in the teen years, the comprehensive high school provides an intense locus of peer culture that resists adult intervention.[8] In their study of active church-attending teens, Kara Powell, Brad Griffin, and Cheryl Crawford found that most parents do not talk with their children about matters of faith, particularly avoiding details of their own faith journeys. In addition, she found that only 9 percent of these adolescents had regular dialogue with parents about Scripture.[9]

This trend appears to continue in emerging adulthood. In his research, Christian Smith found that relationships with parents tend to improve between the ages of 18 and 23. Removed a bit from the parental strictures of adolescence, many emerging adults are able to forge stronger "bonds of understanding and affection" with their parents.[10] At the same time, this improvement does not seem to foster a mentoring connection during these years. As Smith suggests, most parent-child relationships in these years are "renegotiated to selectively keep parents in the dark or at a distance about many of the important things going on in emerging adults' lives."[11] While bonds improve, the desire for differentiation and autonomy often means that emerging adults fail to engage parents on issues related to faith, identity, and lifestyle.

Compounding this gap is the fact that, beginning in adolescence, parents seem to willingly abdicate any form of mentoring role. Anchored by the cultural myth that peers supplant parents in importance during these years, many parents abandon all hope of significant dialogue regarding issues of meaning, purpose, and behavior. Responding to cues from children that they would rather be left alone on such matters, parents seem to accommodate these requests, convincing themselves that their influence is no longer needed. Once emerging adults leave home, such a mentality is embraced all the more. While they may provide financial support and practical advice on matters of education, they often resist exerting any influence on matters of faith, vocation, and lifestyle, issues deemed too "personal" for parental guidance.[12] In short, structural elements complicate parents' ability to serve as mentors, but parents also appear willing to adhere to the cultural scripts and relinquish this role.

Upon leaving the nest, emerging adults do not see a marked improvement in mentoring prospects. Changes in higher education have generated a climate inhospitable to active mentoring. Even acknowledging the tangential presence of faculty and staff, college represents a concentrated monogenerational existence. Many higher education institutions have largely abandoned any sense of a philosophy of in loco parentis ("in the place of a parent"), choosing instead to turn a blind eye to student life outside of the classroom. Because professors are often rewarded for scholarship more than for teaching and mentoring, they have little incentive to carve out time for investment in students' lives. In addition, the institutional separation of facts and values typically means that professors' sole responsibility comes in the communication of factual information, leaving values to be formed within the peer-dominated world of the co-curriculum.[13] This is often done in the name of granting students freedom, but it is also a structure that frees faculty from the "onerous" responsibility of serving as teacher-mentors. As William Willimon and Thomas Naylor put it, "We say we are disengaged from our students' lives because we 'trust them,' we 'give them responsibility,' or we 'allow them to be adults.' This is rather thin rationalization for our abandonment of them."[14]

Despite the presence of adult colleagues, even postcollegiate experience tends to isolate emerging adults among their peers. In the hours outside of work, as such shows as *Friends* and *The Big Bang Theory* depict, social life is generally found among peers. Mobility means that most postcollegiate emerging adults lack close geographical ties with family members. In addition, social networking further dilutes mentoring relationships, drowning what little adult influence there may be in a sea of peer input. Overall, emerging adult life tends to be lived in the absence of older adults, restricting the potential for mentoring relationships. As Smith summarizes,

> One of the most striking social features of emerging adulthood is how structurally disconnected most emerging adults are from older adults. . . . Most of the meaningful, routine relationships that most emerging adults have are with other emerging adults. Emerging adults most often live with other emerging adults, hang out with other emerging adults, go to school with other emerging adults, party with other emerging adults, engage in sports and recreational activities with other emerging adults, have romantic relationships with other emerging adults, and so on.[15]

Combined with generational segmentation in the church, such a reality confirms David Kinnaman's discovery that most emerging adults have never had an adult friend other than their parents.[16]

Yet beyond these critical social factors, a number of personal forces may also inhibit a strong culture of emerging adult mentoring. In some cases, they may see mentoring as a sign of weakness, an admission of need that seems to go against the desire for independence and self-efficacy. As one scholar notes, "When kids go off to college, society expects that their identity will shift from being dependent children to being responsible adults. . . . The societal pressure to become more autonomous and independent comes at a time when college students are entering a new world where they need extra support and guidance."[17] Ironically, therefore, many emerging adults are led to believe that mentoring will serve as a barrier to growing adult autonomy.[18] In reality, at a time when they are leaving behind the family and community supports that sustained them in adolescence, they need the encouragement and guidance of caring mentors more than ever.[19]

The possibility of mentoring can also be threatened by emerging adult opinions of the older adults in their midst. This can work in two ways. In some cases, they are intimidated or overawed by the older adults around them, especially if these individuals occupy esteemed positions as professors, pastors, or leaders in their fields. In such cases, emerging adults may feel unworthy to make demands on the time of such "important" individuals. For this reason, while emerging adults may seek out mentors on their own, it will also be necessary for potential mentors to take the initiative and prayerfully seek out those who appear hungry for such input.[20]

Alternatively, emerging adults may feel that they have little to gain from mentoring relationships with those of older generations. This may be the result of the negative connotations associated with adulthood in general. If adulthood is something that they are trying to avoid at all costs, why would they seek the help of those who had crossed that dreaded line? Older adults often represent stability, commitment, and routine—sure signs of loss.[21] Adults may also seem to represent flawed political or spiritual ideologies. For example, many emerging adults see older adults as ignorant on issues that are important to them: poverty, environmental concerns, the AIDS crisis, and many others. They may view older adults as overly materialistic, culturally conservative, or spiritually bound to church structures that seem inadequate for contemporary life patterns. While such thoughts often reflect a generational arrogance, it is true that many emerging adults feel that they have more to teach than to learn. Such "de-idealization" of adults is a necessary developmental move, to be sure, but if taken to an extreme it can negate the possibility of learning from both the strengths and weaknesses of adult mentors.[22] Like King Rehoboam in the Old Testament, many emerging adults would rather consult "the young men who had grown up with him" rather than the "elders who had served his father" (1 Kings 12:6–15).

Furthermore, older adults may appear "out of touch," unable to understand or relate to the changing cultural trends influencing emerging adult lives.[23] Particularly in a culture dominated by technology and media, older adults who are not attuned to the latest trends in social networking, web surfing, or smartphone usage can appear irrelevant to emerging adult life patterns. While adults are typically those who possess the wisdom and expertise to be handed down to the next generation, the importance of technology in daily life and the rapidity of technological change can actually begin to reverse generational hierarchies. Movies and television sitcoms often portray adults as clueless, obsolete, and irrelevant, hopelessly outdated when compared to the younger generations. The situation is similar to that of immigrants in a new country where youth more quickly achieve a facility with new cultural forms, leaving parents to feel less capable than their children. Similarly, today's emerging adults, as "digital natives," are often able to swim more naturally in the contemporary cultural stream.[24] This reversal of hierarchies threatens to derail the intergenerational mentoring process before it can even begin.

Such a reality accords well with Margaret Mead's classic description of a "prefigurative" society. Mead proposed a theory of cross-generational relationships defined by three potential modes: "postfigurative, in which children learn primarily from their forebears, cofigurative, in which both children and adults learn from their peers, and the prefigurative, in which adults learn also from their children."[25] In a postfigurative culture, change is so gradual that the younger generation simply learns from the older generation how to prepare for the future. In a cofigurative culture, adults and children must learn from their peers because of new situations for which they are unprepared (yet there is still an assumption that values will be retained across the generations). In a prefigurative culture, on the other hand, change is so dramatic that the older generation is perceived as having little to offer those coming after them. Since they cannot know what the future holds, their perspectives are automatically considered anachronistic. Mead posited that "there are now no elders who know more than the young themselves about what the young are experiencing. . . . In this new culture it will be the child—and not the parent and grandparent that represents what is to come."[26] The whole concept of mentoring can seem quaint—even regressive—in such a culture.

This can go both ways, however. Older adults may themselves feel inadequate to mentor emerging adults because of their lack of proficiency in a technologically and media-saturated world. Perhaps they feel they cannot relate to the strange world of the emerging adult, or perhaps they fear embarrassment at their own lack of cultural savvy. Furthermore, some older adults may not be sure they want to take on a role as mentor because this serves as an admission of advancing age. Because our culture unabashedly communicates that emerging adulthood is the best time of life, those beyond these years seem driven to grasp or recapture the fading cultural cache of this decade. They may wish to be around young people, to join in their activities and "look the part." Mentoring, however, seems to impose a separation and distance from emerging adulthood that is resisted because of its association with aging.[27]

Without question, the "mentoring gap" in emerging adulthood is one of the most significant factors blunting spiritual formation in these years. Emerging adults have little direct access to the wisdom and experience of older adults, lacking settings in which to hear the stories of success and failure of those who have gone before them. They miss out on tangible role models of exemplary adult living, lacking settings in which to see clear pictures of faithful adult practice. Their views of the world are shaped primarily by those in the same stage of life, and they are rarely challenged by alternative points of view. In addition, the absence of mentoring means that emerging adults are left vulnerable to the all-pervasive influence of media, advertising, and consumer culture. External forces can easily manipulate and enslave them because they lack the traditional and communal resources that might call them to replace cultural norms with different standards. "This means," Smith notes, "most emerging adults live this crucial decade of life surrounded mostly by their peers—people of the same age and in the same boat—who have no more experience, insight, wisdom, perspective, or balance than they do. It is sociologically a very odd way to help young people come of age, to learn how to be responsible, capable, mature adults."[28]

The absence of mentoring also tends to encourage the cynicism that can so easily arise in emerging adulthood. According to Joseph Chilton Pearce, the growth of the brain in adolescence engenders a burgeoning capacity for idealism.[29] As adolescents move into emerging adulthood, they need to see these ideals modeled and communicated by adults whose lives are overflowing with purpose. If they fail to find such individuals—or if these individuals are limited to the distant and spurious exemplars of the entertainment and sports world—emerging adults may experience despair, disillusionment, and deflated expectations. When it seems as if there are no "real" models of the "ideals" they generate in their minds, many fall prey to cynicism at the very time when a future-driven anticipation should be beckoning them forth to kingdom living. As Sharon Parks suggests, "To varying degrees and in differing forms, mentors worthy of the name embody and inspire the possibility of committed and meaningful adulthood. On the other side of the formation of critical awareness, a good mentor is an antidote to mere cynicism."[30]

The Postures of Emerging Adult Mentoring

Because of the lack of informal and expected contact between emerging and older adults, intentional mentoring is more necessary than ever. In a healthy emerging adult context, such mentoring roles can be shared both by parents and by nonparental adult figures. Despite the previously mentioned limitations on parents, such mentoring connections should be encouraged. With the advent and ubiquity of cell phones, many in this age group remain more closely tethered to their parents even after they have "left the nest." College students often interact with their parents daily via calls or texts, sometimes to ask questions and often just to chat. Furthermore, a growing number of students return home after college or graduate school. While supervisory oversight is often reduced in these settings, it is still true that this so-called boomerang effect places the emerging adult in close proximity to parental influence for an extended period of time. Recent statistics show that between 40 and 50 percent of emerging adults return after college to live at home, a significant increase over previous historical periods.[31] As one study indicated, "The leaving-home transition has become more renewable, less a one-way street, and more like a circular migration."[32] While the wisdom of such arrangements can and should be debated, it certainly does seem to bestow on parents (whether they want it or not!) a heightened role in the emerging adult mentoring process.

Yet it is also important to have nonparental adult mentors as resources for emerging adult spiritual formation. While most still appreciate affirming comments from parents, it is natural for emerging adults to assume that such support is a function of their position: that is what parents are "supposed to do." Commendation from nonparental adults, however, may be received as more "objective" and interpreted as more legitimate.[33] Similarly, parental challenges and demands may be viewed as impositions or attributed to past issues rooted in personal history. The very same demands—sometimes phrased in the exact same way—coming from a nonparental adult may be interpreted as a healthy challenge or proper push toward personal improvement. Some of this speaks to the simple reality of reinforcement. The emerging adult often needs to hear a charge several times, from multiple sources, for it to gain legitimacy and achieve the power necessary to drive action. However, emerging adults also hear comments from parents within a historical context. Parental praise and admonition will always be interpreted in light of a lifetime of past interactions, but comments from nonparental adults may be given more credence precisely because they are not historically charged. All of this points to the necessity of "mentoring communities," settings in which a variety of adults can exert influence and provide diverse pictures of faithfulness to furnish the emerging adult imagination.[34]

As mentioned at the beginning of the chapter, mentors must help emerging adults consider their past, present, and future stories in light of God's work in their lives and in redemptive history. By fostering postures of remembering, attentiveness, and envisioning, mentors can facilitate an intentional and comprehensive vision of life that places God at the very center. The remainder of this chapter will consider these postures and provide concrete ways in which they can be nurtured in emerging adults' lives.

Looking Back: The Posture of Remembering

Emerging adult mentoring must always foster a backward gaze, a purposeful engagement with God's work in biblical history, church history, and one's own personal history. Such a posture is often quite challenging at this stage of life, which is often oriented exclusively toward the present and future. With so many transitions unfolding and with an eye to preparing for careers and relationships, looking back can seem counterintuitive, even unhelpful. However, through drawing emerging adults' attention to the past goodness of God in history and in their own lives, mentors can lay the foundation for present and future growth. The repeated commands throughout Scripture to "tell the next generation / the praiseworthy deeds of the LORD" (Ps. 78:4) cannot be dismissed as mere cultural transmission. Far from wistful reminiscence, active remembering is a potent tool for spiritual formation in these years.

The word "remember" in the Old Testament often implies far more than simple recall. Instead, it refers to the process by which individuals hold events from the past before their eyes, summoning them into the mind so that they can inform and empower action in the present. Critical here is that emerging adults are confronted with the particular story of the Christian faith, the narrative of God's redemptive work throughout history. Yet the church rarely teaches biblical redemptive history or church history to those of emerging generations. Very often, perhaps because of a misguided application of developmental psychology, the stories of Scripture are pictured as relevant for children alone. Once students reach the teen years and beyond, leaders often assume that the stories have all been learned and that they should now focus on principles and life needs.

By neglecting these stirring stories, however, we miss out on a powerful opportunity to establish a firm sense of Christian identity in the next generation. Elementary and secondary teachers often have an implicit understanding of the power of this process. They recognize that the teaching of one's national history—the stories, the battles, the heroes, and the sacrifices—provides not only information but also a deep sense of emotional loyalty and allegiance to the next generation of citizens. As students hear about their heritage and celebrate their leaders, they gain a growing desire to carry on the legacy of those on whose shoulders they stand. Likewise, emerging adults need to hear the Christian biblical story and the stories of the great men and women of faith so that they will cultivate an allegiance to their positions as citizens of the kingdom of God. We are all forgetful people who have experienced the muffling of God's redemptive story amid the din of the world. Unless this narrative is continually rehearsed and reinforced in their minds—that is, unless it is continually *remembered*—the story of the broader culture will set the agenda for their lives.[35]

In addition to the formation of Christian identity and allegiance, active remembering of God's work is also a helpful practice in virtue formation. In the Old Testament, God's command to remember was often linked with specific spiritual benefits. In Deuteronomy, for example, the Lord implores the Israelites to remember his work in bringing them out from Egypt. If they did not remember, he warns, "When you eat and are satisfied, when you build fine houses and settle down, and when your herds and flocks grow large and your silver and gold increase and all you have is multiplied, then your heart will become proud. . . . You may say to yourself, 'My power and the strength of my hands have produced this wealth for me'" (Deut. 8:12–14, 17). For emerging adults in the process of establishing themselves—buying houses or renting apartments and beginning to secure an income—there is always a tendency to see one's advancement as a product of personal power and competence. Because this is a time of growing self-efficacy, those in their twenties are quite prone to the pride and autonomy that can obscure a sense of God's patient and pervasive work in their lives. Active remembering, considering the goodness of God in their lives and throughout history, is a powerful means of helping them acknowledge ongoing dependence on the grace and blessing of God. Humility is irrevocably linked to remembering.

Scripture also clearly demonstrates the connection between remembering and courage. In preparation to meet the nations occupying Canaan, Moses said to the people of Israel: "You may say to yourselves, 'These nations are stronger than we are. How can we drive them out?' But do not be afraid of them; remember well what the LORD your God did to Pharaoh and to all Egypt" (Deut. 7:17–18). For emerging adults who are in the process of taking on new responsibilities, new relationships, and new areas of service, anxious fear is an ever-present reality. Many emerging adults fall prey to what Thomas Aquinas called "pusillanimity," the fear-based tendency to "shrink back from all that God has called them to be."[36] Focusing on their own abilities and perceived insufficiencies, they, like the Israelites, may feel inadequate to move forward into God's call upon their lives. Remembering God's past faithfulness can be a potent means of achieving confidence for the future, a boldness rooted in his strength rather than their weakness. As emerging adults bring to mind

God's power in history and on their behalf in the past, they are better able to trust him for present challenges and therefore resist shrinking from daunting opportunities that come their way.

While there are many other virtues formed in the process of remembering, a last important one is its capacity to strengthen an other-directed posture of service and compassion. Throughout Scripture, there is a consistent relationship between remembering God's goodness in one's own life and serving others. In his command to free one's Hebrew servants after six years (and to supply these servants liberally upon their release), God explicitly states that the Israelites were to "Remember that you were slaves in Egypt and the LORD your God redeemed you" (Deut. 15:15). The Israelites were liberated from Egypt, so they were to exercise similar liberality in offering release to their servants. Sending them out to minister, Jesus also reminds his disciples, "Freely you have received; freely give" (Matt. 10:8). Isaiah proclaims, "Here am I. Send me!" (Isa. 6:8) as the overflow of his gratitude for the atoning grace of God. As these passages would indicate, remembering the great works of God in one's own life history is a powerful incentive to demonstrate goodness to others. Perhaps the lack of service and compassion toward others evidenced in contemporary emerging adulthood is in part related to a lack of active remembering, a lack of conscious reflection on the mercy and grace of God.[37] Remembering produces gratitude, and gratitude is in many ways the engine that drives compassion for others.

If remembering is linked to identity, humility, courage, and compassion, how can this potent practice be encouraged? Retelling the stories of God's great works in Scripture and throughout church history is one obvious means of commending his works to the next generation (Ps. 145:4). Emerging adulthood is also an excellent time to begin journaling, documenting in writing the works of God in their lives so that they can revisit these memories on a regular basis. Just as the Israelites used altars and piles of stones to serve as physical and geographical markers of God's faithfulness, mentors can encourage emerging adults to fashion reminders of God's faithful provision, assistance, and presence. At a time when everything seems new and unfamiliar, emerging adults desperately need "Ebenezers"—places to pitch their flags in the ground to signify that "thus far the LORD has helped us" (1 Sam. 7:12). Celebration would be another means of helping emerging adults actively remember God's goodness in the past. The early Hebrews institutionalized the process of remembering through feasts and festivals that commemorated God's miraculous acts on their behalf: the Passover, the Feast of Tabernacles, the Feast of Pentecost, Purim, and many others.[38] We, of course, have similar rituals in the Eucharist ("This do in remembrance of me"), Christmas, and Easter, but it is fair to say that we are somewhat deficient when it comes to celebratory remembrance.

This will also happen as we help emerging adults intentionally reflect on their lives in order to locate and remember key moments of divine work. By tracing the key people, experiences, challenges, and deliverances of their lives, emerging adults can begin to "see" and reflect on God's hand in their personal stories, locating his power and grace in the mundane and memorable moments of their lives. As Frederick Buechner suggests,

> We cannot live our lives constantly looking back, listening back, lest we be turned into pillars of longing and regret, but to live without listening at all is to live deaf to the fullness of the music. Sometimes we avoid listening for fear of what we may hear, sometimes for fear that we may hear nothing at all but the empty rattle of our feet on the pavement. But *be not affeard*. . . . Listen for Him. Listen to the sweet and bitter airs of your present and your past for the sound of him.[39]

As mentors help emerging adults see Christ in their stories—generating personal spiritual time lines—they can begin to recognize that their lives are filled not with random events but with a God who is "hiddenly at work in all our working."[40] In short, remembering can be a critical tool in helping emerging adults "renarrate" their lives, retelling their stories in the light of divine action. "The gift of mentoring," Keith Anderson and Randy Reese note, "helps transform mere chronology into sacred story, mere biography into spiritual autobiography."[41] At a hinge moment of life, active remembering can provide a sense of pause, a time to listen to their lives for the presence of the One who worked in their pasts but is also the same yesterday and today and forever (Heb. 13:8).

Looking Around and Within: The Posture of Attentiveness

In describing his collegiate experience at Western Kentucky University, singer-songwriter Michael Card articulated the importance of a mentoring relationship cultivated with Dr. Bill Lane, a professor of religious studies:

> Those of us who were together at Western still refer to those college days as "the golden years." They were golden for two reasons. First, practically everything that can be good about being nineteen and in college was happening to me. I was free to pursue any subject that interested me, and for the most part, my professors were all men and women who loved the subjects they taught. But golden also because, with Bill's help, I was awake and alive to how good it was, all while it was happening around and in me. After all, that's one of the tasks of the discipler, to wake us up to what is really going on around us, to encourage

us to take our eyes off ourselves and see that our world is not the only world. That outside the narrow confines of the self there exists a world that truly is golden. And they allow us to borrow their eyes until we can see it for ourselves.[42]

Card's depiction of this relationship speaks to a powerful dimension of mentoring: fostering a context within which emerging adults can "wake up" to what God is doing in and around them. A mentor will work to help the mentee pay attention to the presence of God and his work in their lives, in their learning, in the lives of those around them, in creation, and in the broader world. And, as Card indicates, mentors will also allow emerging adults to "borrow their eyes" so that they can begin to see the unseen spiritual world. Jesus did this repeatedly with his disciples. His parables, for those who had eyes to see, were means of helping the disciples see the reality beyond what they could see with their eyes. His very life displayed the reality of a kingdom not of this world. He wanted desperately for them to recognize that, in the midst of their daily activities and seemingly mundane tasks, the kingdom of heaven was "near." Eventually, as the book of Acts reveals, they began to see it for themselves.

In his classic work *Letters to Malcolm*, C. S. Lewis spoke of the critical role of this attentiveness in the spiritual life: "We may ignore, but we can nowhere evade, the presence of God. The world is crowded with Him. He walks everywhere *incognito*. And the *incognito* is not always hard to penetrate. The real labor is to remember, to attend. In fact, to come awake. Still more, to remain awake."[43] As mentors, we are called to help emerging adults "come awake" and "remain awake," to help them develop a consistent and habitual awareness of God's presence and activity in their lives. As Anderson and Reese suggest, "The extraordinary events of epiphany or revelation are few and rare, but the gentle or firm probing of a mentor's questions draw us back to the central action of spirituality: *to pay attention for the presence of God in everything*. . . . Spiritual mentoring is a relationship that helps us pay attention to our stories and to recognize there *the already present action of God*."[44] The Spirit is already active and working in emerging adults' lives and in the world around them. The mentor's purpose is to open up spaces to help them become more attentive, receptive, responsive, and obedient to that work. In the midst of multiple distractions that blind the eyes to spiritual reality, the mentor is therefore to help foster an awareness of the presence and work of the true Mentor.

Mentors can foster attentiveness in many ways. Timely questions will often alert emerging adults to look for God and his work in everyday activities. For example, a mentor may ask questions such as, What events, situations, or people has God brought into your life over the last week and what might

he want you to see in them? What joys and disappointments have you experienced recently and how have they brought you closer to or driven you away
from God's presence? How is God speaking to you through his Word about
current struggles and victories? In what ways did you encounter God through
his creation today? How might you view this difficult situation differently in
light of a recognition of God's care? The very process of asking such questions can enhance attentiveness to God's presence and a continual awareness
of key locations in which they might connect with him throughout the day.
Asking good questions does not represent a *prelude* to effective ministry. It
is the work of effective ministry in the lives of emerging adults, opening eyes
to the unseen world.

While mentors can help open eyes by asking the right questions, the ultimate
goal is for emerging adults to begin asking these questions on their own. Since
questions set the stage for the way they interpret the world, good and bad
questions can serve as key elements leading to positive or negative patterns of
thinking and living. A recent student of mine (David's), going through a time
of intense suffering, could not get past the question, "Why is this happening
to me?" Such a question has its place, to be sure, but it led this student to a
frenetic search for answers and a flawed sense of the relationship between her
sin and the situation. When I asked her, "Where is God's presence especially
evident in this situation and how might this display his loving care for you?"
it was as if a window had opened to a new interpretation of the world. Not
only did this prompt attentiveness to God in the midst of her struggle, but it
also helped her begin to ask a whole different set of questions that moved her
in different interpretive directions.

In the life of a collegian or graduate student, this mentoring must include
attentiveness to the work and character of God in the academic life. Questions can open their eyes to see God's power, beauty, creativity, sovereignty,
wisdom, and rationality in their studies. They can be guided to reflect on how
their class content enables them to see unique aspects of God's nature and
to worship him more fully. Conscious reflection on these themes can serve as
powerful goads to the development of postures of awe and wonder, humility
before the greatness of God, and gratitude for his marvelous character and
works. In addition to asking questions, mentors can also encourage practices
that promote spiritually attentive learning. Journaling can provide space for
students to reflect on the spiritual implications of course content and can
encourage written expressions of awe and gratitude. They can be directed to
personal and corporate prayer over these matters, providing space for worshiping God in light of his character and work. The mentor may also suggest times
of confession regarding personal or corporate sin and brokenness unearthed

in reading, class sessions, or field experiences. When confronted in classes with the pain and injustices of the world, practices of prayer and fasting can channel righteous indignation in ways that depend on God's action.

While course content can be a potent stimulus for such reflection, a mentor can also help students reflect on the forming and deforming aspects of the educational processes that consume so much of their time and attention. Daily experiences of reading, writing, studying for exams, participating in classroom discussions, and performing laboratory experiments are often viewed as irrelevant to the processes of spiritual formation. However, these common activities are filled with spiritual import. The development of cursory reading habits (i.e., skimming) can easily transfer to the way emerging adults read Scripture. The critical habits gained in reading and writing papers, while immensely beneficial, can threaten postures of humble receptivity in formational activities. Other habits—perfectionism, self-reliance, and "work hard, play hard" rhythms—can become hardened patterns in all of life. Academic rituals provide fertile contexts for the development of particular vices: pride and self-importance for those who are successful, fear and insecurity for those who fail, envy of other classmates, sloth, image management in course discussions, and dishonesty through plagiarism, cheating, or fabricated lab results. At the same time, there are many positive intellectual and moral virtues that can emerge: humility, courage, perseverance, and compassion, to name a few.[45] Mentors are called on to help emerging adult students cultivate an awareness of how their souls are shaped through the processes, not only the content, of education.

Obviously, the same kind of attentiveness will be critical in work settings, athletics, meals, and other relational contexts. Such mentoring will help emerging adults avoid the compartmentalization that is so common in these domains. As they look for God's hand in all of these areas, they begin to recognize all areas of life as "spiritual" settings in which God can be known and worshiped. They will be less likely to confine spiritual experience to church activities, seeing him and his work in the office, on the field, and in the dining hall. "To some God is discoverable everywhere: to others, nowhere," Lewis once noted. "Those who do not find Him on earth are unlikely to find Him in space. But send a saint up in a spaceship and he'll find God in space as he found God on earth. Much depends on the seeing eye."[46] For mentors, the development of the "seeing eye" is a chief formational aim. Once cultivated, such vision can enable emerging adults to see that the "whole earth is full of his glory" (Isa. 6:3).

Finally, attentiveness can be cultivated by the ways in which mentors listen and respond to situations in emerging adults' lives. Among the many skills required of an effective mentor, listening stands near the top of the list. When emerging adults share their struggles, mentors are often quick to look for "solutions"—means of changing circumstances so as to alleviate the condition. However, this approach may stifle attentiveness to God. Rather, mentors should help emerging adults listen for God's presence and work in the situation. As Dietrich Bonhoeffer noted, "There is a kind of listening with half an ear that presumes already to know what the other person has to say. It is an impatient, inattentive listening, that despises the brother and is only waiting for a chance to speak and thus get rid of the other person."[47] While Bonhoeffer's words may appear overly harsh, they speak to the reality that fixing problems is often a means of avoiding a deep and attentive posture toward God and the individual. If an immediate solution can be offered, mentors absolve themselves of responsibility and avoid having to remain with people as they process the experience and God's work in their hearts through it. By giving an immediate solution to the "problem," the mentor presumes to know exactly how the Spirit wants to use this situation for the mentee's good and God's glory. Patient and attentive listening, conversely, means the mentor will spend time with the emerging adult seeking the Spirit's guidance and purpose in the situation.[48]

Furthermore, when the focus is placed on the problem or the situation, it is likely that they will miss the opportunity to see how God wants to transform the heart through the experience. As Paul David Tripp suggests, mentors must look for "entry gates" into the person's heart, which are "not the objective problem a person has encountered, but his particular experience of that problem (fear, anger, guilt, anxiety, hopelessness, aloneness, envy, discouragement, desire for vengeance, etc.)."[49] In order to focus on the person rather than just the problem, Tripp suggests tuning our ears to pick up on certain types of words: (1) emotional words—"I'm angry," "I'm afraid"; (2) interpretive words—"This shouldn't happen," "I guess I'm getting what I deserve"; (3) self talk—"I'm such a failure," "This always happens to me"; and (4) God talk—"I thought I was doing what God wanted," "How could God let this happen to me?"[50] Such words provide "entry gates" because they unlock the heart and reveal root causes beneath their emotions. They can help mentors see some of the false belief structures and idols that underlie emerging adults' views of self, God, and the world.

For example, consider a mentor who is working with an emerging adult in the midst of a discouraging job search. If the mentee shares his sense of shame and discouragement after being turned down by a third company, there might be a temptation for the mentor to respond immediately to the situation rather than the heart: "Let me give you some interviewing tips," "Let me take a look at your resume so that we can make it more attractive," "Did you make good eye contact with the boss?" All of these have their place, but the opportunity for spiritual formation may be lost if the mentor misses out on the mentee's experience of the situation. There might be opportunities to probe the emerging adult's sense of shame, seeking to trace its source and discussing the unfailing and unconditional love of God in the midst of failure. There may be opportunities to discuss the true and enduring source of identity in Christ as his child. Questions might reveal an underlying current of fear that is rooted in the sense that he or she will never find a job, leading to a redemptive conversation about God's sovereign hand and presence. There may be opportunities to discuss emerging idols: counterfeit gods of prestige, reputation, money, and security. By getting to these heart issues, mentors can turn the gaze away from problem solving and toward the opportunity it presents for the attentive, soul-shaping work of the Holy Spirit.

A spiritual mentor is also someone who is willing to help emerging adults be attentive to the areas of their lives that have become skewed due to the effects of sin. Sin, by its very nature, tends to produce blindness and deception, leaving the individual unable or unwilling to acknowledge its presence or see its crippling effects. We are all potential victims of what Cornelius Plantinga calls "self-swindling," in which "we prettify ugly realities and sell ourselves the prettified versions."[51] Therefore, emerging adults often need someone outside of themselves to penetrate the darkness and expose areas of sin.

Such work cuts deeply against the grain of both our human nature and the unspoken contours of emerging adult culture. Mentors tend to avoid confrontation on matters of sin for a variety of reasons. Perhaps they fear rejection or a breach in the relationship with the emerging adult. Perhaps they resist because they know the words of rebuke will be hurtful and wounding, perceived as unloving by the recipient. Perhaps they recognize their own struggles and sin (the "log" in their own eye) and therefore feel inadequate to call attention to the "specks" they see in others' eyes. Perhaps they reason (often correctly) that the mentee will respond defensively and come back with a rebuke of his or her own. Of course, these personal barriers arise within a culture that spurns confrontation and rebuke. Smith found that most emerging adults operate from an ultimate value of tolerance, fueled by the notion that beliefs and actions are "up to the individual" to decide. As he summarizes, emerging adults believe that "the most one should ever do toward influencing another person is to ask him or her to consider what one thinks. . . . You can't make anybody do anything, so don't even try to influence them."[52] Since most emerging adults believe that hurting another person is the only absolute moral affront, confrontation is often vilified as a positively immoral practice.

Yet despite these personal and cultural barriers, the biblical call to enter into such work is clear. James 5:20 implores us to "remember this: Whoever turns a sinner from the error of their way will save them from death and cover over a multitude of sins." Scripture seems to imply a kind of moral complicity in our silence about others' sin. Leviticus 19:17 states clearly: "Do not hate a fellow Israelite in your heart. Rebuke your neighbor frankly so you will not share in their guilt." True gospel love—what Bonhoeffer termed "spiritual love"—is willing to sacrifice personal comfort for the sanctifying good of the other. Culture often defines love as bringing no pain to the other, but in Scripture we hear that "wounds from a friend can be trusted" (Prov. 27:6). True love will not sit idly by while the emerging adult takes part in destructive patterns of thinking or living. As Bonhoeffer notes, this kind of love reverses typical cultural beliefs: "Nothing can be more cruel than the tenderness that consigns another to his sin. Nothing can be more compassionate than the severe rebuke that calls a brother back from the path of sin."[53]

Of course, the recognition of the importance of correction does not mean that all methods are equally helpful. Ideally, confrontation will occur dialogically, using questions to help emerging adults see for themselves the ways in which sin is threatening their growth. It will come within relationships marked by trust over time, a key requirement for emerging adults jaded by distant or broken relationships with authority figures. It will also be regular. Confrontation is not something that takes place only on rare occasions with sins of sufficient magnitude. In the best cases, it is a natural part of a relationship, a pathway of mutual help and encouragement. Furthermore, it should come within a relationship marked by a history of listening, active service, and the bearing of burdens. As Bonhoeffer rightly suggests, "If [confrontation] is not accompanied by worthy listening, how can it really be the right word for the other person? If it is contradicted by one's own lack of active helpfulness, how can it be a convincing and sincere word?"[54] Listening and care are necessary prerequisites to confrontation.

In addition, rebuke must always come as both a "comfort" and a "call."[55] The comfort is rooted in the gospel—the reality that Jesus paid the full price for their sin, redeeming them and clothing them in the righteousness of Christ. Emerging adults must be reminded of the love and grace of God if they are to have any hope of forgiveness and any motivation to be released from the self-protective patterns that promote hiding and shame. As Tripp notes, "We do not need to give in to fear, denial, blame-shifting, self-righteousness, or rewriting our own history. These are all attempts at self-atonement, which is no longer needed because Christ has made full atonement for our sins."[56] But the gospel is also a call, an admonition to turn from sin and to be led "by the Spirit" rather than the flesh (Gal. 5:16). Mentors often emphasize one of these dimensions over the other. The emphasis on the *comfort* of the gospel can produce a tendency toward antinomianism, "cheap grace" without obligation. The emphasis on the *call* without the comfort (of the gospel) can quickly produce legalism and discouragement. As Bonhoeffer notes, one leads to false "security," the other to "despair."[57] Loving confrontation must invoke both of these dimensions of gospel truth.

If this is true, mentors must be very careful about the ways in which they respond to emerging adults' confession of sin. Just as they should not condemn emerging adults with legalistic appeals to self-generated piety, so they must also avoid a misplaced comfort that diminishes the seriousness of sin. One common response is to soften the blow, assuring the mentee that "everyone struggles" with similar issues. They may, in other words, downplay the sin (or make it appear so universal as to blunt its sting) to alleviate the emerging adult's fear and pain. At other times, mentors may simply indicate that they struggle with the same issues, attempting to identify with their mentees. This well-intentioned misdirection, however, can short-circuit the path to transformation. Sin is serious, and true repentance comes with the recognition of a breach between sinner and God. When the mentor foregrounds his or her own identification with the mentee, this may obscure the direct relationship between the emerging adult and God.[58] This does not mean that the mentor should avoid sharing his or her own struggles, but it does mean that such sharing should not come in this context as a means of deflecting attention away from the hard work of confession. After recognizing the sin and calling to obedience, the mentor can then proclaim God's forgiveness and celebrate "what will be" in the light of God's grace.

Helpful here is the example of Samuel confronting Israel about the sin of asking for a king. Samuel provides comfort, telling the people, "Do not be afraid," and reminding them, "For the sake of his great name the LORD will not reject his people, because the LORD was pleased to make you his own" (1 Sam. 12:20, 22). Samuel also provides a strong call to flee useless idols and serve the Lord with all of their hearts. He reminds them of the devastating effects of continued sin in their lives by predicting a grim future if they persist in doing evil. He does not attempt to diminish the seriousness of sin, proclaiming instead, "You have done all this evil" (v. 20). As a worthy mentor, however, he also pledges his own support: "As for me, far be it from me that I should sin against the LORD by failing to pray for you. And I will teach you the way that is good and right" (v. 23). This combination of comfort and call, gospel and law, represents the grace-driven balance that commends appropriate rebuke.

Looking Forward: The Posture of Envisioning

The final posture fostered by mentoring is one of "envisioning," helping emerging adults picture an adult future, pursue worthwhile dreams, and prepare for future realities. Envisioning, as the name implies, involves a sanctified imagination. As Thomas Groome suggests, Christian education always involves a dialectical relationship between the present and the future.[59] As mentors, we help emerging adults think hard about the future consequences of their present thoughts, attitudes, and behaviors. In other words, we use the creative imagination to consider what the adult future might look like if the trajectory of their current lives continues. With added experience, the mentor can at times help the mentee see the likely consequences of present actions if maintained for five, ten, or fifteen years. At the same time, we also work backward from the future to the present. We help emerging adults describe a vision for a future of adult faithfulness—spiritually, intellectually, vocationally, and relationally—and then help them think about the shape of present life that will lead in that direction. We help them see the kinds of thoughts, attitudes, and practices that will, by virtue of the experiential continuum of life, lead to growth. The articulated tension between the default future and the ideal future can generate motivation to transform the present.

Mentors must also help emerging adults construct "worthy dreams" for their future lives. Paul Wadell and Darin Davis rightly note that many emerging adults struggle with the particular vice of *acedia*.[60] More than just "sloth," acedia speaks to a pervasive lethargy regarding human aspirations. Emerging adults afflicted with this vice lack motivation for excellence either because they feel it doesn't matter or because they fear it cannot be attained. Linked closely with cynicism, acedia ends up diminishing ambition and promoting lives marked by perpetual distraction or bland material success. It promotes a self-protective and cautious mentality that sets sights low so as to avoid risk and disappointment. Such "calculated indifference" sets up barriers to passionate dreams that should flood the emerging adult years.[61] At times, this may stem from fears and insecurities that generate feelings of inadequacy. At other times, it may arise naturally from life in a culture that views cool detachment—a stance of "whatever"—as an essential quality of emerging adulthood. The result, according to Dorothy Sayers, is a pervasive apathy: "Acedia is the sin which believes in nothing, cares for nothing, enjoys nothing, loves nothing, hates nothing, finds purpose in nothing, lives for nothing and only remains alive because there is nothing for which it will die."[62]

Mentors can cut the root of acedia by encouraging a courageous response to God's call. Mentors can help emerging adults develop a sense of self-efficacy, a belief that, in God's strength, they are capable of entering into situations that require deliberate action. Albert Bandura argued that self-efficacy often emerges as individuals are provided with mastery experiences, social modeling, and social persuasion.[63] In other words, they need to be given opportunities to develop expertise in various areas, they need to see examples of people who complete important tasks, and they need verbal affirmation that they are capable of completing challenging work. While all of this must be bathed in a sense of God's ultimate power, self-efficacy is often an important posture gained in the emerging adult years. Like Mordecai encouraging Esther to take action to protect her people, mentors are called on to challenge emerging adults for future influence (Esther 4:14).

The call for social modeling implies that imagination must be balanced with concrete examples of the adult Christian life. Emerging adults need tangible exemplars of lives that are infused with divine purpose, providing pictures of faithfulness that inspire them to emulation. Scripture, both in precept and example, is clear on the essential nature of modeling for growth in the Christian life. The lives of Jesus and Paul demonstrate the power of this modeling method. Jesus obviously taught his disciples through words, but he also served as a living demonstration of that message through his interactions with people, his life of prayer, his use of Scripture, his love and compassion for others, and his sacrifice. And as Paul mentored his protégé Timothy, he taught him truth but also called him to examine his mentor's life: "You, however, know all about my teaching, my way of life, my purpose, faith, patience, love, endurance, persecutions, sufferings—what kinds of things happened to me in Antioch, Iconium and Lystra, the persecutions I endured" (2 Tim. 3:10–11). The role of a mentor is certainly to communicate truth, but that truth also derives power, clarity, and credibility from the "way of life" of its bearer.[64]

Studies indeed seem to indicate that such modeling is the best means of facilitating Christian faith in the next generation. In one analysis of parent-child religious transmission, Christopher Bader and Scott Desmond found that faith was best formed when communicated both in message and lifestyle. When the message was clear but the behavioral modeling was mixed, children picked up the message but not the lifestyle.[65] Likewise, philosopher Nicholas Wolterstorff noted that modeling is a critical force in faith-based "tendency learning." Citing a number of psychological studies, he found that young people tended to replicate the preaching of a model's preaching and the practice of the model's practice. If preaching and practice did not line up, the child would be far more likely to emulate the practice than the preaching. "Preaching induced *preaching* rather than practice," he concluded.[66]

In this respect, a mentor's life is a continual visual display of the faith in all the areas of which Paul speaks. Emerging adults need to see adults who live out of a life purpose, organizing their very lifestyles around the values and priorities of the kingdom of God. They need to observe mentors who demonstrate lives of prayer, lives of commitment to the local church, lives of dedication to spouses and children, lives that display a passion for service. And like Paul, they also need to learn from mentors who live out those lives through trials and suffering. They will learn truth, to be sure, but they will also learn about ways of balancing life commitments, ways of relating to others, and potential patterns of pursuing spiritual formation in the adult years. The idea here is that the mentor's life of radical obedience to Christ will itself spark cognitive dissonance, forcing the emerging adult to stop and consider new ways of relating to Christ in the world. The mentor's prayer may very well be that of missionary martyr Jim Elliot: "Father, make of me a crisis man. Bring those I contact to decision. Let me not be a milepost on a single road; make me a fork, that men must turn one way or another on facing Christ in me."[67]

These realities highlight some of the key components of effective modeling. First, modeling should occur in the midst of real life rather than exclusively in formal settings. As Lawrence Richards once noted, "Faith should not be communicated only in artificial situations that demand atomic modes of response, but in real situations where affect, interest, motive, perceptions, and behavior are united."[68] In other words, if mentors desire emerging adults to witness their beliefs, practices, virtues, emotions, and relationships, mentoring will have to move beyond the church or classroom to encompass the mundane tasks of daily life. Mentoring will take place in the home, running errands, on the court or playing field, and in various arenas of service and ministry. Observation in this variety of settings can help to develop a deeper sense of the pervasive influence of a kingdom perspective across all of the various domains of life. If a critical component of emerging adult spiritual formation occurs in the development of "loves" through pictures of the good life, as previously indicated, it would seem that the mentor is in a unique position to provide one such image.

Modeling must also take place within the context of intimate relationship, echoing Paul's description of his mentoring role with the Thessalonians: "Because we loved you so much, we were delighted to share with you not only the gospel of God but our lives as well" (1 Thess. 2:8). Paul's desire to share his life with the Thessalonians emerged from a clear love for the people. Likewise, mentoring research indicates that modeling entails not just imitation but also identification resulting from satisfying relationships. In other words, modeling is most influential when it is coupled with friendship, mutual affection serving as a motivating force for the internalization of character qualities admired in the mentor.[69]

In addition, mentoring mandates a willingness to enter the life worlds of emerging adults—to get "on their turf" and to observe their typical life patterns and contexts. Since mentoring is so deeply concerned with helping the mentee pay attention to the work of God in their routines and life patterns, an understanding of this everyday world is absolutely essential. "Spirituality requires context. Always," writes Eugene Peterson.[70] As mentors view emerging adults in their own settings, they can provide contextually relevant insights and gauge the ways in which mentees embody the faith in various domains. Additionally, time spent in their settings also enables the mentor to communicate the inherent worth of the mentee. By entering their worlds, the mentor demonstrates that the emerging adult is not a project but a person of great value, worthy of a boundary-crossing venture.

However, it is also very important that the emerging adult is able to observe the model of the mentor "as an adult." We mentioned previously that many older adults wish to "stay young" and avoid appearing too far removed from the culturally savvy world of emerging adulthood. It is also the case that many older adults feel they must become indistinguishable from emerging adults in order to gain a hearing with them. Daniel Heishman notes, "What I fear most is that through being constantly in touch with our young people we are producing *fusion* with the young, instead of instilling within them a sense of our *influence*."[71] Such a posture can severely limit the very purpose of mentoring. Emerging adults need to see not mirrors or carbon copies of themselves but inspiring exemplars of faithful adulthood. They need what Erik Erikson called "guarantors," mentors who guarantee the possibility of a kingdom-focused adult life.[72] This does not mean that the mentor is to exemplify a dour mode of adult concern for the cares of the world. Instead, it means demonstrating the vitality that true adulthood can possess as one discovers new venues for kingdom influence. While the culture appeals to the joy and wonder of youth, mentors need to proclaim with their lives the joyful possibilities of adulthood.

A word of caution must be added here: the older adult passion for generativity (guiding the next generation) and the emerging adult need for growing self-efficacy can create conflict in this relationship. As mentors model the adult Christian life for the emerging adults under their care, it is tempting to want to steer them in particular directions commensurate with the mentors' own lifestyle and ideals.[73] Many take the Pauline call to "imitate me as I imitate Christ" to mean that the mentee will emerge as a clone of the mentor, emulating all beliefs, practices, attitudes, and passions. In attempting to carve these individuals into their own images, however, mentors can actually become barriers to the development of emerging adults' unique gifts, desires, and personalities. Some mentors take it quite personally when mentees decide to move in a different direction or to pursue a different focus, viewing this as a rejection of the mentors' aspirations. They desire to see the mentee think of God as they do, to grow passions for similar topics, to take part in practices that are identical to their own. However, this fails to treat emerging adults as individuals, uniquely created by God for his purposes. Mentors must always remember that their chief role is not to see emerging adults submit slavishly to the mentor but to enlist as perpetual apprentices of the ultimate Mentor, more fully themselves as they follow Christ.

As Kenda Creasy Dean suggests, our mentoring of the younger generation must not mandate the particular form that the gospel life will take.[74] Like the Jews taking the gospel to the gentiles after Peter's interaction with Cornelius, we must allow the Word to flourish in its own unique way within the cultural framework of its recipients. While circumcision and various cleansing and dietary restrictions were common for the Jews, they decided in Acts 15 not to impose these on the new gentile Christians, opting to allow the gospel to assume its unique form among these culturally distinct converts. There was a risk in this, to be sure. Without circumcision and strict adherence to the Mosaic law, the faith might end up looking quite different. Similarly, when mentors serve as conduits of the gospel for emerging adults, they must recognize that the gospel will take on a unique hue amid the distinct cultural needs and possibilities of the next generation. As Dean notes, "Translating the gospel for young people amounts to entrusting them with matches, for it gives them access to holy fire, which puts the church at risk: what if young people ignite the church? Then where would we be?"[75] This is indeed the risk but also the awesome potential of the mentoring process—the same gospel considered afresh for a new world.

Postures at the Hinge

Mentoring in the emerging adult years must therefore recognize the "hinge" nature of this stage. The three key themes of remembering, attentiveness, and envisioning demonstrate the need to look backward, to look around and within, and to look forward. At this hinge moment, mentors are to help direct emerging adults' eyes to God's past, present, and future work in their lives and to connect this work with God's larger story throughout history.

In this sense, leaders and guides recognize that mentoring during this stage of life always entails the need for both home and journey, abiding and pilgrimage. Emerging adults must be rooted in a solid faith identity, connected to the story of God's great faithfulness and to the people of God who live into that story. At the same time, they are also called to journey forward, building on this foundation to move forward into the specific adult vision God has for them. "Home" reminds them of who they are in Christ; "journey" empowers and sends them forth to be who they are called to be within that identity. As Parks suggests, "We grow and become both by letting go and holding on, leaving and staying, journeying and abiding. . . . A good life and the cultivation of wisdom require a balance of home and pilgrimage."[76] In such a context, mentors need to both anchor and empower, tethering emerging adults to solid foundations while also liberating them to develop their unique voice for kingdom responsibility.

By facilitating these postures, mentors hope to witness the joint development of two virtues essential to this stage of life: gratitude and faith. Looking back on God's past mercies develops a sense of gratitude for his great work, thankfulness for his sustaining blessings and grace. Looking forward requires faith in his future promises, confident that "he who began a good work . . . will carry it on to completion" (Phil. 1:6). Gratitude sees all of life as a gift from God's hand, and faith recognizes that this same God will continue to provide in the future. As John Piper has suggested, this combination of virtues is powerful because gratitude is deeply humble while faith is unflinchingly bold.[77] "Humble boldness" is the character to be forged and honed at the emerging adult hinge.

Conclusion

Spiritual Formation and the Adult Transition

When I was a child, I talked like a child, I thought like a child, I reasoned like a child. When I became a man, I put the ways of childhood behind me.

1 Corinthians 13:11

I tell you the truth, unless you change and become like little children, you will never enter the kingdom of heaven.

Matthew 18:3

Emerging adulthood represents a time of great challenge but also great opportunity for spiritual formation. As Christian Smith has argued, many leaders and social critics use emerging adulthood as a kind of "blank screen" on which to project their own images of idealism or despair.[1] Those in this age group either represent unbridled hope and optimism or the devastating beginning of a tragic future. As indicated throughout this book, emerging adulthood is a formative stage in which beliefs are solidified, life patterns are shaped, and key decisions are made regarding spirituality, identity, church participation, vocation, morality, sexuality, and mentoring. Each area offers the prospect of spiritual growth and transformation, but each also provides space for pain, compromise, and alienation. Emerging adulthood can become a gateway to a vibrant and mature adult faith, but its potential can also be blunted through sin, self-absorption, and a failure to grasp hold of a strong Christian vision and identity. At this hinge moment, when the contours of adult life begin to take shape, emerging adults need guides—mentors, pastors, teachers, and parents—to support the journey toward Christian faithfulness.

In America and in many other industrialized nations, this journey now unfolds in a new and challenging context. A number of personal, cultural, institutional, and theological forces have complicated the transition into adulthood, lengthening the process and eliminating clear boundaries, scripts, and expectations. In the absence of institutional and personal supports, many emerging adults simply go it alone and do the best they can. Many fall prey to the pervasive influence of the entertainment and media industries, molded by its consumer mandates. Many Christian emerging adults settle for a "good enough" version of discipleship that makes peace with the Moralistic Therapeutic Deism that dominates both popular culture and many churches. On the cusp of adulthood, twentysomethings need leaders who can teach and exemplify a vision of human flourishing that beckons them forth into a life of meaning and purpose.

At the end of this exploration, we want to step back and see what we have discovered about this adult transition. Looking at the big picture, there appear to be two inadequate pathways out of adolescence that tend to threaten faithful Christian adulthood. In the first, emerging adults define adult life in terms of freedom, self-fulfillment, and unbounded exploration. Finally removed from the strictures imposed by parents and other authority figures, they are liberated to do what they please while avoiding the responsibilities that will come later in life. Smith notes that emerging adulthood "is about experimenting, exploring, experiencing, preparing, anticipating, having fun, and hopefully not screwing things up too badly in the meantime."[2] If adulthood is viewed this way, it tends to promote a degree of self-absorption and an emphasis on personal freedom and happiness. It also tends to foster an avoidance of responsibility, both for one's own commitments and for the needs of the larger world. It shrinks from such responsibility, assuming that such work is "somebody else's business." There is an overriding sense that this is "my time," an open space to experience all that life has to offer without the intrusion of obligations. This pathway might be termed a "self-absorbed" emerging adulthood.

We have seen evidence of this pathway throughout the preceding chapters. With regard to spiritual formation, few pursue costly discipleship, preferring instead a therapeutic faith that celebrates happiness and pleasure. With regard to identity, many embrace diffusion, avoiding both commitments and exploration altogether and going with the flow of mass consumer culture in order to "enjoy life." Others remain in foreclosure, choosing to let authority figures think for them rather than developing and owning their own commitments.

With regard to church involvement, many eliminate institutional religion altogether, seeing this as a barrier to the freedom they seek. If they do attend church, they shop and hop around, hoping to find a perfect consumer fit for their desires; in addition, many fail to take responsibility for serving others, choosing instead to be "fed" while allowing others to fill leadership and service roles. With regard to vocation, emerging adults on this pathway tend to see adulthood as "freedom from" rather than "responsibility for" others, choosing vocational lives purely based on personal fit and fulfillment. Instead of living as the light of the world, they will choose either to live in the darkness or avoid the pain of dark places altogether. With regard to morality, many divorce themselves from external or objective reference points, becoming attuned solely to their own intuitions. Moral decisions are made on the basis of personal benefit as self-actualization is elevated above care for others. With regard to romance and sexuality, many simply use others (or others' images) for their own gratification, eschewing commitment in favor of easy emotional and physical pleasure. They may quickly sever ties with those that no longer give them the pleasure and happiness they desire. With regard to mentoring, they will likely remain peer centered, viewing "outdated" adults as barriers to their freedom and pleasure.

The second inadequate pathway out of adolescence is one that defines adulthood in terms of independence and self-sufficiency. Jeffrey Arnett notes that most emerging adults define adulthood as taking responsibility for oneself, making independent decisions, and becoming financially independent.[3] Rooted in a growing confidence in one's own abilities, this image embraces autonomy as the key to adult status, elevating the self-made individual as the model. No longer dependent on others, the emerging adult can now go it alone, competent to forge a successful life derived purely from one's own power. Adulthood viewed this way tends to promote what Walter Brueggemann called "self-groundedness," the belief that "our life springs from us, that we generate our own power and vitality, and that within us can be found the sources of wholeness and well-being."[4] Those following such a path often lose the humble trust, playfulness, and wonder of childhood and youth, replacing these postures with arrogance, sophistication, and even cynicism. This pathway might be termed "self-sufficient" emerging adulthood.

We also have seen evidence of this pathway in our examination of emerging adulthood. With regard to spiritual formation, many see spirituality as a performance-based project, something that they can complete as a self-sufficient task. Emerging adults may see competence in spiritual disciplines as a means of ensuring spiritual growth. With regard to identity, strong achievement is likely to be coupled with arrogance and a sense of self-creation, rejecting or belittling previous authorities while separating from the broader community. With regard to church participation, church membership is often viewed as unnecessary since emerging adults are gaining the capacity to stand on their own with self-chosen beliefs and plans for spiritual development. With regard to vocation, many move forward in light of personal talents, rejecting the need for humble listening to God's directing voice. They may develop pride in their gifts, a sense of utter competence that denies God's providential hand in their lives and work. With regard to morality, they may make decisions autonomously, disconnected from others and devoid of a reference point outside of the self. Alternatively, they may see moral rule keeping as a means of achieving a self-sufficient righteousness, a self-generated "good life." With regard to relationships, many pursue or discard these with a sense of autonomy, making relational and sexual decisions without input from others. With regard to mentoring, they may be resistant to input from others because they are attempting to carve out an autonomous set of beliefs and practices.

Throughout our previous discussions, we have identified many of the forces that tend to generate these unhelpful pathways. Self-absorbed emerging adulthood certainly arises through demographic changes in the timing of traditional adult roles, particularly marriage, opening up unprecedented spaces for lengthy freedom without relational and vocational responsibility. In addition, consumer capitalism also plays into this narrowed vision. The advertising and entertainment industries certainly thrive monetarily when emerging adults seek immediate self-gratification, so there is much to gain on their part by promoting and elevating such images in the popular imagination. Media portrayals of college and postcollege life certainly depict the "me-centered" life as the normative pattern of emerging adulthood.

Self-sufficient adulthood is also woven into the fabric of our culture. The "self-made man" remains a strong cultural symbol because of its link to self-creation and the sense that the responsibility—and therefore the credit—for success rests squarely on one's own shoulders. In contemporary culture, women also embrace this, sometimes feeling a need to prove themselves to their male counterparts in the vocational sphere and sometimes relishing the new freedom to craft their own destiny. In our individualistic culture, personal identity is far more important than group identity. Therefore, differentiation from parents and other authorities is automatically invested with deep meaning in the process of adult formation. A capacity to "make it on one's own" is matched by a need to "be one's own person," and both are essential to feeling like an adult in American culture.

Yet we should not neglect the church's potential role in reinforcing these postures. With regard to self-absorption, Thomas Bergler has recently argued that American churches often foster a kind of "juvenilization" among members. Seeking to attract young people, church beliefs and practices often emphasize emotionalism, romantic images of the God-human relationship, and emphases on fun and "feel good" faith.[5] The characteristics of adolescence, he argues, have therefore been accepted as normative for all ages. Moralistic Therapeutic Deism is just one aspect of this, but it exemplifies a faith perspective that places the spiritual emphasis squarely on personal fulfillment. By catering to felt needs and failing to call emerging adults to active service and kingdom responsibility, churches can play right into this trend.

Regarding the second pathway of self-sufficiency, many church leaders describe spiritual formation in individualistic terms, defining growth in faith as a personal project. The church does not always invest people with a sense of communal identity within the body of Christ. Maturity, therefore, is described as a kind of spiritual self-sufficiency, achieving independence and a unique faith that fits one's persona. Spiritual autonomy is often fostered by church settings in which one must appear "perfect," free of the brokenness that might compromise self-sufficiency and spiritual "success." In addition, many depict adulthood as the time in which faith has been "figured out," systematized and divorced from the passion of youth. Idealism and wonder morph into a chastened realism that tempers expectations and settles into predictable spiritual routines.

As Smith and Kenda Creasy Dean have both argued, therefore, we must recognize that the perspective on spiritual formation exhibited by emerging adults is largely a product of pervasive cultural messages and the faith communicated by our churches.[6] While it is easy to point fingers and criticize emerging adult lifestyles and choices, it is likely more accurate to see within them a reflection of our cultural and religious priorities. More often than not, we reproduce what we are.

Whatever their source, it seems evident that current popular definitions of adulthood can serve as barriers to spiritual formation among people in their twenties. In other words, expectations regarding the "normal" cultural and developmental pathways into adulthood may compromise or obscure alternative paths more likely to lead to Christian faithfulness at this life stage. Both self-absorbed and self-sufficient adulthood normalize patterns that threaten the very foundations of the adult faith structure. Those in the self-absorbed category refuse to accept the new responsibilities of adulthood, remaining fixated on their own needs and completely dependent on others, unwilling to assume leadership roles. On the other hand, self-sufficient emerging adults lose all of the admirable childlike qualities that should live on into Christian adulthood: humility, receptivity, trust, and wonder. And some show evidence of both false pathways. These well-worn cultural grooves create challenges for both emerging adults and their leaders as they search for a proper vision of adult spiritual formation.

Throughout the book, we have attempted to outline the framework of a better way. Christian spiritual formation in emerging adulthood cuts against the grain of self-absorption, pointing instead to a life of costly discipleship marked by personal and cultural investment. Rather than a time marked by freedom from authority, emerging adulthood is defined as a time of growing responsibility for others and the world. At the same time, such formation also cuts against the grain of the autonomous, self-sufficient adulthood that "stands on one's own," pointing instead to a life of humble dependence on God and interdependence with others. The growing competence, identity, and responsibility of adulthood becomes a place of wonder and gratitude for God's provision, continued reliance on his grace, and loving stewardship of his gifts for others' good and for his glory. The emerging adult must move beyond childishness while simultaneously sustaining the childlike qualities of humility, trust, and wonder.

This vision provides a helpful vantage point from which to conceptualize the key issues of emerging adult life. In spiritual formation, there should be a struggle against selfishness, marked by a growing capacity to take responsibility for one's soul, to discern and confront idols, and to pursue costly discipleship. Yet there must also be the continual recognition of absolute dependence on God's grace and the transforming work of the Holy Spirit. This is why we define spiritual formation as a form of "active receiving," a conscious willingness to put oneself in a position where the Holy Spirit can act. This perspective avoids both the legalism that can easily emerge in the self-sufficient pathway while also attending to the antinomianism that often accompanies the self-absorbed path. Because maturity is often accompanied by a growing sense of self-sufficiency, the return to a childlike spirit must often come through repentance, the recognition and confession of self-reliance and the restoration of a posture of humble, childlike faith before the cross.

In identity formation, exploration and commitment will call emerging adults to resist positions of passive diffusion and foreclosure. Leaders will facilitate an internalization and ownership of faith that involves a willingness to cultivate one's voice. Christian identity achievement, however, requires a continual posture of humility and an openness to learn from God and others in community. There must be a growing knowledge of God and his Word, a growing identity commitment to certain views and positions, yet there must also be a growing wonder, a breathtaking sense of amazement regarding God's character, works, and promises. There must be a willingness to move beyond childlike understanding, but there also must be the humility necessary to receive input from and demonstrate gratitude toward parents and other mentors along the way.

With regard to the church, participation in a local body represents a fight against self-absorption on many levels. Emerging adults can use their developing gifts to serve others. They can help to lead in certain ministries and to seek deployment in mission. They can begin to develop as theologians, eschewing a passive spectator role in spiritual learning. At the same time, they must recognize their need of others within the local body, seeking out the wisdom of older mentors. They must see the church as a place in which they can submit to authority and discipline, recognizing their need for guidance, admonition, and even rebuke. Joining in the rhythm of the church year, they submit to the larger narrative that defines life and human history. They will help lead in the church, but they will also depend on the church to facilitate and round out their formation. Rather than succumbing to the social script that sheds formative and socializing influences as encumbrances to individuality, the Christian is baptized into an identity-bestowing community seeking the formation of a cruciform life.

Vocationally, emerging adults are called to resist self-centeredness by developing gifts and passions that can be invested in kingdom work in all spheres of life. By taking part in creating, sustaining, and restoring work in multiple domains, they can make an "adult" difference in all of the pain-filled arenas of this world that have been marred by the fall. Yet they must also continue to recognize the need for grace in this arena. All of their gifts are gracious provisions of his hand, and thus they are completely reliant on him for everything they do. In addition, they must be humble and prayerful in seeking out areas of service, recognizing that they are not independently "changing the world" but rather responding to his call with his strength. The need for both grace and cross, both childlike trust and adult investment, anchors the adult vocational vision.

In morality, emerging adults should cultivate their new capacities to grow as people of character. They need to move beyond the self-actualized morality of our therapeutic culture, and they also need to move beyond the rule-keeping postures of childhood. Adult character formation will lead them to cultivate the virtuous dispositions of the adult moral life. Yet they need to humbly submit to a reference point beyond themselves. They need to find inspiration in the lives of moral exemplars, experiencing gratitude with the Psalmist when he declares, "I say of the holy people who are in the land, / they are the glorious ones in whom is all my delight" (Ps. 16:3). This combination highlights what we termed "authoritative" moral education, neither permissive nor authoritarian but rather rooted in a shared vision of the good.

Relationally and romantically, emerging adults grow into an awareness of themselves as sexual beings and can develop ways of conjoining sexuality with spirituality. They can become conscious of the factors that have formed self-perception, patterns of relating, and relational expectations. And they can acquire growing competencies that create satisfying and wholesome relationships. Yet regardless of how skilled one becomes, the deepest relationships require appropriation of the fundamental, childhood development task of trust. Relationships require a humble submission to God's plan for sexuality and awe at the covenantal framework within which relationships unfold.

In the area of mentoring, the emerging adult moves beyond the hero worship of adolescence to embrace a mentor who can draw out and nurture the adult voice on matters of belief and action. Yet emerging adults must also be open for the mentor to lead them back to a childlike awe and reverence for God that produces an attentiveness to his work in their lives. A mentor will help them remember the great works of God in the past and his work in and around them in the present, guiding them to see their lives as a gradual unfolding of his purposes for them in the future. While childlike joy is often dulled and obscured by the routines of emerging adult life, a mentor can continue to elicit a sense of amazement even in the very ordinary things of life. In one sense, the mentor's role is defined by this dual pursuit: to envision and model adult belief and responsibility while also bringing them to a sense of continual and humble reliance on the work of God in and around them.

There is therefore something about true Christian emerging adulthood that must blend the growing capacities of adult life with the childlike spirit. Jesus, of course, told his disciples that they must "become like little children" (Matt. 18:3) and receive the kingdom "like a little child" (Mark 10:14–16; Luke 18:15–17). This by no means implies that Christianity encourages a simplistic faith, avoiding complexities in order to retain a kind of intellectual and cultural naïveté. Paul, in fact, implores the Corinthians to "stop thinking like children" (1 Cor. 14:20). While he wanted them to be infants "in regard to evil," he also implored them to be "adults" in their thinking. Instead, this blend of responsible adulthood and childlike spirit finds common ground with Oliver Wendell Holmes's famous declaration, "I would not give a fig for the simplicity this side of complexity, but I would give my life for the simplicity on the other side of complexity."[7] Moving into adulthood, as we have noted throughout the book, does require the hard work of exploration and internalization, engaging the cultural and thought systems of the world within the framework of biblical truth. Rather than producing a self-sufficient "sophistication," however, this process should generate an owned faith that is still marked by humility, gratitude, wonder, and awe. The balance between adult competence and childlike trust can only come through continual reminders of emerging adults' desperate need for grace—not only for salvation but for sanctification as well. The posture of Christian emerging adulthood is neither self-absorption nor self-sufficiency but self-surrender, an adult capacity to give oneself away.

Jesus's love for those in both false pathways is readily apparent in the Luke 15 parable of the prodigal son. The younger, self-absorbed son simply wants to enjoy life, throwing off his responsibilities and spending his inheritance on "wild living" (13). The older son, by contrast, reflects the self-sufficiency and arrogance of the Pharisees, claiming that he had "never disobeyed" (29). Jesus wants both sons to know and experience the rescuing love of the father. By implication, he wants self-absorbed emerging adults to know that the father runs to them with open arms and a heart brimming with compassion. He wants self-sufficient emerging adults to know that "everything I have is yours" (31), pleading with them to delight in his riches rather than trusting in their own achieved success. He wants both groups to know that surrendering to the father is the pathway to true joy—the pathway to abundant and eternal life.

What a privilege to walk alongside emerging adults as they live in this tension, as the Holy Spirit weaves together the fabric of their lives into a discernible pattern. The threads of spiritual formation, identity, church participation, vocation, morality, relational wholeness, and mentoring can create a tapestry, however imperfect, of costly discipleship, community, and mission. Amid the challenges and opportunities of this unique life stage, the gospel can mark emerging adults with a clear identity rooted in God's story. These gospel-shaped emerging adults, fueled by an irrepressible passion for the kingdom, can then go forward into adulthood poised to bring the healing, power, and hope of the gospel to the world.

Notes

Introduction

1. Jacques Ellul, *Reason for Being: A Meditation on Ecclesiastes* (Grand Rapids: Eerdmans, 1990), 282–83.

2. Friedrich L. Schweitzer, *The Postmodern Life Cycle: Challenges for Church and Theology* (St. Louis: Chalice Press, 2004), 54.

3. While 30 percent of 20-year-old women had attained these five markers in 1960, only 6 percent had done the same in 2000. On these themes, see Jeffrey Jensen Arnett and Susan Taber, "Adolescence Terminable and Interminable: When Does Adolescence End?" *Journal of Youth and Adolescence* 23 (1994): 517–37; Michael J. Shanahan, Erik J. Porfeli, Jeylan T. Mortimer, and Lance D. Erikson, "Subjective Age Identity and the Transition to Adulthood: When Do Adolescents Become Adults?" in Richard A. Settersten Jr., Frank F. Furstenberg Jr., and Ruben G. Rumbaut, eds., *On the Frontier of Adulthood: Theory, Research, and Public Policy* (Chicago: University of Chicago Press, 2005), 225–55; Richard A. Settersten Jr., "Becoming Adult: Meanings and Markers for Young Americans," in Mary C. Waters, Patrick J. Carr, Maria J. Kefalas, and Jennifer Holdaway, eds., *Coming of Age in America* (Berkeley: University of California Press, 2011).

4. Christian Smith, *Souls in Transition: The Religious and Spiritual Lives of Emerging Adults* (New York: Oxford University Press, 2009), 5.

5. Jeffrey Jensen Arnett, *Emerging Adulthood: The Winding Road from the Late Teens through the Twenties* (New York: Oxford University Press, 2004); Arnett and Jennifer Tanner, eds., *Emerging Adults in America: Coming of Age in the Twenty-First Century* (Washington, DC: American Psychological Association, 2005). It is important to note that late marriage ages are not historically unique. For example, late marriage also characterized American culture at the turn of the twentieth century. However, the experience of delayed marriage is quite different in contemporary culture because of the unparalleled freedom for exploration available to individuals between the ages of 18 and 30.

6. http://nces.ed.gov/programs/digest/d11/tables/dt11_196.asp

7. Smith, *Souls in Transition*, 6. Graduate education enrollment grew approximately 18 percent between 1997 and 2007. See US Department of Education, "Digest of Educational Statistics, 2009," accessed at www.nces.ed.gov. The average student loan debt in 2011 was $23,300. While the median balance is only $12,800, ten percent of graduates owe more than $54,000.

8. Smith, *Souls in Transition*, 5; Christian Smith, *Lost in Transition: The Dark Side of Emerging Adulthood* (New York: Oxford University Press, 2011). Smith suggests that parents spend about $38,340 per child in "total material assistance (cash, housing, educational expenses, food, etc.)" between the ages of 18 and 34 (p. 14). See also Settersten Jr., "Becoming Adult: Meanings

and Markers for Young Americans," 174. Close to two-thirds of emerging adults in their early twenties receive financial support from parents while 40 percent still receive support in the late twenties. See Frank F. Furstenberg, Sheela Kennedy, Vonnie C. McCloyd, Ruben G. Rumbaut, and Richard A. Settersten Jr., "Between Adolescence and Adulthood: Expectations about the Timing of Adulthood," Network on Transitions to Adulthood and Public Policy, accessed at www.transad.pop.upenn.edu/downloads/between.pdf. It should be noted that this safety net was expanded by the 2010 Affordable Care Act, allowing children to remain on their parents' health insurance until the age of 26.

9. Arnett, *Emerging Adulthood*, 5.

10. Robert Wuthnow contends that "fully 69 percent of unmarried evangelicals and 78 percent of mainline Protestants had sex with at least one partner during the previous twelve months." See Wuthnow, *After the Baby Boomers: How Twenty- and Thirty-Somethings Are Changing the Face of American Religion* (Princeton: Princeton University Press, 2007), 139.

11. Arnett, *Emerging Adulthood*. It is important to note that not all scholars agree that emerging adulthood is a new "stage" of human development. Others contend that it is a highly variable process or transition that resists stage-like characteristics. For a helpful exploration of this debate, see Arnett, Marion Kloep, Leo B. Hendry, and Jennifer L. Tanner, *Debating Emerging Adulthood: Stage or Process?* (New York: Oxford University Press, 2011).

12. Among the underprivileged, this freedom and optimism is often curtailed by the immediate need to develop the skills necessary for a job. See Frank F. Furstenberg, Sheela Kennedy, Vonnie McCloyd, Ruben Rumbaut, and Richard Settersten Jr., "Growing Up Is Harder to Do," *Contexts* 3, no. 3 (2004): 33–41. Unfortunately, space in this book does not permit a more extensive treatment of the dynamics of emerging adulthood among under-resourced individuals.

13. Jeffrey Arnett, "Emerging Adulthood: A Theory of Development from the Late Teens through the Twenties," *American Psychologist* 55, no. 5 (May 2000): 469.

14. See Alexandra Robbins and Abby Wilner, *Quarterlife Crisis: The Unique Challenges of Life in Your Twenties* (New York: Jeremy P. Tarcher/Putnam, 2001).

15. Smith, *Souls in Transition*; Wuthnow, *After the Baby Boomers*.

16. On this reality, see David Kinnaman, *You Lost Me: Why Young Christians Are Leaving Church . . . And Rethinking Faith* (Grand Rapids: Baker Books, 2011).

17. Smith, *Lost in Transition*, 19.

18. Such risk behaviors often reach their peak during this period of life and are most prominent among those who do not yet consider themselves to be "adult." See Arnett, "Emerging Adulthood: A Theory of Development," 469–80; Arnett, "Still Crazy After All These Years: Reckless Behavior among Young Adults Aged 23–27," *Personality and Individual Differences* 12 (1991): 1305–13. According to Arthur Levine's research, binge drinking is on the rise on college campuses nationwide. More than a quarter of college seniors, in fact, reported drinking heavily "with the goal of passing out." Alcohol abuse is linked with missed classes, declining grades, and an escalation in unprotected sex and date rape. According to the undergraduates surveyed, prominent reasons for drinking included stress relief, fun, reducing "social and sexual inhibitions," and peer pressure. Many indicated that students feel it is impossible to have a good time without alcohol. According to the study, marijuana use is also on the rise while hallucinogens and tobacco appear to be declining. See Arthur Levine and Diane R. Dean, *Generation on a Tightrope: A Portrait of Today's College Student* (San Francisco: Jossey-Bass, 2012), 59–63.

19. On this theme, see Smith, *Lost in Transition*; Mark Regnerus and Jeremy Uecker, *Premarital Sex in America: How Young Americans Meet, Mate, and Think about Marrying* (New York: Oxford University Press, 2011).

20. On self-focus, see especially James Côté, *Arrested Adulthood: The Changing Nature of Maturity and Identity* (New York: New York University Press, 2000); Jean M. Twenge, *Generation Me* (New York: Free Press, 2006); Robert Bly, *The Sibling Society: An Impassioned Call for the Rediscovery of Adulthood* (New York: Vintage, 1996).

21. Smith, *Souls in Transition*, 49.

22. See, for example, Colleen Carroll, *The New Faithful: Why Young Adults Are Embracing Christian Orthodoxy* (Chicago: Loyola University Press, 2002), 45–46.

23. See, for example, Robert E. Webber, *The Younger Evangelicals* (Grand Rapids: Baker Books, 2002); Carroll, *The New Faithful*.

24. Sharon Daloz Parks, *Big Questions, Worthy Dreams: Mentoring Young Adults in Their Search for Meaning, Purpose, and Faith* (San Francisco: Jossey-Bass, 2000).

25. On such movements, see especially J. Edwin Orr and Richard Owen Roberts, *Campus Aflame: A History of Evangelical Awakenings in Collegiate Communities* (Wheaton, IL: International Awakening Press, 1994); David P. Setran, *The College "Y": Student Religion in the Era of Secularization* (New York: Palgrave/Macmillan, 2007).

26. Andy Crouch, *Culture Making: Recovering Our Creative Calling* (Downers Grove, IL: InterVarsity, 2008).

27. We extend gratitude to Dr. Richard Osmer of Princeton Theological Seminary for formulating these questions in a discussion group as part of the Princeton Conference on Emerging Adulthood, May 2009.

28. See, for example, James Dobson, *Life on the Edge* (Carol Stream, IL: Tyndale, 1995); Craig Dunham and Doug Serven, *TwentySomeone* (Colorado Springs: WaterBrook Press, 2003).

29. On this theme, see such works as Dan Kimball, *The Emerging Church* (Grand Rapids: Zondervan, 2003) and Leonard Sweet, ed., *The Church in Emerging Culture: Five Perspectives* (Grand Rapids: Zondervan, 2003).

30. Smith, *Souls in Transition*; Wuthnow, *After the Baby Boomers*.

31. Parks, *Big Questions, Worthy Dreams*; James Fowler, *Becoming Adult, Becoming Christian: Adult Development and Christian Faith* (San Francisco: Jossey-Bass, 2000); Arnett, *Emerging Adulthood*.

32. Books such as Ed Stetzer, *Lost and Found: The Younger Unchurched and the Churches That Reach Them* (Nashville: B&H Books, 2009); David Kinnaman, *UnChristian: What a New Generation Really Thinks about Christianity* (Grand Rapids: Baker Books, 2007); and Kinnaman, *You Lost Me*, form a kind of middle ground, addressing survey data and providing practical applications for churches. These works, however, are less connected to the larger scholarly literature. Richard Dunn and Jana Sundene, in *Shaping the Journey of Emerging Adults: Life-Giving Rhythms for Spiritual Transformation* (Downers Grove, IL: InterVarsity, 2012), do provide links to both scholarship and theological reflection but focus more on general discipleship and mentoring.

33. This conception of practical theology is derived specifically from Richard Osmer, *Practical Theology: An Introduction* (Grand Rapids: Eerdmans, 2008).

34. Smith, *Souls in Transition*, 154–56.

35. Richard Foster, *Life with God: Reading the Bible for Spiritual Transformation* (San Francisco: HarperOne, 2008), 7.

36. Schweitzer, *The Postmodern Life Cycle*.

37. The concept of a "community of truth" is mentioned in Dallas Willard, *The Divine Conspiracy: Rediscovering Our Hidden Life with God* (San Francisco: HarperOne, 1998), 260.

38. Robin Marantz Henig, "What Is It about 20-Somethings?" *New York Times*, August 18, 2010.

39. Rick Dunn, *Shaping the Spiritual Life of Students: A Guide for Youth Workers, Pastors, Teachers and Campus Ministers* (Downers Grove, IL: InterVarsity, 2001), 208.

Chapter 1 Faith

1. C. S. Lewis, *Mere Christianity* (San Francisco: HarperSanFrancisco, 2001), 197–98.

2. Christian Smith, *Souls in Transition: The Religious and Spiritual Lives of Emerging Adults* (New York: Oxford University Press, 2009), 118–21. Many of these emerging adults moved to a category in which they self-identified as "unsure in belief of God."

3. Pew Research Center, *Religion among the Millenials* (Washington, DC: Pew Forum on Religion and Public Life, 2010), 12.

4. Smith, *Souls in Transition*, 119.

5. David Kinnaman, *You Lost Me: Why Young Christians Are Leaving Church . . . And Rethinking Faith* (Grand Rapids: Baker Books, 2011), 24.

6. Pew Research Center, *Religion among the Millenials*, 14, 18.

7. On perceptions of the afterlife, see also Jeffrey Arnett, "From Worm Food to Infinite Bliss: Emerging Adults' Views of Life after Death," in R. M. Lerner, R. W. Roeser, and E. Phelps, eds., *Positive Youth Development and Spirituality: From Theory to Research* (West Conshohocken, PA: Templeton Press, 2008), 231–43. Arnett found that emerging adults tended to believe in heaven, hell, or "nothing."

8. Smith, *Souls in Transition*, 125. For similar data, see Brad J. Waggoner, *The Shape of Faith to Come* (Nashville: B&H Publishing Group, 2008), 268; Thom S. Rainer and Jess W. Rainer, *The Millenials: Connecting to America's Largest Generation* (Nashville: B&H Publishing Group, 2011), 227–51. Such changes are tempered in certain contexts such as Christian colleges. Recent studies of Christian college students indicate that basic beliefs remain fairly consistent across the collegiate years, demonstrating small declines in orthodoxy between freshman and sophomore years but then stability through senior year. See James M. Pennington and Corwin E. Smidt, *Evangelicalism: The Next Generation* (Grand Rapids: Baker Academic, 2002). By contrast, James Davison Hunter claimed more significant erosion of belief among Christian college students in 1982. See Hunter, *Evangelicalism: The Coming Generation* (Chicago: University of Chicago Press, 1987).

9. Smith, *Souls in Transition*, 112.

10. Other scholars are a bit more positive when describing these overall trends. Some, for example, argue that the sense of religion's importance stays about the same during the transition to adulthood. See Carolyn McNamara Barry, Larry Nelson, Sahar Davarya, and Shirene Urry, "Religiosity and Spirituality during the Transition to Adulthood," *International Journal of Behavioral Development* 34, no. 4 (2010): 311–24; Jenny J. Lee, "Religion and College Attendance: Change among Students," *Review of Higher Education* 25, no. 4 (2002): 369–84; E. S. Lefkowitz, "'Things Have Gotten Better': Developmental Changes among Emerging Adults after the Transition to University," *Journal of Adolescent Research* 20 (2005): 40–63.

11. Significant studies reflecting these declines include the National Survey on Youth and Religion (NSYR) and the College Student Beliefs and Values (CSBV) survey, conducted by the Higher Education Research Institute. For more information on the NSYR, see Smith, *Souls in Transition*. For more information on the CSBV, see James L. Heft, *Passing on the Faith: Transforming Traditions for the Next Generation of Jews, Christians, and Muslims* (New York: Fordham University Press, 2006) and Alexander W. Astin, Helen S. Astin, and Jennifer A. Lindholm, *Cultivating the Spirit: How College Can Enhance Students' Inner Lives* (San Francisco: Jossey-Bass, 2011). A recent study of 18- to 29-year-olds conducted by Thom Rainer and Jess Rainer found that 21 percent in this age group read the Bible at least once a week while 67 percent read the Bible "rarely or never"; 50 percent claimed to pray at least once a week. Alternatively, 38 percent said that they prayed "rarely or never." See Rainer and Rainer, *The Millenials*, 239.

12. Smith, *Souls in Transition*, 116.

13. Conrad Hackett, "Emerging Adult Participation in Congregations," 2009, accessed at www.changingsea.net/essays/Hackett.pdf.

14. Smith, *Souls in Transition*, 102. It is important to keep in mind that such statistics reflect a moment-in-time snapshot rather than a picture of historical trends. According to Smith and the Pew Research, there has been very little change in emerging adults over the past forty years in such measures as frequency of prayer, belief in God, belief in the Bible as the literal Word of God, and perceived importance of religion. In other words, while emerging adults are by all

measures less religious than either teenagers or older adults, they are not markedly different from 18- to 29-year-olds in previous generations. With the exception of religious affiliation and church attendance—where historical changes are more pronounced—the "slump" appears to be more closely related to age than to generational cohort. See Smith, *Souls in Transition*, 88–102 and Pew Research Center, *Religion among the Millenials*.

15. Smith, *Souls in Transition*, 142.

16. Astin, Astin, and Lindholm, *Cultivating the Spirit*, 3.

17. Heft, *Passing on the Faith*, 83.

18. Astin, Astin, and Lindholm, *Cultivating the Spirit*, 27–48.

19. Alyssa Bryant, "Gender Differences in Spiritual Development during the College Years," *Sex Roles* 56, no. 11–12 (2007): 835–46. The most robust differences between women and men come in areas of charitable involvement, equanimity, and religious skepticism.

20. Sharon Daloz Parks, *Big Questions, Worthy Dreams: Mentoring Young Adults in Their Search for Meaning, Purpose, and Faith* (San Francisco: Jossey-Bass, 2000).

21. Alyssa N. Bryant and Helen S. Astin, "The Correlates of Spiritual Struggle during the College Years," *The Journal of Higher Education* 79, no. 1 (2008): 1–27.

22. Barry et al., "Religiosity and Spirituality during the Transition to Adulthood," 312.

23. Astin, Astin, and Lindholm, *Cultivating the Spirit*; Heft, *Passing on the Faith*. See also A. W. Astin, *What Matters in College? Four Critical Years Revisited* (San Francisco: Jossey-Bass, 1993); E. T. Pascarella and P. T. Terenzini, *How College Affects Students* (San Francisco: Jossey-Bass, 1991); A. N. Bryant, J. Y. Choi, and M. Yasuno, "Understanding the Religious and Spiritual Dimensions of Students' Lives in the First Year of College," *Journal of College Student Development* 44, no. 6 (2003): 723–45. As Rodney Stark contends, most people who qualify as "spiritual but not religious" are those who reject churches and major religious traditions but embrace the supernatural in eclectic fashion. See Stark, *What Americans Really Believe* (Waco: Baylor University Press, 2008), 87–94. In his classic work on the subject, Robert C. Fuller suggests that those claiming to be "spiritual but not religious" are more likely than other Americans to have a college education, to belong to a white-collar profession, to be liberal in their political views, to have parents who attend church less frequently, and to be more independent in the sense of having weaker social relationships. See Fuller, *Spiritual, But Not Religious: Understanding Unchurched America* (New York: Oxford University Press, 2001).

24. Brian J. Zinnbauer, Kenneth I. Pargament, and Allie B. Scott, "The Emerging Meanings of Religiousness and Spirituality: Problems and Prospects," *Journal of Personality* 67, no. 6 (December 1999): 889–919; Paul Wink and Michelle Dillon, "Spiritual Development across the Adult Life Course: Findings from a Longitudinal Study," *Journal of Adult Development* 9, no. 1 (January 2002): 79–94. As D. A. Carson notes, the interior and subjective turn in discussions of spirituality can easily miss the centrality of the gospel, the church, and the Word of God in the process of spiritual development. See Carson, "When Is Spirituality Spiritual? Reflections on Some Problems of Definition," *Journal of the Evangelical Theological Society* 37, no. 3 (September 1994): 381–94.

25. Astin, Astin, and Lindholm, *Cultivating the Spirit*, 4.

26. Tim Clydesdale, *The First Year Out: Understanding American Teens after High School* (Chicago: University of Chicago Press, 2007), 49.

27. As Rodney Stark notes, those under the age of 30 are more likely to be "spiritual but not religious" than those in older age categories. He claims that 18 percent of Americans under the age of 30 would fit this characterization while 16 percent of 30- to 49-year-olds, 6 percent of 50- to 69-year-olds, and 3 percent of those over 70 would qualify under this category. See Stark, *What Americans Really Believe*, 8. Robert Wuthnow estimates that between one-sixth and one-third of all 21- to 45-year-olds could be characterized as religiously uninvolved and yet interested in spiritual matters. Wuthnow, *After the Baby Boomers: How Twenty- and*

Thirty-Somethings Are Changing the Face of American Religion (Princeton: Princeton University Press, 2007), 134.

28. This largely confirms the statistics found in other prominent studies. See, for example, Leile Shahabi, Lynda H. Powell, Marc A. Musick, Kenneth I. Pargament, Carl E. Thoresen, David Williams, Lynn Underwood, and Marcia A. Ory, "Correlates of Self-Perception of Spirituality in American Adults," *Annals of Behavioral Medicine* 24 (2002): 59–68.

29. Smith, *Souls in Transition*, 167.

30. Ibid., 166–67.

31. Smith estimates that 30 percent of all emerging adults are "selective adherents," engaging in certain aspects of their religious traditions but neglecting or ignoring many others. They tend to compartmentalize religious beliefs from lifestyle choices. He notes that at least 25 percent of emerging adults are "religiously indifferent," meaning they are neither opposed to religion nor personally invested in it; 5 percent of emerging adults are "religiously disconnected," suggesting that they have little exposure to religious faith. Finally, "irreligious" emerging adults make up roughly 10 percent of this population. These individuals are actively critical of religion and antagonistic toward religious claims. See Smith, *Souls in Transition*, 166–68.

32. Smith, *Souls in Transition*, 297. There is some evidence to indicate that college students are more likely than adolescents to make distinctions between spiritual people and religious people. See Stephen W. Cook, Patricia D. Borman, Martha A. Moore, and Mark A. Kunkel, "College Students' Perceptions of Spiritual People and Religious People," *Journal of Psychology and Theology* 28, no. 2 (2000): 125–37; Jennifer A. Lindholm, "The 'Interior' Lives of American College Students: Preliminary Findings from a National Study," in Heft, ed., *Passing on the Faith*, 75–102; Christian Piatt and Amy Piatt, *MySpace to Sacred Space: God for a New Generation* (St. Louis: Chalice Press, 2007).

33. Rainer and Rainer, *The Millenials*, 256.

34. Smith, *Souls in Transition*, 144.

35. Ibid., 145.

36. Wink and Dillon, "Spiritual Development across the Adult Life Course."

37. Arnett, "Learning to Stand Alone: The Contemporary American Transition to Adulthood in Cultural and Historical Context," *Human Development* 41, no. 5–6 (1998): 295–315.

38. Jeremy E. Uecker, Mark D. Regnerus, and Margaret L. Vaaler, "Losing My Religion: The Social Sources of Religious Decline in Early Adulthood," *Social Forces* 85, no. 4 (June 2007): 1683. It is important to note that many emerging adults, especially those who marry early without the benefit of higher education, spend a great deal of time and energy trying to "make ends meet." See Richard Settersten and Barbara E. Ray, *Not Quite Adults* (New York: Bantam Books, 2010), xii.

39. Clydesdale, *The First Year Out*, 205.

40. Ibid., 50.

41. Tim Clydesdale, "Abandoned, Pursued, or Safely Stowed?," Social Science Research Council website, accessed at www.ssrc.org.

42. Dietrich Bonhoeffer, *The Cost of Discipleship*, rev. ed. (New York: Macmillan, 1963), 69–76.

43. W. C. Buboltz, F. C. Brown, and B. Soper, "Sleep Habits and Patterns of College Students," *Journal of American College Health* 50, no. 3 (2002): 131–35. These authors found that only 11 percent of surveyed students were getting enough sleep. Sleep deprivation also leads to depression, anxiety, general cognitive difficulties, and increased use of drugs and alcohol.

44. Nicholas Carr, *The Shallows: What the Internet Is Doing to Our Brains* (New York: W. W. Norton & Company, 2011).

45. Smith, *Souls in Transition*, 74; Mark Edmundson, "Dwelling in Possibilities," *The Chronicle of Higher Education* 54, no. 27 (2008); Maggie Jackson, *Distracted: The Erosion of Attention and the Coming Dark Age* (Amherst, NY: Prometheus Books, 2008). According to

Jill Dierberg, emerging adults spend more time online than any other age group: 85 percent visit social networking sites, like Facebook and Twitter, regularly, and 36 percent visit a video-sharing site like YouTube on a given day. While they average four hours of television viewing per day, emerging adults have greatly curtailed their use of print media. See Jill Dierberg, "Media in the Lives of Young Adults: Implications for Religious Organizations," accessed at www.changingsea .net/articles/Dierberg.pdf.

46. Steven Covey, *The Seven Habits of Highly Effective People*, rev. ed. (New York: Free Press, 2004), 152.

47. Ibid.

48. Ibid, 153.

49. Smith, *Souls in Transition*, 56. See also Jeffrey Jensen Arnett, *Emerging Adulthood: The Winding Road from the Late Teens through the Twenties* (New York: Oxford University Press, 2004), 6, 182.

50. Arnett, *Emerging Adulthood*, 10–12.

51. Smith, *Souls in Transition*, 76.

52. Because of the delay of marriage and parenting, friendships now exert more influence for a longer period of time. Decisions previously made with spouses are now more commonly made with friends. See Settersten and Ray, *Not Quite Adults*, 104.

53. Hunter, *Evangelicalism: The Coming Generation*, 157–86; Phillip E. Hammond and James Davison Hunter, "On Maintaining Plausibility: The Worldview of Evangelical College Students," *Journal for the Scientific Study of Religion* 23, no. 3 (1984): 221–38.

54. Lee, "Religion and College Attendance." Lee states that only 13 percent of her sample reported a weakening of religious beliefs during college.

55. Mark Regnerus and Jeremy Uecker, "How Corrosive Is College to Religious Faith and Practice?," Social Science Research Council website, accessed at www.ssrc.org. See also Robert D. Putnam and David E. Campbell, *American Grace: How Religion Divides and Unites Us* (New York: Simon & Schuster, 2010), 102; H. V. Hartley, "How College Affects Students' Religious Faith and Practice: A Review of Research," *College Student Affairs Journal* 23, no. 2 (2004): 111–29.

56. Lindholm, "The 'Interior' Lives of American College Students," 81–82.

57. "Religious Engagement among Undergraduates," Social Science Research Council website, accessed at www.ssrc.org.

58. This might also explain why college seems to have a less liberalizing effect than it did in the past. See Bruce Hunsberger, "The Religiosity of College Students: Stability and Change over Years at University," *Journal for the Scientific Study of Religion* 17, no. 2 (1978): 159–64.

59. Uecker, Regnerus, and Vaaler, "Losing My Religion," 1683.

60. Regnerus and Uecker, "How Corrosive Is College?" Additionally, few professors in non-religious institutions seem to raise issues related to faith. Recent surveys have revealed that college and university professors are far less religious than the general population. Community college professors are the most likely to believe in God while those in elite doctoral institutions are the least likely. See Neill Gross and Solon Simmons, "How Religious Are America's College and University Professors?," Social Science Research Council website, accessed at www.ssrc.org.

61. Christian Smith, *Soul Searching: The Religious and Spiritual Lives of American Teenagers* (New York: Oxford University Press, 2006), 124.

62. Arnett, *Emerging Adulthood*, 185. On this theme, see also Penny Edgell, "Faith and Spirituality among Emerging Adults," accessed at www.changingsea.net/essays/Edgell1.pdf; Nancy Ammerman, "Golden Rule Christianity: Lived Religion in the American Mainstream," in David Hall, ed., *Lived Religion in America* (Princeton: Princeton University Press, 1997), 196–216; Michelle Dillon and Paul Wink, *In the Course of a Lifetime: Tracing Religious Belief, Practice, and Change* (Berkeley: University of California Press, 2007).

63. Kara E. Powell, Brad M. Griffin, and Cheryl A. Crawford, *Sticky Faith: Practical Ideas to Nurture Long-Term Faith in Teenagers* (Grand Rapids: Zondervan, 2011), 29.

64. Smith, *Souls in Transition*, 154.

65. Smith, *Soul Searching*, 165.

66. Smith, *Souls in Transition*, 154.

67. Larry Crabb, *The Pressure's Off* (Colorado Springs: Waterbrook Press, 2002), 77.

68. Smith, "Is Moralistic Therapeutic Deism the New Religion of American Youth? Implications for the Challenge of Religious Socialization and Reproduction," in Heft, *Passing on the Faith*, 61.

69. D. Hervieu-Leger, "Present-Day Emotional Renewals: The End of Secularization or the End of Religion?" in W. H. Swatos, ed., *A Future for Religion? New Paradigms for Social Analysis* (Thousand Oaks, CA: Sage, 1993). See also Carolyn McNamara Barry and Larry Nelson, "The Role of Religion in the Transition to Adulthood for Young Emerging Adults," *Journal of Youth and Adolescence* 34, no. 3 (2005): 245–55; Dennis P. Hollinger, "Spirituality on Campus: Cultural Impacts at Christian Colleges and Universities," *Christian Education Journal* 5NS, no. 1 (2001): 67–78.

70. Kenda Creasy Dean, *Almost Christian: What the Faith of Our Teenagers Is Telling the American Church* (New York: Oxford University Press, 2010), 29.

71. Smith, *Souls in Transition*, 287.

72. Jeffrey P. Greenman, "Spiritual Formation in Theological Perspective: Classic Issues, Contemporary Challenges," in Jeffrey P. Greenman and George Kalantzis, eds., *Life in the Spirit: Spiritual Formation in Theological Perspective* (Downers Grove, IL: IVP Academic, 2010), 28–31.

73. Smith, *Souls in Transition*, 290.

74. Dallas Willard, "Spiritual Formation as a Natural Part of Salvation," in Greenman and Kalantzis, eds., *Life in the Spirit*, 45–60.

75. Lewis, *Mere Christianity*, 198.

Chapter 2 Spiritual Formation

1. C. S. Lewis, *Mere Christianity* (New York: Macmillan, 1960), 191–92.

2. Dallas Willard, *The Divine Conspiracy: Rediscovering Our Hidden Life with God* (San Francisco: HarperOne, 1998), 35–59.

3. Paul David Tripp, *Instruments in the Redeemer's Hands* (Phillipsburg, NJ: P&R Publishing, 2002), 63.

4. Ibid., 62, 64. See also Kara E. Powell, Brad M. Griffin, and Cheryl A. Crawford, *Sticky Faith: Practical Ideas to Nurture Long-Term Faith in Teenagers* (Grand Rapids: Zondervan, 2011), 37–40. As with teenagers, emerging adults must recognize that "obedience flows out of their trust in God and the Holy Spirit's work in and through them" (p. 40).

5. James K. A. Smith, *Desiring the Kingdom: Worship, Worldview, and Cultural Liturgies* (Grand Rapids: Baker Academic, 2009), 54.

6. On this theme, see especially Cornelius Plantinga Jr., *Not the Way It's Supposed to Be: A Breviary of Sin* (Grand Rapids: Eerdmans, 1995), especially chap. 3. Plantinga notes that the images of idolatry and adultery signify both pollution and division, both impurity and separation.

7. Saint Augustine, *On Christian Teaching* (New York: Oxford University Press, 1999), 21.

8. Smith, *Desiring the Kingdom*, 52.

9. Craig Dykstra, *Growing in the Life of Faith: Education and Christian Practices* (Louisville: Geneva Press, 1999), 24.

10. Dallas Willard, *Renovation of the Heart: Putting on the Character of Christ* (Colorado Springs: NavPress, 2002), 35.

11. Skye Jethani, *The Divine Commodity* (Grand Rapids: Zondervan, 2009), 110.

12. Søren Kierkegaard, *Purity of Heart Is to Will One Thing*, translated by Douglas V. Steere (New York: Harper & Row, 1956).

13. Timothy Keller, *The Prodigal God* (New York: Penguin Group, 2008), 36.

14. Timothy Keller, *Counterfeit Gods: The Empty Promises of Money, Sex, and Power, and the Only Hope That Matters* (New York: The Penguin Group, 2009), 168.

15. Ibid.

16. Ibid., 155.

17. John Piper, *Future Grace* (Sisters, OR: Multnomah Books, 1995), 336.

18. C. S. Lewis, *The Weight of Glory, and Other Addresses* (New York: HarperOne, 2001), 26.

19. Willard, *The Divine Conspiracy*, 323.

20. Richard Foster, *Life with God: Reading the Bible for Spiritual Transformation* (New York: HarperOne, 2008), 157.

21. Sarah Arthur, *The God-Hungry Imagination: The Art of Storytelling for Postmodern Youth Ministry* (Nashville: Upper Room, 2007), 148.

22. Smith, *Desiring the Kingdom*, 76. See also Smith's *Imagining the Kingdom: How Worship Works* (Grand Rapids: Baker Academic, 2013).

23. On this theme, see Jeffrey Arnett, "High Hopes in a Grim World: Emerging Adults' Views of Their Futures and of 'Generation X,'" *Youth and Society* 31 (2000): 267–86.

24. Dietrich Bonhoeffer, *Spiritual Care* (Philadelphia: Fortress Press, 1985), 44.

25. Plantinga, *Not the Way It's Supposed to Be*, 84.

26. Cited in Dykstra, *Growing in the Life of Faith*, 26–27.

27. Arthur F. Holmes, *Shaping Character: Moral Education in the Christian College* (Grand Rapids: Eerdmans, 1991), 59.

28. James Wilhoit, *Spiritual Formation as if the Church Mattered* (Grand Rapids: Baker Academic, 2010), 60.

29. On this theme of the sovereignty of the self, see Christian Smith, *Souls in Transition: The Religious and Spiritual Lives of Emerging Adults* (New York: Oxford University Press, 2009), 49; David Wells, *Losing Our Virtue: Why the Church Must Recover Its Moral Vision* (Grand Rapids: Eerdmans, 1998), 65–80; James Davison Hunter, *The Death of Character: Moral Education in an Age without Good or Evil* (New York: Basic Books, 2000), 184–92.

30. Lewis, *Mere Christianity*, 195–97.

31. Dietrich Bonhoeffer, *The Cost of Discipleship*, rev. ed. (New York: Macmillan Publishing Co., 1963), 48.

32. Lewis, *Mere Christianity*, 197.

33. As H. Richard Niebuhr put it, God "requires of us the sacrifice of all we would conserve and grants us gifts we had not dreamed of." See Niebuhr, *The Meaning of Revelation* (New York: Macmillan, 1960), 138.

34. On this theme, see David A. Horner, *Mind Your Faith: A Student's Guide to Thinking and Living Well* (Downers Grove, IL: IVP Academic, 2011), 215–26.

35. Smith, *Souls in Transition*, 57.

36. Ibid.

37. John Dewey, *Experience and Education* (New York: Macmillan, 1938), 28.

38. Jeffrey Satinover, *Feathers of the Skylark: Compulsion, Sin and Our Need for a Messiah* (Westport, CT: Hamewith Books, 1996), 4, 8.

39. Ibid., 57.

40. Eugene Peterson, *A Long Obedience in the Same Direction* (Downers Grove, IL: InterVarsity, 2000).

41. On the concept of "tendency learning," see Nicholas Wolterstorff, *Educating for Responsible Action* (Grand Rapids: Eerdmans, 1980).

42. Rebecca Konyndyk DeYoung, *Glittering Vices: A New Look at the Seven Deadly Sins and Their Remedies* (Grand Rapids: Brazos, 2009), 13–14. Craig Dykstra refers similarly to developing the "patterns of intentionality that constitute a person's fundamental orientation in life." See Dykstra and Sharon Parks, eds., *Faith Development and Fowler* (Birmingham, AL: Religious Education Press, 1986), 61.

43. Lewis, *Mere Christianity*, 86–87.
44. Willard, *The Divine Conspiracy*, 322.
45. Smith, *Desiring the Kingdom*, 83.
46. Ibid., 90–91.
47. Foster, *Celebration of Discipline: The Path to Spiritual Growth*, rev. ed. (San Francisco: HarperSanFrancisco, 1988), 7.
48. Willard, *The Spirit of the Disciplines: Understanding How God Changes Lives* (San Francisco: HarperSanFrancisco, 1988), 158.
49. Willard, *The Divine Conspiracy*, 322.
50. Ibid., 353.
51. Saint Augustine, *The City of God*, Book XVI, Section 32 (New York: Random House, 1950), 554.
52. On the larger cultural shift from inner-directed character to other-directed personality, see especially David Riesman, *The Lonely Crowd: A Study of the Changing American Character* (New Haven: Yale University Press, 1950); Wells, *Losing Our Virtue*, 96–103; Hunter, *The Death of Character*, 69–70.
53. Dietrich Bonhoeffer, *Life Together* (San Francisco: HarperSanFrancisco, 1954), 79.
54. Tim Clydesdale, *The First Year Out: Understanding American Teens after High School* (Chicago: University of Chicago Press, 2007), 49.
55. Kierkegaard, *Purity of Heart Is to Will One Thing*, 107.
56. Foster, *Celebration of Discipline*, 97.
57. John Piper, *A Hunger for God: Desiring God through Fasting and Prayer* (Wheaton, IL: Crossway Books, 1997), 19.
58. Ibid, 23.
59. Jeffrey P. Greenman, "Spiritual Formation in Theological Perspective: Classic Issues, Contemporary Challenges," in Jeffrey P. Greenman and George Kalantzis, eds., *Life in the Spirit: Spiritual Formation in Theological Perspective* (Downers Grove, IL: IVP Academic, 2010), 28–29.
60. M. Robert Mulholland Jr., *Invitation to a Journey: A Road Map to Spiritual Formation* (Downers Grove, IL: InterVarsity, 1993), 112–15. On *lectio divina*, see also Ivan Illich, *In the Vineyard of the Text: A Commentary to Hugh's Didascalicon* (Chicago: University of Chicago Press, 1993); James C. Wilhoit and Evan B. Howard, *Discovering Lectio Divina: Bringing Scripture into Ordinary Life* (Downers Grove, IL: InterVarsity, 2012).
61. Smith, *Souls in Transition*, 41.
62. Bonhoeffer, *Life Together*, 114.
63. Ibid., 110.
64. Mulholland, *Invitation to a Journey*, 131–32. See also Foster, *Life with God*, 156.
65. See Foster, *Life with God*, 7.
66. Lewis, *Mere Christianity*, 191-92.

Chapter 3 Identity

1. Christian Smith, *Souls in Transition: The Religious and Spiritual Lives of Emerging Adults* (New York: Oxford University Press, 2009), 6.
2. See the history of the LIFE game at www.hasbro.com/default.cfm?page=ci_history_life.
3. Friedrich L. Schweitzer, *The Postmodern Life Cycle: Challenges for Church and Theology* (St. Louis: Chalice, 2004), 8.
4. Ibid., 9–10.
5. For a good sociological analysis, see James E. Côté and Charles Levine, *Identity Formation, Agency, and Culture: A Social Psychological Synthesis* (Mahwah, NJ: L. Erlbaum Associates, 2002).

6. For a helpful discussion of the subjective meanings young women attribute to adulthood, see Pamela Aronson, "The Markers and Meanings of Growing Up: Contemporary Young Women's Transition from Adolescence to Adulthood," *Gender & Society* 22, no. 1 (2008): 56–82.

7. Michael J. Shanahan, "Pathways to Adulthood in Changing Societies: Variability and Mechanisms in Life Course Perspective," *Annual Review of Sociology* 26 (2000): 667–92.

8. See Côté and Levine, *Identity Formation, Agency, and Culture*.

9. M. Zavalloni, "Social Identity and the Recording of Reality: Its Relevance for Cross-Cultural Psychology," *International Journal of Psychology* 10 (1975): 197–217.

10. Alasdair MacIntyre, *After Virtue: A Study in Moral Theory*, 2nd ed. (Notre Dame: University of Notre Dame Press, 1984), 33.

11. Orrin Klapp, *Collective Search for Identity* (New York: Holt, Rinehart and Winston, 1969).

12. H. R. Markus and S. Kitiyama, "Culture and the Self: Implications for Cognition, Emotion, and Motivation," *Psychological Review* 98 (1991): 224–53.

13. Côté and Levine, *Identity Formation, Agency, and Culture*, 1-87.

14. Stanley Grenz, "Christian Spirituality and the Quest for Identity: Toward a Spiritual-Theological Understanding of Life in Christ," *Baptist History and Heritage* 37, no. 2 (2002): 87–105.

15. Côté and Levine, *Identity Formation, Agency, and Culture*. There are definite cultural variations in this search for adult identity. Chinese emerging adults, for example, tend to stress norm compliance, family capacities, and relational maturity instead of individual self-determination. See S. Badger, L. J. Nelson, and C. M. Barry, "Perceptions of the Transition to Adulthood among Chinese and American Emerging Adults," *International Journal of Behavioral Development* 30 (2006): 84–93.

16. Jeffrey Jensen Arnett, *Emerging Adulthood: The Winding Road from the Late Teens through the Twenties* (New York: Oxford University Press, 2004), 6.

17. Jeffrey Arnett, "Learning to Stand Alone: The Contemporary American Transition to Adulthood in Cultural and Historical Context," *Human Development* 41 (1998): 295–315.

18. See a broader treatment of this in James Côté, *Arrested Adulthood: The Changing Nature of Maturity and Identity* (New York: New York University Press, 2000), 37.

19. On this theme, see S. J. Schwartz, J. E. Côté, and J. J. Arnett, "Identity and Agency in Emerging Adulthood: Two Developmental Routes in the Individualization Process," *Youth and Society* 37 (2005): 201–29. If families are unstable, adolescents often look to accelerate traditional adult roles in order to separate themselves from their current situations. On such "role exits," see J. Hagan and B. Wheaton, "The Search for Adolescent Role Exits and the Transition to Adulthood," *Social Forces* 71 (1993): 955–80.

20. See Côté, *Arrested Adulthood*, 3.

21. Richard Kadison and Theresa Foy DiGeronimo, *College of the Overwhelmed: The Campus Mental Health Crisis and What to Do about It* (San Francisco: Jossey-Bass, 2004), 95.

22. Ibid., 116–17.

23. Côté, *Arrested Adulthood*, 33–34.

24. Ulrich Beck, *Risk Society: Toward a New Modernity* (London: Sage Publications, 1992).

25. Côté and Levine, *Identity Formation, Agency, and Culture*.

26. Orrin Edgar Klapp, *Collective Search for Identity* (Austin: Holt, Rinehart and Winston, 1969). On cultural narcissism, see Christopher Lasch, *The Culture of Narcissism: American Life in the Age of Diminishing Expectations*, rev. ed. (New York: W. W. Norton and Company, 1991).

27. Christian Smith, *Lost in Transition: The Dark Side of Emerging Adulthood* (New York: Oxford University Press, 2011), 80.

28. Ibid., 86.

29. Côté, *Arrested Adulthood*, 34.

30. Erik Erikson, *Childhood and Society*, 2nd ed. (New York: Norton, 1963).

31. Richard Catalano, Lisa Berglund, Jean Ryan, Heather Lonczak, and David Hawkins, "Positive Youth Development in the United States: Research Findings on Evaluations of Positive Youth Development Programs," *Annals of the American Academy of Political and Social Science* 591 (January 2004): 98–124.

32. Arnett, *Emerging Adulthood.*

33. James E. Marcia, "Development and Validation of Ego Identity Status," *Journal of Personality and Social Psychology* 3 (166): 551–58; Marcia, "The Status of the Statuses: Research Reviewed," in J. E. Marcia, A. S. Waterman, D. R. Matteson, S. L. Archer, and J. L. Orlofsky, *Ego Identity: A Handbook for Psychological Research* (New York: Springer-Verlag, 1993), 22–41. Marcia Baxter Magolda describes this shift as a move from adopting "externally derived plans for success" to developing a "coherent internal self-system from which to operate." See Magolda, "Constructing Adult Identities," *Journal of College Student Development* 40, no. 6 (1999): 633. More recently, G. A. Valde suggested the existence of a fifth identity status called "identity closure," describing an achieved individual who then becomes closed off to continued exploration. See Valde, "Identity Closure: A Fifth Identity Status," *Journal of Genetic Psychology* 157 (1996): 245–54.

34. W. Meeus, "Studies on Identity Development in Adolescence: An Overview of Research and Some New Data," *Journal of Youth and Adolescence* 25 (1996): 569–98.

35. Diffusion is similar to what James Côté calls "default individualization," going with the flow of mass consumer culture and failing to engage the identity formation process. See Côté, *Arrested Adulthood*, 129.

36. Others have used James Marcia's model to describe spiritual identity, racial and ethnic identity, and the identity postures of college men and women. On spiritual identity, see Chris Kiesling, "My Sense of Spiritual Self: A Qualitative Study of Adult Spiritual Identity" (Ph.D. diss., Texas Tech University, 2002). On racial and ethnic identity, see J. S. Phinney, "Ethnic Identity in Adolescents and Adults: Review of Research," *Psychological Bulletin* 108 (1990): 499–514; W. E. Cross Jr., *Shades of Black: Diversity in African American Identity* (Philadelphia: Temple University Press, 1991). For emerging adults of color, positive identity development may also be linked to the development of ethnic identity, bicultural identification, and a growing consciousness of the complex expectations of both majority and minority cultures. See R. F. Catalano, M. L. Berglund, J. A. M. Ryan, H. S. Lonczak, and J. D. Hawkins, "Positive Youth Development in the United States: Research on Findings on Evaluations of Positive Youth Development Programs," *Annals of the American Academy of Political and Social Science* 591 (2004): 98–124. For a theory of female identity development during emerging adulthood, see R. Josselson, *Finding Herself: Pathways to Identity Development in Women* (San Francisco: Jossey-Bass, 1987) and *Revising Herself: The Story of Women's Identity from College to Midlife* (New York: Oxford University Press, 1996). Josselson uses the intuitive terms "drifter," "guardian," "searcher," and "pathfinder" to describe Marcia's diffusion, foreclosure, moratorium, and achievement. Research seems to indicate that men achieve identity through competence and knowledge, often through the career decision process and in the formation of a solid political and intellectual ideology. Women, on the other hand, are more likely to locate identity through relationships, perhaps making them more apt to be identified as foreclosed. See Nancy J. Evans, Deanna S. Forney, Florence M. Guido, Lori D. Patton, and Kristen A. Renn, *Student Development in College: Theory, Research, and Practice*, 2nd ed. (San Francisco: Jossey-Bass, 2009).

37. Sharon Daloz Parks, *Big Questions, Worthy Dreams: Mentoring Young Adults in Their Search for Meaning, Purpose, and Faith* (San Francisco: Jossey-Bass, 2000), 55.

38. David Riesman, *The Lonely Crowd: A Study of the Changing American Character* (New Haven: Yale University Press, 1950), 8.

39. Parks, *Big Questions, Worthy Dreams*, 75–76.

40. Riesman, *The Lonely Crowd*, 15. Along these lines, it may not be surprising that those in achievement and moratorium are more likely to have reflective decision-making styles while

those in foreclosure and diffusion have more impulsive decision-making styles. See Caroline K. Waterman and Alan S. Waterman, "Ego Identity Status and Decision Styles," *Journal of Youth and Adolescence* 3, no. 1 (March 1974): 1–6; Michael Berzonsky and Koen Luyckx, "Identity Styles, Self-Reflective Cognition, and Identity Processes: A Study of Adaptive and Maladaptive Dimensions of Self-Analysis," *Identity: An International Journal of Theory and Research* 8, no. 3 (2008): 205–20.

41. John Van Wicklin, Ronald J. Burwell, and Richard R. Butman, "Squandered Years: Identity Foreclosed Students and the Liberal Education They Avoid," in D. J. Lee and G. G. Stronks, eds., *Assessment in Christian Higher Education: Rhetoric and Reality* (Lanham, MD: University Press of America, 1994).

42. Richard Settersten and Barbara E. Ray, *Not Quite Adults* (New York: Bantam Books, 2010), 122–29.

43. Chris Kiesling, Gwendolyn T. Sorell, Marilyn J. Montgomery, and Ronald K. Colwell, "Identity Research and the Psychosocial Formation of One's Sense of Spiritual Self: Implications for Religious Educators and Christian Institutions of Higher Education," *Christian Education Journal* 3, no. 2 (2006): 252.

44. For studies on helicopter parents, see Wayne F. Pricer, "At Issue: Helicopter Parents and Millenial Students, an Annotated Bibliography," *Community College Enterprise* 14, no. 2 (2008): 93–108.

45. Daniel R. Heischman, *Good Influence: Teaching the Wisdom of Adulthood* (New York: Morehouse Publishing, 2009), 27.

46. Melinda Denton and Lisa Pearce, *A Faith of Their Own: Stability and Change in the Religiosity of America's Adolescents* (New York: Oxford University Press, 2011).

47. Parks, *Big Questions, Worthy Dreams*, 137–38.

48. See Kara E. Powell, Brad M. Griffin, and Cheryl A. Crawford, *Sticky Faith: Practical Ideas to Nurture Long-Term Faith in Teenagers* (Grand Rapids: Zondervan, 2011), 143.

49. Ibid., 66. See also Bruce R. Norquist, "An Exploration of the Relationship between Student Engagement with 'Otherness' and Faith Development in Evangelical Higher Education" (Ph.D. diss., Loyola University, 2008); Gay Holcomb, "Faithful Change: Exploring the Faith Development of Students Who Attend Christian Liberal Arts Institutions" (Ph.D. diss., University of Kentucky, 2004).

50. Kenda Creasy Dean, *Almost Christian: What the Faith of Our Teenagers Is Telling the American Church* (New York: Oxford University Press, 2010), 160, 174–78; Parks, *Big Questions, Worthy Dreams*, 66–69; Jennifer Kerpelman, Joe Pittman, and Leanne Lamke, "Toward a Microprocess Perspective on Adolescent Identity Development: An Identity Control Theory Approach," *Journal of Adolescent Research* 12 (1997): 325–46.

51. On the tour guide theme, see Lois LeBar, *Education That Is Christian*, rev. ed. (Wheaton: Victor Books, 1995), 166–67.

52. Denton and Pearce, *A Faith of Their Own*, 145.

53. Robert Kegan, *In Over Our Heads: The Mental Demands of Modern Life* (Cambridge: Harvard University Press, 1994), 42.

54. Côté, *Arrested Adulthood*, 179–80.

55. David A. Horner, *Mind Your Faith: A Student's Guide to Thinking and Living Well* (Downers Grove, IL: IVP Academic, 2011), 180–81.

56. G. K. Chesterton, *The Autobiography of G. K. Chesterton* (San Francisco: Ignatius, 2006), 217.

57. Valde, "Identity Closure."

58. For a wonderful exploration of this form of arrogance, see Helmut Thielicke, *A Little Exercise for Young Theologians* (Grand Rapids: Eerdmans, 1962), 16–20.

59. French philosopher Paul Ricoeur had something like this in mind when he spoke of moving beyond the "first naivete" of unthinking adherence to a "second naivete" that re-embraces

truth after conscious exploration. See Ricoeur, *The Symbolism of Evil* (New York: Harper & Row, 1967), 349.

60. W. Sibley Towner, *Daniel: Interpretation: A Bible Commentary for Teaching and Preaching* (Atlanta: John Knox Press, 1984), 23.

61. Ibid., 25.

62. Joyce Baldwin, *Daniel: Tyndale Old Testament Commentary* (Downers Grove, IL: InterVarsity, 1978), 82–83.

63. E. Stanley Jones, *Abundant Living* (Nashville: Abingdon-Cokesbury, 1942), 22.

64. Towner, *Daniel*, 27–28.

65. D. H. Williams, *Evangelicals and Tradition: The Formative Influence of the Early Church* (Grand Rapids: Baker Academic, 2005). Paul also utilized a similar strategy, setting up identity boundaries in opposition to the norms of gentile culture. See James W. Thompson, *Moral Formation according to Paul: The Context and Coherence of Pauline Ethics* (Grand Rapids: Baker Academic, 2011), 43–62.

66. Dallas Willard, *The Divine Conspiracy: Rediscovering Our Hidden Life with God* (San Francisco: HarperOne, 1998), 260.

67. Towner, *Daniel*, 26–27.

68. Willard, *The Divine Conspiracy*, 260.

69. Tory Baucum, *Evangelical Hospitality: Catechetical Evangelism in the Early Church and Its Recovery for Today* (Lanham, MD: Scarecrow Press, 2008).

70. Ibid., 27.

71. Lewis Rambo, *Understanding Religious Conversion* (New Haven: Yale University Press, 1995).

72. Peter Berger and Thomas Luckman, *The Social Construction of Reality: A Treatise in the Sociology of Knowledge* (New York: Anchor Books, 1967), 158.

73. Baucum, *Evangelical Hospitality*, 83–105.

74. For a classic work on rites of passage, see Arnold van Gennep, *The Rites of Passage* (Chicago: University of Chicago Press, 1960). In recent years, Christian leaders have been attempting to recover some of these practices for adolescent and adult transitions, particularly for young men. See, for example, Robert Lewis, *Raising a Modern-Day Knight: A Father's Role in Guiding His Son to Authentic Manhood* (Wheaton: Tyndale, 2007); Patrick Morley, *The Young Man in the Mirror: A Rite of Passage into Manhood* (Nashville: Broadman & Holman, 2003); Chris McNair, *Young Lions: Christian Rites of Passage for African American Young Men* (Nashville: Abingdon Press, 2001).

75. A helpful book in this regard is Stephen Rankin, *Aiming at Maturity: The Goal of the Christian Life* (Eugene, OR: Cascade Books, 2011).

76. Jones, *Abundant Living*, 22.

77. Steve Chalke and Brian McLaren, "A Tale of Two Gospels," presentation given at Asbury Seminary, January 20, 2009. In narrative theory, identity emerges in the telling of one's personal story as one weaves together diverse aspects of life into a meaningful whole. Religious identity is fashioned when individual self-stories link to religious stories and communities. See Justin Poll and Timothy Smith, "The Spiritual Self: Toward a Conceptualization of Spiritual Identity Development," *Journal of Psychology and Theology* 31, no. 2 (2003): 129–42.

78. Dean, *Almost Christian*, 29. On this theme, see also Craig Dykstra, *Growing in the Life of Faith: Education and Christian Practices* (Louisville: Geneva Press, 1999), 121.

79. The identity-shaping power of this can be seen, for example, in the Mormon two-year mission. For a good discussion of this, see Dean, *Almost Christian*, 56–58.

80. A helpful perspective in this direction is David White, *Practicing Discernment with Youth: A Transformative Youth Ministry Approach* (Cleveland: Pilgrim Press, 2005).

Chapter 4 Church

1. Robert Wuthnow, *After the Baby Boomers: How Twenty- and Thirty-Somethings are Changing the Face of American Religion* (Princeton: Princeton University Press, 2007), 12.

2. Jefferson Bethke, "Why I Hate Religion, But Love Jesus," January 12, 2012, video clip, 2012, YouTube, www.youtube.com/watch?v=Q0p6lVdtGKI.

3. Andrew Sullivan, "Christianity in Crisis," *Newsweek*, April 2, 2012.

4. Ibid.

5. Christian Smith, *Souls in Transition: The Religious and Spiritual Lives of Emerging Adults* (New York: Oxford University Press, 2009), 112.

6. In Jeffrey Arnett's estimation, 46 percent of those in this age span attend church 1–2 times per year or less while only 25 percent attend 3–7 times per month. Twelve percent attend 1–2 times per month while 17 percent attend "every few months." See Arnett, *Emerging Adulthood: The Winding Road from the Late Teens through the Twenties* (New York: Oxford University Press, 2004), 168.

7. Conrad Hackett, "Emerging Adult Participation in Congregations," accessed at www .changingsea.net/articles/Hackett.pdf. It is also important to recognize that there is a class dimension at work here. Lower-income emerging adults are now less likely than middle-class emerging adults to participate in institutional religion. Some have noted that this may be related to the tighter relationship middle-class emerging adults have with social institutions, seeing them as important tools of growth and advancement. See Rebekah P. Massengill and Carol Ann MacGregor, "Religious Nonaffiliation and Schooling: The Educational Trajectories of Three Types of Religious 'Nones,'" in Lisa A. Keister, John McCarthy, and Roger Finke, eds., *Religion, Work, and Inequality* (UK: Emerald Group Publishing, 2012).

8. Scott McConnellon, "Lifeway Research Finds Reasons 18- to 22-Year-Olds Drop Out of Church," August 7, 2007, accessed at www.lifeway.com/ArticleView?storeId=10054&catalogId=10001 &langId=-1&article=LifeWay-Research-finds-reasons-18-to-22-year-olds-drop-out-of-church.

9. David Kinnaman, "Most Twentysomethings Put Christianity on the Shelf Following Spiritually Active Teen Years," September 11, 2006, accessed at www.barna.org/barna-update /article/16-teensnext-gen/147-most-twentysomethings-put-christianity-on-the-shelf-following -spiritually-active-teen-years. Kara Powell estimates that 57 percent of former youth group students attend church during the fall of freshman year. Her overall estimate is that 40–50 percent of those connected to a youth group fail to stick with the faith in college. She also states that only 20 percent of those who disengage had actually planned on leaving. See Kara E. Powell, Brad M. Griffin, and Cheryl A. Crawford, *Sticky Faith: Practical Ideas to Nurture Long-Term Faith in Teenagers* (Grand Rapids: Zondervan, 2011), 167.

10. Alyssa Bryant, Jeung Yun Choi, and Maiko Yasuno, "Understanding the Religious and Spiritual Dimensions of Students' Lives in the First Year of College," *Journal of College Student Development* 44, no. 6 (2003): 733.

11. Smith, *Souls in Transition*, 113.

12. David Kinnaman, *You Lost Me* (Grand Rapids: Baker Books, 2011), 23.

13. Ibid., 22.

14. Smith, *Souls in Transition*, 97. Kinnaman, however, notes that before 1960, people in their midtwenties were as likely to attend church as those in older age groups. See Kinnaman, *You Lost Me*, 45.

15. Smith, *Souls in Transition*, 95–97. See also Daniel Mueller and Phillip W. Cooper, "Religious Interest and Involvement of Young Adults," *Review of Religious Research* 27 (1986): 245–54.

16. Wuthnow, *After the Baby Boomers*, 74.

17. Ibid., 69.

18. Arnett, *Emerging Adulthood*, 172.

19. Kinnaman, *You Lost Me*, 70. He notes that the average emerging adult "nomad" spends about three years separated from the local church (p. 64), though he also claims that many leave for much longer.

20. Smith, *Souls in Transition*, 251.

21. Ibid., 254. Wuthnow similarly contends that "the dominant pattern among young adults is not spirituality or religion but spirituality and religion" (*After the Baby Boomers*, 134).

22. Powell, Griffin, and Crawford, *Sticky Faith*, 15.

23. Jonathan Hill, "Religious Involvement during the Transition to Adulthood" (Ph.D. diss., University of Notre Dame, 2008), 138.

24. T. P. O'Connor, D. R. Hoge, and E. Alexander, "The Relative Influence of Youth and Adult Experiences on Personal Spirituality and Church Involvement," *Journal for the Scientific Study of Religion* 41 (2002): 723–32.

25. Wuthnow, *After the Baby Boomers*, 12–13.

26. Christian Smith, "Getting a Life: The Challenge of Emerging Adulthood," *Books and Culture* (November/December 2007): 6.

27. Kinnaman, "Most Twentysomethings Put Christianity on the Shelf."

28. D. R. Hoge, B. Johnson, and D. A. Luidens, "Determinants of Church Involvement of Young Adults Who Grew Up in Presbyterian Churches," *Journal of the Scientific Study of Religion* 32 (1993): 242–55.

29. Wuthnow, *After the Baby Boomers*, 54–55.

30. Alexander W. Astin, Helen S. Astin, and Jennifer A. Lindholm, *Cultivating the Spirit: How College Can Enhance Students' Inner Lives* (San Francisco: Jossey-Bass, 2011), 90.

31. Smith, *Souls in Transition*, 77.

32. See Astin, Astin, and Lindholm, *Cultivating the Spirit*, 90–91; Robert T. Gribbon, *Developing Faith in Young Adults: Effective Ministry with 18–35 Year Olds* (New York: The Alban Institute, 1990), 20; Jeremy E. Uecker, Mark D. Regnerus, and Margaret L. Vaaler, "Losing My Religion: The Social Sources of Religious Decline in Early Adulthood," *Social Forces* 85, no. 4 (June 2007): 1685; O'Connor, Hoge, and Alexander, "The Relative Influence"; Hoge, Johnson, and Luidens, "Determinants of Church Involvement," 253.

33. Astin, Astin, and Lindholm, *Cultivating the Spirit*, 89.

34. Uecker, Regnerus, and Vaaler, "Losing My Religion," 1676. Wuthnow, however, notes one exception. Women who pursue graduate degrees seem less likely to attend. See *After the Baby Boomers*, 61–62.

35. Wuthnow, *After the Baby Boomers*, 60–62. Studies of particular college settings have found that church attendance is quite high among students in colleges affiliated with the Coalition of Christian Colleges and Universities (CCCU). Up to 90 percent say that they "frequently" attend services. See Gary Railsback, "Faith Commitment of Born-Again Students at Secular and Evangelical Colleges," *Journal of Research in Christian Education* 15 (2006): 39–60. Relative attendance declines are actually higher in mainline and Catholic institutions than they are in public institutions. See Jonathan Hill, "Higher Education as Moral Community: Institutional Influences on Religious Participation during College," *Journal for the Scientific Study of Religion* 48, no. 3 (2009): 515–34.

36. Smith, *Souls in Transition*, 78.

37. Jeffrey Jensen Arnett and Lene Arnett Jensen, "A Congregation of One: Individualized Religious Beliefs among Emerging Adults," *Journal of Adolescent Research*, 17 (2002): 464–65. See also George Gallup Jr. and Jim Castelli, *The People's Religion: American Faith in the 90s* (New York: Macmillan, 1989).

38. Charles Taylor, *The Ethics of Authenticity* (Cambridge, MA: Harvard University Press, 1992).

39. Arnett, *Emerging Adulthood*, 171

40. Wuthnow, *After the Baby Boomers*, 114–17; Dennis P. Hollinger, "Spirituality on Campus: Cultural Impacts at Christian Colleges and Universities," *Christian Education Journal* 5NS, no. 1 (2001): 67–78.

41. Wuthnow notes that 42 percent of young adults (age 21–45) say they "sometimes" attend other churches while 16 percent do so "frequently" (*After the Baby Boomers*, 116).

42. Robert Wuthnow, *After Heaven: Spirituality in America since the 1950s* (Berkeley: University of California Press, 1998).

43. Mike Genn, *In Real Time: Authentic Young Adult Ministry as It Happens* (Nashville: B&H Publishing Group, 2009), 38.

44. Wayne Grudem, *Systematic Theology: An Introduction to Biblical Doctrine* (Grand Rapids: Zondervan, 1994), 855–57.

45. Stanley Grenz, *Renewing the Center: Evangelical Theology in a Post-Theological Era* (Grand Rapids: Baker Academic, 2000), 299.

46. Dietrich Bonhoeffer, *The Cost of Discipleship*, rev. ed. (New York: Macmillan, 1963), 277.

47. Smith, *Souls in Transition*,135.

48. Ibid., 136.

49. The recent National Survey of Youth and Religion revealed that, while most American emerging adults respect organized religion, 71 percent of both conservative and mainline Protestants see religious people as "negative, angry, and judgmental." See Smith, *Souls in Transition*, 133.

50. Kinnaman, *You Lost Me*, 192.

51. For these issues, see Kinnaman, *UnChristian* (Grand Rapids: Baker Books, 2007). See also Dan Kimball, *They Like Jesus But Not the Church: Insights from Emerging Generations* (Grand Rapids: Zondervan, 2007).

52. On this theme, see Schweitzer, *The Postmodern Life Cycle*, 77; Brian Simmons, *Wandering in the Wilderness: Changes and Challenges to Emerging Adult Faith* (Abilene, TX: Abilene Christian University Press, 2011), 12–13.

53. Christine A. Colon and Bonnie E. Field, *Singled Out: Why Celibacy Must Be Reinvented in Today's Church* (Grand Rapids: Brazos, 2009).

54. James L. Heft, ed., *Passing on the Faith: Transforming Traditions for the Next Generation of Jews, Christians, and Muslims* (New York: Fordham University Press, 2006), 105–6.

55. Dietrich Bonhoeffer, *Life Together* (San Francisco: HarperSanFrancisco, 1954), 27–28.

56. It is worth noting that churches have made significant attempts to re-create the church experience for those in post-boomer generations. As Ronald Flory and Donald E. Miller suggest, "innovators" have attempted to provide holistic experiential forms of teaching and worship, "appropriators" have attempted to provide popular and attractive services, "resisters" have attempted to restore a focus on right belief and solid orthodoxy, and "reclaimers" have attempted to bring back the symbolic and liturgical aspects of traditional church forms. See Flory and Miller, *Finding Faith: The Spiritual Quest of the Post-Boomer Generation* (New Brunswick, NJ: Rutgers University Press, 2008). Aspects of all of these movements will be evident in the paragraphs to follow.

57. Kenda Creasy Dean, *Almost Christian: What the Faith of Our Teenagers Is Telling the American Church* (New York: Oxford University Press, 2010), 112–21.

58. Elliott Eisner, *The Educational Imagination: On the Design and Evaluation of School Programs*, 2nd ed. (New York: Macmillan, 1985).

59. Schweitzer, *The Postmodern Life Cycle*, 80.

60. Kinnaman, *You Lost Me*, 116.

61. John Dewey, *Experience and Education* (New York: Macmillan, 1938), 49.

62. On this theme, see Felicia Wu Song, *Virtual Communities: Bowling Alone, Online Together* (New York: Peter Lang, 2009). Robert Wuthnow suggests that many small groups simply foster individualistic goals rather than communal identity. See his *Sharing the Journey: Support Groups and America's New Quest for Community* (New York: The Free Press, 1994).

63. Bonhoeffer, *Life Together*, 37. On this theme, see also Matthew Lee Anderson, *Earthen Vessels: Why Our Bodies Matter to Our Faith* (Minneapolis: Bethany House, 2011), 220–21.

64. Bonhoeffer, *Life Together*, 21.

65. Powell, Griffin, and Crawford, *Sticky Faith*, 75.

66. Wesley Black, "Stopping the Dropouts: Guiding Adolescents toward a Lasting Faith Following High School Graduation," *Christian Education Journal* 5, no. 1 (Spring 2008): 28–46.

67. Robert Bellah, *Habits of the Heart: Individualism and Commitment in American Life* (Berkeley: University of California Press, 1985), 72.

68. Andy Crouch, "For People Like Me: The Myth of Generations," *Re:Generation Quarterly* 5, no. 3 (Fall 1999), 30.

69. Kevin DeYoung and Greg Gilbert, *What Is the Mission of the Church? Making Sense of Social Justice, Shalom, and the Great Commission* (Wheaton: Crossway, 2011).

70. Kinnaman, *You Lost Me*, 203.

71. Powell, Griffin, and Crawford, *Sticky Faith*, 68.

72. On this theme, see Grudem, *Systematic Theology*, 894–900.

73. Smith, *Souls in Transition*, 49.

74. Peter Berger and Thomas Luckman, *The Social Construction of Reality: A Treatise in the Sociology of Knowledge* (New York: Anchor Books, 1967), 158.

75. Ibid.

76. Barry Danylak, *Redeeming Singleness* (Wheaton: Crossway, 2010), 19.

77. On this theme, see Rodney Clapp, *Families at the Crossroads: Beyond Traditional and Modern Options* (Downers Grove, IL: InterVarsity, 1993).

78. Danylak, *Redeeming Singleness*, 214–15.

79. Marcy Hintz, "Choosing Celibacy," *Christianity Today* 52, no. 9 (September 2008): 49.

80. Bonhoeffer, *Life Together*, 110.

81. Colleen Carroll, *The New Faithful: Why Young Adults Are Embracing Christian Orthodoxy* (Chicago: Loyola University Press, 2002).

82. Dykstra, *Growing in the Life of Faith*, 86–92.

83. James K. A. Smith, *Desiring the Kingdom: Worship, Worldview, and Cultural Liturgies* (Grand Rapids: Baker Academic, 2009), 157.

84. Ibid., 202.

85. Kinnaman, *You Lost Me*, 101.

86. On this theme, see Robert Webber, *The Younger Evangelicals* (Grand Rapids: Baker Books, 2002), 205–15.

87. See J. Lave and Etienne Wenger, *Situated Learning: Legitimate Peripheral Participation* (New York: Cambridge University Press, 1991).

88. Sharon Daloz Parks, *Big Questions, Worthy Dreams: Mentoring Young Adults in Their Search for Meaning, Purpose, and Faith* (San Francisco: Jossey-Bass, 2000), 146.

89. Carroll, *The New Faithful*, 45.

90. Kinnaman, *You Lost Me*, 95–112; Kinnaman, *UnChristian*, 121–52.

91. Darrell L. Guder, *Missional Church: A Vision for the Sending of the Church in North America* (Grand Rapids: Eerdmans, 1998), 108.

92. Dean, *Almost Christian*, 63.

93. Kinnaman, *You Lost Me*, 207.

94. Benson Hines has produced an excellent ebook on campus ministry, "Reaching the Campus Tribes." It can be accessed at reachingthecampustribes.com.

95. Guder, *Missional Church*, 108.

96. On this theme, see Francis Schaeffer, *The Mark of the Christian* (Downers Grove, IL: InterVarsity, 1970).

97. Webber, *The Younger Evangelicals*, 113.

98. Bethke, "Why I Hate Religion."

Chapter 5 Vocation

1. James Fowler, *Becoming Adult, Becoming Christian: Adult Development and Christian Faith* (San Francisco: Jossey-Bass, 2000), 113, 117.

2. Christian Smith, *Souls in Transition: The Religious and Spiritual Lives of Emerging Adults* (New York: Oxford University Press, 2009), 294.

3. Sharon Daloz Parks, *Big Questions, Worthy Dreams: Mentoring Young Adults in Their Search for Meaning, Purpose, and Faith* (San Francisco: Jossey-Bass, 2000), 138.

4. Jeffrey Jensen Arnett, *Emerging Adulthood: The Winding Road from the Late Teens through the Twenties* (New York: Oxford University Press, 2004), 208–13; Arnett, "Learning to Stand Alone: The Contemporary American Transition to Adulthood in Cultural and Historical Context," *Human Development* 41 (1998): 295–315. See also Arnett, "Are College Students Adults? Their Conceptions of the Transition to Adulthood," *Journal of Adult Development* 1 (1994): 231–24; Arnett, "Young People's Conceptions of the Transition to Adulthood," *Youth and Society* 29 (1997): 3–23; Jeffrey Jensen Arnett and Susan Taber, "Adolescence Terminable and Interminable: When Does Adolescence End?" *Journal of Youth and Adolescence* 23 (1994): 517–37; Michael J. Shanahan, Erik J. Porfeli, Jeylan T. Mortimer, and Lance D. Erikson, "Subjective Age Identity and the Transition to Adulthood: When Do Adolescents Become Adults?" in Richard A. Settersten Jr., Frank F. Furstenberg Jr., and Ruben G. Rumbaut, eds., *On the Frontier of Adulthood: Theory, Research, and Public Policy* (Chicago: University of Chicago Press, 2005), 225–55; Richard A. Settersten Jr., "Becoming Adult: Meanings and Markers for Young Americans," in Mary C. Waters, Patrick J. Carr, Maria J. Kefalas, and Jennifer Holdaway, eds., *Coming of Age in America* (Berkeley: University of California Press, 2011).

5. Arnett, *Emerging Adulthood*, 209. Arnett suggests that a good number of emerging adults do mention "becoming less self-oriented" as a helpful factor in achieving adult status. However, he is quick to note that "emerging adults who place concern for others at the center of their conceptions of adulthood are relatively rare." When they speak of "taking responsibility," this generally means responsibility for themselves rather than for others (p. 214).

6. According to the research, this shift may be especially important for men. Male adolescents tend to see altruism as something that can potentially develop in adulthood, whereas females see it as inherent within personhood rather than indicative of adult status. See A. L. Greene, S. M. Wheatley, and J. F. Aldava, "Stages on Life's Way: Adolescents' Implicit Theories of the Life Course," *Journal of Adolescent Research* 7 (1992): 364–81.

7. William H. Willimon and Thomas H. Naylor, *The Abandoned Generation: Rethinking Higher Education* (Grand Rapids: Eerdmans, 1995), 38–51.

8. Steve McDonald, Lance D. Erickson, Monica K. Johnson, and Glen H. Elder, "Informal Mentoring and Young Adult Employment," *Social Science Research* 36 (2007), 1328–47.

9. Christian Smith, *Lost in Transition: The Dark Side of Emerging Adulthood* (New York: Oxford University Press, 2011), 236–37.

10. Ibid., 236.

11. Frederick Buechner, *The Sacred Journey* (San Francisco: HarperSanFrancisco, 1982), 91.

12. On this theme, see, for example, Nancy Pearcey, *Total Truth: Liberating Christianity from Its Cultural Captivity* (Wheaton: Crossway, 2004), 31–49.

13. Lee Hardy, *The Fabric of This World* (Grand Rapids: Eerdmans, 1990).

14. Fowler, *Becoming Adult, Becoming Christian*, 84. In such a setting, the elevation of leisure is also a real temptation. Therefore, modern life moves toward "either a fusion or a disassociation of work and private life." See Marlis Buchman, *The Script of Life in Modern Society* (Chicago: The University of Chicago Press, 1989), 66.

15. On this theme, see Os Guinness, *The Call: Finding and Fulfilling the Central Purpose of Your Life* (Colorado Springs: NavPress, 2000); R. Paul Stevens, *The Other Six Days: Vocation, Work, and Ministry in Biblical Perspective* (Grand Rapids: Eerdmans, 1999).

16. Brian J. Walsh and J. Richard Middleton, *The Transforming Vision: Shaping a Christian World View* (Downers Grove, IL: InterVarsity, 1984), 99; John A. Bernbaum and Simon M. Steer, *Why Work? Careers and Employment in Biblical Perspective* (Grand Rapids: Baker, 1986), 10–11.

17. Miroslav Volf, *Work in the Spirit: Toward a Theology of Work* (New York: Oxford University Press, 1991), 70.

18. Douglas V. Henry and Michael D. Beaty, eds., *The Schooled Heart: Moral Formation in American Higher Education* (Waco: Baylor University Press, 2007), 111.

19. Darrell Cosden, *The Heavenly Good of Earthly Work* (Peabody, MA: Hendrickson, 2006).

20. Stevens, *The Other Six Days.*

21. Such a mentality has only been accentuated by the loss of readily identifiable connections between religion and public life. On this, see Douglas J. Schuurman, *Vocation: Discerning Our Callings in Life* (Grand Rapids: Eerdmans, 2004), 9.

22. Amy L. Sherman, *Kingdom Calling: Vocational Stewardship for the Common Good* (Downers Grove, IL: InterVarsity, 2011), 71.

23. M. Robert Mulholland Jr., *Invitation to a Journey: A Road Map to Spiritual Formation* (Downers Grove, IL: InterVarsity, 1993), 35–40.

24. Sherman, *Kingdom Calling,* 16–17.

25. Dietrich Bonhoeffer, *Letters and Papers from Prison,* ed. Eberhard Bethge, trans. Reginald Fuller and others, rev. ed. (New York: Macmillan, 1967), 193.

26. Darrell L. Guder, *Missional Church: A Vision for the Sending of the Church in North America* (Grand Rapids: Eerdmans, 1998).

27. Walter Brueggemann, "Covenanting as Human Vocation," *Interpretation* 33, no. 2 (1979): 125.

28. Ibid., 125–26.

29. Ibid., 126.

30. Guinness, *The Call,* 31.

31. Schuurman, *Vocation,* 47.

32. Fowler, *Becoming Adult, Becoming Christian,* 77.

33. On this theme, see Cornelius Plantinga Jr., *Engaging God's World: A Christian Vision of Faith, Learning, and Living* (Grand Rapids: Eerdmans, 2002), 108–17.

34. Cited in Paul Marshall, "Calling, Work, and Rest," in Mark A. Noll and David F. Wells, *Christian Faith and Practice in the Modern World: Theology from an Evangelical Point of View* (Grand Rapids: Eerdmans, 1988), 202.

35. Paul Althaus, *The Ethics of Martin Luther* (Philadelphia: Fortress, 1972), 10.

36. Timothy Keller, *Every Good Endeavor: Connecting Your Work to God's Work* (New York: Dutton, 2012), 49.

37. Cosden, *The Heavenly Good of Earthly Work,* 46–47.

38. On this theme, see also Volf, *Work in the Spirit,* 88–102; Andy Crouch, *Culture Making: Recovering Our Creative Calling* (Downers Grove, IL: InterVarsity, 2008), 160–74; Sherman, *Kingdom Calling,* 71–72.

39. Crouch, *Culture Making,* 170.

40. Ibid., 171.

41. Cosden, *The Heavenly Good of Earthly Work,* 115.

42. Cornelius Plantinga, Jr., *Not the Way It's Supposed to Be: A Breviary of Sin* (Grand Rapids: Eerdmans, 1995), 197.

43. On this theme, see also Ronald Habermas and Klaus Issler, *Teaching for Reconciliation: Foundations and Practice of Christian Educational Ministry* (Grand Rapids: Baker, 1992); Plantinga, Jr., *Engaging God's World;* Perry L. Glanzer and Todd C. Ream, *Christianity and Moral Identity in Higher Education* (New York: Palgrave Macmillan, 2009).

44. Plantinga, Jr., *Engaging God's World,* 119–20.

45. Keller, *Every Good Endeavor,* 42.

46. Crouch, *Culture Making*, 10.

47. On the importance of "faithful presence," see James Davison Hunter, *To Change the World* (New York: Oxford University Press, 2010). On pages 213–19, Hunter contrasts this vision with three other orientations toward cultural engagement: "defensive against," "relevance to," and "purity from." On this theme, see also Bruce Main, *If Jesus Were a Senior* (Louisville: Westminster John Knox, 2003), 53–59; Gabe Lyons, *The Next Christians* (New York: Doubleday, 2010); Guinness, *The Call*, 213–24.

48. Arnett, *Emerging Adulthood*, 144–45. Work prospects differ a great deal depending on socioeconomic and racial background. On these themes, see especially S. Halperin, *The Forgotten Half Revisited: American Youth and Young Families* (Washington, DC: American Youth Policy Forum, 1998); M. Csikszentmihalyi and B. Schneider, *Becoming Adult: How Teenagers Prepare for the World of Work* (New York: Basic Books, 2000); Richard A. Settersten, Jr., Frank F. Furstenberg, Jr., and Ruben G. Rumbaut, eds., *On the Frontier of Adulthood: Theory, Research, and Public Policy* (Chicago: University of Chicago Press, 2005), 356–95.

49. Smith, *Souls in Transition*, 5.

50. Arnett, *Emerging Adulthood*, 144.

51. Gary Badcock, *The Way of Life: A Theology of Christian Vocation* (Grand Rapids: Eerdmans, 1998); Jerry Sittser, *The Will of God as a Way of Life*, rev. ed. (Grand Rapids: Zondervan, 2004).

52. Dale S. Kuehne, *Sex and the iWorld: Rethinking Relationship Beyond an Age of Individualism* (Grand Rapids: Baker Academic, 2009), 67.

53. Varda Konstam, *Emerging and Young Adulthood: Multiple Perspectives, Diverse Narratives* (New York: Springer, 2007), 82.

54. Robert Nozick, *Philosophical Explanations* (Cambridge, MA: Harvard University Press, 1981), 596.

55. Sittser, *The Will of God as a Way of Life*, 22–23.

56. Walsh and Middleton, *The Transforming Vision*, 59.

57. John Wesley, "The Nature of Enthusiasm," sermon 37, in Thomas Jackson, ed., *The Sermons of John Wesley* (London: Wesley Conference House, 1872).

58. Hardy, *The Fabric of This World*, 92.

59. Fowler, *Becoming Adult, Becoming Christian*, 84.

60. Karl Barth, *Church Dogmatics*, III, 52.2 (Edinburgh: T&T Clark, 1961).

61. Frederick Buechner, *Wishful Thinking: A Theological ABC* (New York: Harper and Row, 1973).

62. Parker J. Palmer, *Let Your Life Speak: Listening for the Voice of Vocation* (San Francisco: Jossey-Bass, 2000), 25.

63. Jeylan T. Mortimer, Melanie J. Zimmer-Gembeck, and Mikki Holmes, "The Process of Occupational Decision Making: Patterns during the Transition to Adulthood," *Journal of Vocational Behavior* 61 (2002): 452–53.

64. Palmer, *Let Your Life Speak*, 22.

65. David Riesman, *The Lonely Crowd: A Study of the Changing American Character* (New Haven: Yale University Press, 1950).

66. Brueggemann, "Covenanting as Human Vocation," 116.

67. Fowler, *Becoming Adult, Becoming Christian*, 84.

68. Laurent Daloz, *Common Fire: Lives of Commitment in a Complex World* (Boston: Beacon Press, 1996), 196.

69. Crouch, *Culture Making*, 262.

Chapter 6 Morality

1. James Davison Hunter, *The Death of Character: Moral Education in an Age without Good or Evil* (New York: Basic Books, 2000), xv.

2. Christian Smith, *Lost in Transition: The Dark Side of Emerging Adulthood* (New York: Oxford University Press, 2011), 69.

3. Ibid., 19–69.

4. Ibid., 45–46. Smith reported that 17 percent of the emerging adults they interviewed referred to karma in their explanations of how morality works.

5. Christian Smith, *Souls in Transition: The Religious and Spiritual Lives of Emerging Adults* (New York: Oxford University Press, 2009), 68.

6. On this shift, see Carl Kaestle, *Pillars of the Republic: Common Schools and American Society, 1780–1860* (New York: Hill and Wang, 1983); B. Edward McClellan, *Moral Education in America* (New York: Teachers College Press, 1999); Hunter, *The Death of Character*.

7. McClellan, *Moral Education in America*; David P. Setran, "Character Education and the Kingdom of God: Liberal Progressivism and the Search for a Modern Morality" (Ph.D. diss., Indiana University, 2000).

8. David F. Wells, *Losing Our Virtue: Why the Church Must Recover Its Moral Vision* (Grand Rapids: Eerdmans, 1998), 96–103; David P. Setran, "Character and the Clinic: The Shift from Character to Personality in American Character Education," in Donald Warren and John J. Patrick, eds., *Civic and Moral Learning in America* (New York: Palgrave Macmillan, 2006), 173–90.

9. Warren I. Susman, *Culture as History: The Transformation of American Society in the Twentieth Century* (New York: Pantheon Books, 1984), 273–74.

10. Wells, *Losing Our Virtue*, 120–39.

11. Ibid.

12. On this shift, see George Marsden, *The Soul of the American University* (New York: Oxford University Press, 1994); Julie Reuben, *The Making of the Modern University* (Chicago: University of Chicago Press, 1996); Jon H. Roberts and James Turner, *The Sacred and the Secular University* (Princeton: Princeton University Press, 2000); David P. Setran, *The College "Y": Student Religion in the Era of Secularization* (New York: Palgrave/Macmillan, 2007).

13. Dallas Willard, *The Divine Conspiracy: Rediscovering Our Hidden Life with God* (San Francisco: HarperOne, 1998), 184.

14. Roy Baumeister and Mark Muraven, "Identity as Adaptation to Social, Cultural and Historical Context," *Journal of Adolescence* 19 (1996): 405–16.

15. Without question, we have won important freedoms through battles to protect and advance individual expression. Yet when freedom is regarded as the capacity to do "whatever one wants" without regard for the common good, this is more characteristic of "license."

16. Smith, *Lost in Transition*, 23.

17. Smith, *Souls in Transition*, 46.

18. Smith, *Lost in Transition*, 51; Dallas Willard, *Knowing Christ Today: Why We Can Trust Spiritual Knowledge* (San Francisco: HarperOne, 2009), 82.

19. David Kinnaman, *UnChristian: What a New Generation Really Thinks about Christianity* (Grand Rapids: Baker Books, 2007), 44.

20. Smith, *Lost in Transition*, 50–52.

21. Ibid, 30, 47. Contemporary adolescents seem to believe in similar ways. See Chap Clark, *Hurt: Inside the World of Today's Teenagers* (Grand Rapids: Baker Academic, 2004), 147.

22. Smith, *Souls in Transition*, 49.

23. Ibid., 24.

24. On this tension, see Stephen Armet, "Religious Socialization and Identity Formation of Adolescents in High Tension Religions," *Review of Religious Research* 50, no. 3 (2009): 277–97.

25. Kohlberg's stages of moral development can be found in W. C. Crain, *Theories of Development* (Englewoods Cliff, NJ: Prentice-Hall, 1985), 118–36. For a good critique of Kohlberg's Theory see John C. Gibbs, *Moral Development and Reality: Beyond the Theories of Kohlberg and Hoffman* (Thousand Oaks, CA: Sage Publications, 2003), 57–77.

26. William G. Perry, Jr., *Forms of Ethical and Intellectual Development in the College Years: A Scheme*, reprint ed. (San Francisco: Jossey-Bass, 1999).

27. Ronald Duska and Mariellen Whelan, *Moral Development: A Guide to Piaget and Kohlberg* (New York: Paulist Press, 1975), 70–72.

28. James Estep and Jonathan Kim summarize Christian critiques of moral development theory in *Christian Formation: Integrating Theology and Human Development* (Nashville: B&H, 2010), 134–41.

29. Werner Greve, Angelika Anderson, and Gunter Krampen, "Self-Efficacy and Externality in Adolescence: Theoretical Conceptions and Measurements in New Zealand and German Secondary School Students," *Identity: An International Journal of Theory and Research* 1, no. 4 (2001): 321–44.

30. Chris Kiesling, "A Long Adolescence in a Lame Direction? What Should We Make of the Changing Structure and Meaning of Young Adulthood?" *Christian Education Journal* 3 (Spring 2008): 11–27.

31. Smith, *Lost in Transition*, 22–23.

32. Ibid., 61.

33. See also Donald Joy, *Moral Development* (Nashville: Abingdon, 1983).

34. Richard Dunn and Jana Sundene, *Shaping the Journey of Emerging Adults: Life-Giving Rhythms for Spiritual Transformation* (Downers Grove, IL: InterVarsity, 2012).

35. See Mark Wheeler, "Relationship between Parenting Styles and the Spiritual Well-Being and Religiosity of College Students," *Christian Education Journal* 11, no. 2 (1991): 51–61; Laura Berk, *Development through the Lifespan* (Needham Heights, MA: Allyn and Bacon, 1998), 266–67.

36. Diana Baumrind, "Authoritarian vs. Authoritative Parental Control," *Adolescence* 3, no. 11 (1968): 255–72. Using her scheme, Scott Myers found that authoritative parenting styles best aided intergenerational faith transmission and enhanced parent-offspring relations. See Myers, "An Interactive Model of Religious Inheritance: The Importance of Family Context," *American Sociological Review* 61, no. 5 (1996): 858–66.

37. "Hardwired to Connect: The New Scientific Case for Authoritative Communities: A Report to the Nation from the Commission on Children at Risk," available at www.americanvalues.org.

38. Armet, "Religious Socialization," 285.

39. N. T. Wright, *After You Believe: Why Christian Character Matters* (San Francisco: HarperOne, 2010), 1–26. This duality, addressed as "desire" and "law," is also confirmed in Willard, *Knowing Christ Today*.

40. John Coe, "Resisting the Temptation of Moral Formation: Opening to Spiritual Formation in the Cross and the Spirit," *Journal of Spiritual Formation and Soul Care* 1, no. 1 (Spring 2008): 54–78.

41. Wright, *After You Believe*, 27.

42. Ibid., 26.

43. Nikki Tousley and Brad Kallenberg, "Virtue Ethics," in Joel Green, ed., *Dictionary of Scripture and Ethics* (Grand Rapids: Baker Academic, 2011), 814.

44. Others have emphasized the emotional aspects of moral formation. Carol Gilligan and Nel Noddings, for example, highlight an ethic of care, both for self and for others. See Gilligan, *In a Different Voice: Psychological Theory and Women's Development* (Cambridge: Harvard University Press, 1993) and Noddings, *Caring: A Feminine Approach to Ethics and Moral Education*, 2nd ed. (Berkeley: University of California Press, 2003). Martin Hoffman proposes that morality occurs not simply with a cognitive conception of what is good, but with an emotive compulsion to do the good. Hoffman argues that the roots of morality are in empathy or empathic arousal, which has a neurological basis but can either be fostered or suppressed by environmental influences. See *Empathy and Moral Development: Implications for Caring and Justice* (New York: Cambridge University Press, 2000).

45. Jay Wood, *Epistemology: Becoming Intellectually Virtuous* (Downers Grove, IL: IVP Academic, 1998), 44.

46. Tousley and Kallenberg, "Virtue Ethics," 814.

47. Wright, *After You Believe*, 29.

48. Ibid., 17.

49. There is consistency in what we are naming here and what is developing in social science research. Intervention strategies have moved from prevention models with a single problem-behavior focus toward consideration of a range of both positive behaviors and problem behaviors. Empirical science is now establishing a number of positive constructs identified as critical in promoting successful transitions into adulthood, many of which align well with aims sought by Christian colleges and campus ministries: the promotion of healthy bonding with an adult; resiliency when encountering stressful events; emotional and interpersonal competence; moral maturity and empathic arousal; self-efficacy; spirituality that includes relating to God and belonging to a church; dynamic, internal organization of a coherent identity; the fostering of hope; and opportunities for involvement within contexts that foster prosocial norms and recognize positive behavior. See Richard Catalano, Lisa Berglund, Jean Ryan, Heather Lonczak, and David Hawkins, "Positive Youth Development in the United States: Research Findings on Evaluations of Positive Youth Development Programs," *Annals of the American Academy of Political and Social Science* 591 (January 2004): 98–124.

50. Wood, *Epistemology*, 71.

51. Perry L. Glanzer and Todd Ream, *Christianity and Moral Identity in Higher Education* (New York: Palgrave Macmillan, 2009), 27–28.

52. Wright, *After You Believe*, 80.

53. Ibid., 243.

54. Kinnaman, *UnChristian*, 53.

55. Wright, *After You Believe*, 93.

56. Ibid., 243.

57. Ibid., 35–36.

58. Paul J. Griffiths, *Intellectual Appetite: A Theological Grammar* (Washington, DC: Catholic University of America Press, 2009), 20.

59. Ibid.

60. Parker Palmer, *To Know as We Are Known: A Spirituality of Education* (New York: Harper and Row, 1983), 6–8.

61. Griffiths, *Intellectual Appetite*, 22.

62. Palmer, *To Know as We Are Known*, 8.

63. Wood, *Epistemology*, 20–21.

64. Stanley Hauerwas, *A Community of Character: Toward a Constructive Christian Social Ethic* (Notre Dame, IN: Notre Dame University Press, 1981), 151.

65. Alasdair MacIntyre quoted in Warren A. Nord, "Liberal Education, Moral Education, and Religion" in Douglas V. Henry and Michael R. Beaty, eds., *The Schooled Heart: Moral Formation in American Higher Education* (Waco: Baylor University Press, 2007), 33.

66. Stanley Hauerwas and Thomas Shaffer, "Hope Faces Power: Thomas More and the King of England," in *Christian Existence Today: Essays on Church, World, and Living in Between* (Durham, NC: Labyrinth Press, 1988), 217.

67. Glanzer and Ream, *Christianity and Moral Identity in Higher Education*, 28.

68. Christine Pohl, *Living into Community: Cultivating Practices that Sustain Us* (Grand Rapids: Eerdmans, 2012).

69. Ibid.

70. Arthur Holmes, *Shaping Character: Moral Education in the Christian College* (Grand Rapids: Eerdmans, 1991), 67.

71. Ibid., 34–40.

72. David White, *Practicing Discernment with Youth: A Transformative Youth Ministry Approach* (Cleveland: Pilgrim Press, 2005).

73. Smith, *Lost in Transition*, 69.

Chapter 7 Sexuality

1. Frederick Buechner, *Listening to Your Life: Daily Meditations with Frederick Buechner* (San Francisco: HarperSanFrancisco, 1992), 264.

2. Judith Balswick and Jack Balswick in *Authentic Human Sexuality: An Integral Christian Approach*, 2nd ed. (Downers Grove, IL: IVP Academic, 2008) distinguish between sexual and erotic energy. By doing so, it becomes clear that most healthy adults engage in many sexual, nonerotic relationships (opposite sex friendships, extended family, and work and community relationships).

3. Space does not permit any significant treatment of important issues related to homosexuality. For helpful explorations of this important issue, see Mark Yarhouse, *Homosexuality and the Christian: A Guide for Parents, Pastors and Friends* (Bloomington, MN: Bethany Publishing, 2010) or Mark Yarhouse, Steve Stratton, J. Dean, and H. Brooke, "Listening to Sexual Minorities on Christian College Campuses," in *Journal of Psychology and Theology*: 37, no. 2 (2009): 96–113.

4. Jeffrey Jensen Arnett, *Emerging Adulthood: The Winding Road from the Late Teens through the Twenties* (New York: Oxford University Press, 2004), 74.

5. Beth Bailey, *From Front Porch to Back Seat: Courtship in Twentieth-Century America* (Baltimore: Johns Hopkins University Press, 1989).

6. Balswick and Balswick, *Authentic Human Sexuality*, 23.

7. Arnett, *Emerging Adulthood*, 74.

8. Ibid.; Bailey, *From Front Porch to Back Seat*.

9. Balswick and Balswick, *Authentic Human Sexuality*, 23.

10. Arnett, *Emerging Adulthood*, 75.

11. Ibid., 75.

12. Ibid.

13. Balswick and Balswick, *Authentic Human Sexuality*, 23–24.

14. Mark Regnerus and Jeremy Uecker, *Premarital Sex in America: How Young Americans Meet, Mate, and Think about Marrying* (New York: Oxford University Press, 2011), 23–24.

15. Christian Smith, *Lost in Transition: The Dark Side of Emerging Adulthood* (New York: Oxford University Press, 2011), 152–53.

16. Ibid., 154.

17. Ibid.

18. Elizabeth Morgan, Avril Thorne, and Eileen Zurbriggen, "A Longitudinal Study of Conversations with Parents about Sex and Dating during College," *Developmental Psychology* 46, no. 1 (2010): 139–50.

19. Donna Freitas, *Sex and the Soul: Juggling Sexuality, Spirituality, Romance, and Religion on America's College Campuses* (New York: Oxford University Press, 2008).

20. Derek Kreager and Jeremy Staff, "The Sexual Double Standard and Adolescent Peer Acceptance," *Social Psychology Quarterly* 72, no. 2 (2009): 143–64.

21. Regnerus and Uecker, *Premarital Sex in America*.

22. Ibid.

23. Ibid., 53.

24. Ibid., 66.

25. Balswick and Balswick, *Authentic Human Sexuality*, 23.

26. Christian Smith, *Souls in Transition: The Religious and Spiritual Lives of Emerging Adults* (New York: Oxford University Press, 2009), 58.

27. Arnett, *Emerging Adulthood*, 98–99.

28. Ibid., 102.

29. Ibid., 105.

30. Ibid., 97.

31. Elizabeth Fussell and Anne H. Gauthier, "American Women's Transition to Adulthood in Comparative Perspective," in Richard A. Settersten, Jr., Frank F. Furstenberg, Jr., and Ruben G. Rumbaut, eds., *On the Frontier of Adulthood: Theory, Research, and Public Policy* (Chicago: University of Chicago Press, 2005), 76–109. It should be noted that marriage is also rapidly dividing along class lines. While college-educated elites can expect to enter a relatively stable marriage, this is less and less true for middle- and working-class Americans. On this issue, see especially The National Institute of American Values, A Call for a New Conversation on Marriage. Their report can be found at www.americanvalues.org.

32. On this theme, see Marlis Buchman, *The Script of Life in Modern Society* (Chicago: The University of Chicago Press, 1989).

33. Andrew J. Cherlin, *The Marriage-Go-Round: The State of Marriage and the Family in America Today* (New York: Alfred A. Knopf, 2009), 140.

34. Mark Regnerus, "The Case for Early Marriage," *Christianity Today* 53, no. 8 (2009): 25.

35. Cherlin, *The Marriage-Go-Round*, 142.

36. Timothy Keller, *The Meaning of Marriage* (New York: Dutton, 2011), 27.

37. David Popenoe and Barbara Dafoe Whitehead, *The State of Our Unions: 2002—Why Men Won't Commit* (National Marriage Project), 13.

38. Balswick and Balswick, *Authentic Human Sexuality*, 163; Pamela Smock, "Cohabitation in the United States: An Appraisal of Research Themes, Findings and Implications," *Annual Review of Sociology* 26, no. 1 (2000): 1–20. Education seems to be a factor in predicting cohabiting relationships; 60 percent of high school dropouts cohabit, while 37 percent of college graduates do the same.

39. Balswick and Balswick, *Authentic Human Sexuality*, 163.

40. Larry Bumpass and Hsien-Hen Lu, "Trends in Cohabitation and Implications for Children's Family Contexts in the United States," *Population Studies* 54 (2000): 29–41.

41. Balswick and Balswick, *Authentic Human Sexuality*, 164.

42. Ibid., 109.

43. Scott Stanley, Galena Rhoades, and Howard Markham, "Sliding Versus Deciding: Inertia and the Premarital Cohabitation Effect," *Family Relations* 55, no. 4 (2006): 499–509.

44. Ibid., 505.

45. In the mid-to-late 1960s, several authors, including Margaret Mead, proposed a graduated step process toward marriage that included "trial marriage" or short contracts that would enable a couple to avoid feeling "trapped for life." This was likely the precursor to cohabitation in North America (see Balswick and Balswick, *Authentic Human Sexuality*, for an elaboration).

46. Stanley, "Sliding Versus Deciding."

47. Ibid., 163.

48. Ibid.

49. Mark D. Regnerus, *Forbidden Fruit: Sex and Religion in the Lives of American Teenagers* (New York: Oxford University Press, 2007), 127.

50. Ibid., 1. Christian Smith estimates this number at a lower 73 percent. See *Lost in Transition*, 149.

51. Morgan, Thorne, and Zubriggen, "A Longitudinal Study of Young Adults' Conversations with Parents." About 71 percent have had oral sex. See Smith, *Lost in Transition*, 149.

52. Regnerus and Uecker, *Premarital Sex In America*, 1.

53. Monte Morin, "Nearly 1 in 4 Teens Has 'Sexted' Nude Pictures, Study Says." www.chicagotribune.com/health/la-heb-teens-sexted-pictures-study-20120703,0,2190428.story.

54. Bill McCarthy and Eric Grodsky, "Sex and School: Adolescent Sexual Intercourse and Education," *Social Problems* 58, no. 2 (2001): 213–34. See also Stephanie Coontz, "Romance and Sex in Adolescence and Emerging Adulthood," in Ann C. Crouter and Alan Booth, eds.,

Romance and Sex in Adolescence and Emerging Adulthood: Risks and Opportunities (Mahwah, NJ: Lawrence Erlbaum Associates, 2006).

55. Mark Regnerus, "Sexual Behavior in Young Adulthood," 2009, accessed at www.changing sea.net/essays/Hackett.pdf.

56. Smith, *Souls in Transition*, 196.

57. Ibid., 294.

58. Robert Wuthnow, *After the Baby Boomers: How Twenty- and Thirty-Somethings Are Changing the Face of American Religion* (Princeton: Princeton University Press, 2007), 138–39.

59. For an excellent description of these issues, see William M. Struthers, *Wired for Intimacy: How Pornography Hijacks the Male Brain* (Downers Grove, IL: InterVarsity, 2009).

60. J. S. Carroll, L. M. Padilla-Walker, L. J. Nelson, C. D. Olson, C. M. Barry, and S. Madsen, "Generation XXX: Pornography Acceptance and Use among Emerging Adults," *Journal of Adolescent Research* 23 (2008): 6–30.

61. Ibid.

62. L. J. Nelson, L. M. Padilla-Walker, and J. S. Carroll, "I Believe It Is Wrong But I Still Do It: A Comparison of Religious Young Men Who Do Versus Do Not Use Pornography," *Psychology of Religion and Spirituality* 2, no. 3 (2010): 136–47.

63. Carroll et al., "Generation XXX."

64. Laura Kastner and Jennifer Wyatt, *The Launching Years: Strategies for Parenting from Senior Year to College Life* (New York: Clarkson Potter, 2002).

65. Roy Baumeister, Sarah Wotman, and Arlene Stilwell, "Unrequited Love: On Heartbreak, Anger, Guilt, Scriptlessness and Humiliation," *Journal of Personality and Social Psychology* 64 (1993): 377–94.

66. Arnett, *Emerging Adulthood*, 87.

67. McCarthy and Grodsky, "Sex and School," 213–34.

68. Smith, *Lost in Transition*, 148.

69. Ibid., 193.

70. Timothy Keller, "The Gospel and Sex," www.qideas.org/essays/the-gospel-and-sex.aspx.

71. David Kinnaman, *You Lost Me: Why Young Christians Are Leaving Church . . . And Rethinking Faith* (Grand Rapids: Baker Books, 2011), 157–60.

72. Freitas, *Sex and the Soul.*

73. Jeremy Uecker and Mark Regnerus found that campus sex ratios seem to influence patterns of dating and sexuality. Where women comprise a higher percentage of the student body, more negative appraisals are made of campus men and relationships. Women on these campuses reported fewer traditional dates, a smaller likelihood of having a college boyfriend, and yet were more likely to be sexually active. See "Bare Market: Campus Sex Ratios, Romantic Relationships, and Sexual Behavior," *Sociological Quarterly* 51, no. 3 (2010): 408–35.

74. Stanton L. Jones, "How to Teach Sex: Seven Realities that Christians in Every Congregation Need to Know," *Christianity Today* 55, no. 1 (January 2011): 37.

75. Keller, "The Gospel and Sex," 4.

76. Ibid.

77. Gerald Hiestand and Jay Thomas, *Sex, Dating, and Relationships* (Wheaton: Crossway, 2012), 28.

78. Lisa McMinn, *Sexuality and Holy Longing: Embracing Intimacy in a Broken World* (San Francisco: Jossey-Bass, 2004), 69.

79. Marva Dawn, *Sexual Character: Beyond Technique to Intimacy* (Grand Rapids: Eerdmans, 1993), 58.

80. Keller, "The Gospel and Sex," 2.

81. David P. Gushee, "A Sexual Ethic for College Students" (paper presented at the CCCU Consultation on Human Sexuality, Calvin College, November 2004).

82. Ibid.

83. *The Confessions of Saint Augustine: A New Translation with Introduction*, trans. E. M. Blaiklock (Nashville: Thomas Nelson, 1983).

84. The following discussion of Augustine's "disordered love" is drawn from Samuel Enoch Stumpf, *Philosophy: History and Problems*, 3rd ed. (New York: McGraw Hill, 1983).

85. Ibid.

86. Ibid.

87. Ibid.

88. C. S. Lewis, *The Four Loves* (Orlando: Harcourt Brace and Company, 1960), 6–8.

89. McMinn, *Sexuality and Holy Longing*, 8.

90. Patrick Carnes's seminal work in *Out of the Shadows: Understanding Sexual Addiction* (Minneapolis: CompCare Publishers, 1983) continues to provide one of the most helpful frameworks for understanding the addictive system, a framework that enables one to consider multiple strategic places for intervention.

91. Dallas Willard, "Beyond Pornography: Spiritual Formation Studied in a Particular Case," paper presented at the Talbot School of Theology's "Christian Spirituality and Soul Care" Conference, September 2008.

92. Ibid.

93. Ibid.

94. Ibid.

95. Ibid.

96. Ibid.

97. Ibid.

98. Peter Bearman and Hannah Bruckner, "Promising the Future: Virginity Pledges and First Intercourse," *The American Journal of Sociology* 106, no. 4 (2001): 859–912. The National Longitudinal Study of Adolescent Health sampled 14,000 youth in 1995, 1996, and 2001. They report that 52 percent of teens who took the pledge reported having sex within a year (see McCarthy and Grodsky, "Sex and School"). These individuals were also less likely to use birth control or contact a physician if they contact a sexually transmitted infection.

99. Dawn Eden, *The Thrill of the Chaste: Finding Fulfillment While Keeping Your Clothes On* (Nashville: Thomas Nelson, 2006).

100. Lauren Winner, *Real Sex: The Naked Truth about Chastity* (Grand Rapids: Brazos, 2005), 126; Eden, *Thrill of the Chaste*.

101. Clifford Stevens, "The Trinitarian Roots of the Nuptial Community," *St. Vladimir's Theological Quarterly* 35, no. 4, (1991): 351–58.

102. Ibid.

103. Wendy Shalit, *Return to Modesty: Discovering the Lost Virtue* (New York: Touchstone, 1999).

104. Christine Gardner, *Making Chastity Sexy: The Rhetoric of Evangelical Abstinence Campaigns* (Berkeley: University of California Press, 2011), 61.

105. Ibid., 77.

106. Orrin Klapp, *Collective Search for Identity* (New York: Holt, Rinehart and Winston, 1969).

107. For more on this topic, see Chris Kiesling, "A Long Adolescence in a Lame Direction? What Should We Make of the Changing Structure and Meaning of Young Adulthood?" *Christian Education Journal* 3 (Spring 2008): 11–27.

Chapter 8 Relationships

1. W. H. Auden, "Oh Tell Me the Truth about Love," in *Collected Poems* (New York: Vintage, 1991), 142.

2. A helpful articulation of this kind of accompaniment can be found in Richard Dunn and Jana Sundene, *Shaping the Journey of Emerging Adults: Life-Giving Rhythms for Spiritual Transformation* (Downers Grove, IL: InterVarsity, 2012), 164–190.

3. Shoveller et al. found that alienation and increased anxiety often emerge when adults pathologize or silence conversation about romance and sex. See Jean Shoveller, Joy Johnson, Donald Langilec, and Terry Mitchell, "Socio-Cultural Influences on Young People's Sexual Development," *Social Science and Medicine* 59 (2004): 473–87.

4. Erik Erikson, *Childhood and Society*, 2nd ed. (New York: Norton, 1963).

5. James Marcia, "Identity and Psychosocial Development in Adulthood," *Identity: An International Journal of Theory and Research* 2, no. 1 (2002): 7–28.

6. A helpful overview of John Bowlby's work that connects it to early childhood attachment can be found in Lee Kirkpatrick, "An Attachment-Theory Approach to the Psychology of Religion," *International Journal for the Psychology of Religion* 2, no. 1 (1992): 3–28.

7. The most widely used classification of attachment theory is Mary Ainsworth's "Strange Situation Experiment" in which children's behavior was observed following a brief separation from the primary caregiver. Ainsworth and her team discovered four general patterns of attachment: secure, avoidant, ambivalent, and disorganized. See Eun Sim Joung, *Religious Attachment: Women's Faith Development in Psychodynamic Perspective* (New Castle, UK: Cambridge Scholars Publishing, 2008).

8. Malcolm West and Adrienne Sheldon-Keller, *Patterns of Relating: An Adult Attachment Perspective* (New York: Guilford Press, 1994).

9. Brooke Feeney and Joan Monin, "An Attachment-Theoretical Perspective on Divorce," in Jude Cassidy and Phillip R. Shaver, eds., *Handbook of Attachment: Theory, Research, and Clinical Applications*, 2nd ed. (New York: Guilford Press, 2008), 934–57.

10. West and Sheldon-Keller, *Patterns of Relating*.

11. Feeney and Monin, "An Attachment-Theoretical Perspective on Divorce."

12. West and Sheldon-Keller, *Patterns of Relating*.

13. Ibid.

14. The linkages between attachment styles, divorce effects, and the faith journey is explored in Chris Kiesling, "An Attachment Theory Approach to Narrating the Faith Journey of Children of Parental Divorce," *International Journal of Children's Spirituality* 16, no. 4 (2011): 301–13.

15. Christopher Lasch, *Haven in a Heartless World* (New York: Basic Books, 1979), quoted in Jeffrey Jensen Arnett, *Emerging Adulthood: The Winding Road from the Late Teens through the Twenties* (New York: Oxford University Press, 2004), 62.

16. West and Sheldon-Keller, *Patterns of Relating*.

17. Ibid.

18. The concept of "becoming conscious" is elaborated in Harville Hendrix, *Getting the Love You Want: A Guide for Couples* (New York: Henry Holt and Company, 1988). Judith Wallerstein reported in her original research with adult children of divorce that about one-half of females and one-third of males felt they could change and create a new mental model of relating. See Judith F. Wallerstein, Julia M. Lewis, and Sandra Blakeslee, *The Unexpected Legacy of Divorce: The 25 Year Landmark Study* (New York: Hyperion, 2001).

19. Andrew Collins and Manfred van Dulmen, "The Course of True Love(s) . . . Origins and Pathways in the Development of Romantic Relationships" in Ann C. Crouter and Alan Booth, eds., *Romance and Sex in Adolescence and Emerging Adulthood: Risks and Opportunities* (Mahwah, NJ: Lawrence Erlbaum Associates, 2006).

20. Ibid.

21. On the specific practices of truthfulness, promise keeping, gratitude, and hospitality, see Christine Pohl, *Living into Community: Cultivating Practices that Sustain Us* (Grand Rapids: Eerdmans, 2012).

22. Collins and van Dulmen, "The Course of True Love(s)," 67–68.

23. Some have argued that peer relationships are dissimilar from intimate affiliations, suggesting that success with peers does little to prepare one for competence in romance. Friendships, it is argued, provide comfort and social ease, carrying a sense of settled quality to them. Romantic relationships, by contrast, heighten emotionality, promote awkwardness, and involve wrestling with exclusivity and commitment. From this perspective, the crossing over process from homosocial bonds (homophily) to heterosexual dyads is discontinuous.

24. A comprehensive analysis of the relationship between attachment style and religious faith can be found in Pehr Granqvist and Lee Kirkpatrick, "Attachment and Religious Representations and Behavior," in Jude Cassidy and Phillip R. Shaver, eds., *Handbook of Attachment: Theory, Research, and Clinical Applications*, 2nd ed. (New York: Guilford Press, 2008), 906–33.

25. The notion of extending oneself for the sake of a partner's emotional or spiritual need comes from Scott Peck, *The Road Less Traveled: A New Psychology of Love, Traditional Values and Spiritual Growth* (New York: Simon and Schuster, 1978).

26. Judith Balswick and Jack Balswick in *Authentic Human Sexuality: An Integral Christian Approach*, 2nd ed. (Downers Grove, IL: IVP Academic, 2008).

27. Christine Colon and Bonnie Field, *Singled Out: Why Celibacy Must Be Reinvented in Today's Church* (Grand Rapids: Brazos, 2009), 171, 195.

28. Ibid.

29. Lisa McMinn, *Sexuality and Holy Longing: Embracing Intimacy in a Broken World* (San Francisco: Jossey-Bass, 2004), 69–70.

30. Colon and Field, *Singled Out*, 171.

31. Stanley Hauerwas, *A Community of Character: Toward a Constructive Christian Social Ethic* (Notre Dame, IN: Notre Dame University Press, 1981), 190.

32. Richard Hays in *The Moral Vision of the New Testament: Community, Cross, New Creation, A Contemporary Introduction to New Testament Ethics* (New York: HarperCollins, 1996) proposes a similar schema of three focal images—community, cross, and new creation—that form biblical moral vision.

33. Joshua Harris, *I Kissed Dating Goodbye* (Colorado Springs: Multnomah Books, 2003).

34. Joseph Myers, *The Search to Belong: Rethinking Intimacy, Community and Small Groups* (Grand Rapids: Zondervan, 2003).

35. Ibid.

36. See Mark Regnerus, "The Case for Early Marriage," *Christianity Today* 53, no. 8 (2009): 25.

37. Ibid., 26.

38. Stanley Hauerwas, "Sex and Politics: Bertrand Russell and 'Human Sexuality,'" *Christian Century* (April 19, 1978): 417–22.

39. Scott Stanley, Galena Rhoades, and Howard Markham, "Sliding Versus Deciding: Inertia and the Premarital Cohabitation Effect," *Family Relations* 55, no. 4 (2006): 499–509.

40. Desmond Morris, *Intimate Behavior* (New York: Random House, 1971), 73.

41. Ibid, 73–78.

42. Donald Joy, *Bonding: Relationships in the Image of God* (Nappanee, IN: Evangel Publishing, 1999), 42.

43. Morris, *Intimate Behavior*, 74.

44. Ibid.

45. Stephanie Rosenbloom, "Love, Lies and What They Learned," *New York Times*, November 12, 2011.

46. Ibid.

47. Morris, *Intimate Behavior*, 75.

48. Ibid.

49. Ibid.

50. Joy, *Bonding*, 45.

51. Morris, *Intimate Behavior*, 76.

52. Joy, *Bonding*, 46–47.

53. Ibid.

54. Ibid, 45.

55. Morris, *Intimate Behavior*, 76.

56. Joy, *Bonding*, 48.

57. Morris, *Intimate Behavior*, 76.

58. Ibid., 77.

59. Joy, *Bonding*, 51.

60. Helen Fisher, "Broken Hearts: The Nature and Risks of Romantic Rejection," in Crouter and Booth, eds., *Romance and Sex in Adolescence and Emerging Adulthood*, 3–28.

61. Morris, *Intimate Behavior*, 77.

62. Mark Regnerus and Jeremy Uecker, *Premarital Sex in America: How Young Americans Meet, Mate, and Think about Marrying* (New York: Oxford University Press, 2011), 33.

63. Morris, *Intimate Behavior*, 77.

64. Regnerus and Uecker, *Premarital Sex in America*, 35–36.

65. Colon and Field, *Singled Out*, 107.

Chapter 9 Mentoring

1. Sharon Daloz Parks, *Big Questions, Worthy Dreams: Mentoring Young Adults in Their Search for Meaning, Purpose, and Faith* (San Francisco: Jossey-Bass, 2000), 5.

2. Richard Kadison and Theresa Foy DiGeronimo, *College of the Overwhelmed: The Campus Mental Health Crisis and What to Do about It* (San Francisco: Jossey-Bass, 2004). See also Arthur Levine and Jeanette S. Cureton, *When Hope and Fear Collide: A Portrait of Today's College Student* (San Francisco: Jossey-Bass, 1998), 94.

3. Kadison and DiGeronimo, *College of the Overwhelmed*, 14.

4. On these concerns, see, for example, Susan E. Chase, *Learning to Speak, Learning to Listen: How Diversity Works on Campus* (Ithaca, NY: Cornell University Press, 2010); Richard Seltzer and Nicole E. Johnson, *Experiencing Racism: Exploring Discrimination through the Eyes of College Students* (Lanham, MD: Lexington Books, 2009); R. M. Hall and B. R. Sandler, *The Campus Climate: A Chilly One for Women?* (Washington, DC: Association of American Colleges, 1982); E. T. Pascarella, L. S. Hagedorn, E. J. Whitt, P. M. Yeager, M. I. Edison, P. T. Terenzini, and A. Nora, "Women's Perceptions of a 'Chilly Climate' and Their Cognitive Outcomes during the First Year of College," *Journal of College Student Development* 38 (1997): 109–24; Jerry G. Gebhard, *What Do International Students Think and Feel? Adapting to U.S. College Life and Culture* (Ann Arbor: University of Michigan Press, 2010).

5. Alyssa N. Bryant and Helen S. Astin, "The Correlates of Spiritual Struggle during the College Years," *The Journal of Higher Education* 79, no. 1 (2008): 20.

6. Ibid., 23. See also Barbara Heckman, "Co-Journeying: Fostering Student Faith Development in College" (Ph.D. diss., North Carolina State University, 2008). Interestingly, attending a Christian college may actually increase spiritual struggle in the short term because it provides a setting within which matters of faith are discussed, debated, and analyzed for potential reinterpretation.

7. Christian Smith, *Soul Searching: The Religious and Spiritual Lives of American Teenagers* (New York: Oxford University Press, 2006), 267.

8. James Côté, *Arrested Adulthood: The Changing Nature of Maturity and Identity* (New York: New York University Press, 2000), 19.

9. Kara E. Powell, Brad M. Griffin, and Cheryl A. Crawford, *Sticky Faith: Practical Ideas to Nurture Long-Term Faith in Teenagers* (Grand Rapids: Zondervan, 2011), 117–20.

10. Christian Smith, *Souls in Transition: The Religious and Spiritual Lives of Emerging Adults* (New York: Oxford University Press, 2009), 43. It is interesting to note that when college students are polled about their "heroes," most choose their parents above more distant figures.

See Arthur Levine and Jeanette S. Cureton, *When Hope and Fear Collide: A Portrait of Today's College Student* (San Francisco: Jossey-Bass, 1998), 36–37.

11. Christian Smith, *Lost in Transition: The Dark Side of Emerging Adulthood* (New York: Oxford University Press, 2011), 234.

12. Ibid., 283–84. Dunn and Sundene, however, note that in 2008, 86 percent of adults had given adult children advice (compared to 50 percent in 1988), and two in three gave practical help (compared to one in three in 1988). See Richard Dunn and Jana Sundene, *Shaping the Journey of Emerging Adults: Life-Giving Rhythms for Spiritual Transformation* (Downers Grove, IL: InterVarsity, 2012), 111.

13. On the historical events fostering this change, see George Marsden, *The Soul of the American University* (New York: Oxford University Press, 1994); Julie Reuben, *The Making of the Modern University* (Chicago: University of Chicago Press, 1996); David P. Setran, *The College "Y": Student Religion in the Era of Secularization* (New York: Palgrave/Macmillan, 2007).

14. William H. Willimon and Thomas H. Naylor, *The Abandoned Generation: Rethinking Higher Education* (Grand Rapids: Eerdmans, 1995), 87.

15. Smith, *Lost in Transition*, 234.

16. David Kinnaman, *You Lost Me: Why Young Christians Are Leaving Church . . . And Rethinking Faith* (Grand Rapids: Baker Books, 2011), 29.

17. Kadison and DiGeronimo, *College of the Overwhelmed*, 12.

18. This is especially true for men, who often define identity in terms of separation, differentiation, and independence. Women, on the other hand, define identity more in terms of attachment, investment, and connection. See Alyssa Bryant, "Gender Differences in Spiritual Development during the College Years," *Sex Roles* 56, no. 11–12 (2007): 835–46.

19. Côté, *Arrested Adulthood*, 135.

20. Smith, *Lost in Transition*, 241.

21. Côté, *Arrested Adulthood*, 49.

22. B. Liang, R. Spencer, D. Brogan, and M. Corral, "Mentoring Relationships from Early Adolescence through Emerging Adulthood: A Qualitative Analysis," *Journal of Vocational Behavior* 72, no. 2 (2008): 170.

23. Kinnaman, *You Lost Me*, 29.

24. John Palfrey and Urs Gasser, *Born Digital: Understanding the First Generation of Digital Natives* (New York: Basic Books, 2010).

25. Margaret Mead, *Culture and Commitment: A Study of the Generation Gap* (Garden City, NY: Doubleday, 1970), 1.

26. Ibid., 82, 88.

27. On this theme, see Daniel R. Heischman, *Good Influence: Teaching the Wisdom of Adulthood* (New York: Morehouse Publishing, 2009).

28. Smith, *Lost in Transition*, 234.

29. Joseph Chilton Pearce, *The Magical Child* (New York: Plume, 1992).

30. Parks, *Big Questions, Worthy Dreams*, 131. Research seems to indicate that current emerging adults are a bit more cynical and distrusting than previous generations. See K. H. Trzesniewski and M. B. Donnellan, "Rethinking 'Generation Me': A Study of Cohort Effects from 1976–2006," *Perspectives on Psychological Studies* 5 (2010): 58–75.

31. Richard Settersten and Barbara E. Ray, *Not Quite Adults* (New York: Bantam Books, 2010), x. These authors note that this represents a 37 percent increase since 1970. See also Francis Goldscheider and Calvin Goldscheider, *The Changing Transition to Adulthood: Leaving and Returning Home* (New York: Sage, 1999), 49–50. About 27 percent of 25- to 35-year-olds live with their parents.

32. Goldscheider and Goldscheider, *The Changing Transition*, 54.

33. Parks, *Big Questions, Worthy Dreams*, 129.

34. Ibid., 158.

35. On this theme, see Perry L. Glanzer and Todd C. Ream, *Christianity and Moral Identity in Higher Education* (New York: Palgrave Macmillan, 2009), 186–200.

36. Rebecca Konyndyk DeYoung, *Glittering Vices: A New Look at the Seven Deadly Sins and Their Remedies* (Grand Rapids: Brazos, 2009), 9.

37. Donald B. Kraybill, *The Upside-Down Kingdom* (Scottdale, PA: Herald Press, 1978), 101–102.

38. William Barclay, *Educational Ideals in the Ancient World* (London: Collins, 1959).

39. Frederick Buechner, *The Sacred Journey* (San Francisco: HarperSanFrancisco, 1982), 77–78.

40. Ibid., 95.

41. Keith R. Anderson and Randy D. Reese, *Spiritual Mentoring: A Guide for Seeking and Giving Direction* (Downers Grove, IL: InterVarsity, 1999), 41.

42. Michael Card, *The Walk: A Moment in Time When Two Lives Intersect* (Nashville: Thomas Nelson, 2000), 12.

43. C. S. Lewis, *Letters to Malcolm: Chiefly on Prayer* (New York: Hardcourt Brace & Company, 1964), 75.

44. Anderson and Reese, *Spiritual Mentoring*, 40–41.

45. On this theme, see Jay Wood, *Epistemology: Becoming Intellectually Virtuous* (Downers Grove, IL: IVP Academic, 1998); Wood, "Educating for Intellectual Character," in Jeffry C. Davis and Philip G. Ryken, eds., *Liberal Arts for the Christian Life* (Wheaton: Crossway, 2012), 162.

46. C. S. Lewis, *Christian Reflections* (Grand Rapids: Eerdmans, 1994), 171.

47. Dietrich Bonhoeffer, *Life Together* (San Francisco: HarperSanFrancisco, 1954), 98.

48. This posture is similar to what Kenda Creasy Dean and Ron Foster termed "hand holding." See Dean and Foster, *The Godbearing Life: The Art of Soul Tending for Youth Ministry* (Nashville: Upper Room Books, 1998), 140–41.

49. Paul David Tripp, *Instruments in the Redeemer's Hands* (Phillipsburg, NJ: P&R Publishing, 2002), 128.

50. Ibid.

51. Cornelius Plantinga, Jr., *Not the Way It's Supposed to Be: A Breviary of Sin* (Grand Rapids: Eerdmans, 1995), 105.

52. Smith, *Souls in Transition*, 49.

53. Bonhoeffer, *Life Together*, 31.

54. Ibid., 104.

55. Tripp, *Instruments in the Redeemer's Hands*, 213–18.

56. Ibid., 215.

57. Bonhoeffer, *Spiritual Care* (Philadelphia: Fortress Press, 1985), 43.

58. Ibid., 37.

59. Thomas H. Groome, *Christian Religious Education: Sharing Our Story and Vision* (San Francisco: Jossey-Bass, 1980), 186.

60. Paul J. Wadell and Darin H. Davis, "Tracking the Toxins of *Acedia*: Reenvisioning Moral Education," in Douglas V. Henry and Michael D. Beaty, eds., *The Schooled Heart: Moral Formation in American Higher Education* (Waco: Baylor University Press, 2007), 133–54.

61. Ibid., 137.

62. Dorothy Sayers, *Creed or Chaos?* (New York: Hardcourt, Brace, 1949), 81.

63. Albert Bandura, "Self-Efficacy: Toward a Unifying Theory of Behavioral Change," *Psychological Review* 84 (1977): 191–215.

64. On this theme, see Greg Ogden, *Transforming Discipleship: Making Disciples a Few at a Time* (Downers Grove, IL: InterVarsity, 2003).

65. Christopher D. Bader and Scott A. Desmond, "Do as I Say and as I Do: The Effects of Consistent Parental Beliefs and Behaviors upon Religious Transmission," *Sociology of Religion* 67 (2006): 313–29.

66. Nicholas Wolterstorff, *Educating for Responsible Action* (Grand Rapids: Eerdmans, 1980), 57.

67. Elisabeth Elliot, *Shadow of the Almighty* (San Francisco: Harper and Row, 1958), 59.

68. Lawrence Richards, *A Theology of Christian Education* (Grand Rapids: Zondervan, 1980), 82.

69. Ibid.; Urie Bronfenbrenner, *The Ecology of Human Development* (Cambridge, MA: Harvard University Press), 1979.

70. Eugene Peterson, *Under the Unpredictable Plant: An Exploration in Vocational Holiness* (Grand Rapids: Eerdmans, 1992), 75.

71. Heischman, *Good Influence*, 22.

72. Erik H. Erikson, *Insight and Responsibility* (New York: W.W. Norton, 1964), 125.

73. Robert T. Blackburn, David W. Chapman, and Susan M. Cameron, "'Cloning in Academe': Mentorship and Academic Careers," *Research in Higher Education* 15, no. 4 (1981); Dana D. Anderson and Wendelyn J. Shore, "Ethical Issues and Concerns Associated with Mentoring Undergraduate Students, *Ethics and Behavior* 18, no. 1 (2008).

74. Kenda Creasy Dean, *Almost Christian: What the Faith of Our Teenagers Is Telling the American Church* (New York: Oxford University Press, 2010), 128–30.

75. Ibid., 130.

76. Parks, *Big Questions, Worthy Dreams*, 51.

77. John Piper, *Life as a Vapor* (Sisters, OR: Multnomah Publishers, 2004), 51.

Conclusion

1. Christian Smith, *Lost in Transition: The Dark Side of Emerging Adulthood* (New York: Oxford University Press, 2011), 227.

2. Ibid., 231.

3. Jeffrey Jensen Arnett, *Emerging Adulthood: The Winding Road from the Late Teens through the Twenties* (New York: Oxford University Press, 2004), 209.

4. Walter Brueggemann, "Covenanting as Human Vocation," *Interpretation* 33, no. 2 (1979): 116.

5. Thomas E. Bergler, *The Juvenilization of American Christianity* (Grand Rapids: Eerdmans, 2012), 224.

6. Christian Smith, *Souls in Transition: The Religious and Spiritual Lives of Emerging Adults* (New York: Oxford University Press, 2009), 287–92; Kenda Creasy Dean, *Almost Christian: What the Faith of Our Teenagers Is Telling the American Church* (New York: Oxford University Press, 2010), 36–37.

7. Holmes is quoted in Max Depree, *Leadership Is an Art* (New York: Dell Publishing, 1989), 22.

Index

acedia, 225–26
Acts, 95, 136
Alpha Movement, 75–76, 77, 79
Althaus, Paul, 121
Anderson, Keith, 217, 218
Aquinas, Thomas, 116, 215
 on love, 35–36
Arnett, Jeffrey, 20, 22, 59, 62, 84, 163, 165, 166
 on emerging adult individuality, 89–90, 113–14, 233
Arthur, Sarah, 36
Astin, Helen, 15, 207
attachment theory, 187
 and divorce, 188
 and internal working model, 187–89
 and physical intimacy, 203
 and relationship with God, 189–90
 and secure, anxious, and avoidant bonds, 187–88
Augustine, 31, 46
 on properly ordered love, 175–76

Bader, Christopher, 226
Baldwin, Joyce, 72
Balswick, Jack, 167–68, 190–91
Balswick, Judith, 167–68, 190–91
baptism, 105–6
Barna, 82
Barth, Karl, 131
Baucum, Tory
 on encapsulation theory, 75–77

Baumeister, Roy, 143
Baumrind, Diana, 149
beauty of God
 communicating to emerging adults, 35–36
 and competition with contemporary marketing, 36
Bellah, Robert, 100
Berger, Peter, 102
Bethke, Jefferson, 81
Black, Wesley, 99–100
Bonhoeffer, Dietrich, 18, 37, 39, 92, 221
 on community, 98
 on confession, 52
 on "pious fellowship," 103–4
 on rebuke, 223–24
 on silence, 47
 on "wish-dream" of ideal community, 94
Bowlby, John, 187
"Bride, The" (Lecrae), 110
Brueggemann, Walter, 119, 134
Bryant, Alyssa, 15, 82–83, 207
Buechner, Frederick, 115, 217
busyness, 48

Calvin, John, 37
Card, Michael, 217–18
Carr, Nicholas, 19
Carroll, Colleen, 107
Case Western Reserve, 171
Catechumenate, 75, 76, 77, 78
celibacy, 193
Chalke, Steve, 78
Cherlin, Andrew, 166
Chesterton, G. K., 69

Chicago Tribune, 169
Chilton Pearce, Joseph, 212
"Christianity, Starbucks," 90
Christianity, therapeutic. *See* Moralistic Therapeutic Deism
church, the, 237
 criticisms of, 81–82
 emerging adult concerns with, 92–93
 as foretaste of kingdom of God, 109–10
 and identity formation, 79, 89–90
 invisible vs. visible, 91–92
 and self-absorption, 234–35
church, emerging adult disengagement from the, 82–83
 different denominations/demographics, 83–84
 impact of, 85–86
 institutional disengagement, 84
 prospects to reverse, 95
 and fellowship (*koinonia*), 98–104
 and outreach (*diakonia*), 106–9
 and teaching (*didache*), 95–98
 and worship (*leitourgia*), 104–6
 sources of, 86–87
 church contributors to, 92–95
 church "shopping/hopping," 90–91

275

concerns with church beliefs,
    92–93
delayed marriage, 87
emerging adult factors,
    87–92
higher education, 88–89
idealism, 93–95
lack of emerging adult-
    focused programming, 93
lifestyle choices, 88
need for individuality, 89–90
Protestant individualistic
    faith, 91–92
as temporary, 84–85
church "shopping/hopping,"
    90–91
Clydesdale, Tim, on emerging
    adult religious slump,
    15–16, 17–18
cohabitation, 167–68, 197–98
college, and belief, 21–22, 88–89
College of the Overwhelmed
    (Kadison and Foy Diger-
    onimo), 206
Colon, Christine, 193, 204
Colossians, 34, 51, 52
confession, as discipline, 51–52
conformity and authority, 63–65
consumerism, 32, 60, 234
    and identity, 60
Corinthians, First, 107, 119,
    155, 238
    and sex, 172–73, 174, 177, 178,
    182, 203
Corinthians, Second, 194
Cosden, Darrell, 121
Côté, James,
    on individualization, 57–58,
    59–60
Covey, Steven, 19
Crabb, Larry, 24
Crawford, Cheryl, 208
Creasy Dean, Kenda, 78, 108,
    229, 235
Crouch, Andy, 100, 121, 136–37
culture, and identity formation,
    70–71
    and engagement, 74–79
    and encapsulation theory,
    75–79
    and refusal, 71–74
    and pluralism, 73–74

Dafoe Whitehead, Barbara, 167
Daloz, Laurent, 135

Daniel
    and cultural refusal, 71–74,
    75, 78
Davis, Darin, 225
Dawn, Marva, 174
Deism. *See* Moralistic Thera-
    peutic Deism
Desmond, Scott, 226
Deuteronomy, 215–16
Dewey, John, 41, 97
DeYoung, Kevin, 101
DeYoung, Rebecca, 43
doubt, 69
Duska, Donald, 146–47
Dykstra, Craig, 104–5

Eden, Dawn, 180
Eisner, Elliot, 97
Elliot, Jim, 227
emerging adulthood, 59, 231–32.
    See also identity formation
as "age of instability," 20
    and anxiety, 59–60
    and challenges of college,
    206–7
    and inadequate pathways out
    of adolescence, 232
    and the church, 234–35
    and self-absorption, 232–36,
    239
    and self-sufficiency, 233–36
    and relationships with par-
    ents, 207–8
    and view of future, 40–41
    and habit formation, 42
emerging adults, ministering to,
    67–70, 186. *See also* leader-
    ship, of emerging adults;
    mentoring, emerging adults
    and attachment, 190
emerging adults, religious slump
    of,
    and decline in belief, 12–13
    and decline in Christian prac-
    tice and institutional par-
    ticipation, 13–14, 82–83
    and decline in perceived close-
    ness to God, 14
    and decline in subjective im-
    portance of religion, 13,
    16–17
    sources of, 17
        beliefs about "my time,"
        19–20, 40–41
        college, 21–22
        disruptions in daily patterns,
        20–21

evangelicalism, 26–27
    moralistic therapeutic deism,
    22–25
    new life-demands, 17–18
    Protestantism, 25–26
    technology, 19
emerging adults, spiritual in-
    terests of, 14–15. *See also*
    spiritual formation
    problems with definitions and
    categories, 15–16
    "spiritual but not religious,"
    15, 84
encapsulation theory, 75
    and "matrix of transforma-
    tion," 76–79
    physical, social, and ideologi-
    cal aspects of, 75–76
    scriptural examples of, 76
Ephesians, 36, 107, 119
Erikson, Erik, 61–62, 228
    on "intimacy vs. isolation,"
    187
Esther, 226
Eucharist, 106
evangelicalism, 83
    and sex, 169–70
    and spiritual formation
    and Biblicism, 26
    pitfalls for, 26–27
    and soteriology, 26–27
Exodus, 131, 175
"experiential continuum," 41
Ezekiel, 156

Failure to Launch, 185–86
fasting, discipline of, 49
fellowship (*koinonia*), 98
    and being under authority, 102
    embodied nature of, 102
    healing through, 103–4
    power of intergenerational,
    99–100
        age-segregation by values/
        tastes, 100–102
    and self-choosing, 98–99
    and singles and family-focused
    churches, 102–13
Field, Bonnie, 193, 204
Foster, Richard, 36, 46, 48
Fowler, James, 120, 135
Foy DiGeronimo, Theresa,
    59–60, 206
Freitas, Donna, 173
"fruit-stapling," 30–31

Galatians, 41–42, 118, 156
Gardner, Christine, 181
generativity, 228

Genesis, 173
Gilbert, Greg, 101
Greenman, Jeffrey, 26, 50
Grenz, Stanley, 58–59
Griffin, Brad, 208
Griffiths, Paul, 155
Groome, Thomas, 225
Grudem, Wayne, 91
Guder, Darrell, 109
Guiness, Os, 119

habit formation, 42, 43
  and the body, 44
  and daily routine, 45
  and morality, 158
Hall, Edward T., 194–95
happiness, and spirituality. See
    Moralistic Therapeutic
    Deism
Hardy, Lee, 129
Harris, Joshua, 194
Hauerwas, Stanley, 157, 158,
    193, 197
Hebrews, 35, 110, 157, 194
Heischman, Daniel, 65, 228
"helicopter parents," 65
Higher Education Research In-
    stitute, 14–15, 18, 88–89
Hill, Jonathan, 85
Hines, Benson, 109
Hintz, Marcy, 103
Holmes, Arthur, 37, 158–59
Holmes, Oliver Wendell, 238
hookup culture, 164–65, 200
Horner, David, 69
Hugo, 111–12

identity formation, 236–37
  and adulthood, 59–60, 187,
    232–35
  and anxiety, 59
  and career, 55–56
  1960s vs. today, 55–57
  and the church, 79, 89–90
  and culture, 70–71
  and early church, 73
  and encapsulation theory,
    75–79
  and engagement, 74–79
  example of Daniel, 71–73
  a language of, 78
  and "matrix of transforma-
    tion," 76–79
  and refusal, 71–74
  and separatism, 74
  developmental trajectories of,
    61–62

authority-bound, 62–66,
    69–70
  four quadrant model, 62–63
  goal for, 70
  healthy models of, 65–66
  and interactions with differ-
    ence, 66
  and internalization, 64, 70
  and pride, 69
  and role of good leader,
    67–70
  and "scaffolding," 67–68
  and individuation, 59–61
  and practice of silence, 47–48
  social vs. personal, 57–58
  and contemporary America,
    58
identity, sexual, 190–91
  personal histories of, 191–92
individualism, emerging adult,
    89–90, 113–14, 141, 233–34
  and Protestantism, 91–92
idols, 33–34
  and spiritual disciplines, 47, 49
individualism, liberal, 60
individuation, 57–60
internal working models, 187–89
interpersonal space, 195
intimacy, physical, 198–99
  and Christian leadership on,
    203–4
  and emotional attachment,
    203
  neuroscience of, 202
  rushing, 201
  stages of, 199–203
Isaiah, 40, 134, 216
iWorld, 125–26

James, 222–23
Jesus, 136, 226
  on adultery, 175
  on discipleship, 38, 238–39
  parables on, 38–39, 239
  and moral formation, 159–60
  and the Pharisees, 25
  on the self, 38
  and vocation, 118–19
Job, 175
John, 25, 119, 136
  on discipleship, 39, 40
John, First, 156
John the Baptist, 37
Jones, E. Stanley, 72
Jones, Stanton, 174
Joy, Donald, 199, 201, 202

Kadison, Richard, 59–60, 206
Kallenberg, Brad, 151
Keller, Timothy, 121, 167
  on idols, 33–34
  on rest, 123
  on sex, 172, 174, 175
Kierkegaard, Søren, 32, 48
kingdom(s)
  false, 31, 45
  multiple, and emerging adults,
    32
Kings, 210
Kinnaman, David, 83, 84, 86,
    92–93, 97, 153, 173, 209
  on Christianity and the work-
    place, 108–9
Klapp, Orrin, 182
Kohlberg, Lawrence, 145
Konstam, Varda, 126
Kreager, Derek, 164
Kuehne, Dale, 125–26

Lane, Bill, 217–18
Lasch, Christopher, 188
leadership, of emerging adults,
    67. See also mentoring,
    emerging adults
  and discernment, 68
  goal of, 70
  and openness and doubt,
    68–69
  and "scaffolding," 67–68
Lecrae, 110
lectio divina, 50–51
Letters to Malcolm (Lewis), 218
Levine, Charles, 57–58, 59
Leviticus, 223
Lewis, C. S., 218, 220
  on costly discipleship, 27, 34,
    38–39
  and the light yoke, 39
  on properly ordered love,
    176–77
  on spiritual choices, 43, 53
LIFE, game of, 55–57
lifestyle enclaves, 100
liminal spaces, 66, 205
love
  of Christ as beautiful, 34–36
  properly ordered, 175–76
  as telos, 31, 45
Luke, 32, 38, 239

MacIntyre, Alasdair, 58, 157
  on social identity, 58
Marcia, James
  on identity, 62

Mark, 39, 177
marriage, 166–67, 193–94
  delayed, 87, 165–66
  early, 196
  arguments for/against,
    196–97
  and singleness, 103, 192–93
mate search, among emerging
  adults, 165–66
  and cohabitation, 167–68,
    197–98
  and marriage delay 165–66
  and views of marriage, 166–67
"matrix of transformation,"
  and relationships, 76–77
  and rhetoric, 77–78
  and rituals, 76–77
  and roles, 78–79
Matthew, 32, 76, 175, 178, 216
  on discipleship, 37, 38, 39, 48
McConaughey, Matthew, 185
McMinn, Lisa, 174, 177, 193
Mead, Margaret, 211
mentoring, emerging adults,
  205–6, 238
  and addressing sin, 222–23
    with "comfort" and "call,"
      223–24
  and confession, 224
  and culture of non-confron-
    tation, 222
  challenges of
  and college, 206–7, 208–9
  and cynicism, 212
  and minorities, 207
  and parents, 207–8, 212–13
  and role of nonparental
    adults, 209–12, 213–14
  and spiritual struggle, 207
  and posture of attentiveness
  and being awake to God's
    presence, 217–8, 220–21
  and education, 220
  and listening to mentee,
    220–22
  and practices to cultivate,
    219–20
  and timely questions, 218–19
  and posture of envisioning,
    224–225
  and acedia, 225–26
  and cautions for, 228–29
  and mentor modeling,
    226–29
  and real life, 227–28
  within a relationship, 227
  and "worthy dreams," 225

and posture at the hinge,
  229–230
  and virtues of gratitude and
    faith, 230
  and posture of remember-
    ing, 214
  and pusillanimity, 215
  and spiritual autobiography,
    216–17
  and the stories of Biblical
    faith, 214–16
  and virtues of humility,
    courage, and compassion,
    215–16
mentoring gap, 212
Middleton, J. Richard, 128
modeling, for mentee, 226–29
moral consequentialism, 143–44
moral formation, 156
  and conscience-raising experi-
    ence, 159
  and exemplars and scripture,
    157–58
  and habit, 158
  and Jesus with disciples,
    159–60
  and narrative, 157
  and social context, 158–59
  and friendship, 158–59
moral intuitionism, 143–44
moral privatization, 143–44
Moralistic Therapeutic Deism,
  22–23, 30, 51, 117, 235
  and Christianity as set of prin-
    ciples, 25
  and conservative Protestant-
    ism, 25–26
  and content of Christianity,
    23
  and evangelicalism, 26–27
  and instrumental spiritual-
    ity, 24
  and liberal Protestantism, 25
  and spiritual formation,
    23–24,
  and proper, 36–37, 38–39
morality, 139–41, 237–38
  and character
    vs. authenticity, 149–50
    vs. rule-following, 149–50
  developmental theories of
    dualism, multiplicity, and
      relativism, 145–47
  Kohlberg, 145
  faith community responses
    to, 147–49
  parenting styles, 149

and emerging adults
  challenge for parents and
    leaders, 144–45
  communal context, 142–43
  higher education, 142–43
  history of, 141–42
  moral individualism, 141
  personal choice, 143–44
  values vs. virtue, 141–42
  and subjective moral realism,
    148–49
  and virtue, 141–42, 151,
    215–16
  Christian telos, 152–53,
    155–56
  curiosity vs. studiousness,
    154–55
  dispositions, 151–52
  intellectual virtues, 154–55
  moral purity and holiness,
    153–54, 179–80
  Scripture, 153
Morris, Desmond
  on physical intimacy, 198–203
Moses, 35, 131, 215
  "mountaintop experiences," 43
Mulholland, M. Robert, 50, 52
Muraven, Mark, 143
Myers, Joseph, 194–95

National College Health Asso-
  ciation, 171
National Survey of Youth and
  Religion, 13–14
Naylor, Thomas, 209
Nozick, Robert, 126
"null curriculum," 97

outreach (diakonia), church,
  106–7
  and gifts, 107
  and missional role, 107–9
  and the workplace, 108–9

Palmer, Parker, 132, 155
parable
  of prodigal son, 32–33, 239
  of rich young ruler, 39
Parks, Sharon, 62, 106, 113,
  212, 230
Paul, 31–32, 51, 52, 136, 155,
  157, 203, 238
  on the body, 174, 177, 178, 182
  on the flesh, 34
  on God-given gifts, 130
  on holiness, 154
  on idolatry, 36

and mentoring, 226, 227, 229
on singleness, 192–93
Perry, William, 145–46
personhood, 58
Peter, First, 130
Peterson, Eugene, 42, 228
Pew Forum, 14
Pharisees, 25, 30
Philemon, 97
Philippians, 154, 230
Piper, John, 230
  on fasting, 49
  on overcoming idols, 34
Plantinga, Cornelius, 37, 122,
  123, 222
"plausibility structures," 102
Popenoe, David, 167
postmodernism and the self,
  58–59
Powell, Kara, 22, 99, 101, 207
pornography, 170, 178–79
prodigal son, parable of, 32–33,
  239
Protestantism, conservative,
  25–26
Protestantism, liberal, 25
Proverbs, 31, 154, 159
Psalms, 35, 100, 214, 216, 237
"psychological adulthood," 59

Rambo, Lewis, 76
Reese, Randy, 217, 218
Regnerus, Mark, 22, 165, 166,
  169, 203
Rehoboam, King, 210
relationships, romantic, 186–87,
  238
  and attachment, 187–89
  relationship with God,
    189–90
  formation of
    Christian leadership on,
      195–96, 197–98, 204
    courtship, 194
    emotional attachment, 203
    dating, 194–95
    neuroscience of, 202
    online dating, 196, 199–200
    physical intimacy, 198–99
    rushing into, 201
    stages of, 199–203
    stages of interpersonal space,
      195
  marriage, 193–97
  singleness, 193
  and friendships, 189
religion, instrumental, 24

Revelation, 74
reverence, 154
Richards, Lawrence, 227
Riesman, David, 62, 132
rites of passage, 77
Romans, 38, 40, 130

Samuel, 224
Satinover, Jeffrey, 42
Sayers, Dorothy, 225
Scorsese, Martin, 111
Scripture reading
  devotional, 49–51
  to gather information, 26, 50
secrecy, discipline of, 48–49
self-absorption, 37, 114, 232,
  234–35, 239
Sermon on the Mount, 77, 152,
  156
sex
  increasing levels among
    emerging adults, 169
  and evangelicals, 169–70
  and grief on account of, 171
  and the media, 170–71
  oral, 202–3
  and pornography, 170, 178–79
sexual ethic, emerging adult
  and Christian vision for,
    173–74
  abstinence, 179–80, 181
  addressing lust, 177–79
  adultery, 175
  chastity, 180
  covenant, 174–75
  in East vs. West, 180
  the flesh, 174–75
  modesty, 180–81
  positive virtues for, 179–80
  properly ordered love,
    175–77
  purity, 180
  and First Corinthians, 172–73,
    182
  and "spiritual universities,"
    173
sexual intimacy. See physical
  intimacy
"sexual Platonism," 172, 173
"sexual realism," 172
sexuality, 161–62
  dimensions of, 190–91
  and history of romantic love
    in America, 162–64
  cohabitation, 167–68,
    197–98
  gender, 164–65

hookup culture, 164, 200
marriage delay 165–66
personal histories of, 191–92
Shaffer, Thomas, 158
Shalit, Wendy, 180–81
Sherman, Amy, 118
silence, discipline of, 46
  and identity, 47–48
sin
  and habit, 42
  and love, 31–32
  state of, 37
"sin management," 30
singleness, 102–3, 167
  Paul on, 192–93
Sittser, Jerry, 126–27
Smith, Christian, 36, 60, 143,
  148, 160, 165, 222, 231,
  232, 235
  on decline in emerging adult
    belief, 13–14, 16, 19, 20
  on decline in emerging adult
    church engagement, 82–83,
    84, 88, 92
  on emerging adult relationships
    with adults, 207–8, 209
  on emerging adult sexuality,
    169
  on emerging adults and voca-
    tion, 112, 114–15
  on moralistic therapeutic
    deism, 22, 23, 24, 25
  on "spiritual vs. religious," 16
Smith, James K. A., 31, 45
society
  cofigurative, 211
  postfigurative, 211
  prefigurative, 211
solitude, discipline of, 46, 47
  and identity, 47–48
Song of Solomon, 173, 180
spiritual disciplines, 45–46
  of abstinence, 46–49
    and enjoyment of Christ,
      46–47
  of engagement, 46, 49–52
    and results-focus, 52–53
spiritual formation, 23–24,
  29–30, 236. See also spiritual disciplines
  beyond moralism, 30
  and evangelicalism, 26–27
  and leaving/staying home,
    32–33
  and love, 31, 34
  and multiple kingdoms, 32
  and spiritual renewal, 30–31

beyond therapy, 37
  cost of discipleship, 37–39
  cost of non-discipleship,
    39–40
  the light yoke, 39
  need for repentance, 37
  sowing/reaping to the flesh/
    spirit over time, 41–42
  and child-likeness, 238–39
  developing spiritual tendencies
    over time, 43–44
  the body, 44–45
  daily routines, 45
  spiritual disciplines, 45–53
  and idols, 54
    consumerism, 33
    emotion, 33
    fighting fire with fire, 34
    money, 33
    willpower, 33–34
    worship, 33
  inadequate pathways of,
    232–36
  and saying yes to beauty of
    Christ, 34–35
  how to foster, 35–36, 40–42
  and self-sacrifice, 36–37
Staff, Jeremy, 164
Stevens, Clifford, 180
Sullivan, Andrew, 82
Susman, Warren, 142

teaching (didache), church, 95
  on all topics, 97
  and depth of, 96–97
  as empowering, 98
  as experiential, 97
  and giving testimony, 96–97
Thessalonians, First, 173, 227
Timothy, Second, 226
Titus, 36
Tousley, Nikki, 151
Towner, Sibley, 72
Tripp, Paul David, 30–31, 221,
  223
Tyndale, William, 120–21

Uecker, Jeremy, 22, 165, 169, 203

virginity, 163, 165, 179–80, 203
vocation, 237
  being called, 119

primary vs. secondary,
    119–20
  and Christian discernment,
    112–13
  vita activa and vita contem-
    plativa, 116, 135
  "great commission" and "cul-
    tural mandate," 122
  helping emerging adults see
    broad calling, 122, 124
  and communion, community,
    character, and cultivation,
    122–23
  and creative, sustaining, and
    restorative tasks, 123
  identity and service, 118–20
  and intersection of grace and
    the cross, 136–37
  and the New Jerusalem,
    121–22
  and present-orientation,
    128–29
  providence, 127–29, 136
    and communal input, 133–34
    and God-given gifts, 129–31
    and passion, 131–33
    and providential opportuni-
      ties, 133
  and purpose, 111–13, 136
    and compartmentalization,
      115–16, 118
    and emerging adulthood,
      113–14
    and sacred/secular divide,
      116–17, 120–22
    and self-focus, 113–15,
      117–18
  Reformation vision of, 120–21
  and rest, 123
  selection of, 124
    current challenges of, 125
    and difficulties of choice,
      125–28
    and God-given gifts, 130–31
    and God's will, 126–27, 128
    and waiting on voice from
      God, 135–36
  vices of: pride and envy,
    134–35
  vs. "grateful stewardship,"
    134–35

Wadell, Paul, 225
Walsh, Brian, 128
Webber, Robert, 110
Weight of Glory, The (Lewis),
  34
Wells, David, 141
Wells, H. G., 69
Wesley, John, 128
Western Kentucky University,
  217–18
Whelan, Mariellen, 146–47
White, David, 159–60
"Why I Hate Religion, But Love
  Jesus" (Bethke), 81
Wilhoit, James, 37
Willard, Dallas, 32, 46
  on the body, 44
  on culture and college, 73,
    74–75, 142
  on evangelical spiritual forma-
    tion, 26–27
  on love of Christ, 35–36
  on sexual lust, 178–79
  on "sin management," 30
Williams, D. H., 73
Willimon, William, 209
Winner, Lauren, 180
Wood, Jay, 151
Word, the
  reading, 49–50
worship (leitourgia), church, 104
  and breaking performance-
    based treadmill, 104–5
  and Christian calendar, 105
  and creativity, 106
  and the sacraments, 105–6
Wright, N. T.
  on morality, 149–50, 151–52
  and holiness, 153–54
Wuthnow, Robert, 83–84,
  169–70
  on delayed marriage, 87
  and making decisions outside
    the influence of church,
    85–86

You Lost Me (Kinnaman), 93